FERBER

A BIOGRAPHY

Julie Goldsmith Gilbert

DOUBLEDAY & COMPANY, INC.
GARDEN CITY, NEW YORK
1978

Grateful acknowledgment is made to the following for permission to reprint material copyright or controlled by them:

Excerpt of review of *Bravo!*, by Edna Ferber, reviewed by Brooks Atkinson, the New York *Times*, 1948; excerpt of review of *The Royal Family* by Brooks Atkinson, the New York *Times*, 1951, copyright 1948, 1951 by the New York Times Company, reprinted by permission; excerpt from article by Edna Ferber, Paris, 1945, North American Newspaper Alliance, reprinted by permission; excerpt from Walter Kerr's review of *Dinner at Eight*, the New York *Times*, September 28, 1966, copyright © 1966 by the New York Times Company, reprinted by permission; excerpts of review by George Oppenheimer of *Dinner at Eight*, *Newsday*, 1966, reprinted by permission of George Oppenheimer; a portrait of Edna Ferber by Louis Bromfield, *Saturday Review of Literature*, June 15, 1935, copyright © 1935 by Saturday Review Company, Inc., reprinted by permission.

Excerpts from letters of: Russel Crouse to Edna Ferber, courtesy of Anna Crouse; Alexander Woollcott to Edna Ferber, reprinted by permission of J. P. Hennessey; Frank Sullivan to Edna Ferber and poem dedicated to Franklin P. Adams, reprinted by permission of the Historical Society of Saratoga Springs, New York; Margaret Sanger to Edna Ferber, reprinted by permission of Grant Sanger, M.D.; H. L. Mencken to Edna Ferber, reprinted by permission of Mercantile-Safe Deposit & Trust Company, Baltimore, Md., trustee under Will of Henry L. Mencken; George Kaufman to Edna Ferber, permission granted by Anne Kaufman Schneider; Dan Longwell to Edna Ferber, reprinted by permission of the Dan Longwell Estate; William Allen White to Edna Ferber, reprinted by permission of Mrs. William Lindsay White for the William Allen White Estate; Rodgers and Hammerstein to Edna Ferber, reprinted by permission of Richard Rodgers and Mrs. Oscar Hammerstein II; Rudyard Kipling to Nelson Doubleday, reprinted by permission of the National Trust; Noel Coward to Edna Ferber, reprinted by permission of the Lantz Office, Inc.; Louis Bromfield to Edna Ferber, reprinted by permission of Ellen Bromfield Geld; Karl Honeystein to Edna Ferber, reprinted by permission of Karl Honeystein; excerpts by Franklin P. Adams from his column "Conning Tower," reprinted by permission of Jacob S. Charney.

Excerpts of a telegram and letter to Edna Ferber from Robert Fryer. Courtesy of Robert Fryer.

Excerpts of letter to Edna Ferber from Senator Ernest Gruening. By permission of Huntington Gruening, son of Senator Gruening.

LIBRARY OF CONGRESS CATALOGING IN PUBLICATION DATA GILBERT, JULIE GOLDSMITH. FERBER, A BIOGRAPHY. 1. FERBER, EDNA, 1887–1968—BIOGRAPHY. 2. AUTHORS, AMERICAN—20TH CENTURY—BIOGRAPHY. I. TITLE. PS3511.E46Z67 813'.5'2[B] ISBN 0-385-03960-3 LIBRARY OF CONGRESS CATALOG CARD NUMBER 76–57512 PRINTED IN THE UNITED STATES OF AMERICA FIRST EDITION

This book is for John Weisman, Harriet Pilpel, Digby Diehl, and Joe Linz. All of them gave me the proper courage.

It is also for Henry Goldsmith, a father of the highest quality.

ACKNOWLEDGMENTS

I would also like to thank some of the people who were helpful in pointing me toward *Ferber:*

Rose Alschuler
Dr. Alvan Barach
Fanny Butcher
Frances Chanock
Marc Connelly
Anna Crouse
George Cukor
Julie D'Acci
Morris Ernst
Fannie Ferber Fox
Beatrice Frank
Margalo Gillmore
Henry Goldsmith
Janet Fox Goldsmith
Max Gordon
Ruth Hammond
Kitty Hart
Helen Harvey
Miriam Elkan Heart
Molly Hennessy
Katharine Hepburn
Dennis Hopper
William Hornbeck
Rock Hudson
Garson Kanin
Madge Kennedy
Lilo Klein
Mina Fox Klein
Rudolf Klein
Donald Klopfer
Lucy Kroll
Armina Marshall Langner
Robert Lantz
Irving Lazar
Goddard Lieberson
Lillian MacKesy
Elliot Martin
Barbara Marx
Ken McCormick
George Oppenheimer
Dorothy Rodgers
Mary Rodgers
Dore Schary
Anne Kaufman Schneider
Judy Shorey
Kate Steichen
George Stevens, Jr.
Howard and Evelyn Teichmann
Lon Tinkle
Phyllis Cerf Wagner
Joan Ward

CONTENTS

FERBER

EPILOGUE

TWENTY-FOUR, twenty-five, twenty-six, twenty-seven . . . She was counting in order to keep her mind on the line. In a week she would be gone. On April 17, 1968, the bottom half of the front page of the New York *Times* would read: "Edna Ferber, who celebrated American life in novels, short stories and plays, died yesterday after a long illness at her home, 730 Park Avenue. She was 82* years old . . ."

On that day in April, my father and I stood on either side of her bed in the darkened room. My father, Henry, who I suppose would be referred to as her "nephew-in-law," was a frequent visitor, and had watched the progression of the cancer. I, her great-niece, young, selfish, and caught up in my own career, hadn't paid my respects for a long time. I tried not to cry out when I saw her. She looked like a strange, wizened child, dwarfed by the normal-sized bed. She didn't look lost, only reduced by her impending death. I reached out, and then, before I touched her hand, checked with my father. He nodded yes. As I touched, the volume of her counting went up slighty—thirty, thirty-one, thirty-two—almost as if to say, "No need. I'll go this one alone, thank you, ma'am. I've done the rest by myself; I can do this one too." I began to weep and left the room. My father said later that he'd kept vigil through the count of eighty, and that she'd never lost a beat.

* She was actually eighty-three years old. There are disagreements about her age. Most sources state that she died at eighty-one. Possibly due to an incurable vanity she reduced her age by two years. In her mother's diary is recorded the only known correct date of Ferber's birth, August 15, 1885.

During the preparations for the service, it occurred to my mother Janet and her sister Mina, Ferber's two nieces, that they should arrange for a police barricade in front of Frank E. Campbell's Funeral Chapel in the event that there be unruly throngs. Since our family had lived under the aegis of the Ferber fame, nobody questioned this.

". . . With a love and enthusiasm that gained her world fame, Miss Ferber wrote about the United States for four decades. Her novels became minor classics and earned her a fortune as well as many honors . . . Her books were not profound, but they were vivid and had a sound sociological basis. She was among the best-read novelists in the nation, and critics of the nineteen-twenties and thirties did not hesitate to call her the greatest American woman novelist of her day . . ." quoted her New York *Times* obituary.

On the morning of her service, my great-aunt Edna did not play to a full house. One of the chosen eulogists couldn't make it, and a great many of her friends were "out of town." The illustrious mourners included Mr. and Mrs. Richard Rodgers, Mr. and Mrs. Leland Hayward, Martin Gabel and his wife Arlene Francis, Mrs. Russel Crouse, George Oppenheimer, theatre critic of *Newsday*, Mrs. Franklin P. Adams, widow of the columnist, and Donald Klopfer, an executive at Random House, Inc. The eulogists, Bennett Cerf, the publisher, Marc Connelly, the playwright, Herbert Mayes, the magazine editor, and Ken McCormick, editor-in-chief of Doubleday, all told anecdotes, received with sprinkled laughter. Marc Connelly recalled that one of Ferber's friends had once told her she regretted most never having met a real hero of American folklore. So, at Ferber's next party, she seated the woman beside George S. Kaufman, the playwright, in the guise of Abraham Lincoln. "He was able to talk to her right up to the assassination . . . with a chattiness that was extraordinarily warm and pleasant," Mr. Connelly said. The thin audience issued an anemic laugh. Ferber probably would have remarked about her own funeral, "It was not an unqualified hit."

There were some characteristic things said of her. Bennett Cerf described her as, "the gallant, dauntless, irrepressible champion of causes she believed in. They were great causes, and when she went on the warpath, tomahawk in hand, sovereign states like Texas and Oklahoma crumbled and arrogant adversaries like Alexander Woollcott were reduced to a quivering glob of Jello. Edna asked for no quarter—and she certainly didn't give any . . . In her home, Edna was an absolute monarch who made Catherine the Great look like Little Orphan Annie. She was a wonderful hostess when her dictates were unquestionably obeyed, but heaven help the oaf who stepped out of line." And, there were loving things said. "She was a story teller and there was none better. She told the story of America . . . they just don't make people like Ferb anymore," lamented Herbert Mayes.

It went on, others spoke, a few tears were shed, and Ferber most likely was casting a jaundiced eye over the lot, thinking that the whole thing needed rewriting.

Afterwards, we walked out onto an empty street. No throngs. Not even a curious passer-by. The cops were taking a smoke and wondering why they were there—what the big deal was. The day was brilliant sunshine. No feeling of death in sight. There was no cortege, no burial, no excess. Ferber had wanted to be cremated—totally gone.

And she'd been counting—forty-three, forty-four, forty-five—so determined not to give it all up.

She took center stage again about three days later. William Klein, Mina's husband, had given a statement to the press that said, "She [Ferber] wasn't religious and didn't want a religious service." Phone calls and letters of protest began to come in. The cry was that in death her family had misrepresented her. That she was a much-self-proclaimed Jew (her autobiography, *A Peculiar Treasure*, lays testament to that fact) and deserved no less than a Jewish service with all the trimmings: rabbi, synagogue, shiva . . . Never. She hadn't wanted that. She wasn't that kind of Jew. She was Edna Ferber, who was lucky enough to be an American and a Jew—not The Jew who was lucky enough to be Edna Ferber. She wouldn't have stood for a service that overwhelmed her with a liturgy that she didn't personally practice. But she would have been pleased that some of her best readers just happened to be Jewish.

Time passes. The family begins to adjust to the loss of its matriarch. Ferber's elder sister Fannie Ferber Fox, now must do without her fondest enemy, her financial support, and psychological antagonist for eighty-three years. Always living in the shadows of her extra-famous sister, Fannie emerges for her last seven years as her own person. It's a fraught sort of freedom. "I wake up in the middle of the night and think, Oh, I must tell this or that to Edna," Fannie says over and over. Fannie's daughter, Janet Fox Goldsmith, is ambivalent toward the thought of no more Ferber. It means no more accepting monster checks and constantly kowtowing, yet obeisance becomes a well-worn habit, difficult to give up. To Mina Fox Klein, it is more of an emotional, less of an assessing loss than her sister's. But that's because she had a bit of distance from the Ferber heat. Early on, she and her husband had moved their family away from New York and somewhat beyond the reach of "Aunt Edna." They were determined that their two kids, Peter and Kathy, would not have to spend a greater part of their young lives saying, "Thank you, Aunt Edna, for everything."

To Henry Goldsmith, in later years Ferber's right arm in business affairs, her death means no more being leaned upon, called upon at any hour. No more hopping. An ulcer staved off.

To me, the loss is severe. Occasionally, the very old and the very young, coming from equidistant points, arrive smack in the middle, and are able to provide comfort for each other. We did that, she and I. I felt close to her and loved her as much as I was allowed. She was not at all a tactile person, so if you loved her, it had to surface from way within. Nothing was easy with her, but if she felt good about you, oh, God, was it worth it. To have Edna Ferber back you up provided you with quite a backbone. An example: I had left college in the middle of my sophomore year; it was a mutual abandonment—I had fired them and they had fired me. The family didn't take it well. There was much throwing up of hands and questioning my moral and cerebral character. Shortly after my departure, we celebrated our annual Christmas Eve shindig at my mother Janet's home. She does a beautiful Christmas (Hanukka was never my family's style), and the apartment was festooned with angel's hair, mistletoe, and gifts from Cartier's, Jensen's, Bonwit's, and Bergdorf's. Sumptuous smells were wafting around, and everyone looked glistening and expectant. But, for me, 'twas not the season to be jolly. I felt like Hester Prynne with a scarlet letter emblazoned on my forehead. I was being politely shunned by all. To be fair, I was also saddled with a heavy dose of paranoia and kept to myself, eating too many hors d'oeuvres in order to avoid explaining, should I be asked, why I'd left higher learning. As I gobbled, I would peek at Aunt Edna, who was wearing a very pink silk dress and was sitting in a blue chair. Her shock of beautifully groomed white hair, topping the pink and the blue, was a startling contrast—like a slightly out-of-kilter piece of the American flag. Whenever I looked up, her eyes were on me, her mouth turned up on one side. For those who knew her, that was her best smile. That crooked little curl of lip, an upturned grimace. It signified fondness, amusement, grit, and power. All in one flick. She was studying me, and I knew I was in safe eyes.

Then, around the hors d'oeuvres, I was joined by Uncle Rudi, my father's sister's husband. An Old World figure. A lovely man, but most of all a scholar. I knew it was coming. "Julie," he intoned with shame. "To leave college, Julie. To do what? An unfortunate step." He shook his head at me, which might as well have been his finger. The room gave way to our *mise en scène*. There are those who are graceful in anger. I'm not one of them. I go off like a lopsided top—no momentum. "Had to leave. Couldn't stand it. Hate establishment. Must go on the stage. Can't LEARN to act," I sputtered. Then he said something about Galsworthy, and that young people had no concept of the value of education until it was too late and their receptive pores were closed. And he went on, scoring point after point. Galsworthy, Kierkegaard, the square root of the right triangle, Prokofiev, Fragonard. And then Aunt Edna to the rescue. In one giant step, it seemed, she was across the living room and by my side. (She was always a walker, never a mincer.) Having sat very still in that blue chair, sipping her Dubonnet, listening to and watching all that was going on, she had prepared her defense. Standing five foot two, her voice towered at six foot three. "Rudi," she said so imperiously that Uncle Rudi deferred by almost bowing. "This girl has great integrity, I'll have you know. If she did not like college, then there was something wrong with the college." (By the by, Ferber had toted the bill for my truncated college education.) She continued. "Talent, Rudi dear, is an innate responsibility. Julie has it, and she must fulfill it in whatever way she knows best. If college is not her bent, so what? Many, many gifted boys and girls have never seen a campus and have somehow made their curds and way. As you know, I never went to college, and just look at the wastrel's life I lead. I have read every good, important author—ancient and modern; I have traveled extensively; I speak two languages, understand three, and write, rather well, so I'm told, in one; I have lectured, enjoyed concerts, love the ballet, know the theatre, and somehow, in between, have managed to earn a dollar. Julie can do anything that she sets her cap for. She is a gifted, clever, and dear girl. I believe in her thoroughly." As if out of a Ferber-Kaufman play, capturing their American-comedy-of-manners style, a maid appeared on cue, announcing dinner. Everyone rose and began to file into the dining room. Ferber winged me, and said, "Let's us go in, doll, and break a little bread."

Aunt Edna had said her piece for me, and it had created peace for me. Nobody ever bothered me about college again. The black sheep had been whitewashed.

Although we all felt the loss of our benevolent, often bedeviling fairy godmother, there was one who actively suffered it. A Miss Molly Hennessy. Molly was with Ferber for eighteen years as housekeeper, cook, companion, confidante, and occasionally, I fear, whipping post. During the last whelping hunk of Ferber life, Molly saw it all, bore it all, respected it all, and, for the most part, loved it all. "Oh, I loved her," Molly brogues. Molly still dreams about Ferber. One dream is particularly recurrent: Ferber stands at the door of her bedroom, dressed in a gray suit with a pink silk blouse and a strand of pearls around her neck. She looks like her old, impeccable self. Molly is trying to keep her in her room because she doesn't know how to tell her that all the furniture in the rest of the apartment is gone. She doesn't know how to tell her that she's dead. Molly laughs and shakes her head. "She wouldn't have accepted it. She was tough. But, God knows I loved her." This cannot be disputed, for Molly saw the author through the details of death. A harrowing experience, which Molly, with an almost macabre pride, refuses to forget. Here, I take the liberty, and possibly the chance of offending, of recording the sequence that Molly tells. Ferber's character looms so large while facing imminent death. It is a clue.

"The cancer progressed until you could see it in her stomach—especially when she wore a knitted suit. She knew for a long time before that she had it, and I knew she knew. At one point, they put her in the hospital. She told me she was going in for a hysterectomy. Now, eighty-three is kind of old for that operation. I mean, who was kidding who? Then, after she came home, she told me herself that it was malignant. So she began to take the cobalt treatment, and I would take her to the hospital. You know, if she had only listened to me, but she wouldn't. I wanted her to take a taxi. You're not supposed to walk like that when you're taking cobalt. But no, walking it was. She wouldn't give it up. Then she had to have a second series, and she started out walking again. They wanted to put her in the hospital for that series, but she wouldn't go. She said, 'Molly will take me to the hospital whenever I have to go, but I won't stay.' Well, Molly took her. We got caught in the pouring rain up there one day. We were in the lobby of Lenox Hill Hospital [Note: At that time Ferber lived at 730 Park Avenue, which is at Seventy-first Street; Lenox Hill is located at Seventy-seventh and Park, six blocks.] and I said, 'Now, Miss Ferber, you sit here, and I'll give the doorman a dollar to go and find us a taxi.' Well, she wouldn't hear of it. And so, the two of us walked home in the downpour. We had to take our shoes off and wade. Her coat didn't dry for a week. Well, that nearly killed her before the cancer could . . . She had to stay in the hospital, in bed, for the end of the series. She was there for quite a while. [Note: One month] I used to be there until ten or eleven at night sitting with her. She didn't want me to go home. She had no faith in the nurses. I used to brush her hair and comb it for her. And I did her poor nails; they were turned over something awful. One night I took a scissor and file and did her nails for her. She said, 'Do you mean to tell me you can do that, and I go and have them done at Elizabeth Arden once a month?' . . . Had I known, I would have done them for her in between her writing . . . But, she was a wonderful person; it's a shame she didn't live longer. She had more life in her than anybody I've ever seen. And, she wanted to do the Indian thing so badly. [Note: A novel on the American Indian that had been in the planning stages for two years. Ferber never got down to the actual writing of it. All she had were notes.] You know that knocked her out too. They were rough trips to the Indian reservations. Even for a regular person. And she was so old for all those plane rides and that sun. The last trip was not too long before she died. And then, physically, she just couldn't take it anymore; she wanted to die at home, in her own bed. And when she was going fast, she took my hand. 'Where is Molly's grave?' she asked. Well, the private nurse who was attending her sort of joked about it. 'Molly, she wants to take you with her,' she said. I don't doubt it. She probably did. Because she always used to say to me, 'Molly, you're the biggest angel that God ever put on this earth.'"

Unfortunately, in Molly Hennessy's case, the meek did not inherit much. Came time for the reading of the will. The occasion took place in the quarters of Greenbaum, Wolff & Ernst, Ferber's illustrious law firm—specifically in the office of Mrs. Harriet Pilpel, who was appointed executrix of the estate.

Contrary to the Disney-like sunshine on the day of the funeral, on the day of the will the air was acid, rain hung suspended; a ruinous atmosphere. The participants at the reading were the immediate heirs: Fannie, Janet, Mina, and myself. Peter and Kathy, being under twenty-one, were not of legal age to inherit, and therefore were not present. Their shares were to be entrusted to their mother, Mina. I remember about two days before the "affair" was to take place, my cousin Kathy saying to me, "Your first will. A dubious achievement. I'm glad I'm not grown up enough." An ultimately grown-up statement.

There was a certain awful excitement to the thing. I can't quite place it, or don't want to, but I know it was there in the room. We sat in a séance-like circle and were each given a copy of the will. Harriet Pilpel, holding the master, presided. There was no attempt at small talk. The scene reminded me of the prelude to taking an entrance exam for college. The proctor would say, "You may not look through the contents of your exam until you hear the word 'Begin.' Then, you will turn to page one."

Harriet Pilpel began to read the first page and we all looked down, more at the fine print than in reverence. We began.

Considering that in her lifetime Edna Ferber's literary output had been: twelve novels, twelve short story collections, two autobiographies, nine plays—plus twenty-five of her properties sold to the films—the accumulation of her wealth was not overwhelming. Considering, however, that she had had her will drawn up in 1956, and in the twelve years following the initial deed provided few codicils, the distribution seemed reasonable. Had it been today—with the rapid devaluation of the dollar, the increasingly stiff estate taxes, the tightening up on gift deductions, and the mounting propensity for greed—it would have been chintzy. But as it was, none of us ever looked Ferber's gift-horse in the mouth. In fact, we all rather pranced for it. Fannie Ferber Fox would be more than comfortable for the rest of her life. She would maintain a co-op in New York, a house in Westport, Connecticut, a live-in companion, and would take a trip to Arizona every March. What more could an octogenarian want? Janet and Mina received ample supplements to ample incomes that their hard-working husbands were already bringing in. Peter, Kathy, and I, as conditioned as we were to Ferber handouts, were bowled over by her generosity toward each of us.

Then there was Ferber's apartment full of perfectly beautiful things to dispense. Spode and Doulton and delft china, Dresden figurines, Waterford glasses, Lalique crystal, antique sterling cutlery, Aubusson rugs, Louis XIV pieces, goose-down stuffed sofas and chairs . . . Things to make one's eyes water. Some of the items were sold at auction, a portion was donated to charity, but the "first family" claimed the bulk of the booty. I didn't even consider that I might be asked whether I wanted anything in particular. And I wasn't asked for a while. Had I been, I probably would have declined—more out of naïveté than humility. At that time, I didn't seriously honor beautiful things. It's an art one learns. Besides, I was perfectly pleased to own Ferber's fountain pen and an autographed picture of James Dean—artifacts my father had rescued when her apartment was first dismantled. Much as I still rue it, I lost the pen. The photo of Dean remains intact, hanging wall-center in our study, for all to read and decipher its slightly obscure message: "Dear Edna, It seems that gentleness is always respected and remembered in the cruel man." He signs it "Jett Rink," the character from Ferber's novel *Giant* that Dean brought blazingly, memorably to life in the movie of that name.

Then, one day a few years ago, my Aunt Mina said, "I have some of Ferber's furniture in storage that you might like to take a look at." I looked and I chose. Two pieces: A refectory table and a secretary of mahogany that looks like poured butter. I was ready for them; I would polish them, tend them, preserve them. A friend, upon seeing them for the first time, suggested they be polished with heavy cream. They are loved.

The phrase "Dutch treat" is anathema to my family. Individually and collectively, we were taken care of. My father always used to say, concerning financial matters, "Don't worry about it. It all comes out of the same pot." He meant the Ferber pot. And of course the family would feed off of the Ferber properties that were still circulatory. It was a blood bank provided by a single, posthumous artery.

But blood proved thicker than paid help. Miss Molly Hennessy, who gave cell after cell, year after year, received a menial transfusion from the will. A family caucus was held and it was decided to chuck in some more, in order to see Molly Hennessy through until her social security could take her the rest of the way.

Edna Ferber died hard with those who took from her and those who served her. She was such a massive little woman that even to have been a mere satellite around her threatened one's autonomy. The important thing when dealing with her was to maintain balance, for she provided quite a teeter-totter, and was never the one to fall. Ken McCormick, her longtime editor at Doubleday, and Harriet Pilpel, her lawyer, were witnesses, participants, and survivors of this strange, psychological metric system. They bore the brunt of it, because they understood that for her the business of writing was hell, pleasure, and all there was. Her release frequently was to upset (or try damn hard to) the ones who aided and abetted her in her life's business. In her 1955 diary, there is an entry on Thursday, November 10, that reads: "Worked A.M.–To Ernst office (Pilpel) at 2:30. There until 5. An irritating and profitless period of talk about contracts for ICE PALACE, SARATOGA, SHOW BOAT, etc. A woman lawyer–the last thing I would ever want . . ." Chances are that Harriet Pilpel didn't have a good session either.

Ferber's tempers were legend. Harriet Pilpel referred to them as "spirals." Some speculate that they were a result of immense sexual repression. There is a chapter in that. One never knew with her what the wrong step might be; it was clear only after the step had been completed. It was as though her foot had been trampled, and she would patiently but furiously let it be known.

She gave a rare (for her) opening night party following the 1966 revival of the George S. Kaufman-Ferber play *Dinner At Eight* in New York. It was prior to the reviews, which were not kind, and everybody was behaving with a forced gaiety. We all sensed the doom that would be ushered in with the critics. Fortunately, the guests were made up of family and old slipper friends. Kitty Carlisle Hart, the Bennett Cerfs, Leland Hayward, the Richard Rodgerses–all were cushions for Ferber, who was exceptionally high-strung that night. She was eighty-one years old, knew that she was dying, and wanted a last hit on Broadway as a send-off. Everyone treated her with kid gloves, save for one young man. An interloper, an actor whom I had brought along. Being surrounded by so many media names and faces apparently bewildered him. He lurched up to Ferber. "Oh, Mrs. Ferber," he began to burble but got no further. She was flashing him her warning signal. Her "You are standing on my foot" look. Her dry-ice look. "Mrs. Ferber, my mother," she enunciated with daggers, "is no longer with us. WHAT did you say your name was?" He hadn't, didn't and wouldn't, for with that, she swiveled around, leaving him to face the back of her large head. Demolished, the young man spent the remainder of the evening in a corner, quietly toeing a piece of rug. "Who does she think she is?" he demanded later, with the irate, high-pitched tone of the callow. "She knows she's Miss Edna Ferber," I replied. Then he said something that haunted me into eventually writing this book. He said, "She *was* Edna Ferber. Once. She's pretty much washed up now."

There is a certain tough finality to being washed up. It brings to mind the gangster phrase "So-and-so was silenced." A writer's best hope, aside from making a living, is perpetuity. Rob him of that, and he might as well have been a sanitation worker. Ferber's only progeny were her books, and to wash them overboard in one fell swoop rendered her a totally barren woman. A parent's wishes toward his children could be applied to Ferber's books. Let them live and be well.

Rudyard Kipling certainly had Ferber's longevity in mind when he wrote to Nelson Doubleday in 1931: ". . . I don't think her own people realise her value as a historical painter—yet. They will later . . ." Ferber was immensely flattered that someone as prophetic as Kipling was known to be had handed her a piece of immortality. "I hope he is right," she responded. "I should love to think that when I am dead the chronicles of my own country written by me because I so wanted to write them will be descendants, however puny and short-lived. We are all vain; we all want to perpetuate ourselves beyond the span of our own brief existence."

But the blunt truth is that Edna Ferber just doesn't get around much anymore. She won the Pulitzer Prize in 1924 for her novel *So Big*. She roped up Texas like a great, thick steer with *Giant* —1952. She paved the way for Alaskan statehood with *Ice Palace* —1958. She inadvertently provided every black baritone (who wanted to sing it) with "Ol' Man River" through her writing of *Show Boat*—1926. She aided Gary Cooper, Ingrid Bergman, Irene Dunne, Jane Wyman, Rock Hudson, Elizabeth Taylor, James Dean, and countless others by providing vehicles for their "starships."

She was a precursor of the Women's Liberation Movement by depicting every single one of her fictional heroines as progressive originals who doggedly paved large inroads for themselves and their "race." Her male characters, on the other hand, were usually felled by their colorful but ultimately ineffectual machismo. Ferber lived, worked at, and perfected the American Dream by never wasting time dreaming of it. She wrote only about America and gave its public an introduction to, and an identification with, itself, and a reading joy that lasted for over half a century. Yet, now, she has gone into what literary historians call an "eclipse." "A decline" is another polite term for it. Obscurity is the rude and, I fear, most accurate expression for what has befallen Edna Ferber. Donald Klopfer, a Random House executive, ponders the reasons that a writer with her impact and output becomes an anachronism so shortly after her death. "She was a great craftsman—shrewd, fine and extremely competent, but she lacked—say, what Faulkner has —a universality. She was a public personality of that time, that public. Faulkner is sure to have a place in the year 2000. Ferber??"

Not one Ferber book is required reading in schools, which eliminates tomorrow's people from her storytelling. Even my own contemporaries look shadowy when confronted with her name.

"Gee . . . I . . ."

"Ever heard of *Giant*?"

"Ummm . . ."

"The movie—with James Dean."

"Oh yeah. James Dean, sure. Hey, she write that?"

Most libraries don't have full Ferber collections. And bookstores—well, just try to get a paperback copy of *So Big*, her Pulitzer Prize-winning novel. A while after her death, I decided to see how accredited she was in the bookstores around New York. I tried them all. At Doubleday Book Shops (the namesake of her publisher)—nothing. The same bad luck followed suit with all the others. Who? What? Ferber? No. Finally, at Marboro's, on Fifty-seventh Street near Seventh Avenue, I thought for a brief, shining moment that I'd picked up the scent. Upon hearing my request, the salesperson nodded affirmatively and said, "Oh yes. We have one of her books. We have *Back Street*." "That was Fannie Hurst," I hissed, and stormed out.

Some novelists lead large personal lives—sometimes lurid, sometimes eccentric, and often tragic. Most share with each other a common denominator: that life dictates their art—no matter how fetal the process. There is a brotherhood of "thrombosis" fiction writers who feel they must obstruct normal circulation in order to get to the heart of what they have to say. And by and by, if they are prolific, the reader gets to know their insides. They become "celebrities" by regurgitating their private lives for public consumption. Then there is the breed of novelist who, after one or two major books, finds he is unable to top himself, or to even keep going. He either sinks into his own oblivion or continues to grind out words with the terrible knowledge that he'll never be a writer again. Edna Ferber never fell into psychological traps; she wouldn't even permit herself to know that they did indeed exist. Her life was economic, antiseptic—absolutely no excesses were allowed. She was a Middle Western maiden lady who took care of her mother, her family, and her typewriter. She recycled herself with every book, and each seemed a testament more to her own health and vigor than to inspiration. With themes like Seattle, Oklahoma, Alaska, New England, the West, Texas—she had no time or penchant for personal probing. There was too much to do. Her ego was as mammoth as her scope, and no man, vice, crisis, or illness was going to deter her. An obsessive in the most productive sense, a spinster in the most resolved sense, a plain woman who kept herself in silk purses, and an angry daughter who determinedly made her mother's life roses. Judging by the fact that she could alchemize liabilities into assets, that discipline was first nature to her, that she ate right, slept right, and was a staunch defender of the unjust, one would assume that her bill of mental health was immaculate. A presumption. Her complete devotion to her mother Julia bordered on the incestuous. Her hatred of her sister Fannie was at times close to being pathological. Her need and ability to "play God" was despotism at its worst. There were chinks in her armor. Many.

Once when I was young I asked her if she was ever lonely. She looked startled, and then recovered almost too quickly. Her answer was very sad; it had a rehearsed quality about it. "Oh, never," she said. "The people in my books are my friends. They don't let me down."

Being a romantic realist, not opposed to working within the system, she created a mink-lined rabbit hole for herself. Her "wonderland" was work; her "tea party" was research. Curiouser and curiouser.

There are reams of pungent adjectives to describe Ferber. Dore Schary packages her nicely and simply, with "She was a remarkable woman." But Max Gordon, the producer—the David Merrick of yesteryear—has a unique and accurate way of expressing exactly what she wasn't. With a Damon Runyon inflection and a nostalgic smile, he says, "Well, I'll tell ya. Ferber? She was no schlepper."

I have chosen to write this book backwards—from Ferber's death down into her life, in lieu of the natural progression. Applying the phrase "When she was four" to Edna Ferber seems puerile and a waste of time. Besides, I'm sure she was four very quickly in her eagerness to get on with it. Because she never "schlepped" through life, it seems more fitting to have her descend gracefully back into it. But not so graceful as to be without her quirky, self-satirizing humor. About to become the subject of a biography—a backwards one no less—she would most likely say, "Wheee."

THE LAST WARPATH

1968-1960

THE QUESTION was what to title the novel she knew she would never write. Ferb, as only her dear friends called her, was floundering, feeling beached, for the first time in her life. After a steady output for sixty-seven years, she'd run dry. She'd known for two years that she had cancer and was weary with the knowledge of it. She felt physically and emotionally washed up, which at eighty-two might be considered a natural feeling. To Edna Ferber it was unthinkable.

So, she needed a title for what would be her last novel—the one about the American Indian. It was not the way she usually worked. The title always came last, after the body of the novel had borne itself. It was incidental until she saw that she had a healthy child with a personality. To be sure, she probed around for titles during the arduous years of birthing a novel; when working on *Saratoga Trunk*, she constantly referred to it as "the Saratoga thing," knowing that Saratoga was the key word. Selina Peake was the heroine of her novel *So Big*, and for a while she could only visualize *Selina* on the dust jacket. After her novel *Come and Get It* was already completed, and the first installment about to be published in the popular magazine *Woman's Home Companion*, she was still at a title loss and wrote an SOS to her dear friend William Allen White: ". . . Will you do something for me. Will you and Sallie [Mrs. White] talk together for five minutes and then wire me, pronto, your opinion of two titles. I am in what is known as a quandry (slang for jam). I've got to have a title. Now. The main character's name is Barney Glasgow and they call him Gusto. You know the period of the first part . . . Also you know the underlying theme of the book—the grabbers of the Robber Barons school. So which. GUSTO or COME AND GET IT. Wire me, there's darlings . . ." White's answer came back in the form of a Western Union kind of anagram: COMENGETIT GRANTITLE.

Now, with her career behind her and the Indian book a looming obstacle in front of her, she racked herself for a title; a creative life jacket. Her state of mind was not good but it was clear. It was clear that she'd reached a dead end, but she kept on going—researching between cobalt treatments, trying to think up possible alternative projects, going for dress fittings at Bergdorf Goodman, hairdos at Elizabeth Arden, having dinners with family, walking a mile every morning, and searching, stalking for that book title, which haunted and eluded her. Every time she moved away from the Indian project, her spirits would perk, but then doggedly, perhaps masochistically but always professionally, she would return to her task and her spirits would fall down. She writes in a 1966 diary, ". . . got some slight ideas for 'Manhattan, The Bronx and Queens'. Play? Short novel? Perhaps I'm coming out of the doldrums. How about 'Squaw' for Indian book title? Don't really like it. Preparing for Phoenix Indian trip Friday. Sort of dread it."

Aside from age, physical disability, and spiritual malaise, there was one rather outstanding reason why she was unable to shoulder this last book. Simply, she felt little compassion for, and didn't much like, her subject. She felt that the American Indian as a people tended to be manic depressive—without hope for themselves, whereas the other American peoples that she had dealt with all had the vigor and the guts that excited her into producing them on paper. She writes among her Indian notes: "Title? Sorrow Into Song." And then cryptically under it as a subtitle: "Indians Sit And Sulk."

Out of all the untapped factions of American life, it's curious that she chose this "sulky" subject that caused her such stagnation. What then? It was the Indian women, the squaws—they grabbed her. Ferber, a rampant feminist, although she camouflaged it by wearing baby pinks and blues, could never remain unmoved by the plight of the strong woman forcibly suppressed in a male world. She identified with them and, in creating them for fictional purposes, glorified them. Her divider line between the sexes was apt to be simplistic if not childish. Women were doers; men were dreamers. Women were workers; men were idlers. Women had character; men had plumage. Men were women's fatal flaw. The emotional distance between the two sexes as depicted by Ferber was comparable to that distance between the North and the South during the Civil War. And, interestingly enough, the kind of woman that she found detestable and seldom wrote about was the Southern belle, child-woman type. The kind with an abundance of physical attributes and a deficit of mental ones. The spineless, isn't-life-soft-for-everyone? kind. Ferber condemned and mimicked the utterly fluttery female, and yet secretly envied the easy prettiness of that sort—marveled at their right to captivate without doing anything. Physical loveliness fascinated her as it often does for one without it.

The Indian woman was right up Ferber's alley. In fact, as she grew older, she began to look like some awesome, Aztec princess who planned to live forever. In her notes for the nonexistent book, she writes with pride about the women: "The Indian women were the leaders now—the do-ers—the workers—the planners. They always had been. Perhaps they had learned this from the modern American matriarch—non-Indian. Or perhaps the white American pioneer woman had somehow learned this from the American Indian woman—she who bore the children, cared for them, planted the grain and gathered it, dressed the raw skins and stitched together with sinews the clothing of skins and fur: Cooked the food, carried the burden, tended the children, built the tepee or hogan or wickiup with her own hands. Now, on the reservation, in the later years of the twentieth century, she kept the house, she went out to work, she joined the women's club, she edited the reservation monthly newspaper, she fought to send her children to the schools, either government or reservation or local public schools. She wanted water in the house—even a bathroom, she had her hair done at the beauty parlor, she dressed in correct prints in the hot months and suits in the cooler days; nylons and spiked pumps and the proper handbag." Quite a love letter, and close to what was Ferber fiction. A great many of her notes read like prose. Her own sign language, hardly ever obscure, often glitters—as though she was showing off for herself. In another powerful scribble she writes, "There are hundreds—no, thousands—of lazy resentful dirty drunken North American Indians in the United States. And there are millions of lazy resentful drunken dirty North American non-Indians in the United States. The difference is that if you say this about an Indian you're in trouble. And if you say it about a white he's in trouble."

On April 20, 1966, Ferber wrote in her diary, "Nothing on the Indian novel except filing of notes. Hair done at 2. A drastic cut & much better. Mina and Bill in at 6. Dinner at Passy with them and Janet and Henry and Julie. Pleasant."

It was not at all pleasant. Ferber was having a hard time with herself that night. Usually impeccably groomed, she looked askew, as though her mood had dictated her toilette. A frump she wasn't, but she did look frumpy; her suit was too pink against the too blue rinse of her hair. It was obvious that she needed to vent her spleen that night. It was the night she called the wine steward a eunuch.

Some families have chicken dinner every Sunday, or cold cuts or Chinese food. We had Passy—an extremely elegant French restaurant at 28 East Sixty-third Street. It was the kind of place where one "dressed"; gentlemen without ties or ladies in slacks or those with dirty fingernails were banished. We didn't like it much—mainly because the service and food were pretentious, but it was Ferber's blind spot—one of her favorite pretensions. Perhaps it was because she was treated there like the great white author. They bowed and scraped, snapped menus and emptied ashtrays like mad. Or perhaps she doted on the place because it provided her with a decent, but not too tiring, after-dinner walk home. She had to have her walk home regardless of the elements. At any rate, none of us could quite put our fingers on why Passy was habitual, but we went with Ferber every Sunday night, grudgingly gracious. Occasionally Janet or Henry would try to deter her from the Passy ritual by suggesting some new and highly touted restaurant in town. Actually Ferber would open herself up for it by saying, "If you could choose the most dazzling place in the whole entire city to dine—where would it be?" Then Janet or Henry would give a rapt description of seafood or Northern Italian or French Provincial dining delights. Then Ferber would, without having been to any of the places, rapidly tear them apart. They all sounded too bourgeois, too amateur, too far downtown to be safe, too far uptown to be any good. "Never heard of it," was her key, denouncing phrase. Then she would extol her dear Passy. And then we would go.

Ferber was fond of this particular game. It was as though she flirted with not getting her way when she knew that we knew that she would. She was a creature of habit, evidenced in her diaries, which day by day almost inevitably begin with, "Walked a mile before breakfast." It was also a habit that in every stage of her existence she had to be "king of the castle."

Passy had a foyer followed by several steps leading down into the dining room. The steps served as a grand entrance for those who were so inclined to want to be seen by the whole room. Ferber always enjoyed being recognized—although she pretended it was tiresome—and because she was short, this particular design was perfect for her.

That night nobody recognized her, and the maître d' seemed harried and not as effusive as usual toward her. She went into a private pet, and as we were all being seated she said, an octave too loudly, "What a dreary crowd here tonight"—her way of getting back at the lack of attention being paid her. She'd do that often—turning things around, distorting them to suit her needs.

During the perusing of the menu she was extremely acid, causing a blush of discomfort to spread over all of us. After we had ordered, the wine steward approached the table, and with him Ferber found her target. He was one of those unfortunate fellows with no beard and a dissonant falsetto voice. Although he had probably been there for years, she suddenly saw him with new dislike. Ferber had a cruel streak, and when it came out, it just bowled one over. It was usually unleashed upon those whom she considered "menial" people: waiters, cabdrivers, salespeople, etc. The wine steward fell cozily into this category. He took the order for a very nice bottle of Bordeaux and returned with it shortly. He was overly elaborate in preparing to uncork the bottle, and kept saying, "Such a nice wine, Miss Ferber. You have good taste. You'll enjoy it, I'm sure." Ferber's eyes never left him; she was waiting for him to blunder. He did. For all his fancy gestures with the bottle opener, and flourishes with his elbows, he somehow managed to backfire the cork, submerging it in the bottle and spraying the table with wine. Ferber jumped back as though he had spit, coiled herself up, and then it came—crisply enunciated and loud: "You eunuch. You clumsy ox. How dare you be so inept." The poor offender fled muttering something about a new tablecloth, new wine, and probably a new job. Ferber, never being one to let disturbances die, summoned the captain and lambasted him for allowing such an oaf to be employed there. The captain doused her with a perfume of apologies, brought out a gratis bottle of better wine, and implied that she would not have to see the wine steward again. She'd gotten the attention she'd wanted, but in a sad way. The entire dining room had noticed her—not as Edna Ferber—but as that small lady who made a whopper of a scene.

Needless to say the next Sunday night we were back at Passy. The wine steward wasn't.

During her last ten years when everything began to fail her—health, career ability, relationships—she had one leading source of agony. There is a facial nerve disease called trigeminal neuralgia, more commonly known as tic douloureux, which, according to the medical profession, is one of the worst forms of pain known to man. It is virtually unendurable and almost incurable, its only remedy being to sever the nerves on whichever side of the face it occurs, thereby leaving that side of the face totally paralyzed. The alternatives are ghastly: pain or paralysis. Ferber chose the former, and never for a moment felt that she might renege and undergo the operation. For a plain woman, she had tremendous vanity; the good points that she felt she did have she guarded with a watchdog ferocity. Her hair was her prized possession. Thick, snowy, and gleaming, she brushed it a hundred strokes every morning and every night, and conditioned it with Alberto VO 5. Molly Hennessy would occasionally interrupt this ritual, only to be admonished by Ferber, who would say, "Not now, Molly dear. I'm doing some of my best thinking."

Her teeth were another proud feature. Strong and white, they got to masticate only the finest of steaks, chops, and vegetables. She was near to fetishistic about her toothbrushes. She had three: one for morning, one for after lunch, and one for before bed. She kept each of them in a separate glass, soaking in an alkaline solution, in order to avoid any germs that might otherwise find their way into the bristles. Ferber was a dentist's dream—incomewise and hygienewise. She went too regularly, demanded too much attention, and as a result her teeth were masterpieces. When her smile broke, they dazzled.

Her legs and her eyes were her other shrines. She considered them her lifetime propellers. They worked synonymously—her legs for the autonomy that she needed to provide scope for her eyes. Her legs, short and sturdy, rather resembling drumsticks—were certainly not Lloyd's of London material. But they served her beautifully all of her life—walking her everywhere in lieu of riding—and always showing her the town. The old saying of, "Feet, do the walking," was exactly what Ferber appointed hers to do at every possible moment. They were large for her body—size 8—and always expensively but sensibly shod. Walking was like a religion with her, and anyone who didn't want to or didn't believe in it was blasphemous. She had trouble in California, where if one walks, especially at night, one tempts an arrest for loitering. While out there, she thought she might have a soulmate in Katharine Hepburn, but Hepburn preferred to bicycle and tried to coerce Ferber into pedaling. Ferber refused, held her ground, and continued to walk it.

Ferber's eyes were like laser beams; they burned out of her face in anger, wisdom, and truth. Never soulful, they were her soul. Ferber had an extreme fear of and sensitivity toward blindness. When she was thirteen, her father, Jacob Ferber, began losing his sight. By the time she was sixteen, he was totally blind. His optic nerve had atrophied, or, as a doctor long ago explained his condition to her mother, Julia Ferber, "it had shrunk until it was dead." Ferber watched her father lose sight of his eyes and of his life. She writes movingly of it in her autobiography, *A Peculiar Treasure:* "It was sad when he lost his taste for smoking. Ever since I could remember he had loved to smoke mild pale-brown dapper cigars. As sight slipped from him his enjoyment of this solace went with it. The smoker is usually unaware that he watches the smoke from cigar, cigarette or pipe, and is soothed by it as by the narcotic. It must have been so in his case. As he held his cigar between his teeth a puzzled disappointed look would come into his face. He would take the cigar from his lips and look at it, sorrowfully, as one would survey a treacherous trusted friend. He would quietly put it down, the smoke would curl futilely for awhile, then die. The fragrant weed would be a dead stinking thing, fit only for the ash can. When a friend or a chance traveling man offered him a cigar he would shake his head sadly. "No. I used to love to smoke. But now I can't see it. No sir, I don't enjoy smoking anymore. I don't know why."

When I was at college, Ferber sent me a letter in which she said, "The enclosed check is for, say, steak or something good for the eyes." The check was for five hundred dollars.

Partially because she made a living from her eyes, and partially because her father went blind, she always placed a heavy emphasis on the value of vision. She was a big carrot eater. She'd serve them at dinner parties and order them when she went out. "They make my eyes bright and my hair curly," she used to say, imitating a goody-goody. But she believed it.

In the last ten years of her life, probably her worst fear came to pass. She began to have trouble with her eyes. Glaucoma and cataracts in her left eye, and, later, cataracts in her right. She was operated on, she was in pain, she was severely depressed, but she was not blind, which was all that really mattered.

Ferber was one of the original "health nuts," beating Euell Gibbons, Adelle Davis, and scores of others to the punch. She proselytized to everybody she could get her hands on about the urgency of a balanced diet, clean air, and walking. She ate three squares a day, never snacked, took an occasional sherry before dinner, and perhaps had one cigarette once a month—never inhaling it. Anybody that did otherwise was mistreating his body. One of her largest requisites was a good night's sleep, and anything under eight hours was a personal disaster. She recorded her sleep patterns in her diaries; the entries have a sort of desperation about them: Friday, May 6, 1966—"Practically no sleep Friday night." Saturday, May 7, 1966—"Slept over nine hours result of practically no sleep Friday night." She was not a napper. She felt that only ladies who took long lunches, ate bonbons, and wore peignoirs could afford to nap. She counted on her nighttimes, and when they let her down she became despondent.

She never would reconcile herself to the fact that with aging her body was changing. She demanded the same things of it as she had when she was a young girl. It was a "knock wood" philosophy. If she treated it well—which relentlessly she did—it would return the favor. She also refused to recognize that her psyche was part of her physical tide. When, at age seventy-seven, she got an ulcer, she regarded it as something from outer space, never admitting that the fear that her last book had been written was riding her. It was a duodenal ulcer that she treated with respect, feeding it all the milk and softs that it needed, until eventually it healed itself. The only surprise in the matter is that it was her first ulcer. With all her inner tension, which she rarely allowed herself to release, one would think that ulcers would have made an early entry in her life.

As quickly as the ulcer left her alone, the ghastly facial neuralgia lingered on to torture her. It was as though the scream of a lifetime had landed on the right side of her face. It is a nerve-based disease about which relatively little is known. Its nature is fickle; it can leave its victim alone for months on end, and then suddenly, like a shark's attack, rip into the cheek again. How Ferber endured the pain her family and friends will never know. It was almost a self-sacrifice, a bloodletting. She hardly ever complained when the attacks were upon her, and, curiously, she didn't even let loose in her diaries. The entries emphasize fortitude instead of despair. "Agonizing facial pains all day. The combination of darvon and Bufferin relieves this somewhat, but the dulling effect is, of course, destructive to writing. Nevertheless worked A.M. Shopped. No dresses to be had—for me at least. But bought a coat at Bergdorf's $60, pale blue, and I don't like it. What a state of mind. Walked home, got myself a bit of dinner, ate it in bed. Terribly, inexplicable weary. Slept 8 hours." She did her best to try to divert herself from the pain. "Worked, but not well. Considerable facial pain. With Ada Taylor to see the Rock Hudson picture 'Lover Come Back.' Rather foolish but amusing." There is only one entry that has no pluck at all. "Agonizing facial pains. So distracted I can scarcely manage to bathe and dress. Breakfast. Walked a bit but yielded for the first time. Simply could not work. Dozed for an hour. No better. Took an anecin."

One always knew when Ferber had "The Face." She usually called Henry, Janet, and me every two or three days. She wouldn't call for a while when she was in the throes of it, and she wouldn't receive any calls. But Lord help you if you didn't *try* to call. There would come a very martyred, nasty note—with a check. The money being an attempt to buy her way out of feeling ugly. When she did call, her voice was unusually low, halting, and steeped in pain. Whoever answered would say, "Hello?" and then have to wait ages for a response. It was even an effort for her to say hello. The conversations were usually unpleasant. My mother Janet got the brunt of it. Ferber knew that she was receptive and sensitive, and would use her as an emotional pincushion. My mother understood but resented it. Who wouldn't? It was the worst kind of manipulation. One doesn't step on someone who's down, yet the person who's down often has the power position and steps on everybody else. We all hated it when Ferber had "The Face." Mostly for her sake.

There are a couple of reasons why Ferber refused the operation that could have relieved her of her agony. There is a story that contributes to one of the reasons. It goes like this: Ferber had a massive head; the features were strong, generous, and vital. It was a sculptor's dream, and indeed, during the thirties, a popular artist of that time executed a bust of Edna Ferber. Now there was a writer-raconteur of that era named Corey Ford, who was a known enemy of Ferber's. Ford's comment when he saw the sculpture was that it looked like the head of a buffalo. This gibe got back to Ferber, who called Ford and threatened suit for damage of reputation. Ford replied with, "Well, in that case, I'll just have to bring a buffalo into court." The case rested right then and there. Years later, Ferber gazed at the sculpture and mused, "You know, it looks like a buffalo." The story proves how much Ferber began to enjoy her own physical lore. Her head was her trademark; it signified all of the powerful thoughts going on inside it. To mutilate it in any way, which the operation would have done, would have been facial suicide.

The second reason was more spiritual than physical. Ferber's mother, Julia, in her later years became a devout Christian Scientist. The credo of this religion is based on an interpretation of the Scriptures that disease, sin, and death are caused by mental error and have no real existence. Some of this theory must have rubbed off on Ferber, who had been devoted to Julia and all that she stood for. Her stoic endurance of the racking pain makes sense when put in this light. To bear her hell was to honor her mother.

During the years of "The Face" Ferber managed to write two books: *Ice Palace* and *A Kind of Magic*. Neither was received well and neither was very good. They were certainly not her best efforts, but then she was not at her best while writing them. Considering the duress she was under, they bear an amazing resemblance to her former work.

One day in the middle of 1965, "The Face" disappeared. She waited for months for it to reclaim her, but it never did. In late 1965, cancer took its place.

In the interim before her cancer was diagnosed, she felt relatively positive about writing her novel on the American Indian. She had an instinctive eye about fresh subjects to probe, and at that time the American Indian had not yet been explored as they are today. It was an open field, and she did so love to play pioneer. Her calendars and date books of 1965–66 are filled with Arizona schedules, for she was concentrating on the reservations in Phoenix and Scottsdale. She was no stranger to Arizona. She'd been using Phoenix for years as a retreat from the rigors of New York City's weather. Elizabeth Arden operated an elegant "rest farm" there called Arizona Maine Chance, where Ferber would go to recoup her physical losses. She would often stay at the Arizona Biltmore Hotel and be driven daily to the farm for revitalizing health treatments and exercises. Arden's also served as an elite social club where Ferber would find old friends and acquaintances such as Clare Boothe Luce, Ina Claire, or Kitty Carlisle Hart, and would dine with one or the other in the evenings. There was a definite snob appeal about the place, which Ferber was not at all opposed to. She liked to socialize with "quality" people. It was an unwritten rule that Arden's supplied them—and only them. Once after a spell at Arden's, Ferber came back with her version of a horror story. The Gabors had invaded—all of them. She seriously considered changing her vacation spot.

During the years that Ferber patronized Arden's, there must have been a third eye casting around for book material. Her muse worked in mysterious ways. She would glimpse an idea years before she welcomed it. While she was resisting her vision, her subconscious was broadening it—until finally it would envelop her like Cinemascope. Then she would sit down and write the novel. So, the Indian book had probably been a-borning for as long as she'd been going to Arizona. In fact, in the early sixties, she'd mentioned it to her West Coast agent, Irving (Swifty) Lazar, who had recently made a tremendous film sale of her novel *Ice Palace*. He vaguely remembers the reference. "Oh, yeah—she talked about doing some Indian thing." Strange that she mentioned it to him at all, with it being in such a preliminary state. She knew that agents aren't interested in ideas—only the execution of them. She must have been feeling insecure. She also talked a great deal about it to Ken McCormick, her editor at Doubleday. He shakes his head sadly at the recollection of those discussions, admitting that secretly he felt the project would never get off the ground. However, he tried his best to see that it would. He knew how desperately she needed bolstering, and, gallant gent that he is, he supplied it in concrete terms. In 1964, he wrote to her: "Working on the very sound basis that when you're at work on a book you are happy and we are happy, wouldn't it help you to begin to firm up this Indian idea if we worked out a contract? There isn't any question that we want you to write that novel very much and there isn't any question in my mind that you want to write it. I think that if you had some sort of committment, if not to deliver a novel at least to explore the possibilities, it might help you psychologically in your development of this important theme. Let's talk it over."

Ferber must have had a premonition that the book would never be done, for no contract was ever drawn up. All the coddling in the world couldn't stave off her pessimism. It was as though she was pregnant with an unwanted, too late child and didn't know whether to abort or to go through with it. There was a fierce morality in connection with Ferber and her work; she felt the same obligation toward it as one would feel toward a child. She went through the motions of bringing her Indian book up, but without her old conviction, know-how, and agility.

It is hard to say for sure when Ferber knew that she had terminal cancer, but by 1967 she was dealing with it in a quirky, psychological way. Since she had already amassed reams of Indian research material and notes, and since she had already allied herself with Indian officials in Arizona, Oklahoma, and Washington—she figured why give up in order to die? So she continued with her plans —but questioned them. In March of 1967, she wrote in her calendar: Sunday—March 12 Flight-#114 Amer. Air Line Kennedy—5:30 (arrive) Phoenix—8:37 [the clincher] Round Trip—?

On Friday, October 13, 1967, there is another eerie clue to the way she felt. She writes: "Garden [her personal secretary] see next page. Also order new calendar?"

In another entry on the same day one realizes her full grasp of her situation: "Enter record of Medicare payments compared with own payments of Doctor bills—nurses—hospital room—drugs etc. Additional payment to nurses."

Although not a page of actual prose was written on the Indian book, her "novel notebook," as she refers to it, reads exceptionally well. In some of her jottings, her state of mind seems to blend with the Indian's state of race. "I've been stumbling around for years, really, like a prospector in the Southwest desert mountains. I've visited reservations of The Puablos, The Apaches, The Navajos, The pimas, The Papagoes, The Hopis. I've talked to superintendents, spent days, weeks in Government schools in which Indian boys and girls, young men and women, were being given free, a much more impressive educational program than I ever had had. Equipment, food, teaching staff, libraries, dormitories, sports, games, languages, crafts, arts, sciences, trades, professions. I've entered such Indian houses as I could, though almost invariably I was not wanted in these houses. Mysterious? No, it wasn't mystery that baffled me, any more than a rock is mysterious. It gives back no response, but that does not necessarily give one the effect of a mystery unsolved. The rock is simply there—a rock. Perhaps there is a vein of pure gold in it, once you've split it. But more likely it is just a rock. The more I learn the less I know."

Ferber knew what the spine of her novel would be; it was the same as in all of her other novels—the working through of generations—the youth into aging process. What she was having difficulty with—anxiety with—was in choosing her vertebra of characters. She'd stayed with Southern Indians; surveyed and visited Indians in South Carolina; in Northern Florida she thought she was finally onto them—hence the book. But she was wrong. They remained elusive to her, the rub being that she did not know who the American Indian of the present was. She knew of their history, of their oppression, and of their customs. She knew that she liked the idea of doing them honor by writing about them. Yet, she was looking for an Indian that she liked—and couldn't find one. Judging from her notes, it seems that she kept inserting herself into her possible choice of protagonist. She writes: "Is one of the book's characters a novelist? Man or woman? A Hemingway? A Sinclair Lewis? A Michener? or one of those historian writers who have wrung the Civil War dry?"

She plays around with the possibility of using a young anthropologist character who works with and studies the Indian, and who sounds like Ferber in mufti. She writes a passage in which her own condition and the philosophy of the novel are mixed up into one. "One of the workers on the Reservation—a non-Indian perhaps elderly or perhaps young worker. Ill, but ambulatory. Spoke of her physical state as a 'Terminal illness.' She had, like most of the world, a horror of the word cancer. A terminal illness.

"Young Anthropologist. (With a shrug that conveyed the comparitive unimportance of this.) 'Life itself is a terminal illness. You're a victim of it from the minute you're born until you die. Life itself is the one terminal illness which we're all afflicted by. You have it the moment you're born and you have it until you die of it. Life.'"

The Indian no doubt depressed her, and brought her own recently dour philosophy to the fore. Most of the passages in her notebook yield more Ferber than Indian, but there is one that speaks for itself. It is the kind of background work that Ferber used to excel at in her prime. It is the lead-in to what the book might have been.

"The American Indian, occupying the North American continent for ten—twenty—perhaps forty-five thousand years—did almost literally nothing with it. Used practically nothing of its treasures, its vast and unmatchable riches. They hunted, they fished, they moved from place to place (with a watchful eye on their enemies, the nearby Indians of another tribe.) A vast continent, breath-taking in its beauty and variety: protected on two sides by the embracing arms of vast ocean, later to be known as the Atlantic and the Pacific. Illimitable (?) forrest: lakes as vast as seas: rivers as vast as lakes. Metals of every kind hidden in the mountains, in the streams, in the secret depths of the soil. Grains, fruit, fowl, flesh to be gathered or seized. There never was such richness to be had for the taking.

"The American Indian did little or nothing with all this splendor or natural wealth. They foraged for food, killed or plucked it, brought it to their crude dwelling, ate it if it were a deer or a buffalo or another of the plentitude of animals, wore its hide for clothing, used its tendons for weapons, its bones for utensils. They hadn't the ingenuity to devise a clay pot wherein to cook their food: or to chop down a tree wherewith to build their house: a wheel whereby to transport their burdens in a crude cart or barrow. They ate, slept: made war on other tribes: worshipped nature, apologized to a deer before killing it for food. Made an offering of cornmeal to the gods of nature: the animals, the winds, the rain, the sun, the streams, the forrests. After forty-five thousand years of their occupation the continent was almost precisely as they had found it, except for the slow march of nature itself as the glaciers formed and moved and made their almost imperceptible march and melted: The huge reptiles made their slithering way out of the slime and had their brief day of thousands of years, and vanished forever.

"They made almost no mark on the virgin world they occupied

alone. They dwelt in their tents of skin: they wore it as clothing: they used its sinews, its bones, its hair, its claws. The nearest tribe was their nearest enemy. The most glorious continent on the globe was theirs. They used it (inhabited it) for thousands of years and occupied it almost untouched by their presence. Somewhere along the way they discovered that there was another way to slay an animal other than to club it over the head. As the centuries rolled by someone came upon the fundamental truth that a small hard stone could be filed and sharpened and pointed by a larger stone wielded in the hands of a patient hunter, so that a three cornered thing emerged, called an arrow. This mounted on a quill or a stick, and propelled by a string of animal tendon and bent bow could be aimed to fly between the animal's eyes and no nonsense about clubbing or hammering with a heavy stone. The bow and arrow. But that was all. No cooking vessel. No transportation other than the human leg and foot: no permanent dwelling: no written language: no contact with other Indian tribes: no common language. If an Indian of one tribe were to speak to an Indian of another tribe, not one word was to be understood any more than a Pole who spoke Polish only could understand an Italian who spoke Italian only. The breathtaking plains, the praries, the rivers, lakes, seas, mountains, forrests were unchanged, almost untouched: almost as unknown and virgin as they had been before the foot of the Indian had mysteriously been set upon this magic, this electric land."

In between trips to Arizona, Ferber spent her time feeling ill, weary, and dispirited, seeing and dismissing doctors, dealing with her lawyers, shopping at Bergdorf's and then returning the things that she'd bought, and arguing bitterly with her sister Fan. She did not get along with her older sister and never had, but in the years when she was marking time before death, she also brutally marked the distance between them. One of the reasons for her increase in bile was that she knew that Fan would outlive her. It was painful and distorting to watch the two of them together. It was like a Diane Arbus photo; they were so visually similar and so visually sour. Each raped the good qualities out of the other when they were together. Yet they persisted in being together; they really had nobody else.

Molly Hennessy was alway playing arbitrator for the feudin' and fussin' between Fannie and Ferber. There was one time when they didn't speak for two weeks over something or other infinitesimal.

Molly took it upon herself to phone Fannie, saying, "How would you girls [Fannie and her nurse-companion] like to join us girls for some dinner?" Fannie asked whether Ferber knew about the invitation. Molly said certainly. Fannie accepted. Just as Molly was hanging up, Ferber, with her innate stage timing, came into the kitchen and asked who Molly had just invited to dinner. Molly came clean, thinking that she was really going to catch hell. Ferber asked if Fannie had accepted the invitation. Molly nodded. There was a silence and then Ferber said gleefully, "Why, that's just wonderful." And they went on to plan a sumptuous meal, including all of Fannie's favorites.

Fannie Ferber Fox, who died in January of 1975 at the age of ninety-two, was fond of saying, "I don't know. I just don't know what it was. But something very strange overtook Edna during the last three years before she went. She changed drastically." Fannie didn't know about the cancer until it was in its late stages. Ferber, having never shared her emotional plights with her sister, was certainly not about to share her impending death. The only medium of sharing exchange between them was Ferber's money. Ferber literally supported Fannie all of her adult life—some of which Fannie knew about, and some of which Ferber had arranged for without her knowing. At any rate, Fannie was kept by her own sister, which bred contempt from both sides. What they shared was a bankbook of resentment. Even had Fannie been aware of Ferber's cancer, one doubts whether she could have subtracted the venom in their relationship.

Very few of Ferber's friends saw her through to the end. Several of her dear ones—Moss Hart, George Kaufman, Russel Crouse—had already preceded her and therefore could not possibly oblige her. And most of the others were not too busy to care, perhaps, but too busy to know about her condition. Ferber's friends were never "fair-weather," it was only that they were some of the most talented, glamorous and sought-after people in this country, which puts a tax on any friendship. Noel Coward was in London or Jamaica, Katharine Hepburn was occupied with projects, Danny Kaye was off somewhere being internationally funny, Mary Martin was enjoying Brazil, the Lunts were holed up at their farm in Wisconsin, and Katharine Cornell was not in the best of health herself. The true-blues got narrowed down to Mrs. Richard Rodgers and Kitty Carlisle Hart, both of whom kept constant vigil while Ferber was ill and dying. In remembering that sad time, Kitty Hart offers her thoughts: "I believe that if you've shared a friend's good times, you should darn well stick around to share the bad."

Kitty Hart originally met Ferber as Kitty Carlisle in 1946. They met at Moss Hart's farm in Bucks County, where Kitty Carlisle was taken by another man. There was a standing social weekend arrangement between George S. Kaufman and Moss Hart, who had neighboring farms. Saturday would be spent at Hart's with all of his and Kaufman's guests, and Sunday at Kaufman's—or vice-versa. The guests, of course, were all star-studded mutual friends—a potpourri of crème de la crème of American creative doers. A treat for any host. So, Ferber was among the merry, and she and Kitty Carlisle met and took to each other right away. (Kitty Carlisle must have been a good twenty years younger than Ferber. The pretty ingenue; every crowd needs one.)

The next time they met accidentally spurred the Hart-Carlisle romance. Kitty Carlisle had been invited to a very "showy" party and didn't have an escort. She had no trepidation about going alone but didn't relish the idea of entering solo. Being a plucky girl, she figured that she might meet someone going in who could walk her in. And, in the way that all glamorous fiction goes, getting out of her taxi, she spotted Moss Hart and Edna Ferber getting out of theirs. They minded not at all when she asked whether they would walk in with her. In fact, that night, Moss Hart, as she puts it, "saw me." Within a very brief eight weeks after that, they were married. I'm sure with Ferber's overt blessings but, perhaps deep down, a tad of rancor. It meant the end of the "Mossie" era for Ferber. They had been so very close in one of those carefully built, deeply invested relationships, where there is little room for sexuality with all the cerebral goodies abounding. Although Ferber considered him "My son the playwright—the genius," she still must have felt slightly dispossessed. He was her friend first. But she was genuinely fond of the new Mrs. Hart. "She loved me. I know she did," says Kitty Carlisle Hart, trying to sound matter-of-fact about an ephemeral—especially among career women—emotion. "And I loved her. She always made me feel that I was a little better than I thought I was. She built you up in your own eyes most wonderfully, and without any fraud involved."

So, Kitty Carlisle Hart, with all of her activities, found time to visit an old friend who was rendered inactive.

Ferber used to refer to Mrs. Richard Rodgers as, "Dear, dear Dorothy," and dear and loyal and organized she was, for she would visit Ferber at least once a week when times got bad. "I would bring flowers—Edna adored flowers—and just sit for awhile. Sometimes I wouldn't even go in the room. I think she knew that I came regularly. Edna knew everything."

Granted, it was convenient for Dorothy Rodgers to pay her respects. She and her husband "Dickie," as Ferber used to call him, lived in the same building as Ferber and owned a co-op only a few floors below Ferber's. In fact, Dorothy Rodgers was directly responsible for finding Ferber the apartment. Ferber says of Dorothy in one of her diaries, "Dorothy always seems to find me exactly what I didn't know I was looking for."

The two women met in 1928, before Dorothy was married to Richard Rodgers, but she knew of Ferber prior to their first meeting. Ferber had taken an apartment at the Lombardy Hotel in New York, and while she was vacationing in Europe, Richard Rodgers rented the apartment right next door to hers. The news reached her, whereupon, she sent a scathing letter to the management. She stated that of all the discourteous things they could do, putting a songwriter (not a composer, but a common songwriter) on her floor right next door to her was the worst. The lambasting went on and on, practically demanding that they evict him. The management showed the letter to Rodgers, who got the general idea that Miss Ferber was not pleased. He asked to know the date of her return, and arranged to have her living room filled with flowers. Ferber was a sucker for flowers; it was just the touch, and Rodgers kept the apartment, becoming "the Composer next door." A bit later, Rodgers invited her to a party, where she met Dorothy, and the three of them remained friends for the duration of her life. Had Rodgers not filled her bower with flowers, he probably would have remained, according to the Ferber lexicon, "that songwriter."

Dorothy Rodgers and Ferber had only one large feud—instigated by Ferber—which caused a two-year breach in their friendship. It started with the idea of giving a party in honor of Margaret (Peg) Leech Pulitzer, a well-known writer in the forties. Both planned to give it on the same night. Dorothy had already invited several people and called Ferber to invite her. Ferber got on her uppers, saying that she'd planned it carefully and she would give it on that night and that was that. Dorothy patiently explained that she too had made plans which included already having invited several guests. She suggested they tally up the number of people each had invited and the one with the highest number would give the party. The loser would plan on another night. Ferber bridled and flared, saying how dare Dorothy dictate when she could give a party. She then hung up. (A Ferber trademark. A childish way of guaranteeing the last word.) She refused to speak to Dorothy for two years. One night in Connecticut, Richard Rodgers found himself at the same party as Ferber. When the party was breaking up, he followed her outside, and as she got into her station wagon he leaned in over the window and said, "Edna, we miss you." She warmed immediately. "I miss you too," she said. Rodgers told her that Dorothy would call her in the morning, which Dorothy did—early, before Ferber went to work. Ferber was totally receptive and they promptly made a date for dinner. Just as they were about to hang up—friends again—Ferber said, "Remind me to talk to you sometime, Dorothy dear, about why a bright girl like you could be so stupid as to suggest . . ." and went on about the Pulitzer incident, opening it all up again. Dorothy realized that Ferber's friendship was worth more than getting mad and let it go. Ferber must have thought so too. They never did have that talk.

Dorothy Rodgers saw her friend clearly—and still remained a friend. "I walked on eggs with Edna because you never knew what was going to offend her at what moment, but I loved her. She was worth all the trouble, you know, she really was. She was just a great woman."

Up until the last, Ferber was never unconcerned about her business and finances. She'd built a cartel out of her properties, and as though it were a doll's house, she constantly wanted to see, touch, admire, play with, and move around the pieces. She mistrusted everyone and, in language she would have disapproved of, felt that she was being screwed all the time. It was not classic paranoia because she was always looking around for someone to leave her eggs with, but there never seemed to be anyone invincible enough. She kept fierce tabs on the people who worked for her, and wrote "bawl him or her out" notes on her calendars. Ken McCormick most likely felt her wrath on Monday, August 7, 1967, for she wrote on her calendar for Friday, August 5: "Write Ken McCormick—Doubleday $4000 owed. Also, where the hell $4000 advance paid by Lancer scheduled for July???" Another one addresses Doubleday and Harriet Pilpel: "Doubleday (& Pilpel) Special Dollar Book Club edition of Giant? When? How about royalty rate. Not good enough." And there was one for me: "Julie—Check #5768—Aug. 24—not cashed. Why not? Careless?"

Although she questioned and knew about every dollar that came in and went out, she was basically simplistic about money. She understood it in numbers that she could lay on a table. Her idea of having made a very good deal was when somebody would approach her and say, "I want to buy this property and I'll give you $300,000 for it." She would say, "I want $500,000," and would settle for $400,000 and be pleased as punch. The tax ramifications were beyond her. That she should take $40,000 over a period of ten years was anathema to her. What if the company failed and went bankrupt? What if they lost the contract, and there were somehow no copies of it? Then where would she be?

The Warner Bros. film property of *Giant* was divided into three parts. The shareholders were Ferber and the two producers, Henry Ginsberg and George Stevens, who also directed the film. Henry Goldsmith (nephew-in-law) remembers, not too fondly, trying to help advise her on that deal. "A final part of the *Giant* deal was the selling of her third to Warner Bros. She eventually agreed to it, but only under constant pressure from Morris [Morris Ernst, one of the partners of Greenbaum, Wolff & Ernst—Ferber's law firm], myself, and Harriet (Pilpel). We three would always be in touch with each other and play 'you be the good guy, I'll be the bad guy' kind of game, and say, 'You try and press this, so that when she turns I can take the other side.' She took a lot of manipulating. When we said to her—whatever the thing was with Warner's—let's take that now over ten years or so, she thought that Warner's might not last ten years. And what would happen if Warner's went bankrupt in the meantime? Then she would be standing there with egg on her face and nothing in her hand. She would say, 'Let's take the money now,' and we would say, 'Well, if you take it now you give it all to Uncle Sam.' *Giant* was the single most lucrative deal that she ever made, and to her dying day she felt it was disastrous and that she'd lost money. In simple terms, she was a hoarder of cash."

It is ludicrous to picture Ferber storing bills in her mattress, but figuratively she did. She could have been and should have been an enormously rich person. Many feeble attempts were made over the years to get her to invest in real estate or to buy stocks and bonds, but no, she was convinced that in any adventurous financial venture she would wind up the dupe. It was the kind of pride that prevented her from any fall whatsoever, and from any escalation. There was a canny if extinct rationale behind her playing so safe. During the Depression of 1929, a great many of her illustrious friends had shot their wads by gambling in the stock market, and were left without enough money to pay their taxes. Ferber, never having believed in that kind of nonsense, was one of the few to be left holding ready cash—of which she lent a good deal to help her friends out of the hole. She was the champion; they were the underdogs. She was right; they were wrong. She never saw, or wanted to see, that the economic picture had changed. That period was her frame of reference for all time forward.

When one is ill, it is no time for one's friends to die. But on April 5, 1966, one of Ferber's oldest and dearest friends, Russel Crouse, the playwright, did just that. Shortly following, came a letter from Frank Sullivan—another favorite crony. It's the kind of letter writing that people don't do anymore.

The Art of. "Dearest Ferb, I was about to write you when your letter came, because I have been thinking about you as you have about me. I knew all about your visit to the Crouses and I wish all visits of that kind could be modelled on your visit. I talked with Anna [Mrs. Crouse] and the two youngsters shortly after and they told me about how you had come in and how you all had found yourselves glowing and laughing and telling fond stories about him. Both Anna and Lindsay Ann [Crouse's daughter] said that lovely thoughtful and genuine thing you and Dick did was the kindest thing that happened during those rough days. God will reward you. If He doesn't, I will . . . Now I will confess that the right thing you did, I didn't do. Poor Anna [Crouse] had the thoughtfulness to telephone me Sunday night so that I would not hear it cold over the radio and I rewarded her thoughtfulness by blowing my top and busting into tears. I was ashamed of myself. It didn't make her sad errand easier. I apologized later and it was all right. I talked with Anna last night. She seemed somewhat harassed, the excitement and exigencies following immediately after his death are over and she is now facing all the talks with lawyers, etc. And poor Howard [Howard Lindsay, Crouse's collaborator] is not able to be much of a tower of help. I talked with Dorothy [Dorothy Stickney, the actress, married to Lindsay] and him the day after Russel died and he sounded so ill and, of course, broken by what had happened —and had a really rough cough which I didn't like.

"It is remarkable and consoling the way you and so many other friends have included me in the sympathy . . . The last time I saw Crouse was here, last August, when Anna and he came for an overnight stay and we went to the races. I treasure that memory because it could not have been more pleasant . . . To my surprise I found it was the first time Anna had ever been to a racetrack and won herself a bet that put her in the seventh heaven. Crouse, a veteran horseplayer (he had been here many times in August) also won several good bets. I lost, as is my wont. Even better, he met quite a few old friends he hadn't seen in a long time, like Mike Casale, a racing writer he worked with on the Mail years ago. And Gene Markey, and others; and then who loomed up but Max Gordon, in a gay and festive mood. He delighted us by telling about his system of beating the races, which was roughly to bet on every horse in the race. That of course insured that he would win and it also made sure he would lose. It was Broun's [Heywood Broun] system, too, I recalled . . .

"I suppose it is sententious to say that Crouse had a good life but surely he did, didn't he. He saw to it in part (The Lord helps those who help themselves) but some of it was just bestowed on him because he deserved it. He had a fine if riotous time with dear old Alison [Crouse's first wife] and was loyal to her to her last moment. I remember the tears in his eyes when, along toward the end he told me she no longer wanted a taste of champagne. All she could take in those days. I think about two years passed before he married Anna, and Ferb, take it from me, he was the most lonely man in the world in those two years. He was just not cut out to be a bachelor. Then he had scruples about asking Anna to marry him because of the difference in their ages, and I was so glad when he got rid of those scruples. And how grand his life with Anna has been, and how good she has been for him, and he for her; and those two splendid children coming along after he had passed fifty. He had a score of years of their companionship and I wish he had had ten or more years of it. And with all else a most satisfying and successful career, full of the inevitable aches and pains of playwrighting but full of rewards, too, and with a perfect collaborator to work with for thirty-two years. And above all that born capacity for friendship that brought him the love of everybody who really knew him . . . Yes, Ferb, I do know there's nothing like work and it fills me with guilt to know that I haven't worked. I'd feel absolutely useless and unjustified if I hadn't, along the way, made friends like Crouse and you. That's an achievement. Love, Frank."

Letter writing was a way of life for Ferber and her friends; it was a way of transmitting back-fence gossip; it was a way of revealing emotion, and it was a way of collecting interest on the deposit of a loving friendship. Being a woman of the written word, Ferber usually stated her case better by letter than over the phone. Unfortunately with her family the statements were usually mercenary and the answers humble and apologetic. We were all poor letter writers in the "thank you" department, which was constantly what we had to reply, for almost every letter from Ferber contained a whopper of a check. As her life got shorter, her checks got broader. It was as though she was desperately ringing up final sales of flesh. Ours. It was the old adage: She had nothing money couldn't buy. She had money. She had nothing. There was no emotional harvest for her those last few years. All of her book children had grown up, had gone out into the world to make a living, and had brought home profits. Those profits were all she had to remind herself of her life; it follows that using them on her family was the only way she could remind us of her existence. Her weapon against loneliness was anger and her missile for anger was money. The process often backfired on her. How lonely she must have felt upon receiving this rejection from her niece, Mina Klein:

"Aunt Edna dear, I know this will make you very cross, but I'm returning the birthday check you sent to Pete, with the full approval of both Bill and Peter. The reason for doing so is that it's far more money than you've ever sent before—and out of all proportion to what he can be allowed to accept. Other birthdays and Christmases, as I know you'll discover if you look through your records, you've given him a generous and far more reasonable amount of $300.00—or sometimes $350.00.

". . . It will only serve to destroy his sense of values, even though, as with all the other gifts you've sent, it goes right into his savings account . . . All of us so appreciate the wonderful way you have built up these savings for the children, by the way. It gives them something to really depend upon for the future. But please don't spoil the good feeling we have about it by over-doing it in this way. I hope you'll understand and not be angry about this, Aunt Edna . . ."

Ferber's way of understanding this sort of thing was by sending the returned check right back again. It would go on this way—back and forth—until the episode would reach seriocomic proportions. And the check would be accepted. Mina had always had great pluck in the face of Ferber; she would try doggedly to stave off being seduced by the Midas touch.

Ferber paid for more than we, her family, could give—which reduced us to only taking. She asked for nothing other than that we take, and bow and scrape a bit. The children, Peter and Kathy, still had some innocence about receiving, but in a note from Peter, who was about eighteen at the time, there is a tone that touches on the obsequious.

"Dear Aunt Edna, Thank you for dinner and the show the other night. I enjoyed myself so very much. I love going to Sardi's even if we only saw Betty White. And of course the show was absolutely fantastic. There are very few shows that have been so well done and that I've enjoyed so much.

"Kathy said that she and a friend dropped in to see you yesterday, and as you know she loved the show also.

"Thank you again for the lovely evening. Love, Peter."

I, on the other hand—and I'm rueful about saying it—had by the age of twenty become a veteran taker and asker-of-favors. Apparently Ferber had secured for me a reading for a play that was to be directed by Garson Kanin on Broadway. In my letter, I thank her—and ask her for something else.

"Dear Aunt Ed, You are the best person I know of to relate my theatre ventures to, so here goes. Seeing that Mr. Kanin is still held up on the Coast with a bad throat, David Pardoll is handling the activity. This afternoon he gave me the script, which I am avidly pouring over. I figure that it's not every day one gets a fat Broadway script in his mitts. My reading is slated for Thursday, at the Helen Hayes Theatre. I keep roaming around knocking on wood.

"Now, I must ask you for a favor. I sort of hesitate, because I seem to have besieged you for favors lately. This will probably sound rather sudden to you, but I've been considering enrolling, in the fall, in a theatrical school of some nature . . . I am shooting for

Ferber at 83, shortly before her death in 1968. (Copyright © by Halsman)

James Dean and Edna Ferber on the set of Giant. *(Sanford Roth-Photo Researchers)*

Ferber with some Indian friends from a Hopi reservation in Arizona, 1966.

Researching with a frosty smile at forty degrees below zero in Kotzebue, Alaska, 1956.

Julia Ferber near the end of her life, 1947.

Great-Grandmother Julia Ferber and Great-Granddaughter Julie Goldsmith, 1947.

Janet and Henry Goldsmith, 1945.

Grandmother Fannie Ferber Fox and Granddaughter Julie Goldsmith, 1947.

Treasure Hill, Ferber's treasured house in Easton, Connecticut, 1938–49.

Ferber fishing in her Treasure Hill pool. (Walt Sanders/Black Star)

Rebecca Ferber of Sunnybrook Farm. (Balkin-Pix)

Ferber in her dressing room wiping away the performance with cold cream. (Walt Sanders/Black Star)

Ferber, the temporary actress, with script and cigarette at Treasure Hill, 1940. (Walt Sanders/Black Star)

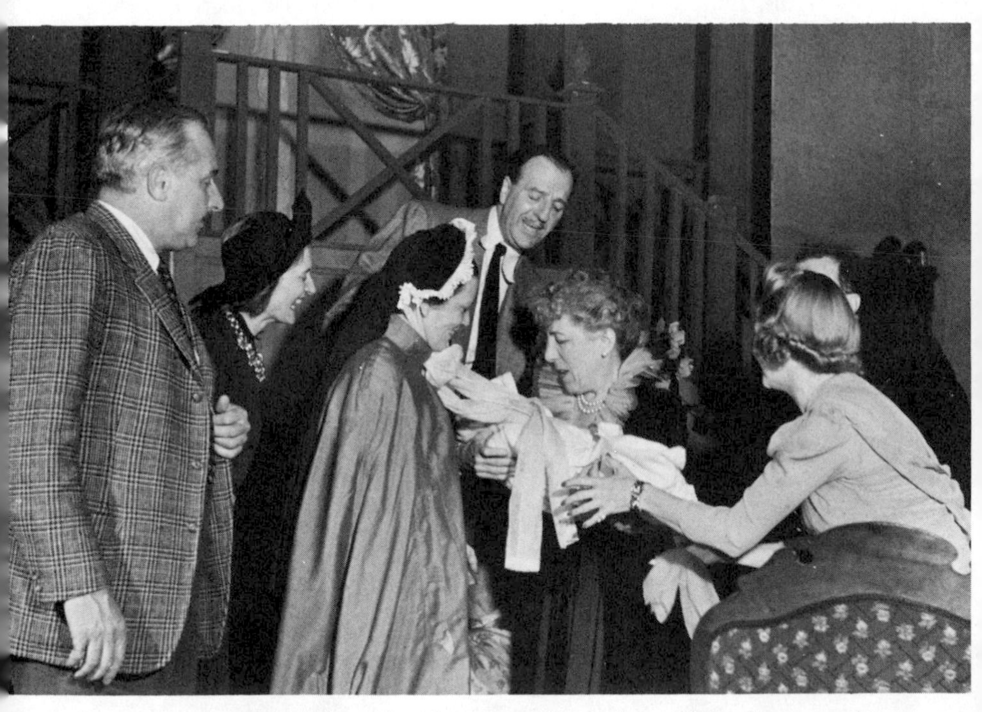

Ferber as Fanny Cavendish in Cheryl Crawford's Maplewood Playhouse production of George S. Kaufman's and Edna Ferber's The Royal Family, *Maplewood, New Jersey, 1940. (Walt Sanders/Black Star)*

Jack Fox and Julia Ferber taking the air, 1941.

Ferber, Mina Fox Klein, and Major Kelmer Le Maaters of the Bombardment Division at a base near Frankfurt, 1945.

Niece Mina Fox Klein and Ferber overseas after World War II, 1945.

a new school called The American National Theatre And Academy, and is sponsored by ANTA . . . The favor entails writing a letter of recommendation for me. I ask you, because I think it would have merit, and also because it should be personal . . ."

Ferber's letter to the school was exemplary—the perfect combination of PR and pride:

"Dear Miss Spears:—This letter is being written by the stage-struck aunt of a young girl who desires above everything else to be accepted as a student in the American National Theatre Academy. The young girl's name is Julie Goldsmith (Julie Gilbert). My name is Edna Ferber. Julie's mother is Janet Fox whom you might have seen in various plays in New York and whose first Broadway appearance was a small part in DINNER AT EIGHT by George Kaufman and myself. A revival of that play to be directed by Sir Tyrone Guthrie, is scheduled for a late September opening.

"A brief dossier on Julie Gilbert: She is nineteen. She has known the atmosphere of the theatre all her life. It's a rock-strewn road and she knows that, too. An amateur, she took part in school plays at Dalton. I saw her in one of these—Albee's AMERICAN DREAM—and she projected a dimensional and believable characterization.

"After graduating she spent a year and a few months of a second year as a student at Boston University's School of the Drama. The following summer she served an apprenticeship at the Ogunquit Summer Theatre. Last summer she was with the Boothbay Theatre. It was good hard tough training. She learned a lot.

"This past winter in New York she has had voice and dance instruction, and some classes at the Berghof—Uta Hagen School of the Theatre. This June she played the lead in an off-Broadway production of Ionesco's THE BALD SOPRANO.

"As to exterior: Julie is small; very blue eyes; dark hair. A dedicated girl and an amusing one, too. I feel confident that she'll make it, appalling though the path is these days.

"She feels that she needs more and more knowledge of the actual technique of acting. As a matter of fact, she could have had a tiny bit both in SHOW BOAT which opens at Lincoln Center Music Theatre July 19 and in the revival of DINNER AT EIGHT due in September. Wisely, she felt that she needed further technical training. Privately, I think she feels, too, that family playwrights are nice and all that, but she'd prefer to launch out on her own keel. And how right she is.

"Sorry to be so long-winded about this. When I was much younger I wrote shorter letters . . . At any rate, my thanks to you for reading it."

Postscript: The school never got off the ground. And, for accuracy's sake—I didn't pass up the "tiny bit" in *Show Boat,* I failed miserably in my audition for it.

In 1966–67 there was the devastating mink coat caper. Janet wanted one for Christmas, and Henry proposed to Ferber that they share the cost. Ferber apparently reneged on their agreement and tried to foot most of the bill herself. What ensued was a family debacle. The letter that Ferber wrote to Janet points up her total obsession with giving.

"Janet, dear girl, I think you must by now know that I have for you (sounds silly to state it, but isn't) the deepest affection and admiration and even a measure of understanding. We are an odd cross-purpose family of women, really—we Neumann-Ferber-Foxes. Full of good intentions and wry results.

"Here, dear, is the complete and brief history of the MINK COAT (Janet Fox Goldsmith ※1) of the late summer and early autumn, 1966.

"Henry telephoned me. He said that you would like a mink coat for Christmas and that he wanted to cover part of the cost and what or how did I feel about this.

"Fur coat purchases or gifts were nothing novel in my life. My first fling at this consisted of two raccoon coats (well, that was considered The Thing at the time, at your age) for you and Mina. You were still students at the University of Chicago School of Education, so-called—, a private school to which you trudged through the long tough Chicago winters. For Fan, a golden-brown caracul coat, in vogue at that time, made of the skins of Asiatic lamb, which was softer than Persian lamb. One doesn't see it any more. Rather pretty and very becoming to Fan.

"I hope I'm not maundering at the moment. There followed mink coats for Fan (two); Persian lamb for my mother and two mink coats for her in the following years. Two mink coats for myself and a third in 1965. There were a couple of other fur coats for you and Mina—broadtail and I dunno what—doesn't matter, really.

"So I said to Henry, has Jan shopped for it? No, she hadn't. Well, let me know. But I'd much rather make it a gift from me alone. I never have given gifts on the partnership basis in this fashion. Henry said he would like to put in with a thousand and I reluctantly let it go under that suggestion, though it was, as I have said, not my habit to split a gift in that way.

"NOTHING WAS SAID AT THAT TIME OR AT ANY OTHER TIME OF YOUR SHARING FINANCIALLY IN THIS PLAN, AND I WOULD HAVE FLATLY REFUSED TO BE PART OF THE PLAN IF YOU HAD." [At this point, Janet writes ON Ferber's letter, "I didn't."]

"The coat's cost, as I have the figures in my books, was $3543.75. By the way, I always wondered what the 75 cents represented. I sent you or Henry (wait a minute, I'll look it up. It was Janet Fox Goldsmith–check #5869–dated November 5, 1966) a check in the round sum of $2600 which was about one hundred dollars more than that agreed on and I suppose–in fact, know–that I did that because it made book-keeping easier for me and certainly chopped off that 75 cents, etc. I had asked Mina about a Christmas mink and she said she had no use for one–suburban living, New York five or six times, for a day or an evening–in the winter–she couldn't use it. So we discussed another kind of gift for her.

"You had the coat, it looked lovely as you wore it, and that was that. Now, ten months later, you turn up with a check for five hundred dollars. You say, in today's letter, that you 'hate the idea of tossing this check back and forth, etc.'

"Honey, it wasn't my idea. And I don't intend to have anyone take over my private, financial, or social or family life as long as I am mentally and physically able to run it myself, to the detriment of no one in the world.

"You can, of course, do as you like with this (again) enclosed check. If you destroy it the result will show up in my carefully balanced monthly bank balance, checked always by Garden and me. If you fail to cash it I shall use another means to credit it to you, and this may not show up until after my death, but at least it won't irk me then.

"Frankly, I don't understand the whole tiresome machination. Perhaps it may stem from some private misunderstanding about the whole transaction, between you and Henry. Certainly it rather spoils the whole idea of the gift, as far as I am concerned. Sordid.

"I love you."

The closing of the letter seems to be an amputation from the body of it; a severed arm reaching out from some distant place. The arm worked as a crowbar, however disjointed. Her love worked in the same fashion.

The coat was a beaut, but Janet never enjoyed it to its full luxury. It was and remains a manipulative mink.

Ferber never gave up her business acumen. She felt jeopardized by anything that might interfere with the sale of her properties. She was, as Dorothy Rodgers puts so aptly, "an injustice collector"; she would root around for possible slander and more often than not come up with a weed. In the fall of 1967, she found a minor weed which she tried to wrap around the neck of CBS. It had to do with *Cimarron*, a novel she had written in 1929; its overt theme being the settlement of the Oklahoma Territory. The book was made into two motion pictures—the first by RKO in 1931, starring Richard Dix and Irene Dunne; the second by M-G-M in 1960, starring Glenn Ford and Maria Schell. Ferber was less than enchanted with both of the films. The origin of her discontent stemmed from the fact that she felt the entire thrust of the book had been misunderstood way back in 1930, and in an arbitrary way never forgave anyone for it. "I was bitterly disappointed. CIMARRON had been written with a hard and ruthless purpose. It was, and is, a malevolent picture of what is known as American womanhood and American sentimentality. It contains paragraphs and even chapters of satire, and, I am afraid, bitterness, but I doubt that more than a dozen people ever knew this. All the critics and hundreds of thousands of readers took CIMARRON as a colorful romantic Western American novel."

Not even the perceptions of Rudyard Kipling could soothe her hurt. He wrote in a letter to Nelson Doubleday: "I am reading CIMARRON (aloud) to C. That's a big bit of work, and dam' good atmosphere. I'm awful glad you got it. Seems to me she's going on from strength to strength. Of course it's melodramatic, but then so was (and so is) Oklahoma and how well she describes the merciless pressure of the respectable women pulling their men folk into line—like mothers chasing up bad boys which, indeed, I suspect all men are."

During her lifetime Ferber's properties were recycled, resold, repackaged, but rarely revaluated. She never gave up on them financially or emotionally and always hoped they'd be reborn to new public applause and new market rewards. In 1967, the Ashley Famous Agency was working on the sale to television of the 1960 M-G-M version of *Cimarron.* On September 3, 1967, Ferber picked up the New York *Times* and saw on the television page a large photo of a man in a stetson with a caption reading: "Cimarron Strip"—U.S. Marshal Stuart Whitman tries to keep law and order in the rough-and-tumble days of Kansas, circa 1880 . . . On CBS Thursdays at 7:30."

Ferber, sensing danger, clipped the picture, drew dagger-like arrows pointing to actor Whitman's head and to the title, "Cimarron Strip," and sent it off to the Ashley Famous Agency. Obviously knowing Ferber was apt to boil kettles, and also that she had no grounds in this case, the agency sent a sedative type letter back. ". . . As to CIMARRON STRIP, neither Ted [Ashley] nor I believe that the program series will in any way influence the sale of the motion picture based upon your novel. Television buyers will continue to be attracted by both literary auspices and the star value of that picture . . . even though you may not believe the picture itself to have been a good one. The key to the sale is, and will continue to be, MGM's planning with regard to its television licensing. I am enclosing here the clippings you had sent me. Kind regards, Karl Honeystein." And that was the end of the episode save for the fact that *Cimarron* was sold to television for a tidy sum. Secretly, what probably irked Ferber was that in the era of hour-long Westerns nobody had considered a spin-off series on the novel of *Cimarron.*

In April of 1969, a year after Ferber's death, a woman named Eta Kitzmiller evaluated all of Ferber's properties with an eye for possible television series ideas. *Cimarron* came out galloping with potential. "This material seems to me as good or better than that used for Bonanza, Lancer, High Chapparel, The Big Valley, etc. I don't know, however, if new shows of this genre are being considered. It would seem to me that Bonanza, for instance, has about run its streak, and if this is true the market for new material would be limited. However, if I am wrong, the story and characters in this have a definite appeal . . . There is more than enough material here to keep a long-lived series going and a lot of it—the Indian sections, the sudden oil riches—haven't been over-told on TV . . . I think this book has possibilities."

Nothing more has ever been done with *Cimarron,* and one doubts that Rudyard Kipling will go down in history as understanding its full merits.

There is a peculiar trait in today's society of meddling with classics—giving them an upbeat, contemporary look—making them germane to the now in lieu of accurate to the yesterday. Shakespeare has taken the worst beating. His plays have been presented in drag, in tie-dye, in glitter-rock, in blackface; the settings have been in Brooklyn, on Mars, on Park Avenue, etc. A great many of the presentations (interpretations) have been not only out of keeping with the intent of the play, but inaccurate and in bad taste. There seems to be a license for tomfoolery to go on with plays written before the twentieth century. Rarely does an American twentieth-century classic get tampered with; it is either revived with dignity or rendered an anachronism.

Edna Ferber's and George S. Kaufman's *Dinner at Eight*—more a period piece than a classic—was about to get its first major revival in September of 1966. The play, originally produced in 1932, opened at the Grand Opera House in New York City, directed by George Kaufman and produced by Sam Harris. The revival was to open at the Alvin Theatre in New York City, directed by Sir Tyrone Guthrie and produced by Elliot Martin, Lester Osterman, Alan King, and Walter A. Hyman, Ltd., with associate producers Leonid Kipnis and Fred J. Antkies. It was to be an illustrious, star-studded, boffo Broadway attraction. It seemed a natural, for as the drama critic George Oppenheimer was to write in his review: ". . . George S. Kaufman and Edna Ferber wrote an entertainment rather than an earth-shattering contribution to the art of drama, but it is intricately and wonderfully constructed, filled with bright dialogue and its characters are varied and, for the most part, absorbing today as well as yesterday . . ."

Although, up until that time, the play had been dwelling in semioblivion, the 1933 film of the same name—directed by George Cukor, with a cast that included Marie Dressler, Wallace Beery, John Barrymore, Jean Harlow, Lionel Barrymore and Billie Burke—was proclaimed a classic gem and redistributed to art movie houses throughout the country in the wave of nostalgia mania. College students seeing Jean Harlow's assets and the Barrymore profile for the first time uttered delighted, "Oh, wows." Parents of college students were allowed to rediscover what they'd never wanted to let go of. But the parents associated the film with Kaufman-Ferber comedy, whereas the kids just knew it was a good movie—Who wrote it? Oh, two old hacks.

The film of *Dinner at Eight* has often been likened to that of *Grand Hotel*, and when Ferber and Kaufman were about to write their play, they had a bit of badinage on that subject. Ferber describes it in her autobiography, *A Peculiar Treasure*. "'Well,' I said, with that grace and charm which so endears me to a collaborator, 'I still think you're wrong . . . and everybody's wrong who says we can't make a fine play of Dinner at Eight. It has stuck in my mind all these years. It can't be so bad.'

"'All right, all right,' George said—a peace-loving man—'if you're still so stuck on it let's dig it up and have a look. But even if we do it now everybody'll say we're imitating Grand Hotel.'

"'They can't. We thought of Dinner at Eight years before Grand Hotel was produced.'

"'They'll say so anyway. After all, we didn't write our play.'

"He was right. But then, I was, too."

Ferber was not terribly interested in the film version. She'd had nothing to do with it—other than to sell it. For her, the play was the thing, and at the ripe age of eighty-one for a new production of that play to be launched, and successful all over again, could be sweet victory indeed. Especially since Kaufman had died in 1961, and she was the only collaborator left to hold down the fort of their memory. During the years of their collaboration, Kaufman's name always preceded hers on the billing—George S. Kaufman and Edna Ferber. Somehow, somewhere she had deferred to him on that matter. But now that he was gone, and their play was about to walk the boards again, he had deferred to her. In a letter that he wrote to her shortly before he died, *Dinner at Eight* seems to have played on his mind. ". . . In an idle moment last week I picked up 'Dinner at Eight' and read a lot of it, and we were certainly good when we were good. It's too bad we can't do another—I am down to about eight fair minutes a day now, which come along about 3:17. So this time I would drive you REALLY nuts . . ."

Dinner at Eight had also played on the mind of Sir Tyrone Guthrie, the noted director and founder of the famed Tyrone Guthrie Theatre in Minneapolis. He had wanted to do an American comedy of manners for ages and had at last hit on the perfect vehicle. His great friend was producer Leonid Kipnis, and when he knew he was coming to New York he made plans to see Kipnis specifically in order to intrigue him with his idea. Guthrie had great charm when he decided to rev it up. In front of Kipnis, he laid both the charm and the project: He wanted to do it with an all-star cast; a first-rate production—as, of course, only Kipnis could give it. Guthrie wanted to treat the play as though it was 1933 celluloid—presenting it in cinematic rather than theatrical terms. He had not seen the film since before World War II, but he told Kipnis that the visuals had remained with him. It wasn't every day that Sir Tyrone wanted to direct on Broadway; he usually had loftier ideas about theatre and kept himself and his productions away from the masses. Kipnis rounded up colleague producers and gave Guthrie the go-ahead—if Ferber agreed. Guthrie wished to approach her himself. "I've got to call on Miss Edna," he said. Ferber responded immediately. She thought Guthrie was a giant in the realm of theatre. She was thrilled that he should offer her his directorial hand. For all her stature, when Ferber thrilled she thrilled hard. A deal was made and the series of problems began.

Guthrie's concept was massive. He wanted a very opulent set—calling for real stone and garrets and bay windows. He got it. The scenery alone cost $80,000. The budget for the entire show was $225,000. Already there was an unbalance of theatrical nature.

At the outset, Guthrie had bent over backwards—it was a far reach; he was over six feet of solid oak—to assure "Miss Edna" that he would seek her opinion at every turn. Blarney. Ferber began to realize that she was titular when nobody, least of all Guthrie, would listen to her. After the gargantuan set had been ordered—without her consultation—she sensed the heavy hand of disaster and tactfully—for her—voiced her opinion. It was still too early in the day for her to conceive that the high and mighty Guthrie could stoop and not conquer. But she sensed that his attack was wrong and tried to give him guidelines to right it. She mentioned that one of the clues to the original play's success was that it was done lightly; it never bogged down in structure, scenery, dialogue, or inflection. Guthrie nodded, smiled, took note, and ignored her.

Guthrie had wanted a star-spangled cast. He also wanted actors who would be comfortable working with him, which was difficult, because he was so demanding. The cost of the set was so high that the management could only afford to hire semistars, which made Guthrie feel uncomfortable because they weren't of the star stature he'd requested. It was a strange assortment: Robert Burr, Ruth Ford, June Havoc, Darren McGavin, Pamela Tiffin, Mindy Carson, Arlene Francis, Walter Pidgeon and Blanche Yurka do not exactly spell box office pizazz.

Ferber remained passive for as long as she could, but when in the script sessions Guthrie began to cut the play, she put her dukes up. As Elliot Martin, one of the producers, puts it mildly, "She wasn't keen on cutting." From then on, the only cutting she was keen on was of Guthrie down to size. Granted, she had an abundance of territorial imperative for her play, but she knew what had worked once and was about not to work again. Her ire grew with every rehearsal. She felt that the casting was dissonant and that Guthrie had done it on purpose—that he had deliberately chosen strident actors in order to poke fun at our American society—that he was imposing his own comment to the play's detriment. Ferber's contention was that the actors should speak in the tone of the day, and that Guthrie didn't have—and wasn't about to get—an accurate ear for American accents. She was strongly opposed to June Havoc's performance in the leading role, and although she felt Havoc was a good actress, she also felt that Havoc was ruining her play. As for the others, she dismissed them as being "all wrong." The only actor who got her nod was Walter Pidgeon, who she felt had the tone of that day down pat.

She would go to rehearsals, sit in the back of the theatre, and take copious notes, which she would rather elaborately present to Guthrie, who would rather elaborately receive them—but with just a slight hint of disdain. Then they would go through a sham-full procedure. He would say, "And how is Miss Edna today?" to which she would reply, "I'm the same dazzling blonde I was yesterday." Then he would chortle and go off and throw away her notes. Always resourceful—and at that point slightly desperate—Ferber tried a new approach. Instead of giving him her notes in longhand, she would send them to him all crisply typed. This tactic seemed to penetrate Guthrie's hide enough for him to take her to lunch. She did not care for the lunch one bit and told him about it. "Dear Sir Tyrone:—I've always thought that a restaurant was the ideal place in which to discuss nothing at all. Yesterday I'd rather have had a sandwich (or nothing at all) in a corner of the empty theatre, quietly—though ordinarily I'm a girl who likes her food.

"I've thought about those significant speeches that might emerge from the mishmash of vapid nothings as the dinner party chatters its way into nowhere.

"Whatever I've contrived since I saw you sounds just that—contrived—pulled in. Nevertheless I've included one or two in the enclosed pages which are random notes, some of which you heard at lunch yesterday (and I want to thank you for being so patient and receptive).

"I plan to come in Monday. I know you'll be able to work smoothness and movement into that complicated dinner scene. How I wish we could have had just a week out of town. But I know that that would have been unrealistic in the case of this play.

"If you care to call me during the weekend (when you should be getting some rest, rather) I expect to be here—or hope to be.

"The play held me yesterday. I've thought about it ever since then. Yours, Edna Ferber."

It's difficult to know why Guthrie didn't see how much Ferber cared, and wouldn't heed to what she cared about. Either he was oblivious or sexist or both. Her notes might have threatened him; they were so knowing:

"At the risk of boring you I want to register (again) my objection to that cigar business of Packard's. The cigar and his entrance with it, and his smoking while Carlotta is talking with him—these register the character. But I've never seen anyone talk-talk-talk through a cigar. It distracted me and it would distract an audience. Packard's telephone speech is a good laugh—or should be—but that waggling cigar between the teeth is a laugh-stopper, and (to me at least) unnatural.

"If Millicent is coquettish with the chauffeur, Ricci, at her desk in the first act (as she was yesterday) the audience is quite justifiably going to expect this relation to continue. Is it going to be a rivalry between Dora [the maid] and Millicent Jordan?? It gives a false meaning to the scene. Millicent, whose society—or social—position is all that matters to her, wouldn't dream of carrying on in that way with a chauffeur in her employ. Misleading to the audience.

"It seemed to me that Millicent did an awful lot of hors d'oeuvres and nut passing to her dinner guests when she had a butler and a waitress for that purpose.

"I still insist that Carlotta Vance wouldn't totter. The Duchess of Windsor doesn't totter, does she? Or Ina Claire. Or Lynn Fontanne. They never will."

Carlotta Vance, as played by Arlene Francis, continued to totter. So did the play. Most big budget shows have tryouts out of town, iron out the kinks, get a feel of the audience's reaction, and then, when relatively secure, open in New York. The *Dinner at Eight* management couldn't foot the out-of-town tab. Most of their budget had gone into eleven lugubrious sets—sets so cumbersome that on the first of ten previews in New York each scene change took a half hour. Panic began its St. Vitus's dance. The management was saddled with impractical sets and very little money left in the till. Ferber willingly, if sadly, put in three shares. She'd never had to invest in one of her plays before. Elliot Martin had recruited Alan King as another one of the producers; King helped tremendously with the financial picture. He would drive up every day in his Rolls-Royce, park it in front of the stage door, and go in to watch the rehearsals. Ferber makes reference to this in her diary: "The stand-up comic with the chariot came again today."

During the run of previews, Elliot Martin got a call from Ferber. She wanted to talk—at her place. Martin went over for tea, with a certain amount of trepidation. Ferber was known for her lovely teas, also for her tempers. He wondered whether the boom would fall before or after the finger sandwiches. She spoke her mind promptly. She said, "I'll tell you what's wrong with the play. When we did the original, the dialogue went like wild fire. The tone of the day was bright, brittle and unsentimental. The way Sir Tyrone is orchestrating it, it goes like swamp. The solution is not to cut but to pick up the pace. It's too mannered, too heavy, and the audience won't like it."

Martin conceded that she was absolutely right, but he chose to ignore her subtext, which implied the firing of Guthrie. After that, he recalls that for the remainder of their acquaintance she was caustic. Martin again concedes that she was absolutely right in being so. He had let her down.

Progress seemed to be inching its way when they finally got the sets to change smoothly and quickly by flying them in. But on the Sunday before the opening Sir Tyrone Guthrie did an unforgivable thing. He wrote a piece for the New York Times *theatre* section in which he lambasted American critics. It was not a good move. Ferber was choleric. In her eyes he had gone from Guthrie the giant to Guthrie the lout to Guthrie the fool. She felt that his article had personally issued her doom. She couldn't have been more right.

On the morning after the opening night of *Dinner at Eight*, the critics were less than kind, responding to Guthrie's critique of their art by flexing their power. Walter Kerr, of the New York *Times*, did his own brand of lambasting: "There is one thing about a dinner party, no matter how it is going. You can always get off in a corner with someone you like. 'Dinner at Eight', the George S. Kaufman-Edna Ferber confection of 1932 which director Tyrone Guthrie chose to disinter at the Alvin last evening, is a play almost completely made up of corners, and in various of the red plush, white satin and Japanese-wallpapered nooks you can find such agreeable company as Walter Pidgeon, June Havoc, Jeffrey Lynn, Blanche Yurka and Phil Leeds. I mention these five names so quickly because they do help to take your mind off the others . . . What is most curious about the evening is that Mr. Guthrie has elected to stress, rather than to hide, what is most transparent in the manufacture. Too many of his actors have been urged to become even more papier-mache than the text strictly requires . . . Mr. Guthrie's gesture has been generous: we do need to investigate the theatre of 30 odd years ago to see what is, and what is not, cheerful and alive in it still. But he has neither uncovered the original energy of 'Dinner at Eight' nor devised a pastiche staging for it that might provide it with long-distance charm. There it is, getting about rather stiffly. And there are the actors, some friendly, some feeble, some forced."

Most of the critics went on in this vein. Ferber had expected no more. She had hoped that someone would spot the fault as being more Guthrie's than the play's. Her old friend and Newsday's theatre critic, George Oppenheimer, came through for her by serving Guthrie his deserts: ". . . Some of the reviewers based their criticism of 'Dinner at Eight' on the old-fashioned and hollow material. I do not think this is valid . . . it's characters are varied and, for the most part, absorbing today as well as yesterday. Or they should be, had Mr. Guthrie assembled a proper cast and directed it in a proper and unified manner. In his staging he seems not to have made up his mind on any particular style . . . At times the actors almost seem to be kidding the play, at others giving it their all and in the process, overacting. There is neither stylization of style, mood or manner . . . Mr. Guthrie has compounded his error by striving for names rather than performances. Maybe he had in mind the MGM film of the Broadway play, which had an all-star cast . . . I wonder what would have happened, had Mr. Guthrie chosen a cast of lesser fame and greater accomplishment and directed it with his accustomed aptitude. I feel confident that 'Dinner at Eight' would have proved far less dated and a lot more timely than it does in its present production."

What more was there to say? Elliot Martin made a halfhearted attempt at a cheery eulogy note: "Dear Miss Ferber: Thank you so much for your good wishes to me on opening night. You had to prove DINNER AT EIGHT long ago. I had to prove that I could put it on as well and as successfully. I am afraid we did not quite come up to that measure but I have enjoyed my many telephone conversations with you and I have appreciated working with such a wonderful 'pro.' Warmest regards, Elliot Martin."

Ferber was not as despondent as she might have been; in fact, she was more social than she had been in quite a while. She loathed long lunches at hifalutin places—only those who weren't working as hard as they should be took them. Yet, she was spotted by Leonard Lyons and plunked into his column as one of the "lunch set":

". . . At the Four Seasons the President of Senegal was given a luncheon party by Pan Am. And Edna Ferber was at the Colony. Miss Ferber was with her agent, I. P. Lazar, and his wife. They ordered chicken hash. 'I find it strangely decadent,' said the novelist, 'to order hash in the most expensive restaurant in New York. It means we've come full-cycle, in a way.' It reminded her of her first day in N.Y. when, at the Ritz, she saw a man ordering one apple . . ."

And because of the *Dinner at Eight* production, flagging though it was, Ferber's name appeared in other columns—among them Radie Harris's in *The Hollywood Reporter*. Ferber wrote an amusing letter to Lazar about her reported comings and goings:

"Irving dear, the Radie Harris column in the Reporter was almost as correct as Leonard Lyon's item about our Colony lunch. I didn't attend the DINNER AT EIGHT opening. I was at home. I haven't seen the play since the night before it opened.

"Anne Kaufman [George S. Kaufman's daughter] telephoned me to say that she was at the opening and seated not down front as the column said, but on the balcony steps with one of the ushers. Still, any publicity is better than no publicity. And DINNER AT EIGHT seems to be so far luckier than BREAKFAST AT TIF-

FANY'S [a David Merrick show that laid one of the most expensive eggs in Broadway history].

"How about you, Mary [Mrs. Lazar] and I collaborating on a play entitled LUNCH AT THE COLONY, just to fill out the three-meals-a-day routine.

"My love to you and Mary. Yours, Edna."

The death knell had been ringing faintly, since *Dinner at Eight* had opened. At last the production was about to be put out of its misery. The New York *Times* paid its respects: "Dinner at Eight", the George S. Kaufman-Edna Ferber revival staged by Sir Tyrone Guthrie, will close Saturday night at the Alvin after its 127th performance.

"In an effort to extend the run, twofers (two tickets for the price of one) were distributed last week but not enough have been redeemed at the box office for the engagement to continue. The post-Broadway tour will be dispensed with.

"The $200,000-production will wind up with a loss of $100,000, it was estimated by Lester Osterman, one of the producers who also owns the theatre . . ."

Not only did Ferber lose money on the show, she lost the hope that she and Kaufman would ever be revived auspiciously. *Dinner at Eight* was her last professional supper.

Dinner at Ferber's was something else again. She never had a flop. Garson Kanin, Ruth Gordon, Mrs. Bennett Cerf, Kitty Carlisle Hart, George Oppenheimer, Goddard Lieberson, Marc Connelly, Irving Lazar, Danny Kaye, Alfred Lunt, Lynn Fontanne, Dorothy Rodgers, Richard Rodgers, and countless others can attest to that fact. She applied the same sort of discipline toward her dinner parties as she did toward her work. Nothing was left to improvisation or informality. Her parties were researched weeks in advance, so that if anything went wrong it would be due to the guests, not to the hostess. Ferber was a perfectionist about her home, and anyone who entered that realm reveled in its grace. And she never had just anyone; she was careful. She would never dream of saying, "Oh well, bring So-and-so along." There were no interlopers, no aliens, no germs. Her guests were as tasteful as her décor.

George Oppenheimer, a man who savors a good time, recalls her prowess for entertaining. "She was a most gracious hostess, who gave marvelous, 'hit' parties. She always had a limited amount of guests—eight or ten at most. She fed her guests wonderfully well and the talk was always superb." Was Ferber always diplomatic in choosing her guests? Oppenheimer smiles ruefully, probably remembering several verbal fracases of the past. "Almost always," he says.

Oppenheimer and Ferber had two blockbuster arguments—one of them being about two Olympian battlers: George and Martha. Oppenheimer had recommended that Ferber go and see Edward Albee's hit Broadway play *Who's Afraid of Virginia Woolf?* She did and found it unbearably detestable. After dressing him down for sending her, she asked him if he would invite the four characters in the play, George, Martha, Nick, and Honey, to his home for dinner. (Her criterion for sympathetic characters.) He replied, "No, Edna, but neither would I invite the Macbeths."

It was common knowledge that Ferber would get terribly irritated—crushed, really—when she couldn't get her way. For instance, she would call Oppenheimer on a Wednesday noon and ask him to dinner that same night. She would say, "Just a spur-of-the-moment thing. Just a few of us. Nothing fancy. Molly has put up a small roast . . ." And when Oppenheimer would refuse in favor of another appointment, he'd hear a sigh over the phone and then, "Well, where ARE you going, George?" indicating a tone of, "Can't you break it?"

But then, when one expected her to become irate, she didn't. One evening, during a dinner party at Ferber's, Oppenheimer accidentally knocked over and broke a beautiful crystal goblet. Ferber was kind and absolutely forgiving—trying to take away the boorish feeling that follows a blunder. As far as she was concerned, the incident was forgotten. But not by another member of the party, an actress friend of Ferber's, who kept mercilessly carping at Oppenheimer about it all night. Apparently they had both been at a previous dinner party where he had fallen back in his chair and had broken two very valuable Meissen vases. So, when Oppenheimer had his third breakage at Ferber's, the actress turned to Herbert Bayard Swope—another guest—and said, "George is a sick man." Whereupon, Swope swooped down on her with, "You're the one who's sick."

At another one of Ferber's dinner parties, George Kaufman was seated to her right, and to her left was seated a fellow who had the misfortune of asking Ferber the wrong question. The question was:

"Is it true that your mother did the laundering in a loggers' camp?" Ice fell on the room. Ferber finally answered him with a murderously quiet, "Never." Kaufman said quietly, "I think we'd better go home."

Ferber offered lavish meals—always beautifully prepared and served. She had a zest for food that bordered on the sybaritic. One could read a certain amount of sexuality into this and not be entirely off base. It was as though Emily Post had gone wanton in the kitchen. Her dinners were usually too rich, usually too much, and always irresistible. She would start with opulent hors d'oeuvres consisting of such sundries as: caviar and chopped egg, cream cheese and watercress, water chestnuts wrapped in bacon, hot cheese puffs, and thin little smoked salmon sandwiches with a sprinkling of capers on top. Then at the table she might serve a lobster or crab meat cocktail or individual cheese soufflés for starters, to be followed by squab, say, or a leg of lamb, accompanied by two fresh vegetables, which were her forte. She doused the habit of pushing vegetables to the other side of the plate; hers were gobbled. Carrots in herbed butter, puréed spinach with nutmeg, green beans with mushrooms or almond slivers—to name a few. She kept her potatoes simple—new potatoes with parsley and butter, usually. Then there'd be rolls with curls of butter, a green salad laced with endive, perhaps a Brie, finger bowls to rinse (once someone even ate the lacy doily beneath the finger bowl, thinking it was part of the repast), and finally the *pièce de résistance*—a *crème brûlée* for dessert. This being a concoction of the purest cholesterol: brown sugar, egg yolks, and heavy cream. Ferber used to say, "Miss Molly Hennessy's recipe is love and calories."

"When we told Edna," says Margalo Gillmore, "that some of us were trying to diet, she'd scoff and say, 'Do it on your own time.' She took feeding us like Strasbourg geese very seriously."

Molly Hennessy remembers one near catastrophe before a large dinner party. She calls the episode The Drapes. Ferber had had her living-room drapes cleaned. They'd arrived back and Molly was administering their rehanging. As the workman was putting them up, Molly observed that there were huge blotches of discoloration all down the front of them. She said, "Oh, Miss Ferber's not going to like this—take them down." A cue for Ferber's entrance. Ferber became livid immediately, working up into apoplexy. Molly made her sit down, and tried to quiet her saying, "Miss Ferber, they're only drapes—only drapes—material, that's all." Ferber kept ranting about a dinner party that she was to hold a week hence, and now she would have to go drapeless, which meant she would have to call off the party, which sent her into new paroxysms. Molly suggested that with her pull she could order new drapes to be made in time for the party. Which is exactly what she did, and the party lived happily ever after.

Ferber thought that material mishaps were the end of the world. Yet there was a certain relish connected with them. It was as though she almost looked forward to things going wrong in order to afford her an outlet for all her pent-up child's anger. What she would have were tantrums, not mild annoyances. Her rage against workmen and inanimates was infantile—totally out of control.

Ferber was insecure about people not showing up after she had invited them. She would send little reminder notes like the one received by Moss and Kitty Hart:

"This is just to say, dear Moss and Kitty, that I'm looking forward to seeing you here next Wednesday, the 14th, at 7:30. Just plaid tie." And then, as an interesting and rather moving afterthought, "I've never taken a tranquilizer, but I think that hour or two we spent at your home last Sunday served as the same sort of bridge between emotion and reality. How good of you to have arranged this. My love to you. Edna."

Ferber was literally famous among the cognoscente for her food. Moss Hart used to champ at the bit before going to chomp on her viands. He used to say that he never liked to read any Ferber before retiring because the way she described food made him starve all night. There is a passage from *A Peculiar Treasure* that would make anyone have nocturnal gnawings:

"The pantry was as fragrant as a garden with spices and fruit scents and the melting delectable perfume of brown, freshly baked dough, sugar-coated. There was one giant platter devoted wholly to round plump cakes with puffy edges, in the center of each a sunken pool that was pure plum, bearing on its bosom a snowy sifting of powdered sugar. There were others whose centers were apricot, molten gold in the sunlight. There were speckled expanses of cheese kuchen, the golden-brown surface showing rich cracks through which one caught glimpses of the lemon-yellow cheese beneath. There were cakes with jelly, cinnamon kuchen, and cunning cakes with almond slices nestling side by side. And there was freshly baked bread; twisted loaf with poppy seeds freckling its braid, its sides glistening with the butter that had been swabbed on just before it had been thrust into the oven."

Part of Ferber's bead on food was due to the extensive research she did whenever she wrote a book. The food of the various peoples she dealt with was telltale of their personalities. She used the subject of food as historical and regional background. On her sojourns, when she was digging up source material, she often ate what was indigenous to the area she was studying. She was a sensory writer and rarely waxed on about what she hadn't experienced. In her novel *Giant*, there is a passage in which she transfers one of her own culinary experiences onto her heroine, Leslie Benedict—a young bride new to Texas ritual.

"These men were carrying a large sack, dark, wet, and steaming. This outer sack they deftly slit with sharp bright knives. Beneath it was another cloth, lighter and stained with juices. Still thus encased, the burden was carried to the table and placed on a great flat wooden board. They were crowded all round the table now, and in each hand was a wedge of the crisp thin bread.

"The feast dish. Cloths that covered it were unrolled carefully, there floated from the juice-stained mound a mouth-watering aroma of rich roast meat . . .

"The final layer of wrapping was removed. A little Vesuvius of steam wafted upward on the hot noonday air. There on the table was the mammoth head of an animal. It was the head complete. The hide—hair and the outer skin—had been removed, but all the parts remained, the eyes sunken somewhat in the sockets but still staring blindly out at the admiring world. The tongue lolled out of the open mouth and the teeth grinned at the Texans who were smiling down in anticipation. Collops of roast meat hung from cheeks and jowls.

" 'M-m-m-m!' cried the Girls.

" 'There's another down in the pit where this came from,' shouted Pinky Snyth jovially. 'Can't fool me. I saw it.'

" 'We'll sure enough need it,' Bale Clinch bellowed. 'Appetites these girls have they're liable to leave us boys with nothing but the ears.'

"Curiously enough they stood as they ate. Deftly Eusebio jerked the tongue out, he sliced off the crown of the head, someone began to peel the smoking tongue and to cut it neatly on the wooden board. The hot spicy tidbits were placed on the pieces of thin crisp bread held out so eagerly and there arose little cries of gustatory pleasure.

" 'Here,' Vashti said, and hospitably extended to her erstwhile rival a moist slice on a wedge of bread. 'If you don't say this is about the best barbecue you ever ate.'

" 'It's been eighteen hours cooking,' Ollie Whiteside explained . . .

" 'How interesting,' Leslie murmured faintly.

" 'Needs a sprinkle of salt,' Vashti cautioned her.

". . . Through her mind, as she smiled and accepted the food held out to her, went an argument founded on clear reasoning against instinct. You're being silly and narrow-minded. You've eaten cold sliced tongue, where did you think it came from—did you think it was born on a silver platter bordered with sprigs of watercress? After all, perhaps Texans wouldn't like the idea of lobsters and oysters and crabs, they're not very attractive either when they come up from the baking pit, with all those claws and tails and whiskers.

"Bick was talking, he was explaining something to her. His low charming voice flowed over her soothingly. 'This is the real Spanish-Mexican barbecue, Leslie. They despise what we Americans call a barbecue—meat roasted over coals. This pit-cooking is the real Mexican barbacoa. That's where we get the word.'

" 'How fascinating,' Leslie managed to murmur again. 'Barbacoa.'

" 'You see, we take a fresh calf's head and skin it and place it in a deep pit dug in the ground on a bed of hot mesquite coals. We wrap the head in clean white cloths and then tightly in canvas and down it goes the night before, and it cooks down there for eighteen hours—'

"Now spoons were being used. With glad cries the Girls were dipping into the top of the head and removing spoonfuls of the soft gelid brains and placing them on fresh pieces of bread with a bit of salt sprinkled on top. Joella Beezer, a hearty matron, brought up an eye with her spoonful. Leslie turned away, she felt she was going to be very sick, she steeled herself, she turned back, she smiled, she felt a little cold dew on her upper lip and the lip itself was strangely stiff.

" 'Eat while it's hot,' Miz Wirt Tanner urged her. 'They's plenty more.'

"'I'm not very hungry, really. Perhaps if I just had a little of the rice and some coffee. I'm not accustomed to the—the heat—yet.'

"'My gosh, this ain't hot. Wait till July!'

"She ate. She drank. She talked. She laughed. She said delicious how do they make it the rice is so yes indeed we eat it in the East though we usually think of Virginia as the South but of course it must seem East to you there is a dish we sometimes calves' brains with a black butter sauce.

"The second head was brought up from the pit, was eaten though perhaps without the gusto of the first. Replete, then, the little company wandered off and left the littered table to the vaqueros and to old Eusebio. 'It was wonderful,' Leslie said to him. Her new word came to mind. 'Delicioso. Gracias.' The old mummy face with the live-coal eyes bowed statelily, accepting his due as a culinary artist.

"She had not disgraced herself, she had not disgraced Jordan, she drew a long breath of achievement . . . In a corner under the open shed another of the Mexicans had got hold of the calf's head from which the company had so recently eaten. As she watched him he took a piece of bread and plunged his hand into the open top of the empty skull, he wiped the interior briskly, round and round with the bit of bread, he brought the morsel up, dripping, and popped it into his eager open mouth.

"Someone asked her a question, she turned her face up to the questioner, she smiled a stiff contortion of the mouth, she even arranged a reply of sorts in her mind, but it never was uttered. At that moment the bunkhouse tipped toward her, the sky rolled with it and the ground rose up in front of her and rapped her smartly on the head.

"For the first time in her healthy twenty-odd years Leslie Lynnton had fainted dead away."

Savory or not, Ferber's descriptions of food were fully packed.

It was difficult for Ferber to thoroughly enjoy a social gathering, for her eyes were always taking notes, scavenging around for material—how this one talked, how that one chewed, how So-and-so had developed a tic, and how the fellow who had piles excused himself to go to the bathroom. She could never shrug off having been a newspaper reporter as a girl. When among people, she was always on the job. Even when among friends she delved for snippets that might be useful later on for her "character palette." Her observations and reportings run rampant through her diaries—some bitchy, some loving, some dull. But always she filed a piece of story —some remnant of news. "Dressed (in my old last summer's chartreuse) called for Terry, heard broadcast of Edward [Note: G.] Robinson and Una [his wife]. Simply incredible in its mawkishness and stupidity. It costs $10,000 a week. To a party for Katharine Hepburn given by Laura Harding. Not very good." . . . "With Fan to see 'The World We Live In', Kingsley's [Note: playwright Sidney Kingsley] dramatization of 'The Outward Room'. Unconvincing and shallow. All poor people are good and sweet, according to this little opus." . . . "At seven, to my horror Constance Collier walked in, ready for dinner & the theatre. I was a mess. Dressed, had dinner at the Algonquin. Saw Muni [Note: Paul Muni, the actor] in 'Key Largo.' Very bad. Anderson's [Note: playwright Sherwood Anderson] a pretentious bore." . . . "Met Kate Hepburn and her friend Laura at Iceland. Kate learning to waltz. Lunched at Iceland. With the girls to see 'Gone With The Wind.' A superb spectacle. Leigh and Gable good. Too long. Could have been cut an hour." . . . "Met Bob Nathan. He's had his third divorce, poor lad . . . To Fan's briefly. Her demon sister-in-law, Elsie Fox, there and too offensive for words." . . . "Dinner and the ballet with Moss [Note: Moss Hart] and to Lindy's for tea (in glasses). Moss told me about the play he is writing alone—a psychiatric play about a woman editor told in half realistic half dream terms." (Note: the play turned out to be the tremendous hit *Lady in the Dark.*) . . . "To Ritz. Larry Hart telephoned for matinee seat. Saw show. [Note: the show was Rodgers and Hart's musical *Higher and Higher,* which was trying out in Boston. Ferber's niece, Janet, then a young actress, had a part in it.] Janet bad, looked unattractive, costumes unbecoming. Sad. Dinner with Dicky, Dorothy, Jan, etc. Saw show again. Tried to help Jan with lines. She is very unhappy. Talked with Dicky after show. Second act needs rewriting." . . . "Mina in with little Janet French, 3 yrs. A charming child with tragic eyes—probably near-sighted." . . . "Rollin Kirby in with Corey Ford. Ford an odd neurotic fellow; his nose is too small." . . . "Dinner at Florence March's. A not very interesting evening with an appalling supper of strange smorgasbord." . . . "Janet called by Garson Kanin from Hollywood in offer of part in Carol Lombard-Charles Laughton picture. Paris bombed from the air by Nazis." . . . "Dinner at the Dicky Rodgers: Ten of us. The Jack Wilsons,

Moss, Josh Logan, an Italian refugee couple, Florence March. Dicky played for us for hours. Lovely."

For all her reclusive traits, in her good years, Ferber was quite social and usually had herself a gay old time. But in her last ten years—Fannie, her sister, shakes her head. "Edna turned queer, that's all—just queer." Define queer. "Well . . . perhaps it could have been something physical. Something wrong." Define wrong. "Well . . . perhaps Edna found out something terrible about herself." Such as? "Oh, I don't know . . . I think that perhaps she found out that she wasn't quite a woman." Fannie made this statement at the age of ninety-two. The reason behind it is that once she had seen a copy of *The Well of Loneliness,* by Radclyffe Hall, one of the first novels to deal with lesbians, in Ferber's study. She had stored the viewing of it in her recesses, and during the years the sight of it had become subconsciously deformed into a damning conclusion. Ferber was a woman who enjoyed good women as well as good men. On the surface, she seemed to be asexual toward both. But she certainly could wither either sex when she chose to. Mary Rodgers, the daughter of Richard and Dorothy Rodgers, remembers that acid side all too well. For some reason Ferber was not overly fond of Harold Prince, who was and is a dear friend of Mary's. Mary always believed in mixing ages at her dinner parties. One night, during one of Mary Rodgers' dinner parties, Ferber, who was seated next to Prince and obviously found the going tedious, turned to him and said, "And what good books have you read lately?" A withering thing—to make small talk and to parody it at the same time. Ferber didn't seem partial to brash young men on the move. Women, yes. They were to be greatly admired, but young men seemed to threaten her, and she felt the need to squash them. Mary Rodgers recalls that Ferber also didn't care much for the young wizard Stephen Sondheim. It was probably for the same reason.

". . . I might say that though I enjoy the company, the friendship and the affection of both men and women, I prefer, if given the choice, the company of men. They act more directly, they have not been obliged, for centuries, as women have, to dissemble, to resort to subterfuge. I find their company more stimulating, more challenging, no matter how young or how old. Having lived a somewhat adventurous life and since young girlhood the life of a worker, I am impatient of evasion and pretense as I would be of hoopskirts and pantalettes in a New York yellow taxi in the rush hour. Mine has been a long and eventful life in which the routine of work was not only accepted but sometimes fought for. More men than women live this sort of life. The male has been running up and down the world for thousands of years, bopping animals over the head, bopping other humans over the head, fighting foolish exciting wars in a kind of lethal game; exploring new continents, writing love poems, competing in politics, in fisticuffs and in business, the professions, the arts. So the masculine viewpoint is likely to be a refreshing one. No one has said to him, 'Your place is in the home. Your place is in the office—the shop—the factory.' His place is in the world. He had experience, he acted and spoke with incalculably greater freedom than the female. When he said, 'Funny thing happened at the office today,' it may not have been so very funny, but it was likely to be funnier than the funny thing that happened in the kitchen today."

This rather covertly feminist discourse was taken from *A Kind of Magic,* Ferber's second autobiography and last book. It reads well on paper, but to know Ferber was to not quite believe that she relished men all that much. She was a bit of a charlatan to her reading public, but most of all to herself. She wrote down things that she would have dearly liked to stand behind, but perhaps didn't. She was never spiritually content to be just a woman, and certainly in output, she felt more male than female—which must have caused her great ambivalence when it came time for emotional input. She was good with men, understood them, enjoyed their conversation, and knew that they enjoyed hers, which doesn't mean to say that she liked them. She observed them too much as a species to relate to them organically. She connected with them, and, as the old saw goes, familiarity often breeds contempt.

Kitty Carlisle Hart has said about Ferber, "She had the charm of the devil." True. It was a sort of glistening, bristling charm—like a brand-new hundred-watt bulb just screwed into a lamp. A jolting, blinding charm that had nothing to do with flirtation. It protected her from intimacy, at the same time condemning her to a sterile safety.

Mary Rodgers talks about the gap created by, ostensibly, no man in Ferber's life. "Not to need doesn't necessarily make one live her kind of life. Edna probably couldn't find anybody smart enough. And by the time someone did come along, if they did, she was probably too impenetrable." Mary Rodgers doesn't remember ever having seen Ferber respond to men like a woman—in the flirting sense. She draws a parallel to make her point: "I was once at a party to which Lillian Hellman had been invited. This was before I knew about Hellman and Dashiell Hammett. I had always thought of Hellman as being an abstinent sort of woman, and was surprised to see her actually behaving in a flirtatious manner toward the men around her. She positively glowed." The subtext of Mary Rodgers' anecdote was that Hellman, while enjoying a tremendous literary reputation, also enjoyed men as a woman—whereas Ferber didn't, couldn't.

"She adored Hank," Mary Rodgers says, referring to her second husband, Henry Guettel. She reveals that her "Hank" is tender and sweet—qualities which Ferber always sought out in a man. She says so herself. "For me there is no greater bore than a one hundred percent male or a one hundred percent female. Confronted by a massive two-fisted, heavy-breathing, barrel-chested all male he-man . . . I run from [his] irksome company . . . A man who is masculine with a definitely female streak of perception, intuition, and tenderness is a whole man; he is an interesting man, a gay companion, a complete lover . . . The feminine in the man is the sugar in the whiskey . . ."

Ferber was a dinner guest at the Guettels' relatively often during the year. She always sent flowers—before or after or both. When she came to the Guettels' home, no matter who else was there, she was the center of attraction. "As she got older, she felt—I think—that it was special to be invited by young, vital people," Mary Rodgers says, and then lovingly, "Whenever she came she was interesting, interested, amusing and flattering. There was never a scene."

Kitty Carlisle Hart and Garson Kanin hail back to a time when Ferber made scenes. Gloriously disgraceful ones that shook the rafters. There was a particular humdinger that took place at the dinner table of Kitty and Moss Hart. There is a preface to the story. Cecil Beaton, the well-known photographer, had shot a cover for *Vogue* magazine on which he featured pictures of many prominent Jews in the arts. Out of the mouth of each photo he had doodled a bubble, and inside the bubble he had placed a blurb of a rather vulgar nature. Goddard Lieberson, who was a dear friend of Beaton's, feels that it was merely a cartoon with no slander intended and should not have been taken so seriously. Others weren't inclined to be so benign. The cover caused a hue and cry among Jews particularly in New York, who felt that Beaton's slant was, without a doubt, anti-Semitic. Ferber thought it execrable, inexcusable, and that night at dinner at the Harts', she certainly didn't keep it to herself.

Kitty Hart had a seating of twelve, with Ferber at the far end next to Moss Hart, and Garson Kanin at the opposite end next to the hostess. Kanin was in the midst of a story about being photographed by Beaton that morning. (It was a photograph of popular authors sitting atop ladders, peeping through holes in a curtain, to give the effect that they were disembodied.) Kanin was telling it in his usual twinkly, witty style. Kitty Hart was laughing at the idea of a bunch of dignified authors wobbling on ladders. Suddenly, cutting the laugh—and the story—like a squirt of lemon came Ferber's voice from the far end of the table: "Nothing amusing seems to be going on at this end—what's so amusing at your end?" Kitty Hart, ever gracious, asked Kanin to repeat the story for Ferber's benefit. He began but got no further than the name Cecil Beaton, when Ferber let out an indignant yell, demanding for Kanin to tell her how he could ever, ever allow himself to be photographed, or even in proximity of the dreadful anti-Semite Beaton. Kanin, trying to be polite but firm, said, "I'll tell you after dinner, Edna." "NOW," she bellowed. "After dinner," Kanin insisted. "NOW," she laid down the gavel. A pall fell on the table. Moss Hart called in dulcet tones across to his wife, "Now, my dear, is the perfect time for a good hostess to say something sparkling. It's up to the good hostess to smoothly change the conversation." Bedlam had begun. The next thing Kitty Hart knew, she had been dragged up to the bedroom by a shaken woman guest whose mother had been on the famous *Vogue* "kike" cover done by Beaton. The woman practically backed Kitty Hart against a wall, and told her her side of her mother's side of Beaton. When Kitty Hart finally emerged downstairs at about ten-thirty, her entire party had left. She still refers to it as the night Edna Ferber cleared the room.

Dorothy Rodgers contributes another Ferber flambé. "One day at Rock Meadow, we had some guests for lunch, who were making sort of anti-Semitic remarks. Well, you know Edna was a fiercely proud Jew—irreligious—but very much a Jew. And she just took this on so brilliantly. All I remember is that they said something about it not being possible for Jews to do so and so, and Edna said, 'Well, one of our boys made it'—meaning Jesus, and it was a marvelously well-taken point that Jesus was a Jew. And she was witty and forceful and very clear about it."

The technique of the put-down never left Ferber; in fact, it became more barbed as she got older. She never failed to get her inning when the topic of being a Jew arose. Once at a luncheon Ferber made reference to her race. A venal woman in a silly hat responded with nasal distate. "Oh, Miss Ferber," she said, "I didn't know you were Jewish." Ferber sniffed, held her throat as though to protect a war cry, smiled a below-zero smile, and said, "Only on my mother and father's side."

Although she usually rose majestically to the occasion, she was not immune to being put down. Dorothy Rodgers smiles. "One day she was having lunch at our house and Anita Loos was there. People were talking about their first jobs and Edna was making rather a point that she had been a newspaperwoman when she was sixteen —supporting her family and so on. And Anita Loos was sitting there not saying a word, and finally Edna said, 'Anita, when did you do your first work?' And Anita said, 'Well, I sold my first scenerio when I was twelve.' I'm afraid that was a put-down for Edna."

The biggest put-down for Ferber was age. Each year seemed to dictate to her how many fewer books she could fit in. She was terrified of losing her sensibilities, which never did happen. To imagine Ferber frail would be like imagining Lillian Gish with muscles. Alvan L. Barach, M.D., Ferber's onetime friend and doctor, wrote in the introduction to his essay "Aging Without Abdication": "Aging is unpopular. The body wrinkles, and the mind undergoes a wrinkling of its own. However, science has recently contributed an extraordinary bit of cheerful evidence which indicates that aging need not force men to retreat from their chosen professions. The brain, the peak evolutionary achievement of man's anatomy and the one which most distinguishes him from animals, may receive a blood flow in men over 70 only slightly less than that of the most youthful idealist on the university campus.

"Aging is not an inevitable process that affects all equally; men in their 70's and even in their 80's have made remarkable achievements in the arts, the sciences, and technology. Society would be far different if all men over 65 had been deprived of the opportunity to work."

Women too. Old gal Ferber, she just kept rolling, she kept on rolling along. And so did *Show Boat.*

In May of 1966, yet another major revival of Jerome Kern-Oscar Hammerstein's musical classic *Show Boat* was being mounted at Lincoln Center in New York. Ferber, of course, had a little something to do with the property, although it's surprising—shocking, really—how many people are not cognizant of that fact. They think it was born a musical, not having a clue that it was a 1926 best seller born out of the head of Edna Ferber. Of course, every *Show Boat* marquee reads: "Jerome Kern and Oscar Hammerstein's *Show Boat,*" and then underneath, in much smaller print, "Based on the Novel by Edna Ferber." The public's eye doesn't readily go to a "based on."

Through the decades *Show Boat*'s honors were attributed to Jerome Kern's rather immortal score. Ferber certainly never begrudged him that; she thought it the top-notch score in American musical history—the most melodious, virtuous thing that could have ever happened to one of her "children." She was genuinely proud of this *wunderkind* and pleased as punch each time it stepped forth into the limelight. If she did sing in the shower, which is possible but hard to visualize, it would probably have been something from the score of *Show Boat*. How she loved that score, and Kern for composing it. Her original meeting with Kern was accidental, as is the usual case with most eventual marriages.

"It was Alexander Woollcott who acted as schatchen in the marriage between the novel entitled SHOW BOAT and the musical play presented by Florenz Ziegfeld at the Ziegfeld Theatre in 1927.

"One night I went to a first night with Alexander Woollcott, then dramatic critic on the New York Times . . . After the first act we drifted out to the lobby and my courtly cavalier bounded off to talk with someone else, leaving me to my own devices, of which I had none. A pixie-looking little man with the most winning smile in the world and partially eclipsed by large thick spectacles now fought his way through the lobby throng toward Woollcott. He said (I later was told): 'Look, Aleck, I hear you are a friend of Edna Ferber. I wonder if you'll kind of fix it for me to meet her. I want to talk to her about letting me make a musical from her SHOW BOAT. Can you arrange an introduction or a meeting or something?'

"Mr. Woollcott, with a dreadful relish for the dramatic plum which had thus fallen into his lap (if any), said, musingly, 'M-m-m, well, I think I can just arrange it if I play my cards right.'

" 'Thanks,' said Kern. 'Thanks awfully, Aleck, I'll be—'

"Woollcott now raised his voice to a bellow: 'Ferber. Hi, Ferber. Come on over here a minute.' Then, 'This is Jerome Kern. Edna Ferber.' It was done . . .

"Since then I suppose I've heard the Show Boat music, and Ol' Man River especially, a thousand times. I must break down and confess to being one of those whose eyes grow dreamy and whose mouth is wreathed in wistful smiles whenever the orchestra—any orchestra—plays Ol' Man River. I've heard it played in the bar of the King David Hotel in Jerusalem, at Pre Catelan in the Paris Bois, at the Savoy in London (we writers get around). I never have tired of it. I just happen to think that when Jerome Kern wrote the Show Boat score he achieved the most beautiful and important light-opera music that has ever been written in America."

Ferber's emotional structure tended to be child-like, her feelings, ingenuous when it came to her own turf. She would look forward to one of her revivals much like a child looks forward to a birthday. Mine, all mine, was the sentiment behind the worldly lady. And, if the revival fell short of her expectations, she would blame the incompetents (one of her favorite words, incompetent) who were behind it. She really only trusted herself, which gave her a lot of leeway to expect disaster. Much like the Walter Mitty sequence of Oscar Levant's in the film *An American in Paris,* where he not only conducts an orchestra but plays all the instruments, Ferber, ideally, would have liked to have written, directed, and played all the parts.

But this time, with this projected revival, Ferber was fairly confident that it was in good hands. It was to be presented by the Music Theatre of Lincoln Center and Richard Rodgers (dear Dickie), president and producing director. She trusted Rodgers' reputation, if not Rodgers himself. After all, he was the pillar of the American musical theatre; he would not be as unpatriotic as to give *Show Boat* a dud production. And he would never be as unfriendly as to not grant her a small favor. She had a great-niece. An aspiring actress. Could sing. Could dance. Very talented. And if the leading soprano role of Magnolia was up for grabs . . . or even a part in the chorus . . .

I was nineteen and had had two singing lessons in my whole life. With this vast range of vocal experience, I went to audition for

Richard Rodgers. The tryouts were being held at Lincoln Center. It was a diamond-studded day. With nepotism holding my hand, I was not particularly nervous. I did, however, become faintly uncomfortable when the woman who was taking names asked me where my sheet music was. It wasn't, I told her, I hadn't known to bring any. I didn't like the look she gave me; it was not encouraging. Then I felt true discomfort when I heard the caliber of a female singing voice wafting under the closed door of a room nearby. It was a glorious, resonant, soaring voice. A highly trained voice. I was in trouble. I asked the woman taking names if the voice belonged to someone auditioning for one of the leads. "Oh no," she said, "this is strictly a chorus audition." I started to perspire. I was in fierce straits if that was the quality that they wanted to hear in that room.

The singing stopped. The door opened, and the woman with the voice that would put me to shame came out. She even looked trained. High cheekbones, dancer's body, LOTS of sheet music.

Then my sentence was pronounced: "You may go in now."

A young man ushered me into the room. I had expected to see Richard Rodgers and perhaps one other officious person; I had expected it to be an intimate, cozy disaster. What I had not planned on seeing were fifteen hard-eyed men, sitting in judgment at a long board table. At the very end was Richard Rodgers, looking the most flinty of all. I thought to myself that if I died and tried to get into heaven, without credentials, this was what it would be like.

I think I was introduced as Edna Ferber's great-niece. I might as well have been. I had nothing else going for me.

"What are you going to sing for us?" asked the first hard-eyed man.

"I don't know."

"Well, where's your sheet music?"

"I didn't bring any. I thought I'd wing it."

The fifteen grim reapers looked grimmer. Richard Rodgers put his hand over his eyes. I was told to go to the back of the room and discuss with the accompanist what I might like to sing. I remembered Ferber's word to the wise: Never sing a Richard Rodgers' song in front of Richard Rodgers. So I chose instead to massacre a song by Lerner and Loewe instead. It was a little ditty from *Gigi* called "The Night They Invented Champagne." The accompanist wasn't sure he knew it. I told him to play it anyway; there were thirty hard, impatient eyes waiting for me. With both of us winging it, I began—off-key. To complicate matters, I tried to smile and be winning, and in trying to do those two things promptly forgot the entire middle of the song. My presentation was this: "The night they invented champagne, they absolutely knew that all we'd want to do is fly to the sky on champagne, and shout to everyone in sight are tonight." The sum total of my performance took three seconds.

I staggered out. They never said, "What did you say your name was?" All I was was Edna Ferber's great no-talent.

I cried so hard in the taxi going home that the driver finally asked me what could possibly be so tragic. I told him. "Oh, Jesus," he said, "glad it wasn't me."

Ferber had asked me to call her after it was over. I called her—three days later.

"Aunt Ed?"

"Hello, doll."

"I failed miserably."

"So I've been told."

"I'm sorry."

"You shouldn't have gone unprepared."

"I know. I feel awful—especially about using your name and . . ."

"Don't worry about my name. Worry about yours."

"I feel awful."

"It can happen to anybody. I love you. Don't do it again."

Perhaps *Show Boat* should not have been done again, or at least not when she was still alive. She was old enough to be nostalgic about the days of its glory, but not young or supple enough to realize that those days were no more—that *Show Boat,* in the year 1966, could well be regarded as a relic.

Ferber didn't attend opening night. She had her dinner alone at home on a tray, and retired early. Her secretary, Y. B. Garden, left a cryptic note for her, which she was to find the next morning:

"Miss F, After leaving 730 earlier, it occurred to me you might like to see one of the reviews of SHOW BOAT. So I got a Times, and here it is. I think its enthusiasm sounds about as restrained as my own. Anyway, here it is. G."

Stanley Kauffmann's review was not a good thing for Ferber to wake up to.

"What keeps 'Show Boat' afloat is its songs. The dialogue is a bit warped, the daring subjects a bit weather-worn, but those songs. Oh, Jerome Kern, thou art mighty yet . . . Oscar Hammerstein's book from Edna Ferber's novel, was once considered the harbinger of a new American popular opera; but someone always says something like that whenever a musical doesn't hew exactly to the chorus line. The show is historically noteworthy because it made some attempts at characterization, touched a few then-forbidden subjects, and reveled in some authentic Americana. But perhaps the large terms like 'classic' and 'great work' are dimming a little with time. What of it? We are left with a serviceable show with one of the best scores ever written in the American musical theater."

A Philadelphia paper, not that it helped, gave Ferber a bit more of her due: "The Edna Ferber book is a classic tear-jerker, but in many ways it contains more brutal reality than seen in many more modern musicals. It considers the plight of the subjected and discriminated against Negro, before it was fashionable to do so, part of the plot revolves around miscegenation and the characters suffer the disillusionment of love and the despair of poverty. You can't get much more meat than that."

She cared about reviews, said she didn't, saved them all, and occasionally, when deeply miffed at what she felt was some injustice done her, would write the critic a letter of indignation. After the opening of the revival of *Show Boat*, she jotted in her diary: "Musical 'Show Boat' opened at Lincoln Center, New York. Bad review S. Kaufman [Note: she spells his name incorrectly—as in George Kaufman.], N.Y. Times. Take it up with him?"

George Oppenheimer was the only theatre critic who was able to remain her friend. Personally, he kept on her good side, and professionally he kept her in good reviews. Alexander Woollcott, her great crony in the heyday of the Algonquin Round Table, feuded bitterly with her, and later dismissed her in his play reviews, giving most of the credit to George S. Kaufman, her collaborator. She had as little to do as possible with other theatre critics along the way.

When I approached the former New York *Times* critic Brooks Atkinson about discussing Ferber, his response was cool: "I have to reply to your letter that I never knew Edna Ferber. Towards the end of her life and my career we had a speaking acquaintance, but that was all. I don't think she really liked me as a critic, which was a valid attitude, but not conducive to friendship. I started to read

Edna Ferber when I was an adolescent . . . I admired her then, and it seems to me that I liked her plays."

Some of them he liked—others he panned. She remembered him for the others.

Whenever Ferber had a defeat, she retreated; she got out of New York, away from sympathy, and buried herself in the act of revitalizing. Marc Connelly remembers how Ferber used to stand at her window and say with ire, "How I hate New York." Connelly chuckles knowingly. "It would have taken a sheriff with an indictment to budge Ferber out of New York City for good—and even then she would have fought it tooth and nail." Ferber, as with many things in her life, had a love-hate, pleasure-pain relationship with New York City. She was constantly taking its temperature; when it was feverish, she made threats to leave it forever, but made plans to leave it only temporarily.

Noel Coward, in a letter to her after reading *A Kind of Magic*, writes of her "savage, accurate and loving description of New York." She does seem to capture it.

"No born and bred New Yorker actually can appreciate New York City. Accustomed to it from infancy he must take for granted this schizophrenic Bagdad.

"It is the young cornfed wide-eyed naive Middle-Westerner who meets the impact of this half-sordid half-glittering city, head-on; is stunned by it; and is forever stirred by love and hate for it.

"Half palatial dream city, half foul slum. Rat-ridden tenements; rat-ridden politics. Mountains, man made, walled by glass. Offering daily the talent the genius of the world in music, the theatre, the dance, science, business, designing, architure, merchandise, fashion. Days and weeks of brilliant sunshine, Mediterranean blue skies, exhilarating cold in the winter; salt ocean breezes in the summer; each autumn and spring a delight. The whole besmirched with dirt, crime, carelessness, greed, ignorance. Here were the matchlessly lovely rivers and bays put to no use for the millions who within their limited means, needed the haven of grass and trees and quiet and rest.

"Out for a solitary salutary walk at 9 p.m., a reasonable enough hour for a pre-bedtime amble.

"The building doorman says, 'Taxi?' He has been there for years.

" 'No thanks. I'm walking.'

" 'I don't think you'd better. This hour.'

" 'It's nine o'clock.'

" 'You going far?'

" 'I'm walking a mile. Up Park, down Madison. What is this? A sanitarium or something?'

"But I know he is right.

"New York City the once beautiful enchantress, raddled now and grown careless and neglectful, is slopping about all day in soiled negligee and rundown slippers, uncombed, bleary-eyed. But at day's end she dons the flattering chiffons of dusk and of the kindly night. Her lines and wrinkles are softened, the marks of decadence hidden. She covers herself with jewels—the emerald and ruby and diamond lights, the silks and furs of the brilliant Fifth Avenue windows, she wears the tiaras of the flashing towers and the fountains. Again she is the beauty, the enchantress for a few hours until dawn reveals the wrinkles, the dirt, the grime, the decay."

Getting out of New York seemed to free her physically and emotionally; she could escape the financial albatross of her family, her ambivalent feelings toward her sister Fan, and her own weary self-image. Once out, she seemed to become again the reporter-girl whom she mourned the loss of—vital, probing, relating. Her old self.

Dr. Alvan Barach feels that she withheld herself from the land of living people—especially in New York. That her typewriter was her barricade against letting anyone in. That the tragedy of her life was not so much what she suffered but what she missed. He remembers that she was always much cheerier outside of New York. "New York," he says, "is similar to Paris in that there is the same 'stench of amour'. It upset her. It diminished her." His observation might be a clue to why she was always on the move for her novels—choosing to live right in the locales, and consistently selecting them for their rusticity. There was nothing cosmopolitan about the settling of the Oklahoma Territory, or a showboat, or the emergence of Alaska into statehood, or adjusting to the Texas life. Only in her short stories did she get to urban situations, but in those she was more studied, with less lengthy emotional investment.

When Barach was treating her—back in the thirties and forties—she complained of chest pains that never showed up on a cardiogram. He calls it "an hysterical angina." She went off to Arizona for a spell and rode on a ranch every day. When she returned to New

York, he inquired about the chest pains. He describes her smile. "It was like sunshine on a winter's day—not all that warm." "They're back," she said. When her chest pains became oppressive for her, Barach referred and transferred her to a cardiologist, Dr. Alfred Steiner. She always felt that Barach had rejected her. Once at a dinner party they both attended, Ferber said to Barach with a cordial sting, "I wish you were still practicing medicine." At that point, he was at the peak of his practice. "I am, Edna," he responded. She just smiled frostily. At the end of the evening, she extended her hand to him, shook her head sadly, sighed, and said, "Oh, Alvan, I do wish you were still practicing medicine." Ferber wasn't one to let bygones be.

When in 1965 she went to Arizona to visit the Hopi reservation, she must have been in a period of release with herself, for she wrote in her notebook a telling and provocative passage:

"Scene—Kate and Oil Man. (She cooks lamb stew—String beans—Biscuits. New England food.) After their, or his, love-making. "Oh, dear, I didn't like it." As one who had been disappointed in her first cigarette or a child in a first chocolate éclair. He strikes her. She looks at him, takes his hand and holds it a moment against her cheek with its scarlet mark. 'Oh, my poor boy. I'm sorry. I didn't mean to be rude.'

"'RUDE,' he yelled. 'Out.'

"'Most crusading women like myself are frustrated. My grandmother and my mother. The Carrie Nations, the Sylvia Pankhursts and the Joan of Arcs. Sex-starved, probably. Lived like a nun, with the emotional release of religious ectasy. I'm all wrong, you know.'

"'You talk too much,' he said.

"She laughed her merry, chiming laugh.

"'You laugh too much, too.'"

Ferber didn't bring up sex much in her books, and never in her personal life. It was not her favorite subject. She was a favorite subject, however. "Oh, people used to sit around at dinner tables talking about Edna. She fit the true definition of a 'character,'" says Kitty Hart with a memory twinkle. And people also used to speculate a great deal about her sexual proclivities—or lack of them. A goodly portion of the Harts' pastime was taken up with speculating on whether Ferber had ever slept with anyone or not. Moss Hart felt that she might have because she wrote so romantically of the sexes. That's just the point. Not many who have had much sexual experience can permit themselves to wax overly romantic. In not one of her books does Ferber write about making love. Making kisses, just, but she skirts everything that would naturally follow. She practically writes blackouts when the moment might, and should, arrive. Even in her diaries she draws the curtain. She makes childishly prudish, giggly references occasionally: "When sex reared its ugly head, I left the room," or detached references: "Had dinner with Harry Boyle . . . Boyle a masher and a professional pass-maker. A rather attractive Irishman, manager of the hotel. The only man around, and evidently torn to pieces by the old gals." Then, there is a psychologically disturbing entry when she was having a tussle with the writing of *Saratoga Trunk:* "I couldn't lie down to my work today," she records—as if the typewriter was the male instrument to which she couldn't succumb. There was much sexual identification connected with her work. In her efforts at creativity, it seemed she was often sexually ambivalent; she equated not working well with impotency: "Phoenix Arizona. Worked A.M. but seem to be accomplishing as little as I did in New York. If this keeps on I shall know the fault lies within me, and has little or nothing to do with environment. A thing I have suspected . . . A feeling of futility and emptiness." When she was writing well, "A thousand words today. A full feeling," she felt sated, appeased, womanly.

Ferber craved feeling feminine, and fought to deny the androgenous qualities she perceived in herself. Yet she knew that those were the very qualities that had gotten her ahead, had ensured her success. What a wicked paradox for her. Flowers, doors held open, a coat helped on with—all the small pleasures she savored from a man. On Valentine's Day, 1945, she received, "A terrific valentine from Todd [Note: Mike Todd, the late producer]—a heart-shaped mirror with red roses, orchids, freesias arranged in front of it. But a structure." She was in love with the concept of romance; gallant gestures made her glow. But the larger pleasures she evaded thinking about and avoided experiencing. So it seems.

Dr. Alvan Barach has a special hook into Ferber's libido—or lack of it. Among Barach's illustrious patients were Eugene O'Neill and Ring Lardner, Jr. He states that all of the "glitter folk" that he met in the twenties became his patients. He was introduced to Ferber through Peg Leech [Note: later to marry Ralph Pulitzer, becoming

Peg Leech Pulitzer and winning the Pulitzer Prize] in 1925 when he was "going around with Peg." Barach was quite the fellow back then. Young, good-looking in a large, craggy way, a ladies' man, and, apparently, a brilliant doctor. For a while he was the assistant to Kreplain, who felt that Barach had such promise that he never allowed anyone to call him an assistant. Under Kreplain, Barach began to practice psychosomatic medicine. He would see a patient for a cough, but it was really for a talk. He was officially a pneumonia specialist and developed the ventilated oxygen tent, but psychosomatic medicine was his baby. He felt that most ailments were imagined or brought on by the imagination.

Barach saw a great deal of Ferber socially up until the time of his marriage. She confided in him more as a doctor than as a suitor. He never practiced overt psychotherapy, but cajoled her to discuss herself more freely than she probably ever did again. She told him enough about her early life for him to deduce reasons for her abstinent behavior. He thought that there was a someone with whom Ferber had had some relations early on; however, he didn't feel that she ever had had any sexual affair. He said that he felt she was in love twice in her life and that he was not at liberty to say with whom. That he, Barach, might have quickened her pulse is not unlikely. Trust can be mistaken for love.

Barach told a story about Ferber and a man (anonymous) that she liked, who had the misfortune of being ten minutes late for a date they had made. She said that if he'd really cared for her, he wouldn't have been late. He excused himself with the fact that he was caught in traffic. She continued to scold him, saying that he should have arranged his schedule so as not to be caught in traffic.

Barach stated that Edna never felt attractive, which was true, he added, of a number of writers. Jack London, for example, never did either. His rationale was, "I'll write my way out of it. People will love me because of my words and in spite of my face." Alfred Adler [Note: the renowned psychiatrist] always felt that Madame Lapanchin's long nose in Dostoefsky's The Idiot, was the root of her inferiority—to say nothing of Cyrano de Bergerac or Miles Standish. However, Ferber never used a humble physical front; her tongue and her eyes were her moats.

Barach felt that the form Ferber's love took was an infantile one. The "Love me no matter how bad I am" kind. He observed that an infant pees, defecates, hollers, etc.—expecting that someone will clean up and put up. Infants are that way; no one accuses them of being disagreeable. They take and don't give much, which is as it should be. When one is older, the way to have a friend is to be one. Mature adults seek out people who give them pleasure. Immature ones test out love by being disagreeable because they figure they won't be loved anyway. Edna never had the knack of offering herself. She was too horrified of rejection. She always had to be the first one to reject. There was an undiscernible element in her childhood that never allowed her to let go of the idea of rejection. Her loneliness was a terrible malaise.

Dr. Barach cuts close to the bone in appraising Ferber's emotional deficits, but then it was not difficult for most men to denote what was lacking in her, for she withheld from men her womanliness. Only to the public at large did she present all of her assets—her strength, her courage, her humility, her compassion, her wisdom, her insights, her oversights, her yearnings, her fulfillings, her joys, her sorrows—herself as the woman she would have liked to be.

There was not much magic in *A Kind of Magic,* her second autobiography that came out in 1963. It was intended to be a love letter to life, and specifically to life in America. But something odd happened. Her good intentions caved in on her. What emerged was a testy, preachy, anemic treatise on how she had lived the good life. The book is an undernourished postscript to her brave and nourishing 1938 autobiography, *A Peculiar Treasure.* Why she didn't put her last energies into a novel is a puzzlement. *A Kind of Magic* reads like a long Hallmark greeting card—for the most part full of synthetic wit and wisdom. It spans her life from 1938 through 1960. Somewhere along that life line she lost her zest. It shows. Two autobiographical works, two barings of breast were too much for Ferber. Her writing in *A Kind of Magic* is a ghost of what it once was. She felt bedeviled during her work on it, knew she was in trouble with it. She had a habit of being in trouble with every book she worked on, but this one was different. Usually she enjoyed being asked how progress was coming so that she could complain—as most authors do. But with this one, she was very still. One knew not to ask. I remember my parents receiving the finished manuscript to read. They read it in a single night, sharing the pages, so as not to keep Ferber waiting for their critique. She would want to know how much they liked it—nothing else. That was how the process went when her family read her latest. Janet and Henry or Mina and Bill or Fannie would say, "Edna, it's really marvelous," and she would counter wearily with, "Oh . . . I don't know. Do you really think so?" "Yes, yes—really really," said her frightened family fan club.

I remember the horror-stricken looks on my parents' faces after they'd finished *A Kind of Magic*. Janet: "What are we going to tell her?" Henry: "Lies." It was the only thing to do. Blunt truth to an artist is often destructive and, to an elderly artist, impossible. It wasn't so much the work itself that was at stake as it was Ferber's reputation. She knew that the work wasn't up to snuff, but to hear it from others would have been a blow. She was depressed after having finished it, and instead of letting her self-anger tear at her, she struck out. She had no compunction about dealing blows, especially at the head of her editor, Ken McCormick. On March 22, 1963, she sent him a letter that has little to do with anything concrete; it is more an outlet for her own anguish and rage.

"Dear Ken, you and I must talk, however briefly, on the latest manifestation of destructive behavior on your part. I am writing you in this way because I would like to be of some help to you in this matter, but also because I cannot, in justice to myself and my work, permit it to go on.

"You must face this situation and you must try to stop it completely. Otherwise I, who feel toward you only affection and goodwill in all other facets of our long relationship, must protest more publicly and must find a new editorial contact. I can't and won't go on this way.

"I shall not at this time refer to the ghastly situations with which you have confronted me in the past. The latest affront is infinitesimal in comparison with these.

"In this week's item for the record you have telephoned me—you, editor-in-chief at Doubleday's—to convey a message and request acting as a sort of errand boy for a movie man I do not know and of whom, to the best of my recollection (and it's a good one) I never have heard.

"The request was that I, as author of the novel GIANT, look at a motion picture whose background and characters are, presumably, Texas and Texans, and that I then convey to the motion picture company my comment (favorable, naturally) for which, to quote your own words, they will pay me.

"I am a writer of integrity and achievement. I am not a person who avails herself of the shabby and shoddy offers such as you presented to me on the telephone.

"Why didn't your friend put this request in written form? And why didn't you? The answer to that is clear.

"I think you need to take a good look at the situation in which you and I so deplorably find ourselves. I repeat, I will not be subjected again and again to this kind of contemptuous treatment. Perhaps a talk between us may clear the situation, though I feel that it goes much deeper than that in your own unconscious. You do these ghastly things and then you profess to be 'sorry.' It isn't good enough.

"I stand ready to help clear all this if I can. What do you want to do? I have a book coming out and I think it is a good and arresting book. It was written with a purpose. I will not stand by and see its future jeopardized as it so nearly was in the shocking book-jacket material you so incredibly sent me. Sincerely and affectionately, Edna Ferber"

Her intent surfaces in the last paragraph; it is, in its convoluted way, an SOS. Ferber needed someone to blame for her state of helplessness. She also needed someone to bail her out. She refused to recognize either of those motives.

In one entry in her diary she voices uncertainty: "The book—2nd autobiographical volume called A Kind of Magic finished. good? Bad?" She was incapable of writing bad prose. Her grasp of language was too broad, her structure too provocative, her character studies too visceral, her dialogue too accurate for her to ever make a disgraceful showing. On the whole, what *A Kind of Magic* lacks is *brio*—an Italian word that pops up often in her notes for the book—meaning vitality—dash—spirit—vivacity. Her notes, in fact, contain a lot more *brio* than is found in the book. There was an unpublished section that she titled "Americans Eating Eating Eating Constantly." It shows her preoccupation with other people's preoccupation with food.

"It is common psychological knowledge that the apprehensive or insecure child (or adult) is likely to eat as a panacea against fear or semi-starved for affection or security, eats. He raids the refrigerator. He munches, he is a snacker. Often he isn't hungry, actually, but he eats. The amount of eating done in the United States is beyond anything. It is true that Europe is given to sitting in a cafe or outside at a sidewalk cafe, but there is before him a small cup of black coffee, or an aperitif, or a citronade which lasts him an entire afternoon or evening. But the United States eats. It munches constantly, or so it seems. It walks or sits or sprawls in the parks, dipping into a paper bag. Adult men and women walk along the streets eating vast chocolate confections and ice cream on a stick. They eat chocolate bars, popcorn, peanuts in the movies. Their discarded food litters the highways, the parks, the streets, the sidewalks. Munch munch munch from breakfast to bedtime.

"There is a fantastic plethora of food. The cost of food is fantastic. Bread. Milk. Meat. Butter. Eggs. Coffee. The basic American foods. There is a fantastic profusion of all this, yet its cost mounts. This, it is explained, is due to labor. The oranges to be picked, crated, shipped. The wheat cut, ground, handled. The cattle raised, bred, fed, shipped, cut, sold.

"Strawberries and watermelon and peaches in the icy days of winter, and throughout the year. Perhaps the Second World War started this habit of munching all day long; with rationing in this land of waste and plenty, perhaps there entered for the first time the fear that perhaps food was, after all, something to be devoured quickly, on the spot, in the fear that it might otherwise be snatched away."

There is another amusing page, which she chose to discard, titled, "Oldsters."

"Here we are, oldsters in our sixties and seventies. Burstin with orange juice, T-bone steaks and green vegetables. We are of the generation that still foolishly holds the thought that legs were meant for walking. This accounts for the fact that the leg muscles (the term is muscle tone, I believe) enables us to get about by placing one foot in front of the other. Surely this next generation, if any, will have a sort of spaghetti for muscles.

"We do not bewail the past as much as our forebears. The present is precarious beyond bearing, but exciting. We have everything to gain and nothing to lose. If we have kept alert and receptive we, as a generation, have had the exhilarating ride of all time. I remember when there was really something to remember. Perhaps the sixty-and-seventy lot back in the centuries gone by recalled the thrilling day when the wheel was invented. Certainly it was, in the long run, probably more fundamentally important and useful than John Glenn's contemplated trip to the moon. But I'm the girl who can take a moon or leave it alone. I'd be hard put to it to be forced to do without the wheel, muscle tone or no muscle tone. After all, wheels are necessary all the way from a jet plane to a wheel chair."

The "outtakes" of the book are more fearless and more telling than the actual contents. In them, she seems obsessed with two themes: women and progress. Her notes show that progress was both exhilarating and repellent to her; she didn't feel that mankind used it to grow wise—only to grow wide. She links progress to more produce to more greed to less integrity. She says: "Certainly if the United States of America is in a bad way (which it is) psychologically and physiologically, it is its own fault. Fat. Food. Fun. These have nearly done us in. As the waistline has widened the spirit has shrunk."

Ferber was not known or reviewed as a "heavyweight" writer. She was a popular writer, a palatable writer, one who stirred the public sentiment without outraging it. What she serves up in *A Kind of Magic* is like spiced junket; there is a kick to it, but it's junket all the same. She was a professional writer, as she stressed all the time—somehow making the word professional sound antiseptic, starched. Kitty Hart recalls how she would always preface everything by saying, "I am a writer," as if to excuse herself from all of the mundane, mortal, tedious things in life. She could have as well said, "I am a nun," for she certainly had taken her vows and, from what it appears, was celibate. As a professional writer, she felt she had an obligation to reach the masses—not through mediocrity, but through an emotional common denominator. She had a slick sixth sense about what she could say that would make people hearken. In a sense, she was victimized and compromised by her professionalism in *A Kind of Magic*. She should have pulled out all the stops, but retreated for fear that her public wouldn't recognize her. Her book is manicured. It is a fairly good book. Her notes are the hangnails that could have possibly made it a very good to excellent one. There is a group of notes which she called "White Race Black Race." It has little sentiment, and probably less public appeal. It is not included in the book.

"At the present rate of change it seems inevitable that the white race will take second place. The colored race, black and yellow, will dominate. Already the white race is enormously outnumbered. When a group, race, class is outnumbered it must, if it hopes to retain its position, outwit its opponent in strategy. But brilliance in strategy is not, it appears, necessarily found in the people or nations who eat the greatest number of beefsteaks, drive the biggest and fastest cars, sit longest in front of the television, walk the least, eat the most. Automatic dish washers and washing machines are fine if the time saved by those accommodating gadgets is spent in pursuits of some constructive value. Health measures. Educational measures. Perhaps one day the wheel will revolve slowly again and the white people will rise again to the top, but centuries will have rolled ponderously by.

"The figures are rather unassailable. This alone would not bring about this state of affairs now, and has not in the past. But now one must add to these figures the probability that the millions in India, China, Africa may have one stomach-filling meal a day. Starvation and semi-starvation has been the rule for centuries. Disease has weakened them. Lack of education. Lack of water. Absence of the most ordinary hygiene. All this is vanishing. Two vast world wars have mixed the ingredients into a mass of ferment. White boys in uniform, black boys in uniform, yellow boys in uniform. This is what you eat for strength—for bone, blood, muscle, brain. This is the way you handle a gun. In this airplane you can see the world in a few days time. Listen to this box, it is called a radio, it brings you the news of the people thousands of miles in every direction. This is called a play. This is called a factory. This is a tractor, a magic tool that will bring its magic to your farm. These are minerals, these are vitamins, these are medicines, they will heal your sick, strengthen your children, banish your pain.

"It doesn't take long to learn that sort of lesson. The white race has, for the most part, invented, discovered and devised these tools, machines, medicines, buildings, garments. They took the medicine and felt well. They ate the foods and grew stronger. They used the machines and prospered. Well, what do you know. How long has this been going on says the coolie, the serf, the slave, the drudging peasant, the half-savage. They need not invent it or devise it. They need only make use of it, ready made. Unless an atomic war wipes so-called civilization off the face of the planet Earth, the strong probability is that the outnumbered white race, tricked by its own ingenuity and particularly the United States, notoriously open-handed and sympathetic to suffering, may find itself in a poor second place within, say a half a century from now. Perhaps sooner. It takes so little time to become accustomed to tractors, laundromats, pressure cookers, motor cars, airplanes, televisions. Perhaps then, in another thousand years the white people, hardened and toughened and humbled by adversity may strike for their rights among the luxury fattened and lethargy-slackened black colored race. Certainly a change, whether cataclysmic or beneficial, is rushing toward us all."

Ferber was ahead of her time with her thoughts about the "women's front," or perhaps she was just more articulate than most. She was certainly prophetic about women's capabilities, and we are only beginning to see today what she'd predicted. Had she lived, and had the urge been strong enough, she might have preceded Betty Friedan in writing the first powerful women's manifesto. Her notes indicate that the women's theme was an angry hum in her:

"I've seen a lot of women who were under stress. I've yet to see a woman who behaved—or who appeared potentially to be capable of behaving—like a Kaiser Wilhelm, an Adolf Hitler, a Benito Mussolini, a Fidel Castro. Hitler's hysterics would make any woman's performance sound dulcet as the cooing of a dove; Mussolini, pop-eyed, slobbering with incoherence; Castro, ludicrous in his antics; and Khrushchev—I'd like to show what would be recorded in the way of masculine head-waggings and jokes if a woman were to take off her shoe in the midst of a United Nations session, and while the representative head of one of the most civilized nations in the world actually was speaking to the assemblage—what would be said and recorded if a woman were to remove her shoe and clatter the heel of that shoe on her desk like a machine-gun outburst."

Since her own consciousness had been raised at an early age, she tended to make statements about women that contain hope for what they're capable of doing and at the same time intolerance with their lack of strides.

"Four-footed animals are either male or female. But two legged humans are not only male or female. They are men or women. A woman can be a female and a woman at the same time. My objection to the behavior of my sex in general is that the great majority of them go on being merely female. This isn't good enough. More than half of the United States is largely a loss of talent and force.

"Women are usually smarter than men because through the centuries they have had to be for survival. This now is nonsense. They are smarter for much the same reason that Jews are often smarter than Christians. Jews have been held in subjection for centuries and they have learned to see through the backs of their heads. So have women. If men ever discover how tough women actually are they'll be scared to death. And if women ever decide to throw away that mask, wig and ruffled kimono and be themselves, this will be another monarchy—and perhaps it's about time. Certainly if this is a man's world I'll make you a present of it."

Whenever Ferber proselytized, she also personalized. A self-proclaimed and totally acclimated spinster, she discusses spinsterhood as though it is a scaly condition in the eyes of mankind.

"Woman has been so set apart from her sisters in Europe, Asia, Australia, Africa in that there always has been a greater—though far from perfect—partnership arrangement in the relation between husband and wife, mother and son, brother and sister. In countries other than the United States the son—particularly the first-born or the only son—is a kind of god. If there is an education to be got, he gets it. No questions asked. Spinsters are and always have been a dime a dozen in England, France, Germany, Italy, Spain, Scandinavia. Other than, perhaps, Queen Elizabeth the First, Catherine of Russia and Joan of Arc, most European spinsters have been held in pity, if not contempt."

But where Ferber really makes her personal statements is on the subject of marriage.

"I never have married. And I'm glad I never married. But I should have married. Marriage is a great experience in life which no one should miss. If you are born, and can stand it: live, and can stand it: die and can stand it, one should be able to marry and stand it. Encompass it."

The critics who reviewed *A Kind of Magic* treated Ferber as a phenomenon and the book as an afterthought. They implied that her skills as a person were far greater than her last volume. Jerome Weidman, in his review that appeared in the New York *Times* Sunday book section, evades criticism of the book by discussing Ferber as an edifice.

"'All passes. Art alone enduring stays to us; The Bust outlasts the Throne,—The Coin, Tiberius.' Thus, Henry Austin Dobson. And if his observation contains as much truth as it contains poetry, then Miss Edna Ferber is assured of immortality. For nobody, reading this second installment of her autobiography, can doubt that she has made of her life a genuine work of art . . . Without the strength of character that enabled a 60-inch slip of a girl from Kalamazoo, Michigan, to descend on New York City before the First World War, scoop up the metropolis, and pin it to her shoulder like a corsage, we would not now have that national institution known as Edna Ferber."

Weidman goes on to tell a little-known George S. Kaufman-Edna Ferber story that seems to fill up the space of his nonreview but reveals a softer and more reverent side of Kaufman's relationship toward Ferber.

"Once, many years ago, I heard the late great George S. Kaufman describe to a group of dinner companions a walk with Miss Ferber along the Atlantic City boardwalk. They had gone to the New Jersey shore to woo the muse in an atmosphere that other playwrights before them had found helpful. 'We were there with an act, you might say,' said the dour Mr. Kaufman. 'We were hoping to come back to New York with a second and third.'

"One day after a grueling and not too fruitful session at the typewriter, Miss Ferber suggested a breath of fresh air. Mr. Kaufman, whose attitude toward exercise was not unlike that of Ben-Gurion's toward the Nuremberg laws, slouched along morosely behind the briskly striding Miss Ferber. As they came to a drug store, Mr. Kaufman's famous collaborator suddenly stopped and climbed onto a weighing machine outside the door.

"'Here, hold my purse,' she said. 'And give me a penny.'

"'Why are you suddenly interested in your weight?' asked Mr. Kaufman.

"'I'm not,' said Miss Ferber.' I want that little card that comes out of the slot. You know. The one that tells you all about your character.'

"'It would be cheating the owners of the machine to ask them to tell you all about your character for a mere penny,' said Mr. Kaufman. 'The amount of character YOU'VE got, here, just to be fair, drop this in the slot.'

"And he handed her a silver dollar."

Ferber was probably more pleased with Weidman's words than with those that came out in the Nashville *Tennessean:*

"The author of such perennial favorites as Showboat, Giant, So Big, and Ice Palace, has most certainly carved for herself a niche in the world of modern American fiction. She may be no Melville or Katherine Anne Porter [Ferber circled Miss Porter's name and wrote above it her own initials, E.F., followed by an exclamation point, indicating that this slander was not to be taken gently] but she has proven almost always more than entertaining."

It is surprising that she saved one review in particular coming from the Savannah *Morning News.* It must have caused her a twinge. There is more truth than praise to it.

"Miss Ferber sees her work as living for many generations, and passes herself some bouquets with a kind of naive conviction which is as refreshing as it is boastful. Certainly her record is one of accomplishment and her books have stood up as representative interpretations of the American way of life. Texans may not agree, as she candidly shows by her admissions of the vituperous letters and accusations she received from that state upon publication of GIANT.

"As a record of a life dedicated to writing and one revelling in the good life, the book is interesting and commands respect, but as a production to add stature to her literary reputation we find it questionable."

There is a great deal that is smug in *A Kind of Magic.* Ferber's tone is one of complacency about her lot. Often it rings false. In her review in the Washington *Evening Star,* Mary McGrory's subtext is, "Methinks the lady protests too much."

"After a half century at the writing table, she [Ferber] is understandably complacent about her achievement. Four generations have read 'Show Boat', 'So Big', 'Come and Get It'. As a dramatist collaborating mostly with George S. Kaufman, she has had her share of hits. Of her novels she says, and it is her own punctuation 'They had power they had theme they had protest.' She ticks off her qualities as 'vitality, observation, characterization and readability.'

"Those four virtues, with the exception of characterization, are present in this second installment of her autobiography. The only character present is Edna Ferber herself, sturdy, alert, appreciative, voluble. No wit, no stylist, she is not self-conscious about stating or even belaboring the obvious. Her observation is better than her perception.

"In this longish book, there is no suspense, or even chronology. These are jottings. There is no real emotional content. Miss Ferber protests she is that rare being, a happy spinster."

Mary McGrory strikes fairly close to the jugular. Ferber was unable to see between her own lines in *A Kind of Magic;* there was no way she could perceive how pronounced the hollows were.

Her friends bluffed it through, sending her letters full of hyperbole. Noel Coward, for one, writes a letter that seems slightly insincere in its praise but totally sincere in its affection:

"Darling Ferber. It was YOU who said that it [*A Kind of Magic*] was repetitious here and there. Well, perhaps it is, for the layman, but for a fellow writer NO. All the pains and pangs and sturms and drangs, so eloquently and vividly described, merely made me go on nodding my head like an old Buddha in a state of masochistic euphoria. That awful writer's conscience. That ghastly and rewarding self-discipline that civilians have no idea of. Oh dear Oh dear. I hope that every conceited amateur that lives in this great big world reads your book and has a nice quiet think and goes out to have his or her hair done.

"You also said, with beguiling modesty, that there were some good things in it. This dear was a coy understatement. There are far more than SOME good things in it. There is, for instance, the chapter on Israel: the savage, accurate and loving description of New York. The bit about noise emerging incessantly from the Chatterbox and, above all, the last chapter which I suppose is the most brilliant descriptive writing you have ever done. As I said on the telephone your use of English is, to me, endlessly satisfying. No one, in my experience, has ever equalled you in your sentimental, UNsentimental, shrewd, affectionate, astringent, deeply understanding appraisal of your own country. (You're not the only one who likes adjectives) Nobody but you also, who I have always suspected of having a secretly baleful disposition, would have sent such a book to a poor struggling composer-lyricist on the eve of a major production. For the last three days I have been sitting in a rococco ballroom at the Bradford Hotel spearing wrong notes out of a heavy and complicated score only to return to my bedroom and be compelled to go on reading about all YOUR troubles. Not only that, I have regularly wakened at about three in the morning, eaten some chocolate (My old energy trick) and read just one more chapter. I have now, at last, finished the book. Exactly ten minutes ago and what the hell am I to do when I come home to-night? I shall buy Life magazine that's what I shall do.

"I must add obsequiously and slavishly that without 'A Kind of

Magic' this particular week might have been insupportable. So there.

"I will enlarge upon all this when next I see you which I hope will be here.

"Thank you darling Ferb very very much indeed. Coward"

A lovely letter from a loving and devoted friend. Mr. Coward, certainly not a pushover for only fair literature, had shared the half of life with Ferber that she chronicles in *A Kind of Magic*. Perhaps his fond memories imbued his criticism with favoritism.

Russel Crouse, another dear friend, wrote another supportive letter.

"Dear Edna, I am always the guy who reads the book last. Anna, being younger, pounces on it faster than I can. She had a wonderful time reading 'A Kind of Magic.' I didn't get it until after she had savored every word of it and I'm the boy who is a candidate for a remedial reading course. I'm a slow but thorough reader. I'm also a thorough enjoyer when I enjoy and permit me to say, Miss Ferber, that 'A Kind of Magic' creates a kind of magic.

"I love the joy of living that it breathes. I relived the several occasions on which I visited Treasure Hill [A house in Weston, Connecticut, that Ferber built and lived in from 1938 to 1950.] I even remember its telephone number—Trumbell 221. There was so much I loved in your picture of New Orleans which is the way I first saw it, and if it still isn't that way, I don't want to go back. I was there for Mardi Gras almost by accident. Being a baseball writer, I couldn't take a vacation in the summer and it got so late that the sporting editor of the Kansas City Star finally ran me out of the office before the next season started. I wound up in New Orleans where I spent two weeks with the Newspaper Fraternity including Meigs Frost, who turned out to be a pretty good writer later, and who had a wife with the incredibly lovely name of April Frost.

"There is so much I loved in the book, I can't begin to tell you. But, I do have to spank you for one thing—you, the best reporter I have ever known—failing to remember the name of that fellow at Yale who told you where to dig for the well. Edna, how could you. Anyway, I loved the book and as you've known for many many years, I love you. Sincerely, Crouse."

Yet another form of a love letter came with the notes of her editor, Ken McCormick, after she had delivered her manuscript to him. He starts out by writing:

"This is real vintage Ferber filled with wisdom, wit, savage commentary, wise observation, brilliant contrast, breadth of interest, and alive alive alive.

"I read this book with mounting excitement and ended it with regret because I wanted to go on in this trip through your life with you . . .

"I love your love of people, of life, of places, which Huxley* found only through the use of drugs, and which you have as a daily waking sense. My comments, both praise and critical, follow."

What follows is far more of the former than the latter. And as to Ferber's love of people and of life—well, one could soundly debate that. Professionally, on the written page, yes, she was a lover. Personally, in her soul, in her being, she could never quite master the art of joy. She was an observer of joy, of love, but too removed to be able to sufficiently feel the emotions. The theme of "lacking" threads through all of her diaries, dating back to the mid-twenties when she was a young woman. She constantly jots about being weary burdened by her family and generally fed up. If Ferber's being fed up at thirty-two-ish is added to forty-odd years, there could not have been much love going out or coming in. And by 1963 there wasn't, and it comes through in *A Kind of Magic*. It's as though she's bearing false witness against herself. Ken McCormick seems to sponsor this false witness by ending his notes with:

"You have every right to be proud of this book as you have every right to be proud of your life. The book sparkles with the radiance of your observations and it has a fierce integrity, which is you . . . I'm very happy about this book and I can't wait to get busy telling everybody at Doubleday how great it is. Remember I love you."

At that time Ferber needed all the support, encouragement, and accolades she could get. She was working under a double physical jeopardy. Not only did she have severe attacks of trigeminal neuralgia, she had glaucoma and cataracts in her left eye.

On May 6, 1963, she entered the hospital for an eye operation. She recorded as much as she could of the events:

Monday: "To New York Hospital. Thirteenth floor room. No good can come of that."

* Aldous Huxley.

Tuesday: "Double operation on left eye for glaucoma–for cataract. No pain. Janet–Mina–Molly [Note: she means visitors]."

Wednesday: "Little physical discomfort. One excellent 8 to 4 nurse. Eve Bourguignonne."

Thursday: "Night nurse–4 to midnight not good. Especially bad 4–12. Hanson. Shrill, tough, dreadful."

Ferber needed to have a scapegoat. Most often it was her sister Fan, but occasionally a Nurse Hanson would slip in and do the trick nicely. Fortunately for Nurse Hanson, Ferber only had to endure her until she checked out of the hospital and went home to resume her badgering of sister Fan.

Fannie Fox owned a lovely old house in Westport, Connecticut, upon which Ferber would descend every once in a while during the summer months. Neither sister welcomed the visit, yet it was a ritual–a trial by sibling fire. During one of their get-togethers in June of 1963, Ferber records with bile: "To Fan's at Westport. Molly with me. A wretched week-end. Mrs. Connor [Fannie's nurse and companion] threatened to leave. Fan's behavior unreasonable and saddening. Home Sunday terribly depressed."

One wonders whether Ferber ever considered Fan's feelings. One thinks not. Ferber treated her sister as though their relationship was reversed. She had such *angst* toward Fan, it was as though Fan was the celebrity and she was the one who had been left behind. Ferber always had many more sour grapes to give Fan than vice-versa. Even when Fan was ill, which she was with a bad flu in March of 1962, it stirred little sympathy in Ferber, who testily writes in her diary: "To Fan's at 11 A.M. so that Nurse Connor could go to Mass. Fan a hell cat in mood. If she weren't ill I wouldn't see her for weeks at a time. It's very saddening." Even her sister's birthday turned into a personal holocaust for Ferber: "That great National Holiday Fannie Fox's birthday. She has triumphantly succeeded in making everyone miserable. Went to her apartment at 4:30. Janet, Henry, Julie there . . . Birthday cake, etc. I was asked not to come until late afternoon, so didn't see the Candle Ceremony, etc. Strange woman. Mistakenly stayed a short while after others left. A scene. Fan probably over-tired."

Ferber was unable to make peace with her sister. When occasionally she tried, the effort only turned into a chastisement. Fan, being psychologically the sounder sister, would destroy many of the letters that Ferber sent her. Ferber would keep copies of them. In one particularly vituperative one she writes:

"Dear Fan:—Since I've heard nothing from you following my mistaken drop-in visit of Sunday before last, I am impelled to try to clear what is, to me, an unpleasant situation. As we are sisters, with no other siblings, there always is the danger of a situation such as this deteriorating into a serious schism. I should hate to have that happen.

"Although you and I are almost always in agreement on somewhat superficial things such as books, plays, humor, clothes, decoration, etc., we often are far apart in matters of conduct—particularly emotional conduct.

"To display family friction in public always has seemed to me as offensive as to perform private functions in public. It is a form of pants-wetting that adults abstain from, if they can.

"Your friend seemed to me an interesting, intelligent and attractive woman. I was sorry to have to leave after an hour that Sunday evening, but as you remember I had been up very late at the Rodgers' party the night before, and staying up late has always been difficult for me. When you began to reproach me with the statement that I hadn't been in your apartment since your Thanksgiving dinner I realised that I must try to brush this off lightly and get out quickly. Even if it had been true, which, as you know, it is not, this was not the time or place for such a discussion. So I tried to paste a smile on my face as I said, oh, I wouldn't say that, Fan. Then it began. If you were here, when were you here! Just tell me when you were here.

"I said goodbye and made for the door, but it was no use. You came to the door, you again said you wanted to know when I had been at your apartment, and then you shouted, 'You make me feel like a fool.' Mercifully, the elevator came up, I said, 'Well you may,' and that was that.

"How embarrassing for your friend, and for me, if not for you. I can't imagine what she must have thought, or said.

"You and I, Fan, are really old women, fortunate though we are in being able still to enjoy friends, fun, books, exercise, our home, good food, and even to help other less fortunate people, perhaps, to enjoy these things. In the very nature of things, however, we can't have a very imposing number of years ahead. I wish we could both try at least to skirt the edges of each other's weaknesses so as not to tread on them. Your daily interests, and mine, are not very similar. But fundamentally that should make little difference between us, as sisters.

"If all this sounds solemn or even pompous, heaven forbid, please believe that I didn't mean it to be so. Much love to you. Edna."

It would appear, as twisted as it may seem, that the only way Ferber could show empathy toward her sister was in rage. To express warmth was to lose her temper. When making love or making rage, a person is forced to deal on a one-to-one basis. Both emotions dwell in a very hot zone. Since making love was not a part of Ferber's life, she chose rage, by default, to establish closeness. She used her sister, especially in the later years, to lovingly abuse. Why Fan took it is a mystery. Why didn't she ever tell Ferber where to put her pugilistic tendencies? "It did no good," Fannie says sadly. "When I came back at her, it only stoked her. I think Edna enjoyed not getting along. It gave her something to do when she wasn't writing."

Ferber's rage, frustration, pain, and sense of loss reached a crescendo during the years of writing *A Kind of Magic*. She was unrelenting with herself and everyone else. Small irritants loomed large, and large ones gigantic. She had taken to idle, depressing jottings in which she mercilessly berated herself:

THE VIEW FROM THE WORKROOM WINDOW

I found myself sitting in an armchair gazing idly out at the sky and the view. This is what met my eye. From my fifteenth-floor double French door that leads out to a small balcony I was staring at a huge brick apartment building that was even higher. It was red brick, with terraces and every terrace was empty and of the rows and rows of windows every one was closed and all the shades were pulled down on all the windows so that they stared, sightless and blank, back at me. But on the roof of this blank inhuman deserted manifold dwelling there is a forest. But this was not a forest of trees. It was a grove of television antennae. Antennae, dozens of them pointing skyward, their trunks black metal, their branches black metal. Well, I said to myself as I stared, you are pretty stupid if, after having come past your allotted three score and ten and having worked for more than fifty of those years, you find yourself sitting staring out of your New York home at a lot of blank sightless windows and a half acre of television spikes. If that's the best you can do, it isn't good enough. You're a failure.

The truth was that Ferber rather enjoyed television, although she would never even admit to watching it. She had bought Molly Hennessy a set that Molly kept in her room off of the kitchen. It was an early set—no color, no console—nothing fancy. It was a maid's set. Despite herself, more than occasionally, Ferber would venture "underground" to Molly's room, where the two of them would watch happily while sipping hot chocolate. Ferber would never entertain the thought of buying a set for her own use. She condemned the new and crass medium as though it were her own personal enemy, and in a way it was stealing the reading public—part of which was hers. She felt it was a blight on children's minds, and a pathetic panacea for adult problems. She was about ninety per cent correct to snort at it. For with the advent of television, so many practices that her generation held dear went down the drain. Theatregoing became less and less prevalent; people could always stay home and be entertained. The art of witty conversation was rapidly going to rot, being replaced with TV slang and catch phrases. Novels were being traded for hour-long programs: Michener for "Adventures in Paradise," P. G. Wodehouse for Ernie Kovacs or Sid Caesar, and perhaps even Ferber for "Rawhide." Dinner parties were being cut short in order for guests to beat it home in time for some "special" or other. Even dinner, in many homes, was held, like an offering, in front of the set. No wonder Ferber shuddered. She loathed anything common and television was the most common denominator of all time. Yet, eventually even she succumbed to the normal, average American pleasure of watching it. She was selective. She would choose a Danny Kaye special, or a tribute to Richard Rodgers, or Mary Martin's *Peter Pan*, or, when Kennedy was assassinated, all of the proceedings. It was not so much television, perhaps, but the camaraderie of sitting with Molly Hennessy on an otherwise lonely night that won her over.

During the struggle with *A Kind of Magic*, Ferber retreated more than usual to the rest farms of Elizabeth Arden. There were two—one in Arizona and one in Maine. In the summer months Ferber would head toward Maine, and, in the winter, Arizona. At the Maine Chance branch, Ferber found a friend—a little girl just out of college named Judy Shorey, who was hired as a secretary to the manager. Ferber often lit on people who would faithfully serve her without being slavish about it. Judy Shorey filled this bill. Her recollections of Ferber are more touching and telling than those of some of Ferber's more illustrious friends. Judy Shorey traces the relationship and captures "her" Ferber:

"I first came to [Miss Ferber's] attention my second season at Maine Chance. A quick description of the travel situation in Maine . . . only one airline Northeast, flew into Maine . . . Augusta 20 miles from Maine Chance . . . three flights daily on weekends. Rail travel was available the first few seasons, then all passenger service into the state was cancelled. Greyhound buses were available, as were private hired limousines. Miss Ferber travelled by air. There were two men running the entire Augusta Airport. That literally means flagging all flights in and out of the airport, meeting all passengers, loading and unloading baggage each flight, making all reservations, writing all tickets, answering all incoming calls, recording weather, doing all janitor work, and just anything else entailed in running an airport. When a flight was inbound or outbound, the phone was just left ringing. A recording was used in later years. So you can see the two men who were running this entire operation were too busy to know or care about the name or position of any passenger.

"We always suggested our clients book round trip reservations before coming to Maine due to the limited passenger service (28 seats aboard a plane). Miss Ferber had her confirmed return reservation but decided to change her plans. I believe there were three or four completed, confirmed changes—when once again she changed her mind. Well, neither heaven nor hell was going to get her on her newly desired flight. She was livid. The manager was truly given an impossibly difficult time by Miss Ferber. [She] called Northeast Airlines President threatening suits . . . wrote letters . . . threatened loss of job employment if she wasn't gotten on that flight. The calls, telegrams, and correspondence started early in the day and continued into evening. While at our end in Maine, the airport manager could do nothing. His hands were tied. All flights were booked and confirmed solid. He therefore proceeded to simply hang up on Maine Chance calls. He wanted no more to do with any of it. She still had her last confirmed reservation but was not satisfied. New York, Boston—nobody could or would at this point do anything. This one little lady had the entire Maine Chance staff distraught, not to mention Northeast Airlines in total. I then decided to make one last ole Maine stab. I, of course, had been involved in the phone calls all along. I went into the airport knowing the manager was off duty, but that his assistant was on. I used all my Downeast—us Mainers got to stick together—knowhow. I pulled every Downeast trick in the book—pleaded, begged, bribed, and cried a little. Well, Gene (second in command) was one of these dear, understanding, compassionate men. At least in this situation and to me—and through some pull he said for me and no other person at either end of the line would he even try, but knowing the pressure everyone was putting on me, he'd do his best and be in touch by morning. To this day it is beyond me, but he performed the miracle of getting Miss Ferber on her desired flight. From that time to the end of my Maine Chance career, Miss Ferber always dealt directly with me, and made it known to all, that I was the one and only one who could have gotten her on that flight. 'This little Maine girl,' she would say.

"I think in my eleven years at Maine Chance there were fifteen different managers. Miss Ferber used to bypass them and correspond with me because I guess she felt I could handle her requests.

"She was on her own a 'Giant' of a woman . . . truly. A demanding woman, but nicely. She wanted her schedule exactly as she wanted it and as long as she got it her way her stay went well. When she was writing in Maine, she always took her morning walk. Seldom was there a morning she didn't stop into the office just to say hi and leave mail or discuss travel plans or banking business or something needed in town. But mostly she came to sit and chat. The office was the dining room at Marbury House. The kitchen to the left, the sitting room and five client rooms to the right. Our office sandwiched between the two. Maids, trays, clients and problems were constantly going back and forth in front of my desk and between Miss Ferber and I. She used to comment, 'How do you ever get anything done with these continual interruptions?' I'd smile and say, 'It sometimes isn't easy.' She would always smile back with some little reply.

"She was working on A KIND OF MAGIC one summer at Maine Chance. Working very hard. In fact, forgoing some treatments in order to write. Those mornings her walks would be earlier and sometimes she would only look in and wave as she passed. On her walk she never wore the Maine Chance dress of the day. She always wore a pastel shade of a simple linen sleeveless dress with a sweater, white bobby socks, and white wedge type sensible walking shoes. She always walked softly and spoke in a low soft tone except when upset by something. Then, she spoke slightly louder.

"One season in Maine, Miss Ferber asked me to work for her personally in New York. I thanked her, but said I liked my job, and especially liked being home for the summer months. She then offered to match my salary, pay for my New York apartment and give me the summer in Maine WITH PAY. This was overheard by a co-worker who was in the office with me at the time. He couldn't believe I'd turned it down. Miss Ferber and I left it that if ever I changed my mind, there would still be a job with her as her girl Friday anytime. It was a flattering offer and I'll always be grateful to her for it. I guess she liked my Downeast honest approach to business and life. She was stern, set, even at times a stubborn woman, but she was sincere. You knew where you stood with her at all times. I think she liked me because I was young, level headed, competent in my work, honest and sincere. I was after nothing from her or any of the other clients. I just tried to do my job and meet their requests and demands to the very best of my ability. Miss Ferber liked this approach. I think she found people always after something because of her position and fame in life. She found me unimpressed by this . . . NOT THE PROPER CHOICE OF WORD . . . I was truly impressed, thrilled and flattered and honored to have known her and to have had her genuine friendship, but I wasn't one of those silly, giddy, flighty, flippant types. Oh, how she disliked several managers who all had the above mentioned personality types—so impressed with the clients and their wealth, fame and fortune that they could never settle down and do the job. It took Miss Ferber one or two days to have them figured out. She'd once in awhile wink at me and make some quick comment. We'd smile together and it was our secret. I do know that the treatment staff, maids and chaffeurs that Miss Ferber sang praises of me and my ability to run Maine Chance. She'd be overheard telling the other clients that if they wanted something done and done right, just go to Miss Shorey. This too was flattering, but at times it gave me a great deal more work.

"When I was twenty and at Arizona Maine Chance, I had a reacurrance of an old ulcer. This time doctors were contemplating surgery. I was kept under daily observation and put on a milk only diet every hour, twenty-four hours a day, plus Mylanta, which I was to take every two hours for six weeks. Miss Ferber heard of this although I never missed a day's work. She was truly concerned. Several years later (1964) she arrived at Maine Chance Maine after having an ulcer diagnosed. She had written me telling of this before her arrival, and also that she'd be on a special puree diet and treatment schedule. One day the housekeeper called the office frantically . . . get the chauffeur . . . get the nurse . . . do something. Miss Ferber is out of her medicine. I merely said, 'yes' right away. Well, since I was still taking Mylanta, I always kept two bottles in my desk. I had a full one which I immediately had a chauffeur take up to Miss Ferber. About an hour later Miss Ferber very quietly appeared in my office—in fact, startling me, as I was deep in book work. She held her arms out to me and said something like, 'Thank you, Judy dear, for being so thoughtful and kind to an old lady like me.' (She often referred to herself as an old lady to me). I explained I had the medicine and was only too pleased for her to have it. Tears welled up in her eyes. She squeezed my hands, thanked me again and went on her way to treatments. The next day she sent a full bottle of Mylanta down to me via a chauffeur with her typed note of thank you again . . . signed Affectionately, E.F.

"I found her personally to be a kind, generous, thoughtful and to me, a very considerate person. For all her fame and fortune she was a lonely lady . . . not something she dwelled on or that many people ever knew or realized . . . but I know this from our many personal visits. She'd sometimes talk about her childhood . . . how she used to read to her ailing father . . . how she had never been a pretty child . . . things of this nature. I remember telling her one day that each person has their own beauty . . . some of face, some of body, some of mind, some of personality . . . just like each person has their own God given talent and ability . . . you Miss Ferber for your brilliant mind, imagination and ability to create so much pleasure for so many people in your writings. Again, tears came to her eyes as she said something like, 'My, for such a young girl you have so much adult wisdom.'

"I honestly believe she was a very lonely lady . . . lonely within, a sad sort of thing."

Miss Shorey's limited evaluation of Ferber is decent, touching, and pure. Ferber let her hair down with very few, which renders Miss Shorey very special. Judging from her syntax she seems the type of girl that Ferber wrote about in her early short stories. In particular: "Home Girl" (1922) and "Classified" (1924). Judy Shorey seems to evoke a combination of the two heroines in these short stories. An emerging woman not yet ready to be worldly, a woman who would eventually, if she strayed, always return to her basic values, a woman beginning to be aware of her own shrewdness, a woman beginning not to be malleable. Perhaps Judy Shorey reminded Ferber of her own creations. Also, Judy Shorey was impeccable at her job—a quality that Ferber admired more than any other. God help Judy Shorey had she ever once slipped up, for then, The Wrath would have descended on her Down East head. It's interesting to note that Ferber never once mentioned Miss Shorey in her diaries. It is possible that what was to Miss Shorey a personal relationship was considered by Ferber a service—one on a par with a very good cleaner, dentist, etc.

During this period, there was another young woman who was devoted to Ferber, and of whom Ferber, seemingly, was particularly fond. She, like Judy Shorey, performed her job to the nth degree. Her name was Kate Steichen, and she was the assistant to Ken McCormick at Doubleday. She also happened to be Edward Steichen's daughter. This piece of genealogical luck added a certain cachet to Kate Steichen in the eyes of Ferber, who responded to anyone who made an exceptional artistic mark in the world. That Edward Steichen was who he was made it easier for Ferber to relate to his daughter. Although Kate Steichen left Doubleday to go to work at Macmillan in 1959, she continued to remain in contact with Ferber.

"I loved her from the very first minute and in all those years at Doubleday," says Kate Steichen of Ferber. "She was a devil to work with. She was a heller, but I kept saying that she's worth it. That was to me the keystone of Edna Ferber. She was worth it. She was so damn real. Always. With even the little things. I know when I used to set up the luncheons—the long luncheons that she and Ken had to have when they were working—when they were "in book," and I'd call up and say, 'Good morning, Miss Ferber.' 'Dear Kate, how are you?' Then I'd say, 'Now, about lunch . . .' and I would propose whatever was the best place then—Baroque, Pavillon—whatever it happened to be. 'No,' she'd say, 'I'll meet Ken at Schrafft's.' I would say, 'Schrafft's??' And she would say, 'You know, they make the most delicious chicken hash available.' So off they'd go and have their conference over the chicken hash at Schrafft's."

Ferber was generous. It was one of her known attributes. She not only gave to her family, she gave period. Kate Steichen was one of the recipients.

"One time over lunch with Ken, he told Miss Ferber that Carol [Carol Silverberg, a friend of Miss Steichen's] and I were finally going to build our own house, and she said, 'You know, Ken, I would like to do something really nice for Kate. What do you think I could do?' So Ken thought about it and he said, 'Well Kate's father is giving them a whole hi-fi music system thing for the new house. They have no long-playing records, so why don't you pick some out and send them to her.' And Miss Ferber, Ken then told me, draws herself up to her full height, which I think was probably to my shoulder, standing there on the corner of Madison Avenue after lunch, and says to Mr. McCormick, 'I wouldn't ever *think* of choosing books or records for my friends.' Whereupon I assume Ken threw himself under the nearest taxi and evaporated. Well, a few days later, with a beautiful little note, came a check. It was a check for one hundred dollars to use to start our record collection. I was really shook, and I went into Ken with this check—and of course at Doubleday we just didn't take any lagniappe or gravy from authors—let alone agents. There was really none of that stuff at Doubleday, which was one of the things I loved about it. So, I went into Ken and I showed him the check and I read him the note and I said, 'Ken, I simply cannot accept it, and how can I gracefully refuse?' And Ken looked at me and he said, 'Look, dear, take it because it will give Edna so much pleasure.' And so the basic collection was started at that time, and I mentioned it to her several times, for instance in a little Christmas card I'd say, 'The music is still resounding, thanks to you.'"

Early in the 1960s Ferber decided that she wanted to rent a house for the summer months. Her reasons were more deductive than anything else. She had to get out of New York, was weary of Arden's, and, due to health reasons, did not feel up to going abroad. So instead she rented a mansion in Westport, Connecticut. It was a white elephant, a horror, much too unwieldy for a single lady—even with servants—to manage. Part of her rationale for taking the house was to be near (to torture) her sister Fan, who had her own house also in Westport. The other part is too difficult to decipher, for there seemed to be no pleasure involved in her summer. Kate Steichen recalls the serio-comic aspects of that time:

"When she was up in Westport in that huge mansion with the swimming pool, it was arranged that we would go over and see her. So we beat our way up Long Lots road and we found this place, and then this strong-fragile woman told us this incredible story of vandalism that had apparently been going on ever since she'd moved into this rented place. And the state police had been in on it, and everybody'd been in on it, and they'd all advised her to get out because these kookies had been coming in at night and breaking beer bottles around the swimming pool and it was a very frightening thing. And she was there alone except for two darling housekeepers. But Miss Ferber, being Edna Ferber, would not move. She took us down to the swimming pool and showed us that a telephone had been installed there, and there were all kinds of locks on the house and everything, and she wouldn't move. No, not her. She said, 'I won't go. They can't make me go. I'll stay.' We were terribly concerned. I remember going back to New York and telling Ken about this—that I thought it was incredible that Miss Edna Ferber was being subjected to a frightening situation like this with just two little maids in the house. I think Ken probably talked to her; I think everybody talked to her, but she was adamant as only Edna Ferber could be.

"Several weeks later—midsummer—we were sitting down in the grove of our little cabin house, where the hammocks and outdoor furniture were. We had with us a young architect, Louis Gelders, and we were sitting down there—he and his wife and Carol and I—having iced tea. All of a sudden at the top of this hill we heard a little yoo-hoo, and I waved and thought, oh, God, who's coming now, because we were having such a ball with the young Gelderses. Appears, coming through the brush, Miss Edna Ferber. She had had a terrible time getting there obviously—from vague directions. We had said we'd set a date, but she'd just decided to come. So we asked her, after greeting her with great joy, if she'd found the place all right, if she'd had any difficulty getting there. 'Oh,' she said, 'when I started, I was a black-haired, blue-eyed colleen.' There she sat with her pure silver hair. We just whooped and hollered. Dear Louis was staggered at meeting Miss Edna Ferber, and I was staggered that she came. So we sat for a few hours and chatted away. At one point I asked Miss Ferber to tell Louis what she was going through in Westport, which she did. He was perfectly horrified. He said, in his gentle way, 'Miss Ferber, we have our own home here in Wilton, and we have a little summer cottage up in Maine. We always take off for a month or two every summer, and we're about to leave next week. I'm sure it's nothing compared to what you have over there, but why don't you just pack up and come over to spend the rest of the summer. The house is empty. It's got three bedrooms, two baths and it's very secluded.' She wouldn't hear of it. 'Oh no,' she said. 'I'm going to stick it out; they'll never drive me out of there.' And they didn't."

Ferber must have felt something for Kate Steichen, who felt so much for her.

"When she died, Ken and I met at the funeral. I went into New York. I don't believe in funerals, but once in a while, if it really means something to me, I go. I went simply to make my obeisances. I met up with Ken afterwards and he said, 'Walk down with me.' He had to get back to the office, of course. So we strolled down Park Avenue; it was SUCH a beautiful day, and I said to him that she was a heller but she was worth it. We recalled various amusing things about her. We walked down to 57th Street and parted. It meant a great deal to me to walk down Park Avenue with Ken McCormick and Edna Ferber. It made it all seem real and whole and alive and the circle was complete."

Kate Steichen was never mentioned in any of Ferber's diaries. Not even so much as a passing, "dear girl." If Kate Steichen was just another "utility," who did Ferber, in the last quarter of her life, really care about, feel compassion for, go out of her way for? One is hard put to answer. The name of Noel Coward comes to mind and seems to fit the category, for in Ferber's own words she "deeply adored him." But he wasn't as loyal to her as he might have been, or as she might have preferred him to be. She didn't like to go out with him because she'd always lose him to the boys. One night she went to a party with him and, after they'd walked in the door, she never saw him again and had to go home alone. Theirs was a glamour friendship, based on many years of living in their own and each other's heyday. Each reveled in, and related to, the other's success. They shared a devoted twinkle and any depth in the relationship came from years of being amused and entertained by each other. Their barrier was distance—what with Coward living all over and

Ferber only in New York. Like the title of one of Coward's plays, *Hands Across the Sea,* so was their friendship.

On her own shore, Ferber had two friends who, without debate, were two of the most important men in her life. One helped her earn her bread and butter and the other provided her with the only maternal instincts she ever had. George S. Kaufman and Moss Hart. She lost both of them in 1961. A most grievous loss for Ferber. It was, in a way, the end of a triangle. Hart wrote five plays with Kaufman. Three—*Once in a Lifetime, You Can't Take It with You,* and *The Man Who Came to Dinner*—were tremendous hits. Kaufman wrote five plays with Ferber. Three—*Dinner at Eight, The Royal Family,* and *Stage Door*—were tremendous hits. Ferber and "Mossie," as she called Hart, discussed combining their talents but opted for a safe, loving friendship instead. The one time they considered collaborating on a musical version of Ferber's novel *Saratoga Trunk* resulted in their not speaking for four years. But by 1961 all was forgiven and mellow with them again, and just a few months prior to Hart's death she wrote him a lovely letter, in which she mentions Kaufman's declining health:

"Just now, dear Moss and Kitty, I've returned from that chic and exclusive spa, Atlantic City. Eight days of rain, cold, and a bone-biting northeast wind. I didn't even get much work done, so the whole thing was perfect. But at least I was out of New York, which was the idea.

"I'm writing you because it was refreshing and reassuring to see you two civilized self-possessed, well-dressed and cerebral human beings as contrast to the dullness and bad taste that dominated the Oscar Awards program. You were like beings from another world—or perhaps the inept ones seemed the other-worldlings. Ustinov [Note: Peter Ustinov] and Danny Kaye were intelligent, too. The rest of it was a shambles.

"Yesterday I talked briefly on the telephone to George. He seemed almost like himself. When I said that I'd like to come in if he felt like seeing me, and that I'd stay only fifteen minutes or thereabouts as I knew he wasn't yet enjoying long visits he said with the courtliness that always has marked his every spoken word: 'Three minutes for you.'

"I hope you're both as well and as handsome as you looked on the screen and that it wasn't merely makeup, tailoring and dress-making.

"I called your office for the Palm Springs address. It doesn't sound respectable—467 Via Lola. Lola who? Montez? Fisher? Brigida? It sounds like one of those Art Theatre Italian movies. Yours, Ferb."

On December 20, 1961, Moss Hart died suddenly of a heart attack. Ferber makes no mention of it in her diary. Strange, because she never fails to mention daily some mundane little tidbit such as how she walked 1.6 miles, or how she bought a teal blue dress when she really wanted navy. So on that day instead of recording the death of a cherished friend, she wrote in list fashion: "Giant—gross—returns."

On January 9, 1962, there was a memorial tribute to Moss Hart at the Music Box Theatre in New York, where Hart's first success, *Once in a Lifetime,* opened on September 24, 1930. The speakers were Brooks Atkinson, Dore Schary, Alan J. Lerner, Bennett Cerf, and Edna Ferber. Ferber never spoke at what she called, "these shindigs." Hart's shindig was the exception.

EDNA FERBER'S TRIBUTE TO MOSS HART

"When I first met Moss Hart, he had just been discovered hidden in the bulrushes. A year later, a tall, gangling youth, stunned by his own spectacular success, possessed of an extraordinary zest for life, he had been turned loose on the slippery race track that was Broadway and New York and the world of creative writing. To his amazement he found himself one of a hard-working, realistic, laughing, talented group of people such as George Kaufman, Lillian Hellman, Marc Connelly, Alec Woollcott, Dorothy Parker, Herbert Swope, Helen Hayes, George Gershwin and many others. Moss was like a young spindling colt turned out on the track to compete with Sea Biscuit and Man o' War. He promptly surged ahead and out-distanced many of them.

"He was younger than most; much younger than some. For me he was, I suppose, the son I'd never had—you know—mine son de doctor.

"Many of you here today have experienced the exhilaration of success. I never have known anyone who so savored every luscious morsel of his own victory over hardship. Above all, he battled that enemy we all must face—ourselves. He fought himself, and conquered.

"Often unwise about unimportant things, almost infallible about the things that really mattered; sometimes unreasonable, frequently exasperating, occasionally unpredictable and even outrageous, Moss was never, never dull.

"To his work he brought not only great talent—which alone is not enough—but also integrity, ambition, and above all, discipline, that invaluable tool of the writer. In those early days of his success we were aware of his periods of deep and terrible depression. We reveled in his more customary moods of brilliant high spirits. I worked with him, I quarreled with him. He had the gift of making you feel that you were capable of writing better than you actually could. And so, miraculously, you did. He gave one fresh courage. When he entered a room the lights came on. There was nothing exhibitionistic about this. He just carried with him a built-in incandescence. He was a dazzler with a self-starting dynamo.

"His extravagance with money was a legend. He had got hold of the strange idea that money was for spending, for enjoyment, for helping others less fortunate. For this there was a basic explanation.

"Many years ago, one hot, stifling New York summer Sunday I drove with him up to Westchester to lunch with friends. He was the owner of his first car. There never was a driver more reckless than he since the days of the Ben Hur boys. Returning in the bright early evening we came to the Bronx, which at that time years ago was a welter of elevated tracks, racking noise, swarming streets, grim tenements, suffocating heat and humidity. As we drove through this I pointed to a row of dilapidated tenements.

"'Imagine living in a place like this.'

"Moss said, 'I don't have to imagine. I lived there.'

"It was then I became one of the friends who didn't begrudge him those solid-gold sapphire-studded Cartier eyedroppers.

"In today's world, full of apprehensive human beings, groping, stumbling, frightened, we are urged to see plays all about despairing people presented in terms of despair. This may be good for our souls but it is tough on the nerves and searing to the morale. We see these characters tortured and torturing. Moss Hart, too, wrote of the desperate, the odd balls, the stumbling, the insecure. He wrote of them in terms of compassion and deep, rich humor. No symbolism. We understood them. They were anybody. They were us. We recognized them, all the way from Grandpa in 'You Can't Take It With You' to Liza in 'Lady in the Dark' and on up, up to that radiant, moving and dimensional hero of the autobiography 'Act One.' These people were groping their way as best and as blithely as they could in the fog-choked world of today.

"Long, long ago, when I was very young, I read a line that I didn't understand. It had been written by a gifted man who, too, had been untimely taken away. The puzzling line was, 'A thing of beauty is a joy forever, it will never pass into nothingness.'

"That's silly, I thought. A rainbow, a flower—these pass into nothingness. I know better now. Nothing that exalts the spirit of man, no matter how briefly, ever ceases to exist. We are here today because of the conduct of someone who left the world richer for his having been here. He gave it gaiety, beauty, compassion. It's as simple as that. Though Moss Hart's name, like yours and mine, may one day be forgotten, he will never pass into nothingness. Human beings like Moss Hart are forever and ever."

A bit maudlin, perhaps, but effective, and probably as true to the heart as Ferber could get at that time, for she was beset by her own health problems and still deeply affected by the absence of George Kaufman, who had died shortly before Hart. There was, by all valid accounts, absolutely nothing doing romantically between the two collaborators, which seems to contradict certain invalid accounts that there was. Anne Kaufman Schneider, Kaufman's daughter, responds with a resounding, "Pooh," when questioned about the matter. "Edna was too smart to have carried a torch for Daddy. I think she admired him, enjoyed him, worked well with him—but that was that. On his side, Edna was far too much like my mother [Beatrice Kaufman] to have ever entertained any romantic thoughts. Besides, he liked pretty women."

Neither Kaufman nor Ferber was a looker in the conventional sense. Each had suffered and survived his or her lack of physical beauty in different ways. Ferber defended herself by writing about good-looking people in romantic situations, while warding off physical contact in her personal life. Kaufman dealt with his lot by shunning any romantic shenanigans in his plays, yet devoting himself to them in real life. Ferber and Kaufman were equally matched; each one's protective coloring was the reverse of the other. An even draw. Both had their own one-liners when the subject of their speculative intimacy arose. Ferber: "George treats me like Broadway Rose—bringing brown gardenias." Kaufman: "I'm fond of Edna but I don't like her."

What they really felt about each other was probably, eventually, beyond evaluation. They were simply familiar, and left it at that.

Toward the end of his life, Kaufman suffered from arteriosclerosis. Although there was no massive brain damage evident, he wasn't anywhere near as clear as he'd once been. One of the manifestations of the disease was that he rarely spoke. He would sit way at the end of his long, narrow living room in his wing chair and friends would come to pay their respects, chatting at him for a maximum of forty-five minutes. It was "entertaining George" time, and though one could tell that he was receiving, he hardly spoke or smiled.

One day Ferber came to call, did her forty-five minutes, got up, and was waiting for the elevator—which entered directly into the apartment—when Kaufman, who'd not said a word until then, boomed out, "EDNA," in a hollow, rather frightening tone. Ferber turned, startled, to face the frail figure.

"Yes, George?"

"Are you going to the funeral?" Kaufman called out.

"Whose funeral, George?" Ferber asked, more frightened than puzzled.

"Yours, Edna," was the reply.

The next thing Ferber knew she was standing on Park Avenue, so stunned she could barely walk home.

This type of incident, although unique in itself, was not unusual for Ferber. She seemed to be a conductor of freakish energy, and would often attract the one-chance-in-a-hundred occurrence. Some people carry about them a scent of fear which draws stray dogs, pseudo blind men, prankish boys, and the like. Ferber had this scent of fear making her vulnerable to anything and everything—making her suffer from shocks that to the norm were invisible. She was always caught in the act of trying to lead a private life, and although she was amusing, courageous, and entertaining, sadly comic happenings used to come in at her—as though life was out to get her and she could only battle it off with her output.

When the restaurant Voisin was in its prime it was the home of the muckamuck. All used to go to see and be seen in order to raise their social cholesterol. There was an antechamber that one had to pass through on the way to the dining room and then again on the way out. There, people would have cocktails and little hot hors d'oeuvres and perhaps while waiting for a dinner partner watch the parade go by. The time setting was after the Ferber-Alexander Woollcott feud had gotten off the ground. They only wished each other ill. They were professional enemies and could never let down again—especially not in public. It was Ferber's best feud; one she took very seriously.

One evening Ferber was sitting in the antechamber all decked out in an ermine coat with orchids pinned to the lapel—the style of the day. She was waiting for her vis-à-vis to arrive. Enter Woollcott, accompanied by a party of people. Without a word he sailed past her as portly and haughty as a caricature of himself. Time passed. Ferber was still waiting in the antechamber when he sailed by again, finished with his dinner. It seemed she had been stranded, done dirt, or, in the colloquial phrase of plain women, stood up. Woollcott couldn't help himself. Seizing the sweet bitchy opportunity, as he whisked by he went, "HA," very loudly.

Years later, Kaufman's funeral line was the equivalent of Woollcott's "HA." Moss Hart once said that Ferber was like the Japs—she fired without warning. After the Kaufman episode she took to her bed feeling fired upon, which is, I think, the way she felt most of her life.

Ferber went through periods of having crushes on her friends which lasted for as long as they were extremely kind and thoughtful toward her and behaved exactly as she saw fit. Moss and Kitty Hart were "in" with Ferber in 1960, as was evident in her letters to them:

"How lovely to have your telegram at Christmas time, dear Moss and Kitty. Being a Scrooge-type I always am touched and a bit contrite when my friends rise above my mutterings and imprecations.

"New Year is the event for me. Elated, I'm always certain it will be the best of years. And, do you know, it often is. My fondest wishes for your New Year. You know—don't you—that you are of the few who have everything. Edna."

Hart's fatal heart attack is foreshadowed in the next two letters. One of Ferber's sterling qualities was lending plucky comfort when any one of her friends was ill or low.

"Just as I was about to write you, Moss, I heard of your illness. Too much. But I know you will surmount all this as you have again and again when the barriers confronted you.

"That cliche, as true as it is old—nothing matters, really, except health. The man who wrote ACT ONE and LADY IN THE DARK and ONCE IN A LIFETIME doesn't need to drive himself under ferocious stress.

"We are all more or less frantic in this very odd world in which we find ourselves. Today I'm off to Israel where, I suppose, everyone is frantic all the time, as a way of life. Back October 30th.

"You're a lucky pair, you two, and you have been for many years, and will be. Of course luck is often confused with hard work. Most people don't know the difference but the hard workers—such as you and I—know. Yours, Edna."

"That Toronto hospital, dear Moss, is unknown to me—personally, that is. But I'm an old grad when it comes to Harkness Medical Center, and my story is if you've seen one you've seen them all. Certainly the champagne and cavier they serve you in these places is definitely inferior and sometimes is even presented in the form of oatmeal and weak bouillon. Ferb."

All was well in the last years when Moss Hart's death was imminent, but shortly Moss and Kitty Hart would descend into the depths of Ferber's disfavor. As did Mr. Ken McCormick when Ferber found out that Doubleday was about to publish a first volume of short stories by an author with the unfortunate name of Ellen Ferber. She hit the roof. Her special pique stemmed from the fact that McCormick, her editor for many years, had signed the young author on himself. Ferber's temper spiraled, did a volcanic whip around, sucking up everyone in sight, and didn't subside for quite a while. This was not a temper tantrum; it was a temper tarantula. She would call Ken McCormick for the sole purpose of hollering at him, demanding an explanation for his incredible behavior. He says that he was literally unable to provide one. In fact, he remembers that the "alien's" short stories were nothing remarkable—merely mediocre.

Ferber was not about to let this one lie. She called a meeting at Greenbaum, Wolff & Ernst to be held in the office of Harriet Pilpel, who, aside from being Ferber's lawyer, was a dear friend of Ken McCormick. Ferber demanded the presence of Douglas Black (then head of Doubleday), Morris Ernst, Harriet Pilpel, Henry Goldsmith, and the guilty-until-proven-innocent Ken McCormick. A public hanging. Once inside the chambers Ferber lit into McCormick, lambasting him, basting him with vitriol until everyone present felt sick. The intent, Henry Goldsmith recalls of that afternoon, was to get McCormick fired. The outcome, however, of that afternoon was that all there experienced the horror of witnessing a nearly psychotic fit. Whether Ferber was right or wrong became irrelevant. Her tactics were cruel and pathetic, only serving to point out that she was her own worst enemy.

Afterwards, Ferber told Harriet Pilpel, rather tongue-in-cheekily, that she feared McCormick would lose his job. Mrs. Pilpel reported Ferber's concern to McCormick, but he was agonizingly convinced that he'd surely lost a friend.

Time passed, McCormick remained at Doubleday, Ellen Ferber's book went to press, and Ferber went to London. McCormick found himself in London on business and decided to approach Ferber—to try for a reconciliation. In fact, he recalls, "We were like lovers who had been through the worst." He phoned her at her hotel, Claridge's, and asked if he might stop by. She said, "Come for tea," and he knew that things were on the mend. He found her cordial but with a faint edge of cool. Once tea was poured and amenities spoken, she asked him why he'd done it. He replied that it would take a lot of deep therapy to find out. She heartily agreed with him and the matter was almost dropped.

Ferber was bedeviled by her lack of progress on *A Kind of Magic* during her stay in London. In her diary she wrote: "Floundered around in the mire of MAGIC." Her social life did not suffer; however, she writes dubiously about it too: "To see 'Oliver'. Interesting production [Oliver Twist], but performances—no. To see King Kong [African musical]—no, no, no." . . ."Dinner Mrs. Guiness Portman Square. The Whitney's staying there. Stuffy. Bad dinner. Warm champagne." . . . "Shopped. Some gifts for Fan, Mina. Evening to see 'Beyond the Fringe'. Disappointing. A sort of family joke." . . . "Packed. To see opening of Osborne's play 'Luther'. A history lesson."

There was one pleasure during her stay after all. It was Noel Coward, who, although he was putting together a production of *Blithe Spirit*, managed to make time for his "darling Ferb." "Thank heaven for Noel," she records. "He makes my laughter worthwhile."

It's interesting that so soon before her oppression with *A Kind of Magic* she had such high hopes for it. She wrote a letter to Ken McCormick after lunch and a talk with him at Brussels Restaurant on January 14, 1960:

"By the way, perhaps I've quite unknowingly given you a

mistaken impression of my reason for wanting to write a second autobiographical volume, and my as yet rather groping presentation. I think of what you said about being leisurely and sort of detached in this, in contrast with the emotional and fiery approach to A PECULIAR TREASURE. I am sure you think I have in mind a misty-eyed stroll down the years of memory, stopping to pick a nosegay here, resting a moment on one of those damned wet tree-trunks to contemplate the golden vistas across the valleys of time. Boy, you never were more mistaken in your life. If you think I was indignant, vociferous and shrill in A PECULIAR TREASURE I should, in fairness, tell you that this book probably will make P.T. [Note: *A Peculiar Treasure*] seem a blurred carbon of Rebecca of Sunnybrook Farm. You may not even want to publish it. And I don't want, as you suggested, to write it slowly. There isn't time. I don't mean my time. I mean time in the present world.

"Have fun in Kansas City. I'd like to go to Kansas City, too. I haven't, in these past six or seven years, gone to the Kansas Cities often enough."

Postscript on *A Kind of Magic:* Ferber's intentions for the book were the best, if a bit didactic. She wanted to teach her readers all that she'd digested about America, the world, LIFE. Her readers weren't up to such a broad-scale lesson. She'd wanted too much for the book to be great, an epistle, a sermon on the mount. She wasn't up to such a broad-scale task. Personally, I feel badly about this last book of hers. It is dedicated: "To Julie Goldsmith and to Peter and Kathy Klein, a new young generation in an old tough world. E.F." And then, my private dedication: "Julie dear, a lot of this happened before you were born; and much of it when you were too young to give a thought to the world of then. But read it anyway—won't you?—there's a good girl. With love—Aunt Edna."

It is somewhat ironic that only three years before *A Kind of Magic* was published, Ferber's first autobiography, originally published in 1938, was reissued with moderate success. She very much liked the opening line of a review from *Parade of Books* that was released to Hearst newspapers: "With all due respect to Pearl Buck, Edna Ferber is the first lady of living United States American literature. It is a good thing indeed that her A PECULIAR TREASURE . . . has been revised and reissued with a new introduction, for it is one of the great literary testaments."

Ferber must have felt chatty and even talked to *Parade of Books* about the reissue. Her tone modestly heralds the second coming:

"On rereading this book for necessary corrections some of it seemed to me naive and even schoolgirlish. Some cutting has been done, but very little, really. Slight additions and corrections have been made. Little of that, too. The book is what it originally was—the autobiography of an American Jewish child, girl and woman, born in the Middle West in the middle eighties. I am startled to note certain prophetic pages, written before World War II, for which, in earlier centuries, I might well have been hanged for a witch.

"As I am a somewhat slow worker in the field of writing there are, on my workroom shelves, only thirty published volumes of novels, plays, and collected short stories to which my name is attached. They represent the work of almost half a century. If I were given the choice of only one of these to be saved—for a time at least—while all the others were blotted out forever, I should choose this book as an honest record of a receptive and perceptive human being who has loved life and enjoyed living, and to whom the world owes exactly nothing."

Perceptive she was, for one so wrapped up in herself. On occasion she was also receptive—especially to those who were "connected." Her correspondence was mammoth as it was, but people were constantly seeking her help, her time, her contributions to their own various projects. She gave short shrift to most of them. However, when Jane Grant wrote to her, she took heed. Jane Grant being the first wife of Harold Ross, who originated *The New Yorker* magazine. That counted. In her response to Jane Grant, Ferber lets her know what a lucky girl she is to get such a favor from the busy Ferber. Yet the favor is generous, for she writes a wonderfully succinct composite of Ross.

"Every day, Jane dear, since I had your letter about your proposed book on Ross, I have wanted to write to you. But my daily grist of work goes on day after day, as you know; and that is from for some hours daily, starting in the morning. After that there are appointments, business and otherwise, personal things that must be attended to in that short period between mid-afternoon and six. All this goes on in my daily life, as it has for decades and decades. You understand, I am sure, why you haven't heard from me until now concerning your writing project.

"Yes, I knew Ross for many years, but curiously enough I saw him rarely, and then usually at a dinner, perhaps given by Woollcott in the 47th Street house, or at the Kaufmans' or whatever. None of my own work ever appeared in the New Yorker or was submitted to the magazine.

"This doesn't say that I didn't know Ross. I did. Perhaps I knew him and understood him more genuinely than many others who saw him frequently and more intimately. In his field he was a genius. Perhaps the genius in that profession in this country. He was unique as an individual and as a functioning editor. In appearance, in manner, in background he was, I suppose, the last person in the world to be tabbed by the unknowing as the moving power, the creator, the overall editor of a weekly magazine such as the New Yorker—a weekly presentation of brilliance, of wit, of criticism, of almost surgical honesty, of searing comment, and of fearless comment. He was an iconoclast who snatched ruthlessly the soiled and pretentious garments off the swollen and sickly body of pretense, of social dishonesty, of rapacity or vulgarity. As this was done with the light deadly thrust of the rapier, never with the club of the sledge-hammer, made it all the more deadly and effective.

"Perhaps Ross's physical aspect, too, added to the piquancy of the improbable. When I first saw him, just after the end of World War I, it was at the apartment of Franklin P. Adams [who later became the F.P.A. of the unequaled New York *World* column]. Seated on the living room floor deep in a game of cards of some sort, were Woollcott, Heywood Broun, Robert Benchley, F.P.A. and a strange and improbable character who turned out to be Ross. I assumed that this was a bit of driftwood—a gnarled and weather-beaten bit of driftwood they had picked up in the chaos and adopted in the chaos of war days. None of these named—particularly Broun, known as the human laundry bag—were known for their sartorial or physical perfections. But compared to this unknown companion they were Beau Brummels all.

"Outwardly, this was Mortimer Snerd, complete. The pituitary gap between the two monolithic front teeth; the clay-gray skin; the no-color eyes; the hedge of bristling hair; the flailing arms; the too-frequent and braying laugh; the flat voice which was seldom raised but which compelled attention through the often daring felicity of phrase and the freshness of thought it produced. In his presence the tired phrase, the bumptious manner, the inflated ego died at birth.

"That nervous laugh, not really a gay or amused laugh. A nervous reaction, stemming probably from insecurity. When first you met him and encountered that too-frequent laugh you felt you were a great success. Then you realized that it was, oftenest, merely a nervous reaction. As someone else would have said Yeah? Really? uh-huh.

"In his office he was a perfectionist. The magazine pin-pricked with wit and ridicule and brilliant analysis the balloons of pretense, of civic buffoonery and dishonesty and stupidity. He hated and he destroyed whenever possible the pretense. He was very funny. His critical notes on the margins of copy were a course in how not to write if you were the unfortunate author of the proof-read piece. No comma, no over-written phrase, no superfluous adjective escaped his snickersnee.

"In the American reading and critical public if a piece of writing is dull it must be good. And if it is unreadable it is great. The New Yorker was highly and uniquely readable. This was the New Yorker of that day and during Ross's editorship and lifetime. Every week's issue was a new delight. Thursday was New Yorker publication day; you would have no more missed reading it than you would have missed Thursday."

Ferber's timbre was vastly different in her answer to a letter from an "unconnected" person than it was to Mrs. Harold Ross. The sample serves not so much to point out Ferber's snobbery as it does to show her time priorities. The letter is from an Israeli schoolteacher:

". . . After discovering your two treasures [two autobiographies] at the Information Bureau of the U.S. in Tel Aviv, I plunged hungrily into your works of fiction, all of which I am enjoying thoroughly . . . An Israeli born who has lived many happy years in America, I fully appreciate your love for that country and your criticism of it as of the other countries of the world. I wonder at one of your assertions about Israel, where you claim to have felt most alienated particularly here. How is that possible in a person to whom Jewishness is so important and to which you attribute your success? . . . Needless to say—a reply from your esteemed person —will be an honor deeply cherished, not only because of your literary stature but also because of your human and humane one. Sincerely, Ofra Diron."

Ferber answers the letter, but not the question it poses.

". . . Though I seem to have abandoned all formal religious rites and beliefs I am irrevocably a Jew, I hope. I never have ceased to marvel at the tenacity, the courage, the high intelligence, the warm humanity, the capacity to rise above adversity, the wry humor and the spirit which, combined have enabled us as a whole to survive in this weird world."

Ferber's consciousness about the Jews and of being a Jew was above average. She was not a "professional" Jew; the themes of her novels never incorporated Judaism—save for *Fanny Herself*, written in 1917, which dealt with a Jewish girl growing up in the Middle West. Aside from that one direct character reference, the religion of her other heroines was "American Person." She left the Jewish theme to grapple with in her two autobiographies and in her privately public life. Her little pumps would become soapbox platforms as she railed against what she felt was erroneous Jewish thought. Producer, director, playwright, former head of M-G-M, Dore Schary recalls one particularly heated conversation with Ferber on the subject of Zionism—which she was fervently against. He had gone to her apartment for tea; she hadn't been feeling very well—which never, by the way, prevented her from speaking her mind. It often seemed that the testier she was the more clearly she thought. So as they were taking tea, Schary mentioned that he felt the label Zionist was too readily applied and was often a contradiction of terms. Ferber began to bristle. He went on to say that, although he did not consider himself to be a Zionist, he was certainly devoted to and supportive of Israel, feeling that all Jews had to have a home—Israel being that home. Ferber's quills shot sky high. She couldn't have disagreed more radically. She asserted that the Jews' home was in their spirit, within themselves—that there was no other. Schary recalls that it was not a particularly long tea.

When Ferber got worked up over an issue, there was nobody who could touch her. She was a dervish of indignation. When she was calm she exuded power; when she was upset she exuded great power. Phyllis Cerf Wagner, who was a dear friend, puts it aptly: "Had Edna been a man, she could have been anything. She could have been President. She would have been President."

Ferber's wrath was incurred—to put it mildly—over a statement that Prime Minister David Ben-Gurion made to the twenty-fifth Zionist Congress in Jerusalem on December 29, 1961. He said:

"Since the day when the Jewish state was established and the gates of Israel were flung open to every Jew who wanted to come, every religious Jew has daily violated the precepts of Judaism and the Torah of Israel by remaining in the Diaspora." (Diaspora is the term used for the placement, or in this context displacement, of Jews outside Palestine.) "Whoever dwells outside the land of Israel is considered to have no god."

Ferber may have been speechless with outrage, but certainly not penless. She wrote a letter to the editor of the New York *Times* that in its way was a proclamation of independence.

"Writers who write usually are reluctant to involve themselves in political or sociological or national or international turmoil. To do so invariably results in conflict of a disturbing nature. As writers are emotionally vulnerable (or they wouldn't be writers) this can seriously affect the most cherished thing in their lives; their work.

"Not since Hitler has anyone delivered such a hideous blow to the Jews of the world as that recently dealt by David Ben-Gurion, the Premier of Israel. He has publicly issued the statement, quoting the Talmud, Jewish book of the early religious law, that 'Whoever dwells outside the land of Israel is considered to have no God.' And that it is the duty of Jews in America to dwell in Israel.

"As an American-born Jew, granddaughter of a German Jew who came to the United States one hundred and thirteen years ago with the great exponent of freedom, Carl Schurtz, I consider this Ben-Gurion statement not insolence and arrogance merely; in making it the Premier of Israel joins the ranks of today's dictators—the Castros the Trujillos the Khrushchevs. It is as monstrous as though there should be issued from Rome, seat of the Catholic church, a statement that all Catholics who dwell outside Italy have no God; and that all Catholics should come to Italy. Quite aside from a somewhat crowded condition that would result, this would deprive me, for one, of a terrific young man named John Fitzgerald Kennedy to whose administration as President of the United States of America I am looking forward with the most exhilarating anticipation, having voted for him.

"Well then, as an American, a civilized human being, and a Jew, I find the Ben-Gurion statement not only infuriating but potentially hideously destructive, and I don't scare easily. In October 1960 I returned from a strictly personal visit to Israel. I went under my own steam, as a tourist. I saw the amazing and almost incredible and frequently annoying aspects of this brilliant this gigantic achievement. Millions and millions and millions of dollars and hours of thought and work have been contributed toward it by citizens of The United States for the security of the homeless the suffering of the hopeless and now the new generation of the hopeful the buoyant the resolved of another generation.

"I suggest that Ben-Gurion retract his statement completely or be removed from office, his splendid early work done, before his later work proves the undoing of future plans for Israel."

Ferber had been militantly pro-American all of her outspoken life. She had been a stand-up Jew for most of it. Often it was an oil and water proposition, but through success she had managed to assimilate the two fronts. America had allowed her the right to achieve; for this she blessed and thanked it constantly, and perhaps in her recesses she felt that it was despite the fact she was a Jew. That there was no outright tyranny in this country never ceased to refresh her, and when men like Stevenson and Kennedy came along with goals of making America an idyl of democracy, she became downright ebullient. Had she lived to see the Watergate scandal, and now the exposing and smirching of the Camelot years, the sight would have blinded her spirit—would have diminished her "American religion" to ashes. It would have sapped her, for in a way she considered America as her alter ego.

Ben-Gurion had served as a catalyst for her outburst; she'd actually begun to rev up years before with the advent of Leon Uris's novel *Exodus*. She writes of her feelings about it to Ken McCormick, who had sent her the book.

". . . I am reading it but I can't honestly say that I, a Jew, am with it or against it. By now I suppose Israel cannot be condensed into any definite form. It is incredible that we Jews have survived literally thousands of years of the most brutal persecution. Perhaps it is persecution that has caused our survival. One of the characters in *Exodus* somewhere says that it is, for him, so wonderful to be in a country where everyone is a Jew. How frightful to be as insecure as that. Perhaps the reason why I've so rarely written a word or a line about a country other than my own is that the variety of the North American human being makes this the most exciting country in the world, and the most unartificially vital. In England almost everyone is English, in France French, in Switzerland Swiss, in Holland Dutch. But here every face you pass on the street is what?

You conjecture. Irish? German? Scandinavian? Italian? Spanish? A mixture of two or three or four of these, through the decades? It is like eating one of those steam-table meals in which every dish tastes like every other dish, or one in which every dish has its own flavor—piquant or sweet or bland."

When Ferber went to Israel in 1960, she was very much aware of and disturbed by the "Israeli-firster" attitude, and of course scribbled about it as she went. Her jottings are time bombs. They are planted toward Ben-Gurion's eventual statement.

"Israel is, in one way, a kind of Jewish Texas. It has the brashness and self confidence of Americans in the U.S. without the American citizen's charm and almost incredible innocence. They have accomplished the impossible, but they aren't content to let this speak for itself . . . Israel reminds me, more than anything, of Texas on my trips there for research on the novel, GIANT. Arrogant, uninformed, self-complacent, regarding the world outside itself as definitely second-best. The young boys and girls, men and women of Israel (and, truthfully, many of the middle-aged and older ones) do not see beyond the confines of Israel and the comparatively few miles beyond that barbed-wire fence which separates them from the Arab world. Beyond that, except perhaps for an imaginary jaunt to the moon or another planet, they do nothing, care nothing, know nothing about the great struggling world known as the planet Earth. I talked to a number of them. If they knew anything of the United States—and they are abysmally ignorant of it—they dispose of it with a shrug or a sneer . . . Miles of writing have been done about Israel's political, economic, religious and international situation and importance. Even in the popular novel Exodus all the Jewish characters were tall, blond and more or less heroic. One rarely reads of people in Israel. They are spoken about and written about as though they were scenes carved in a frieze on a door or wall. By and even large, they seem to me to have the worst manners of any people I've encountered in a lot of travel, including the people on a Madison or Lexington Avenue bus or a subway between 5 and 6 P.M. in New York City. Perhaps it is due to the new feeling on the part of refugees who have been under the thumb of dictators or who, for thousands of years, have lived as unpopular minorities. I suppose Jews are the most misunderstood people in the world. This new-found independence, precarious though it may seem to many non-Jews (including, certainly, the Arab countries surrounding them) it is sweet in their mouths. They are not tolerated or snubbed or insulted or sneered at in Israel. They are Israel."

Ferber's emotional yardstick was most peculiar, for it had no peripheral measurements. Everything mattered; everything was upsetting. She had such an overpowering sense of right, of discipline, that it seems all she came upon that wasn't right according to her impossible standards was dead wrong. Her justified outrage at the Ben-Gurion statement was equivalent to her fuming about a topcoat. In her diary she writes: "March 5, 1961—Sort of miscellaneous. Today. Observed in New York. Today there was an advertisement of a topcoat—a blue wool coat to be worn by a woman. There was a drawing of a woman wearing the coat. The price was $475. The woman's bare arms stuck out of the armholes. The coat had no sleeves. The cynicism, the impudence of this ad infuriated me. A wool coat is intended to be worn only in the cool weather. Its purpose is to protect the wearer. A sleeveless wool coat is a paradox as well as an outrage."

Outrage was a household word at Ferber's. She was always in a tempest about something—her publisher and her lawyers being her favorite targets. Since with her own bare fingers she had typed an empire—built a monster of verbiage—the properties that resulted were unwieldy and required meticulous management at all times. And, since she never trusted anyone, whatever management was carried out, according to her, was always bungled. There was one respite for her, however. She was blessed when she inherited, through her niece Janet's marriage, Henry Goldsmith, a man with the ability to untangle and assuage. To my knowledge she never raised her voice at him, which, when dealing on a long-term basis with Ferber, was the highest form of compliment that could be paid. Henry witnessed many of the "blowouts" and arbitrated many of the peace settlements. He was an invaluable go-between. Even when Ferber was away she kept Henry hopping. She kept him so up to date on her business matters that it was difficult for him to find time often, for his own. Her letters to him are full of gratitude, yet the favors that she asks or implies are ongoing. In a letter that she writes from San Francisco, where she was supposedly getting away from it all, she deftly hints that Henry check into a few things.

"Henry dear, how good of you to write me about the GIANT

mess, when you must have been up to here with your own piled-up mail.

"I tried to get Harriet on the telephone but she was out. Two communications have come to me here from her. Neither contained one word about the GIANT-tax situation.

"Nothing can be done I suppose about the proposed motion picture tax expert until I return . . ." Two favors down. Now she complains about her lawyers—which falls under the "outrage" theme. "You know what came of the Ernst's previous selection of the tax expert, Brach. And I think I wrote you that Morris Ernst actually said to me that he knew nothing of the sum of $440,000 sent the Ferber-Goldsmith-Fox-Klein partnership by Warner, and that it was impossible that I would have received nothing from such a sum, had it been received. Unfortunately, I talked with Morris alone. I have, in the past three years, made a rule against talking to him on business matters without a witness.

"I have tried to put this situation into perspective and have in a measure succeeded. In the beginning it again made me ill, and that I want at all costs to avoid. By the way, I wrote Harriet about Morris Ernst's incredible statement. No comment has been received from her . . ." And then, as if to soften her crankiness, she writes a postcard description of San Francisco. "San Francisco is refreshing and fantastic. Like the rest of the world it has changed, but not so sadly. There is still the incredibly blue sky, the white white papier mache buildings, the hills at 180 degree slant, the brilliant bay, the Golden Gate Bridge, the eerie fog rolling in at four. Chinatown now is just a sort of Woolworth's. Its wares are all Japanese, of course.

"My love to you, and my thanks. Edna."

Although Janet, not Henry, was one of the direct recipients of the Ferber fortune, it was always Henry who helped out in matters pertaining to it. And what did Henry Goldsmith receive for his labors? "Lots of tsouris," he answers. And temptations. Ferber did try to tempt him with offers of extravagant gifts—but only on birthdays and Christmases when she felt it was legal to buy him her thanks. Whenever she offered gifts, she got very cute about it as in a letter to him about his approaching birthday.

"Dear, dear Henry, I asked everyone—Janet and Governor Rockefeller and the TIMES information desk. I said, 'What do you think Henry would like for his birthday?' And they said, he has one, or, I got him that last year. How about getting one of those cashmere (or is it vicuna) coats? . . . How about a pearl stickpin for your gray silk ascot tie? How about a muffler that isn't black? There is something so cold-blooded and thoughtless-seeming about a check. Especially for some one whom I love as I do Mr. Henry Goldsmith. Happy Birthday, dear boy. And many thanks for all your thoughtfulness and help."

Ferber was big on birthdays—other people's. She considered her own an inconvenience and an imposition, and would announce a few weeks before it was to arrive that nobody should bother about it. God help those who believed her and didn't. On that day she would make herself scarce—lying in wait to see who would ignore her. When those who were on to her game—her family mainly—found her, she would act surprised and a bit put off. Even with her birthday, she had a love-hate relationship.

Dorothy Rodgers utters a manicured groan when remembering a certain birthday gift bestowed upon her by Ferber. It all started with Richard Rodgers' upcoming sixtieth birthday.

"Edna called Mary and asked for any ideas of what she, Edna, could give Dick for his birthday, and Mary said, 'I don't know what you could give him but I know what you could give my mother. You could do a preface for her book.' I had mentioned sort of off the top of my head to Mary that I would love Edna to do a preface, because she had known us in every place we had ever lived, had known all of our friends, and knew about that side of my life more than anybody else, but that I would never ask her because she was a pro and busy and I thought it would be an imposition. So I put it out of my head. Well, Mary had the nerve to tell her this. So Edna called me up and said, 'I hear you'd like me to do a preface.' She asked what my schedule was, what my deadline was, and I gave them to her. She said, 'Well, if you can wait until this summer, I'll do it in Switzerland.' Shortly before she went abroad I asked if she'd like to read the galleys and she said, 'NO, I'd rather not; I'd rather do it without.' Okay. In the middle of the summer I got the preface and I was simply devastated because it had in it so much of what I had put in my first chapter. To use it would have meant redoing the whole first chapter. Somehow I had to let her know that all was not completely well. So I sent her a cable saying, 'Preface divine—thrilled—would like to talk to you sometime.' I knew she was smart enough to see through that; she would know immediately. I found out when she was due home. I called her and she said, 'Drop by Sunday afternoon.' I didn't sleep for nights before. I went up and my hands were cold and clammy; I was absolutely petrified. Trembling as I was, I told her the truth. I said, 'If you had read the book, Edna, you wouldn't have written this preface. It's almost my entire first chapter.' She was so understanding and so terrific about it. There was no anger at all. This woman who could get furious when you didn't even know you were doing something to offend her, was magnificent about something that she'd really made an effort with, had spent a good deal of time on, and was all in vain. My other fear was that she might offer to do it over. I certainly didn't want her to do that, so I had to forstall any such thought—which I did. I don't recall that she offered to do it over. But, in any case, she did ask me to give it back to her. She didn't want me to have it."

There is something so utterly sad about this story. It was one of the few times that Ferber didn't buy a gift. She gave a gift. There were probably many of the same elements in the preface that there were in Dorothy Rodgers' first chapter, but Mrs. Rodgers could not have possibly written the same tribute to herself as Ferber did. The first paragraph is strewn with compliments enough for a lifetime:

"It is an arresting and significant fact that though Dorothy Rodgers, author and compiler of this book, has a multitude of friends and acquaintances, not one of her women friends hates her. That this is true, too, of the men who are part of her social, professional, business, organizational life—in short, her public and private existence—goes without saying. One glimpse of her would prove that. Married thirty years and more, mother of two married daughters, grandmother of five children, she could today pass for a debutante, though she definitely does not dress or behave like one. This fact alone would not endear any woman to her friends. It is not here presented as an understandable though completely non-existent basis for female enmity. Beautiful, chic, velvet-voiced, she has the look of a compassionate but fashionable wraith, with just a touch of the indomitable Clare Boothe Luce about the softly glowing eyes and the determined jaw. She can do practically everything."

Janet Fox Goldsmith recalls that the very quality that irked

Ferber about Dorothy Rodgers was that she was perfect to a fault. So much for imperfect prefaces.

Despite very little magic in her last years, Ferber descends into a near-perfect career full of ice palaces, giants, peculiar treasures, and dinners at eight. The American beauty rolls up her sleeves.

THE CHILL FACTOR
1960-1954

WITHIN this six-year period there was a Broadway musical, two major movies, a new novel whose research helped give advent to a new statehood and two rip-roaring feuds. Ferber managed to keep herself occupied.

In the late fifties, when the musical stage rights of Ferber's novel *Saratoga Trunk* reverted back to her, Robert Fryer, Lawrence Carr, Yip Harburg, Raoul Pene du Bois, Ray Stark, Melvin Frank, Cheryl Crawford, Frank Loesser, Alan Jay Lerner and Frederick Loewe, Oscar Lerman, Mary Martin and Richard Halliday, Patrice Munsel, Jule Styne, and Sam Spiegel, Meredith Willson, Harold Arlen, Johnny Mercer, William Inge, Michael Kidd, Abe Burrows, all bid for its favors. The applications came in steadily, begging Ferber to allow this combination of producer-director-composer-lyricist or that combination of same to create a Broadway hit. The property certainly had musical possibilities, which was the case with most of Ferber's novels—their romantic sweep led right into love songs, their virility into gusto songs, and their heroines into bring-the-house-down songs. *Show Boat* was potent proof that it could be done. But who could top the strudel beauty and savory know-how of the young Ingrid Bergman cooing, "Clint, Clint cheri" to the impassive yet vulnerable heights of Gary Cooper in the 1945 film version of *Saratoga Trunk*? And where was another Jerome Kern? There were many self-proclaimed contenders. Some, like Melvin Frank, producer, she dismissed kindly: ". . . Successful as you have been, and will continue to be, I cannot convince myself that SARATOGA TRUNK is the type of thing which falls naturally into your sphere of work . . . Perhaps . . . the white-plumed prince may never come along, and SARATOGA will forever be condemned to spinsterhood." Some she cast off not so kindly, such as Jule Styne, man of many talented hats and hit shows—*Peter Pan, Bells Are Ringing,* and *Gypsy* to name a few. She wrote to his lawyer: "I do not know Mr. Jule Styne. I have never met or seen him. No one has ever authorized him to have any connection with SARATOGA TRUNK." Some she disdained altogether—such as the enthusiastic bid of Patrice Munsel, who wrote to her: ". . . I cannot begin to tell you of the challenge (and warmth and interest) 'Cleo Dulane' [misspelled] holds for me." In the margin Ferber wrote, "Gush."

Ferber was, as usual, wary of everyone, but in this instance her standoffishness was entirely comprehensible. She had already been left in the lurch once with *Saratoga* and it had hurt her very deeply. Originally, she and Moss Hart were planning to do *Saratoga Trunk* as a musical. They'd never worked together, had always longed to, and felt that this property would be the perfect meeting of the muse and Mossie. They would collaborate on the book, and, as Ferber insisted, Rodgers and Hammerstein would do the score. Everything would be very cozy indeed. The first wrench was thrown by Rodgers and Hammerstein, who seemed to be pretty tied up and said from the beginning that they doubted whether they could fit it in. But somehow Ferber was sure they'd come around. Meanwhile, Hart was talking to Ferber about the much-established Harold Arlen, who was eager to work with them and would have been just as appropriate as the more venerable Rodgers and Hammerstein. Ferber listened with half an ear. Finally, Rodgers and Hammerstein officially turned the property down:

"Dear Edna and Moss: We are confident that SARATOGA TRUNK, built along the outline you have started, can be a big hit and a beautiful show. For several reasons, however, the other story we have been considering is more interesting to us. It will be a more radical departure from the previous stories and groups of characters with which we have dealt. We don't think its chances of being successful are any greater than the chances of your play—perhaps not as good. We just feel more like working on that one, and that perhaps is the best if not the most analytical way of putting it. It would have been a lot of fun for the four of us to work together on a play, so let us do it sometime on some other play . . .

Our best wishes for the project, and our love to you both. Dick & Oscar."

Hart received the letter first, called Ferber, broke it to her, and again cheerfully and eagerly pitched Arlen.

"WHO," hooted Ferber in her most witheringly imperious tone, "is this Arlen fellow? Never heard of him."

Hart tried to be calm, but despite his efforts began a rapid boil. "Oh, come off it, Edna," Kitty Hart, who was within earshot, heard him snap over the receiver. But Ferber kept it up.

"What's he done? What are his credits? Never heard of him . . ."

Hart let full steam go and hung up. He told his wife that if the project was this gluey at the beginning it would never work. He couldn't, didn't want to, go through with it. Kitty Hart reminded him that of course he'd have to tell Ferber, in person, immediately. He knew that but was not looking forward to what would inevitably take place when he begged off. To put oneself in the vicinity of the Ferber Fury was like ignoring a sign that said Beware of Dog. Kitty Hart implored her rather hotheaded husband to be gentle and patient—that after all, Ferber had been rejected once on the project and he'd be rejecting her a second time.

The day came for him to break it to her. Kitty Hart recalls: "He was grey with fright." But when he came home, he reported that he felt all had gone smoothly enough. The phone rang sometime later that day. It was Ferber, who ranted to Kitty Hart as to how Mossie had called her "an old granite face," and that she couldn't possibly see her way clear to ever, ever forgive him. And she didn't—for four years. For four years they did not speak.

Now, in truth, one can believe that through her hurt and insecurity she had made herself hear that epithet. It is no secret that she was an "injustice collector," and this kind of misinterpretation was right up her alley. What Hart had said, concerning her unyielding stand against Arlen, was that often she was granite-like. He denied ever calling her a cruel name. Perhaps she was looking for a direct insult. However, perhaps in Hart's frustration, coupled with a flare of temper, he did call her the name. If this be true, then understanding Ferber's low profile about her looks—large face and head—perhaps four years of silence was just enough time to soothe the wound.

During the years of the Ferber-Hart estrangement, Hart suffered his first heart attack. He was hospitalized for quite a spell, and each day the first thing he would ask his wife upon her visit was, "Has Edna called?" or "Have you heard from Edna?" Kitty Hart felt that it seemed a step backwards toward his getting well when she had to say that, no, Edna hadn't called.

While Hart was ill, Kitty Hart was starring in *Anniversary Waltz* on Broadway. It happened to be an especially steamy summer and air conditioning was not *de rigueur* in theatres at that time. One day during the long hot run Kitty Hart got a note from Ferber. It went on and on about the perils of playing in such heat and what a sport Kitty was and so forth—never once mentioning Moss, the heart attack, the hospital. The subtext of the note was Ferber saying how sorry she was, how concerned. But she just couldn't say it; her overwhelming pride allowed her no release in up-front remorse. Although Kitty Hart understood this, she refused to let the note go by. Her response was to write Ferber a sizzler: How dare you talk to me about heat when my husband is lying in the hospital recovering from a serious heart attack, etc. And that was pretty much that for a while—until October, when Ferber chose to reply with an attack-and-defense letter of the highest order:

"Kitty dear, you can, as you wrote me, cease to be my friend. But you can't prevent me from being your friend unless you assume a pattern of behavior which I can't imagine in you.

"My letter to you didn't mention Moss because he had made it impossible to think of him in terms of friendship.

"Moss had just experienced his first success when I met him more than a quarter of a century ago. I've known him through his mounting successes, through the years of his illness, and then when he had health and you and the children. It was a thing for rejoicing. In all those years he had from me friendship, understanding, appreciation and respect.

"In my long life I never had heard directed at me (or at anyone) such undeserved vindicativeness, such venom, as Moss Hart hurled at my bewildered head. Horrified, I could only say, over and over, as I did—but Moss, I don't know what you're talking about, I don't know what in hell you're talking about. And I didn't know. And I don't to this day.

"You must believe me when I say that I didn't resent his decision to discontinue work on Saratoga. I never understood why he decided to do it in the first place . . . Naturally, I was delighted. When, after our few days of preparatory work, he found that he didn't want to go on with it, he would have needed only to say so, quietly and definitely. Instead he opened a barrage of the most savage and uncalled-for abuse. Myself, I hadn't particularly relished the idea of working again on a book I had written years back. It was rewriting, really. But Moss had said he wouldn't do the musical play's book unless I agreed to collaborate.

"In the weeks just preceding this ferocious outbreak Moss had experienced your sudden and shocking illness; the children's mumps; his own virus infection; and his disappointment in the Rodgers-Hammerstein decision on Saratoga Trunk. Perhaps he had to vent his pent-up emotions on some one and that unfortunate someone was me. This is the kindest interpretation I can put upon his conduct.

"As he shouted (among other courtly statements) that he was sick of looking at my granite face, I told myself that I mustn't take this shocking behavior as a normal manifestation. This was, I thought, a man temporarily ill after prolonged strain. I chose to believe this if I could, rather than to believe that this was a deliberate performance for deliberate reasons. It was, in any case, a saddening spectacle. I was, and am, ashamed for this man who was, I had thought, a friend.

"The clobber method may be fine for children. I wouldn't know. I don't meekly permit it to be applied to myself. Edna"

Moss Hart held up his end of the feud. Silence was poison on either side.

Once, when they ran into each other, Hart couldn't help but take a potshot. It was during the run of Mary Martin's *Peter Pan* on Broadway in New York. Hart had taken his then five-year-old daughter Cathy to see a matinee. After the performance he trotted her backstage so that Mary Martin could throw pixie dust on her—which was the big thrill for kids whose parents were friends of Mary Martin. While they were backstage, they happened to cross paths with Ferber, who had brought her darling great-niece to the show, and had gone back for the same pixie-dust fix. Darling niece does not remember much, since the next day she had to be taken to an ophthalmologist for the removal of pixie dust. Her irritated vision blocks out memory. At any rate, Hart and Ferber whisked by each other with nary a word. But Cathy Hart sensed something in the wind, as children, more than adults, are very apt to do. They have amazing powers of picking up scents. "Who was that, Daddy?" Cathy Hart asked. Moss Hart aimed at the receding back of Ferber. "That, my dear, was Captain Hook," he fired.

The chill factor was still very much present between Ferber and Hart when the offers to do *Saratoga* began to come in. Ferber wrote to him, fearing that since he had once been involved he just might sue.

"Again SARATOGA seems to be raising its hydra head, Moss. Apparently it dies hard. I have told the interested people that as you and I worked seven days on our outline I definitely would want to clear with you your position in the matter, following your withdrawal. Naturally, if ever there is a production (and I couldn't care less) the book would follow the story of the novel.

"All this sounds somewhat stilted, but as you and I did work on the original structure, anything that you would want considered would, of course, be necessarily cleared if there's a play in the future. Edna."

Hart sent a terse note back, reassuring her that he would never be so crass as to make trouble:

"There is nothing to 'clear.' Whatever the outline contained stemmed directly from the book—my contribution was purely a technical one—and if it is at all helpful, so much the better. Moss."

Moss Hart was well out of it. He went on to direct *My Fair Lady*—one of the biggest hits in the history of musical theatre; and to write *Act One*, a best-selling autobiography. Rodgers and Hammerstein didn't fare as well with their innovative new project, which was *Pipe Dream*. But, saving the worst for last, Ferber was left to lug the trunk of *Saratoga*.

As dubious as Moss Hart was about working with Ferber on the project, producer Robert Fryer was eager to the point of being bushy-tailed. He wanted, seemingly above all things, to option and produce *Saratoga Trunk* as a musical. His persistence matched Ferber's resistance. He wooed, flattered, telegrammed, candied, and flowered Ferber; he promised her the moon and stars of creative people to work on the show. She waited for him to deliver an instant constellation, and when he didn't she wrote him a rejection slip:

". . . As you know, no rights of any kind in SARATOGA TRUNK were given you when you expressed an interest in the book's musical play possibilities, nor have any rights been granted in the many months that have gone by since then. I think, as you do, that this novel could readily form the basis of a dimensional, romantic and absorbing musical play. But in the months elapsed since we first talked of these possibilities, no action on the part of your office or that of your agent has brought any practical results. Action without results is merely motion . . . After all these months, therefore, I am sorry to say that I do not think your feelings about the possibilities of S.T. can ever come to actual accomplishment. I have liked knowing you and talking with you. I have made absolutely no other plans for the book's stage future, nor have I any in mind. I am by nature a person of action. It is unfortunate that this really promising material has had no development of any kind . . . I need hardly say that no announcement concerning S.T. should come from your office or your agent's office. I mention this simply because the right to make such announcements never, as you know, existed. Sorry if this sounds rude. It is merely a matter of routine business."

Ferber's letter of dismissal served to goad Fryer into action. Shortly, he came up with his trump. Lerner and Loewe—second only to Rodgers and Hammerstein—wanted to do the book, music, and lyrics. The only catch was that they were still at work on *My Fair Lady*, which would prevent them from delving into anything else until its completion. But yes, they wanted to do *Saratoga* and, yes, they would commit themselves to it. How 'bout it Ferb? Ferb agreed and finally granted Robert Fryer his option, to which he replied, "I am so excited about it, I can't wait to start." The contracts were drawn up in 1954, with the understanding that Messrs. Lerner and Loewe would go to work when they were ready.

In April of 1956, Ferber picked up the New York *Times* and read in Sam Zolotow's column a choice little item:

"Alan Jay Lerner and Frederick Loewe, who wrote My Fair Lady, are unable to proceed with their next project, a musical version of Edna Ferber's novel, Saratoga Trunk.

"It was their intention to go ahead in behalf of Robert Fryer and Lawrence Carr. But Mr. Loewe had to leave Monday for a rest in Europe on the advice of his physician. Mr. Lerner feels tuckered out, too . . ."

Aside from Ferber having an immediate attack of trigeminal neuralgia, the following—and to her shattering—events happened mostly through letters. The first one, sent by Alan Jay Lerner, was a courtly but firm rejection of the project. In it, he defuses any blame that she might have put on the producers, Fryer and Carr, insisting that the venture would not be going through due to financial backing, but solely because he and "Fritz" Loewe were not up to it at that time. Actually, he places the burden of the withdrawal on Loewe, who had recently had an emergency appendectomy, from which he needed time to convalesce. He stresses how patient she had been during their work on *My Fair Lady*, and subtly implies that with that show as their tremendous hit, they wouldn't want to launch into something that could well be a flop. He suggests that she not burn the midnight oil for them, because there was no hope that they would work on her property. It is a "that's that" letter. But not where Ferber was concerned. Her response, dated April 18, 1956:

"A sad and dispiriting business, Alan, not only in effect but in execution. In the New York Times of April 11th, I was confronted by the news of your decision regarding SARATOGA TRUNK. It was, at least, news to me, and appalling news. Some hours later, I had your letter. It was dated April 9th, oddly enough.

"Your letter expressed concern regarding what you termed my anxiety to get started. In the year that has passed since I last saw you, and in the time preceding that year, I never have expressed to you the slightest anxiety or concern regarding the starting of my work on the musical that was to have been made from my novel . . . I did think that the Morris office and Robert Fryer and Lawrence Carr were too slow in closing with one of the many financial backers apparently interested in this proposed production. I thought the delay was their fault, and I urged them, quite understandably, to get this settled. I never dreamed that this delay, extending over a period longer than a year, actually was due to your own deliberate planning. In your letter to me, dated April 9, 1956, you say 'Fritz and I have been holding it up on purpose.'

"Why, please, did you not tell me this earlier?

"As to your weariness. It was long ago understood, and discussed at length, that you and Frederick Loewe could not possibly start work on SARATOGA TRUNK until you both had had a period of rest and recuperation sufficient, in your opinion, to enable you to begin work on a new venture. This was so thoroughly agreed on that no date was named for the start of fresh work. It would have been to me unthinkable for you to turn from the completion of MY

FAIR LADY to another long task without a fitting period of complete rest.

"You did not ask for an extension of time for the delivery of the book, lyrics and music of SARATOGA. It would have freely been granted. It was expected. I carefully avoided bothering you in any way while you were engaged in the nerve-racking task of putting on MY FAIR LADY.

"A London company of your wonderful play, and a second or even third United States Company would need your attention for casting, etc. But the leg work, the detail, the working from what amounts to a pattern finished and inviolable, would be done by competent assistants. A rehearsal is a four-weeks period. You know that and I know that. After all, Alan, I'm not a Tennessee mountain girl. I've been wearing shoes for years. You are a creative writer. Frederick Loewe is a creative musician. Doing again and again something you already have done isn't very satisfying to the creative spirit.

"SARATOGA TRUNK was and is a property worth a great deal of money. Its value was in no way dependent on whether MY FAIR LADY had been a success or a failure. Your action has immeasurably degraded this property. In favor of you, I (and the other owners of SARATOGA TRUNK) refused many other offers.

"Finally, you and Frederick Loewe long ago signed a legal and binding contract to write the book, lyrics and music for a musical play based on the novel SARATOGA TRUNK. Some months ago you amazed me by saying on the telephone that you and Mr. Loewe had done a few numbers for this musical. Certainly, I hadn't expected this at that time, or even hoped for it. In your letter dated April 9th, you say that you 'have been in touch with thousands of attorneys.' There still remains a broken contract to account for; a contract which, as you know, involves other owners of SARATOGA besides myself.

"MY FAIR LADY is one of the most enchanting experiences I've ever had in the theater. Witty, gay, tasteful, dramatic, beautiful. It brings new stature to the living stage. And this makes me all the sorrier to find myself confronted with a situation as sordid as the one you have created. Edna Ferber."

Alan Jay Lerner responded to her blast with a letter dated April 24. In it he dutifully, if somewhat sarcastically, deals with all of her points, and turns them, in his perspective, into unreasonable accusations. He ends with a plea for her return to amicability: "I beg you not to feel the 'business is sordid.' Sad it undoubtedly is, but sordid, never. Now I shall phone you. Fondly, Alan."

Whether he did or not is beside the point. He'd already wreaked havoc with Ferber's good faith—and good face. The pain was worse than ever. I remember during this time she wouldn't even call me "Julie doll" or "Miss Gomit," as was her custom. It was just plain "Julie," which upset me. I was still rather young and didn't understand the machinations of her life. There is something chilling about being called your own name when love terms have always been applied.

She was desolate. Robert Fryer, however, was undaunted; he was determined to get this show on the road. He pulled two more rabbits: On December 27, 1957, he presented them in a letter, for she was too ill to receive visitors:

"Dear Edna, I just called your home and of course did not want to disturb you. I only hope that the pain has abated and that you are feeling better.

"I feel strange in a way in coming to you about SARATOGA TRUNK again since there has been such a long period of time involved. However I am still in love with it and still feel that it will be a classic musical.

"Meredith Willson and Morton Da Costa, who did THE MUSIC MAN, are most eager to do a production of SARATOGA TRUNK as their next project.

". . . Both Meredith Willson and Tec Da Costa would love to meet you to present their ideas regarding SARATOGA TRUNK . . ."

Ferber tartly replied that not only did she have facial pain, she had finger pain as well. She had fallen in the bathroom, had broken her finger, and did not feel up to any more SARATOGA TRUNK travails.

Fryer reassured her.

". . . I checked with Da Costa about his doing another musical with Meredith Willson. He said he has considered another show, not with Meredith, but would not of course do anything else if he were able to do SARATOGA TRUNK, as that is the only thing he really wants to do. Meredith Willson feels the same way . . ."

Meredith Wilson did not feel the same way, and turned his energies toward *The Unsinkable Molly Brown.* Ferber found Morton

("Tec," pronounced "Teak") Da Costa to be a most personable and promising theatrical figure, and it was agreed that he would write the "book" of Saratoga and direct it as well. But who would compose the music and write the lyrics? It was a problem that was stewed over for approximately two years, during which time Da Costa was stewing over the writing of the "book." Each time Harold Arlen's name would come up, Ferber would hold her face. Da Costa placated her feeling of Arlen-anxiety in that he also shared her feelings on both Arlen and Berlin. He had finished the first draft and showed it to Ferber, who thought it was a final copy.

Soon thereafter, as irony would have it, Harold Arlen was signed to compose the music. Johnny Mercer was to write the lyrics. The rest of the production names fell into place and they were good: costumes—Cecil Beaton; choreography—Ralph Beaumont; lighting—Jean Rosenthal. At that point, the marquee read far better than the "book," which Da Costa had shown to Ferber. He did not take kindly to the idea of a rewrite with her. He felt that when he took the project on he would do the writing alone, as he did not like to collaborate with anyone. Da Costa thought that Edna should make suggestions, scene by scene, in writing. He also felt that he should have the final say in all matters, as he was more experienced in the theatre than she was. He wanted to be assured that there would be no delay because Edna had, by contract, the approval of the two leading actors. She had approved of Harold Arlen and Johnny Mercer, but Da Costa felt that they had accepted the job because they were guaranteed that they would be working directly with him.

Ferber was beyond umbrage. There was work to be done and her reputation to uphold. She swooped the adopted child up in her arms to recondition it to make it more natural, more her own. In late April of 1959, she took off for Arden's Maine Chance and seven weeks of rewrite. Morton Da Costa and Robert Fryer took off in the opposite direction—to Los Angeles—to scout for the two leads. Ferber would send her rewrites as she finished them out to the Coast, and Da Costa was to contact her as he received them. She heard only from Robert Fryer—two blithe telegrams. The first saying: "Delighted with first act material received from you. Arlen and Mercer doing wonderful work too." Ferber mentions the telegram in her diary, saying, "Nothing to dine out on." The second telegram concerned Rock Hudson, who Ferber thought might be right for the male lead, Clint Maroon. "Tec worked with Hudson three days and finally had Arlen and Mercer hear him. Must have all approvals before Hudson will ask Universal to release him. Have no idea if they will but worth a good try. Would you please wire your approval so that Hudson can go to Universal on Monday. Much Love—Bobby." Ferber wired her disapproval with Fryer's telegram: "As you know I have repeatedly said Rock would be right for Clint if proved to have the stage and musical potentialities. Your telegram whether intentionally or carelessly said absolutely nothing regarding these qualities. However, if you Tec Arlen Mercer have seen heard and approved Rock then my co-partners and I certainly give our approval. Personally, I am fond of Rock, and I have seen how admirably he conducts himself."

The interest in Rock Hudson was dropped because of a suit he was involved in, peculiarly enough with Henry Ginsberg, who was one of the co-producers of the film *Giant*. Ferber did not want to have anything to do with that messiness. She had her own to deal with. She'd not had a word from Da Costa about her arduous rewrites, although he had informed her that he would probably go with Carol Lawrence and Howard Keel in the leading roles—with or without her approval.

On June 29, 1959, she summarized the disgraceful events in a to-whom-it-may-concern letter titled, "JUST FOR THE RECORD OF THE MUSICAL PLAY SARATOGA".

"Perhaps a copy of this informal and (I hope) brief record should be sent to Robert Fryer and to Morton Da Costa . . .

"You will recall that when the Da Costa script was finished and read it was generally agreed that structurally and dramatically it was excellent but that dialogue and characterization and plot and motivation were, in unnumerable instances faulty. Robert Fryer and Morton Da Costa requested me to rewrite. Although I was most reluctant to do this I agreed to undertake the work. I worked on the script for about seven weeks . . . The pages, in four separate lots, were air-mailed to Da Costa and Fryer in Hollywood. I received no word of any kind from Da Costa . . .

"Some weeks before this work was begun I had asked Mr. Da Costa if he would work with me on this writing task. This is the usual proceeding in cases such as this. I felt—and said—that in two weeks or thereabouts we could, working together daily, bring the SARATOGA script into playable shape. This Da Costa refused to do. He said that he could not write with anyone. As I have successfully written thirty published volumes of plays, novels, and short stories, and as I have no record of any written signed by Morton Da Costa, this seemed to me odd . . . I rewrote, making many changes in dialogue, characterization, situations; suggesting new scenes, inserting dramatic scenes from the novel which had not been used, making certain suggestions for numbers, etc. An overall rewrite job.

"I have absolutely no information as to what became of this work. I do not know what Da Costa has chosen to retain in the script. He has never discussed this rewrite. If he had been the acknowledged playwright and novelist and I the tyro the situation might have been somewhat less fantastic.

"Here I wish to stress two or three important matters that have arisen as the result of this situation:

1. A letter from Da Costa to me stated that sometimes his appraisal of the written word might have been slightly different from mine because he had been an actor first and had dealt with actors and knew by experience that the less literate line would give more the illusion of spontaneity and roll off the tongue easier.

"Well, it's too late for me to learn to write illiterately.

2. I talked with Robert Fryer Friday . . . He said that Harold Arlen had come here from California and had been present at an audition—Carol Lawrence and some others. Fryer then said (to my amazement) that Arlen and Mercer had said that anyone that Da Costa might see fit to engage would be satisfactory to them. I never before had heard of any creative person who had so little respect for his own completed work, or its fate.

3. The Ferber-partnership contract stipulates that we (Fannie, Mina and Janet) have the right to approve the two leading players. Robert Fryer said (finally) that he had suggested this when Da Costa refused us the right to manuscript approval. Carol Lawrence had auditioned three times and is the favorite so far. Many others have auditioned, including Keel. Neither I nor my co-partners were notified of these auditions or given any information concerning them . . .

4. Whether intentionally or not, Robert Fryer said that NBC had not yet signed the contract. They are supposed to provide the necessary $400,000 for production. HE SAID THAT THEY WANTED THE NAME OF ANOTHER WRITER IN THE EVENT THAT

SOMETHING HAPPENED TO DA COSTA IN THE MIDST OF TRYOUT OR REHEARSALS.

"I feel sure they'll be able to find some one sufficiently illiterate to suit everyone.

"Fryer said that the Beaton costume and set sketches were enchanting. I haven't seen any of these. He also spoke with great enthusiasm of the music. I haven't heard any of this.

"All this will—or should—explain to you my reasons for bowing out.

"I rather wonder what the situation will be for seats for my family and friends for the opening December 7. Gallery, I assume. Yours, Edna."

Following the opening of SARATOGA, Ferber received two notes of abject apology. The first came from Da Costa in December 1959. In it he told her that he felt there were some good quotes usable in advertising and with a good word-of-mouth campaign they might be able to get the public to disregard the reviews. He was sorry that he was unable to give her a hit show for Christmas and hoped that she would know he had a deep affection for her.

The second, dated February 7, 1959, was Fryer's:

"Dearest Edna: This is one of the hardest letters I have ever had to write.

"Little did I dream a year ago today, that we would be faced with a closing of SARATOGA in such a short time. Looking back I have tried to see where I have failed you . . . the thing that nags my conscience and sits on my shoulder all of the time is that I have failed a great and wonderful person like you. You have demonstrated all of the great human qualities we read about—loyalty, integrity, honor, dignity and wisdom. I have repaid you for all of these great qualities with a failure. A failure that should not have occurred. On top of that—many things occurred that I should be horse-whipped for. If I had only been stronger in many areas.

"Someday—somehow I shall try to make it up to you. Your story is still a great one and should be told in musical terms . . . My love to you, Bob."

Six years of investment for a two-month run. Ferber seemed quite philosophical about it. Her tart humor came to the fore in a letter to Henry: "What a disheartening mess the whole thing has been. Serves me right for being a writer. Still, Steinbeck survived

PIPE DREAM so I'll prolly emerge from this with just another experience to add to my charm bracelet."

The last of *Saratoga* for Ferber, was in a telegram that she sent to the company. The tone is of a general talking to his troops after a battle lost.

"From out here in Arizona dear Members of the Saratoga Company, I want to thank you for the courage and hard work and patience you have contributed in the face of defeat. During the New York run I did not see a performance but my thoughts were with you in the theater each night. Every good wish to you all from one who loves and deeply respects the great arts of acting and playwriting. Edna Ferber."

Yet another defeat for Ferber was the film version of her novel *Ice Palace*. Released by Warner Brothers in 1960, starring Richard Burton and Robert Ryan, it was glacial at the box office. Ferber never even saw it. She did, however, see and appreciate the sale figure that the indomitable agent, Irving "Swifty" Lazar, negotiated for her. Lazar had originally met Ferber through Moss Hart and George Kaufman, and although he'd socialized with her for years, he'd never sold anything for her. Both bantam, inclined toward aggression, one would think they would have sparred. To the contrary. "I never had a single time when Edna raised her voice," Lazar asserts. "I'd heard about it, but it wasn't for us. Ours was a love story. We never had any problems."

Prior to the publication of *Ice Palace,* Ken McCormick felt that the property should go to Lazar for a speedy and hopefully lucrative film sale before the word got out that it was not a very good book. Usually, Harriet Pilpel handled such sales for Ferber, but in this case McCormick felt that Lazar, with his herculean chutzpa, would be more appropriate. Lazar tells the story with as much color as his reputation carries:

"The funny part about ICE PALACE was that I met Jack Warner—who had made GIANT, which had been an enormous success—I met Warner at Charlie Feldman's house—Charlie's himself a producer—and I told Jack that Edna had just finished a novel called ICE PALACE. He says, 'What's it about?' And I told him the story of the book and he was mad for it. He said, 'Will you sell it to me right now—no other competition—What'll ya take?' I said,

'$500,000.' He said, 'I'll give ya four.' I said, 'All right. I'm sure Edna will take that.'

"But meanwhile, I'd told him the story, which was MY conception of ICE PALACE. It happens that it was not exactly HER conception. So when he bought the book, he thought he was buying a specific kind of story. He loved it and he, so enchanted by what I'd told him, told it to a director. The director said, 'That's a great story. I love it.' So Warner gave him the book. But when he read it, it turned out it wasn't exactly what I had said—meaning my version with my embellishments. The director said to Warner, 'What story did you hear? Because the one you told me I loved.'

"So Warner called me over to the studio, and I met the prominent director—whoever he was—can't remember—and he said, 'Look, tell us the story.' And I said, 'Well, I don't remember what I told you six months ago for crying out loud. I'd just read the book then and I told you what I liked about it.'

"So they ended up getting my story. They never got the story that they bought."

Lazar had apparently agreed to submit *Ice Palace* to the producer Harold Hecht, and then passed him over opting for Warner instead. Hecht felt that it was a question of moral ethic—something new in the film industry—and decided to campaign against Lazar's tactics. He sent a telegram to Lazar, with a copy to Ferber, saying:

"I must protest your selling motion picture rights of Edna Ferber's new novel without giving this company opportunity to read and bid for it since your action is clearly detrimental to Miss Ferber's interests as well as unfair to us and all other active companies. Situation especially flagrant in view of fact you advised me you had the manuscript, offered to submit it to me and subsequently confirmed that you would do so, yet sold it without fulfilling your agreement. Miss Ferber cannot know whether offer you accepted was true market value. No other agent repeatedly engages in such practices and I feel industry and writers should cooperate to put an end to your methods of dealing with important literary properties. Harold Hecht."

At that time, Hecht had not read the book. Lazar had; Ferber certainly had; both knew it was not up to par. Both knew that the sale was a coup of camouflage, for if the book had gotten around, its selling price would have rapidly descended.

Despite Hecht's threats to "disbar" Lazar, nothing punitive befell him. He is still swift, shrewd, and today probably the most sought-after agent in the world. Certainly his ability to negotiate didn't harm him in achieving his lofty position. The actual sale of *Ice Palace* was for $350,000, not $400,000. The property was "leased" to Warner's on a fifteen-year deal of which Ferber was to receive 15 per cent of the net profits. The leasing was not Lazar's invention. The original idea is generally attributed to the late great film agent Leland Hayward, and has been a successful ploy in book-into-film contracts ever since, but actually the brainstorm was Ferber's. Ferber and Hayward were in preliminary talks about the selling of the novel *Saratoga Trunk,* for which she had chosen him to be agent. Hayward was spouting off large prospective figures when Ferber asked innocently, "Why sell it, if you could rent it?" Hayward smiled. His bargaining position had just gone up. He would use her idea of less is more, for although the outright purchase price might be higher, the property would revert back to the author in a certain number of years enabling her to resell it elsewhere. Hence leasing for Ferber the Inventor.

Inventor, explorer, discoverer. It is safe to say that Ferber discovered Alaska—for popular use. She says so herself:

"In almost a half century of writing novels, short stories, plays and articles I can clearly recall the spark which touched off every published or produced work—except one. That one is my latest novel, ICE PALACE, published in 1958. I remember how I came to write my first book in 1911. The origin of ICE PALACE is a mystery to me. This may indicate something portentous, good or bad, but there it is. I can't imagine how I happened to write a novel whose background is Alaska.

"Alaska, as a part of the United States, didn't particularly interest me. I was as ignorant of it as were (and are) most of the millions of citizens of my country. I knew a few bare facts only; Alaska was a Territory of the United States; it was vast enough to be termed, without too much exaggeration, a sixth continent; it had been bought from Russia for seven million dollars in 1867 over the protest of most of the citizens of this country who called the transaction Seward's Folly because the purchase had been advised by Secretary of State Seward. Something over seven million had been paid to Russia for this gigantic territory. Vaguely, it was known that Eskimos lived there and that in the 1890's gold had been discovered.

"These sparse facts were about all that the average citizen of the United States knew about Alaska. Certainly they comprised my entire knowledge. In the past five years or thereabouts there was a mild political stirring regarding Alaska's wish to graduate from the status of a Territory of the United States to the position of a State of the United States. The dramatic struggle that grew out of this wish began to penetrate the emotions of millions who never had set foot in Alaska, had thought little if anything about it, and who didn't really know where it was, exactly. I was one of those.

"An airplane flight from New York to Alaska at that pre-jet time took much longer than a flight from New York to a European country. Yet, mysteriously, impelled, I found myself flying across the continent from New York to Seattle; then across the water from Seattle to Juneau, Alaska, and so up, up, up until I had reached the shores of the Arctic Ocean. This I did five times, spending many weeks each time. Those journeys entailed hardship, novelty, adventure, but these were not my reasons for undertaking them. There simply was no reason. The novel ICE PALACE was published in March 1958 in the United States. Alaska has triumphed. It is the 49th state of the Union. These two facts are not related. They only form part of an inexplicable whole."

On Tuesday, July 1, 1958, the headline in the New York *Times* read: "ALASKA TO JOIN UNION AS THE 49th STATE; FINAL APPROVAL IS VOTED BY SENATE, 64–20; BILL SENT TO EISENHOWER, WHO WILL SIGN IT."

Although Ferber was not singlehandedly responsible for this sweet victory, she was a powerful contributing force and was nationally recognized for being so. The Alaskans paid her homage, calling her, "a twentieth century version of Harriet Beecher Stowe." A few months before the statehood was official, before the bill was passed in the Senate, a prophetic editorial appeared in the Anchorage *Daily Times* thanking Ferber for what in all probability was about to happen to Alaska:

". . . Miss Ferber has rendered a great service to Alaska through her newest novel. The book will have a profound and beneficial effect. It contains a tremendous boost for the good qualities of Alaskans and their plea for self-government as a full-fledged member of the union of states . . . Her most sympathetic characters are the ones who, in the contemporary scene, are all plugging for Alaska's acceptance as a state. Contrasted with them are the 'exploiters', who take what they can get from Alaska and would keep the territory in an indefinite state of vassalage . . . Congressmen dallying with the statehood bills, especially the one pertaining to Alaska, will return home next summer to find a great number of their lady constituents have just read Ice Palace and that they have suddenly become tremendously interested in the book's locale. They are apt to have greater faith too, in Miss Ferber's report than in any alibi a congressman can invent. And right when the November election comes up, Ice Palace will doubtless be at the peak of the best seller lists. A shrewd politician will not underestimate the power of a lady novelist . . ."

Ferber worked on *Ice Palace* for five years. During that time she dealt closely with one very honorable politician, who always estimated her as the forceful person she was—nothing less. His name was Ernest Gruening. He was, at that time, Senator-Elect of the Alaska Statehood Delegation; he was to become, with the emergence of Alaska, its full-fledged senator. He helped Ferber to get inside the crannies of the power struggle existent in Alaska. She in turn, eventually, and ironically—through her book paving the way to statehood—helped him come to power. The right kind of power —pro-pipeline, anti-canned salmon—the things, again ironically, that Thor Storm, the hero of *Ice Palace*, believed in.

They had a rather formal relationship, Ferber and Gruening, each regarding the other as noble. He signed his letters to her, "Cordially yours," and her salutation to him was usually, "Dear Ernest Gruening." Both shared the same passion for Alaska, and when it was finally admitted to the Union, he embraced her with the victory:

". . . Really, Edna, it's a wonderful sensation, and most wonderful of all is that ICE PALACE contributed substantially to the result. In the last few weeks, just about everybody appears to have read it. Whenever people talked about Alaska—as scores did, in the closing hours of the fight—they talked about ICE PALACE, and they had gotten the message. How wonderful that you synchronized it just the way you did! . . ."

It was no accident that the book was the banner that led the way. Ferber was no waiter-in-the-wings; her sense of drama always propelled her to center stage. Back in July of 1957, she knew. She wrote to Ken McCormick from Arden's Maine Chance:

". . . Though you thought that Statehood would make no difference in the book's timeliness, I feel that it should come out before that possible event. Certainly I didn't mean to write a first-page book. When I first thought of the Alaska background the Statehood drive was not on in any degree of intensity. I didn't even think about it, except in terms of injustice . . ."

Following the statehood decision, Ferber was the toast of her friends, who always gathered round when she did something great but were, for the most part, dispersed in her off-hours, days, weeks, years.

John Mason Brown tipped his hat in a telegram: "I can imagine what a state you are in. You are the real star of the 49th. Congratulations."

Dear Dickie and Dorothy Rodgers made a funny in theirs: "Now let Ellen [referring to Ferber's name nemesis, Ellen Ferber] come up with Hawaii."

Mary Martin was so enthusiastic that she got out her parka and booked a tour through Alaska, saluting Ferber in a postcard with: "Adore YOUR Alaska."

In Hollywood, Hedda Hopper did her hat dance: "Our story editors are burning the midnight oil reading Edna Ferber's latest book, Ice Palace about modern Alaska. She's been there many times. I hear the book is as hot as that country is cold."

Ferber was nonplussed by all the tumult. Although she was thrilled with Alaska's victory, she was tepid about her own book—and to her, the book was the thing. Her attitude was, "Look what I've done for Alaska, but what have I done for my art?"

Not much said Charles Poore in his New York *Times* review: ". . . Her story is too repetitious and disorderly to win a prize in the world of literature. But I shouldn't be surprised at all to hear that it had helped measurably to win statehood for Alaska . . ."

Elizabeth Janeway, in the New York *Times* Sunday magazine review, slapped Ferber twice—for a poor book and for her prudish tendencies: ". . . Miss Ferber seems definitely more interested in the facts that her research has turned up than in the perfunctory structure she has thrown together to hang them on, for when she is faced with a choice between romance and a description of the Alaskan canned-fish industry, the cannery wins every time. A wedding breakfast is followed by no honeymoon scene, but by a survey of the housing shortage in the city the author has named Baranof.

The volume of instruction covered by a sugar-coating of fiction to make it palatable has been with us for a long time. Miss Ferber, however, has now carried the process so far that she has produced a pill of fiction with a sugar-coating of good honest research. A few old-fashioned readers with an anachronistic affection for fiction will regret that such a production should be billed as a novel."

The difference between friends and critics is vast. Here is Noel Coward's review:

"Darling Ferber, I know you endured blood and sweat and tears and knocked yourself out and that we didn't see nearly as much of each other as we should have done while I was in New York. However having just finished Ice Palace I can only say that it was all worth it.

"I was held by it from beginning to end and nobody, nobody but you could have dreamed up a Floosie called Butterfly Magrue.

"The fabulous vitality of your writing is entirely undiminished and your trained, observant eye misses nothing. I never thought that I should want to go to Alaska, but now I do. Bridie is enchanting, both the Grandfathers utterly real and uncompromising, Christine of course a darling. The love story is handled with such sureness and delicacy, and the devotion of those people to their own territory is moving and completely convincing.

"I tremble to think what an enormous amount of research you had to do to absorb all that detail and I am lost in admiration because not once, with all the detail, does the story and the narrative quality falter. There is no dullness anywhere in the whole long book; it moves along with speed and your particular brand of urgency from the first page to the last.

"I really do congratulate you darling and thank you for such a satisfying and stimulating treat . . ."

Frank Sullivan's book review:

"Dearest Ferb, I want to tell you how much I enjoyed Ice Palace. What a comfort to know there is a writer still around who can tell a story beautifully and make all the people in it come to life. There aren't too many left who hold with Maugham that a story ought to have a beginning, a middle, and an end, but you do, so thank the Lord for Ferb . . ."

Ferber's own assessment and review to Ken McCormick, dated November 15, 1958:

"Don't think, Ken, that I'm such a befuddled fool as to think that

Doubleday was responsible for the comparatively low sale on ICE PALACE. In no day is 75,000 (correct?) considered a small book sale. You all did a fine intelligent enthusiastic job on the book, it just happened to come along at a time which was good or bad—I'll never know—for the book's publicity . . . ICE PALACE got bad reviews. It was a faulty book, a tapestry, really, of the vast, varied, incredible region. People are almost entirely ignorant of Alaska, they are curious about it, it will, I think, have fantastic growth and drama in the next ten or fifteen years. It isn't a land for sissies. Juneau, Anchorage, Fairbanks aren't what I mean when I say and think Alaska . . ."

There are many versions concerning the facts of a person's life. Often they are more colorful than what actually went on. There is a rather well-known story about the feud between Ferber and Peg Pulitzer. It comes from a variety of sources, with a variety of shadings, but the gist of it remains the same. It happened at the time when *Ice Palace* had just come out. Supposedly Peg Pulitzer sent Ferber a letter telling her how much she'd enjoyed *Giant*—mixing up the two novels. Such an error wouldn't sit well with any author. A few days later, Peg Pulitzer received an envelope addressed to her in Ferber's hand. Inside was her own letter that she had written to Ferber. She knew she was in big trouble. Ferber had circled the word GIANT, and in the margin had written, "If you haven't yet, why not read SHOW BOAT, or SO BIG if you get a chance." Ferber didn't speak to Peg Pulitzer for two years, but eventually pardoned her.

A tasty story. The bland-diet fact of the matter is a letter from Peg Pulitzer, dated March 31, 1958:

Dear Madam, I read—devoured—ICE PALACE, and like it fine . . . Thank you for the treat—You are a woman of wonderful vitality and unsurpassed powers of observation. I wish you'd give me one of those photographs of you in a parka. Love, Peg."

Ferber got inside a new book with the relish of approaching a new lover. She was eager and reckless, probing and taking. No detail was too small to be revealing.

She charted her course for Alaska again and again before committing herself to it. She was determined to be faithful to her subject of research. Almost as with a difficult, challenging, and draining courtship, the family objected. It was too rigorous for her—at her age and all. The hardships—starting all over again—not a good idea. But when Ferber was infatuated with a locale, she always forgot what the marriage to the typewriter would be like. There was no stopping her when she was in the throes of romance. She was like a smitten young "gel," as she would say. We would sit in the safety of Passy on a Sunday night, and she would regale us with her latest exploits in the tundra, and that igloos had kitchens, and did we know that Eskimo means man who eats sea animals? Gradually the family began to accept Ferber's new, strange, and exciting young man, Alaska. In June of 1955, when she was off to Fairbanks, Janet played maid of honor:

"Darling—I hope you'll find this trip satisfactory as well as necessary. I know it's going to be worthwhile—and feel it's going to be fascinating, fresh and wonderful. It's really unexplored as far as fiction goes, and you're the girl that can do it. I love the contrast—sleds and planes. The Jewish family—the beautifully furnished home you went to—the Eskimos, whom no one really knows anything about except the Nanook of the North stuff. You're really amazing. You love luxury and yet it really means nothing to you when you're searching and exploring. You love good food, and yet you forget about it under research conditions. I admire you."

There was an absolute dichotomy about Ferber. As snobbish and constrained as she was in her normal surroundings, she was free-spirited and a sport in her abnormal ones. Once she had her "sea legs" on, there was nobody she wouldn't talk to. She flirted ruthlessly to get her story. On the plane to Seattle, she apparently struck up a conversation with a fellow named Bayard. Her notes convey that she was intrigued by him:

"Bayard. (Bay). He is 33 or 34. Had been an aviator in World War II. A quiet moody rather handsome and compelling man who is curiously withdrawn. His family background is New England—later Seattle. Annis, his wife."

Then she wrote a list of possible fictitious surnames for him:

"Bay Crawford, Bay Grafton, Bay Corbett, Bay Constant, Bay Condact, Bay Cornwall, Bay Garrison, Bay Gilbert, Bay Gorham, Bay Goodwin."

Eventually, he turned into a full-fledged character named Bay Husack. Her description of him in *Ice Palace* is not remote from the young man she met on the plane:

"He had returned from the War in late 1945, handsomer than

ever, feminine Seattle agreed . . . But six years had gone by, he was thirty-one, and whatever it was that he had been supposed to take hold of had eluded him."

Ferber's notes were like laying salt on a slippery ground so that later she would be able to walk. Many of them she discarded in her final work; all of them tell a great deal about her sweet 'n' sour grasp of the human condition. From her Alaska notebook:

"Seattle flight: Airline stewardess who married new millionaire and who gradually became a hostess in a much more perilous atmosphere than a mere nineteen thousand feet."

"Observation on American service men (Air and Army). They stuff too much. All that pork chops and steak and sweet potatoes and pie and cake and ice cream and milk and butter and gravy. They've got the biggest behinds of any fighting force in the world."

"Fairbanks: Everywhere women pretty and pregnant. Babies and small children like walking flowers in the arctic sun . . . Overheard in Fairbanks dress shop—'I want something real dressy, but not on the cocktail side.'"

"Folks in Fairbanks: SADIE MCKEEGAN—associate editor. Wispy, Gish-ish, white bangs, girly hats, scarves, Greenwich Villagey, middle west born, lives in cabin five miles out of Fairbanks. Persistent, strange, loyal, prolly in love with old Jessen . . . ZEKE LACEY. Intelligent, boardering on effeminate. Learned he used to be mama's boy, didn't get away, unmarried. Knows old Alaska pioneers, knows a lot about Alaska. Not very electric, but pleasant and informative . . . GLORIA RAINEY—Woman reporter on Fairbanks News-Miner. White fur parka. Hard eye. Capable. Surface. Attractive looking . . . MRS. AVA MCGINTY—Former city hostess. Was a photo bride but won't admit it. Came from Ireland. Rich Irish brogue which she clings to and exaggerates. Fussy, bustling, fidgety, high blood-pressure, partly phony, warm-hearted, pretty trying. A character. Fired when I was in Fairbanks. Gives the effect of wearing a sweeping cape but doesn't . . . ROGER WOUK—Lawyer. Firm of F. Banfield & Boochever. Wouk head of all the lobbies. The real governor of Alaska. Power behind the throne stuff . . . Nameless Character—He carried a smart swagger-stick like a small staff of ivory. Explained that it was made from the penis of a male walrus. And so it was. This flustered the wives of the air base officers."

She didn't camouflage the characters she used in *Ice Palace* as carefully as she used to in her younger books. Ernest Gruening, Governor of Alaska, and George Sundborg, editor of Juneau's progressive newspaper *The Weekly Independent*, turned up in the novel without much protective coloring. Ferber used to say that there was always somebody who would claim direct identity with one of her characters, be secretly flattered by it, and would threaten legal action. It didn't seem to bother her much.

What did bother her during, but mostly in between, those treks to Alaska was The Face. Curiously, it seemed to strike most savagely when she was at home, near her family. Yet, she persisted in seeing us as much as possible, and paying for our lives. The self-imposed burden of the latter was what probably gave her the trigeminal neuralgia.

I was cautioned that during the times when her malaise was fierce I was to be extra understanding and polite. One night, in what must have been late 1958, Janet, Henry, and I had dinner with Ferber at "21." Her face looked as though she had an impacted wisdom tooth. The pain, she informed us, was that of a thousand impacted wisdom teeth. She could barely eat. After dinner, as we were making our way downstairs, a man and a lady converged upon Ferber. The man I didn't know. The lady everyone knew—or so I thought. She was Vivien Leigh. She was so beautiful. In my, at that time, prepubescent state, this was ecstasy. She was my total heroine. To meet her would launch my high school career. I couldn't wait. There was much kissing between Miss Leigh, the man, and Ferber—who winced each time she was bussed. When that was over, Ferber turned stiffly toward us. "Surely you remember Mr. Leland Hayward," she said, "and his terribly pretty friend." That was it. No Vivien Leigh introduction. The two of them went off. Ferber looked as if she wanted to fan herself. "Wasn't that awful," she said. "I simply couldn't remember the woman's name."

I was unforgiving. "Oh, Aunt Edna," I reproved. "If you couldn't remember Vivien Leigh, at least you could have remembered Scarlett O'Hara."

She turned to me with a bleary eye. "Who?" she asked.

When Ferber had The Face, even her favorite friends were in disfavor. She jots in her diary of displeasing social events: "Dinner at Terry Helburn's. Weird" . . . "Dinner with George Oppenheimer at Barberry Room. Jascha Heifetz and his wife there . . . All pretty dull stuff." . . . "Felt the delayed shock of Lerner withdrawing from Saratoga. To Peg Pulitzer's for dinner. Madelaine Sherwood, Mrs. John Mason Brown–Peg astonishingly belligerent and unpleasant. Too many scotches the cause. Not good." . . . "Rodgers, Gordons, Mark Connelly to dinner. Fair. Max ominously silent, ate prodigously." . . . "Dinner at Emanie Arlings for Rebecca West and Henry A. Harrison Smith there (Editor Saturday Review) I found I couldn't speak to him and didn't except when he twice asked me a direct question. Horrid little man. Dullish evening, bad dinner." . . . "Dinner at Stork Club with Dick Rodgers and to visit Dorothy at Special Surgery Hospital. Dorothy had calcium removed from right shoulder. Dick looked the sicker of the two."

Dorothy Rodgers remembers how irritable Ferber was at that time.

"Edna wanted to know when she could come and see me. So I wrote her a little note and said why don't you come late some morning–because I really wanted to enjoy her alone and other people tended to come in the late afternoon. I got back a letter from her–they seldom started 'Dear'–it would break in the middle–'I thought you would have known, dear Dorothy, that I work in the morning. If I didn't work in the morning, I would not have twenty-seven books on the shelf. I only break this rule for an emergency–for someone in my own family.' Well, here I was in the hospital having a hell of a time. I was so mad when I got that letter that I was going to write her back and tell her what my mornings were like. But then I thought, oh, forget it. We'd already been through one feud. So, I just wrote a note and said, Edna, come whenever you like."

Robert Sherwood, the playwright, died in 1955. He had been a "socially" close friend of Ferber since the late twenties. During the thirties, he too had suffered recurring attacks of the treacherous "tic douloureux." John Mason Brown tells of the agony of Sherwood while writing his classic American play *Abe Lincoln in Illinois:*

"Then would come hours of torturing doubts when, laid low by attacks of Tic Douloureux, he found himself harassed by the episodic form he had chosen."

On the morning of Sherwood's funeral, there was a tremendous downpour of rain. Ferber's face was crippled with pain. George Oppenheimer called for her at 10:45 and with him and Peg Pulitzer she went to the service. Death was one of the few exceptions for breaking her morning writing regimen. "Alfred Lunt gave a moving eulogy," she wrote in her diary of that day, and then, "I now know, and, too late, can be empathetic to what Bob suffered then. Poor, poor fellow. That he could get past the AB in Abe to write a masterly play is astonishing. The chore of ICE PALACE looms larger than ever."

The translation into film of Ferber's novel *Giant* cast a kinder shadow. It was released in October 1956 to wild public and enthusiastic critical praise. To Ferber, it was a commercial *pièce de résistance* because she was a co-partner in production and, as its author, it was the most satisfying of any of her books-into-films. To George Stevens, producer and director, it was, "the last of the really big pictures."

One of the more salient statements that the film made had not much to do with its artistic integrity. In a sense, its sensationalism overshadowed its many merits—for *Giant* meant the last of James Dean. Killing himself in his Porsche racing car on the heels of the picture's completion, he became the giant of *Giant*. His death, perhaps, was greater than his performance; the knowledge of it, combined with his screen presence, made for an electricity that was ineffable. His reviews were luxuriantly morbid—all in the tone of Bosley Crowther's evocative epitaph, which went thus:

"However, it is the late James Dean who makes the malignant role of the surly ranch hand who becomes an oil baron the most tangy and corrosive in the film. Mr. Dean plays this curious villain with a stylized spookiness—a sly sort of off-beat languor and slur of language—that concentrates spite. This is a haunting capstone to the brief career of Mr. Dean."

Actually, Dean never completed his work on *Giant*. His scenes on camera were in the can, but since one of them in particular was inaudible, he was scheduled to come back for looping—a postproduction technique that involves dubbing in clarified dialogue to match the picture. Dean was not available to do this for one of his key scenes. It was the banquet speech, where Jett Rink was supposed to be just at the edge of falling down drunk; Dean took it to heart, and although visually he was splendid, he fell down verbally. George Stevens and William Hornbeck, the film editor, recruited Dean's former roommate and best friend, a young actor named Nick Adams, to complete the vocal role of Jett Rink. Adams, by stuffing his cheeks with wads of gum, assimilated a clearer version of Dean's slur. The result of the necessary trick was perfect, went completely undetected, and, in fact, the scene was cited as one of Dean's best. Eerily, Nick Adams died several years later in the same self-destructive vein as his friend, Dean. That tiny portion of film is known as the late looping.

Ferber chose to save all the clippings from *Giant* featuring Dean as the top dog. She had been deeply affected by his death, although she'd felt that it was probably imminent. In Dean's case, she certainly was a seer. The events chill:

"I . . . had received in the mail a large photograph which he had sent me. It was inscribed and it showed him in character and in costume as Jett Rink, the ranch hand. It was not characteristic of him to send his photograph unasked. I was happy to have it and I wrote to thank him: '. . . when it arrived I was interested to notice for the first time how much your profile resembles that of John Barrymore. You're too young ever to have seen him, I suppose. It really is startlingly similar. But then, your automobile racing will probably soon take care of that.'

"I was told that the letter came the day of his death. He never saw it."

The very fine character actress Mercedes McCambridge was featured in *Giant*. During the endless filming—nearly four months, most of it on location in Marfa, Texas—she played a leading role in Dean's life. She got as close to him as he would allow anyone. She was chief mamma and emotion washer. She wrote a letter to Ferber describing how she was uncannily drawn into his death. In it she told how she and Fletcher, her husband, started out in their car for a vacation in San Francisco, where they were going to live it up after the long and arduous filming of *Giant*. They spent the first night of their journey in Terra Bella, and the following morning, Saturday, October 1, headed for Pebble Beach, where they would spend the second night. They'd gone about sixty miles on a flat, barren highway (reminding McCambridge of the *Giant* terrain in Texas) when they noticed their tank was low, and began to scout for a gas station. What they finally came upon in the middle of that nowhere zone was a seedy station with a tin-roofed garage. A hulking girl came out to fill the tank, and while Fletcher stayed by the car, McCambridge went inside to get some Cokes. The girl told Fletcher that they had James Dean's car in the garage, and he, knowing that Dean liked to tool around in that area, thought that the Porsche was in for repairs. Then he heard his wife exclaim from inside, "Oh, my God," and deduced that she'd seen Dean coming out of the men's room, and that she was simply expressing joy at seeing him. But what had happened was that someone had told her that Dean's car was there, and had then pointed her to what was left of it: a demolished, smoking accordion, surrounded by blood. It was then that she shrieked. The accident had occurred about a half mile down the road they'd just traveled.

The owner of the car that killed Dean was named Turnupseed. McCambridge mentions wryly that Dean was probably getting a chuckle out of that name.

All the provocative adjectives have already been applied to Dean. But he just must have been something extra for two more than middle-aged, rather salty women to have felt so bereft by his passing.

Although Rock Hudson and Jimmy Dean did not get along—due to charisma conflicts, one suspects—he is still affected by his last meeting with Dean:

"The last scene I had with Jimmy Dean was down in the basement and he was drunk. We shot it. He left. That was that. Our work together was over. Then he was killed. The last thing I ever said to him was, 'You know what, Jett—you're all through.'"

Ferber had always had a penchant for glamour, which appeared to have its outlet during the long and well-publicized filming of *Giant*. She took a particular shine to Dean, calling him ". . . an original. Impish, compelling, magnetic . . ." and to Hudson, who she thought was "as dear as he was tall."

Both actors reciprocated her fondness—in diametrically opposite ways. Hudson, when he came to New York, would have tea with her, would squire her to the theatre, and would listen to her talk about her past—a ruse of hers when she wanted to hold somebody spellbound. He was held.

"She used to talk about her girlhood and the fight she knew she had in front of her. I remember she said something like, 'I had to learn to fight early because I was too little and too ugly.' Edna had a knack of telling things in the palm of her hand . . . She was a power—but an elderly power—which is so much more commanding. Old ladies of authority command much more attention than younger women, middle-aged women, or even men—even old men of authority. Edna was authority."

Hudson appealed to Ferber's gracious-lady side. Dean got closer to the truth of her; he got whimsy out of her—a quality that lay dormant from too many years of neglect. There were glimmers of it, but too few people really sparked her. One day on the Warner's set, just after Dean had bought his fatal Porsche, he plunked Ferber into it and raced around the lot with her at top speed. She loved it.

Perhaps these two actors were so special to her because they embodied the characters that she'd written. They didn't betray her.

Neither Hudson nor Dean fit into the original concept that George Stevens had for Bick and Jett. He was thinking more along the lines of Forrest Tucker as the roughhewn Bick, who had to age more than thirty years during the course of the picture. Not only was Hudson a stripling at that time, but so was his film career. He had read the novel and ached to do the role—as did William Holden, Clark Gable, and every other major Hollywood star. Hudson must have somehow conveyed his longing to Stevens' secretary, who later became his wife. She told Stevens about a small Western that Hudson had made, where he had aged up and was successful at it. She advised Stevens to run a print of the film, which he did, and immediately snapped-to, wanting Hudson for Bick without ever having met the actor. Complications. Hudson was under contract to Universal, who sensed that if Hudson was wanted by Stevens for the plum part of the year, he must be a hot property that they had neglected to put on their own front burner. They refused to lend him out to Stevens at Warner's. Hudson fought, applying granite-like tactics, and eventually won his case. After all the contracts were signed and the first day of filming was scheduled, he finally met George Stevens. In retrospect, Hudson is surprised that he ever got the role. In the book, Bick Benedict was written as a blond. Had Ferber had casting approval, he might have remained as a blond.

Dean was the real long shot in the casting of *Giant*. He was chosen prior to the release of *East of Eden*. He was awfully young, relatively untried—save for *Rebel Without a Cause*—and already known for causing rebellion. Stevens felt that the prototype for Jett Rink was Montgomery Clift, whom he'd cast earlier, with wonderful results, in the award-winning *A Place in the Sun*. But Clift was already on an emotional downslide, Dean's test was brilliant, and his price was right. He was paid very little. In fact, it is said that he wanted to be Jett Rink so badly that he made Stevens an offer: he would pay back his salary twofold if, by the end of three weeks' filming, his work was deemed unsatisfactory. The rest is history.

None of the three stars commanded the astronomical fees that they would have later in their careers. George Stevens, Jr., now head of the American Film Institute, worked intermittently with his father on the picture, and remembers what a humble position they were all in then:

"Neither Rock nor Elizabeth—and certainly not Jimmy—were hot at the time. So they all took a flat fee and no percentage. It was a job."

Productionwise, *Giant* had a prodigious financial appetite. There is a clipping that Ferber saved which explains how Stevens arranged for the film's survival and profit:

". . . If Producer Stevens had not been as good a businessman as Director Stevens is an artist, GIANT might never have been made. Hearing the high Hollywood price on Novelist Ferber's bestseller, Stevens did not even consider bidding for GIANT, although he admired it as a story. Later, hearing that there were no Hollywood takers for the novel, he decided to do it if the money went into the film rather than into buying the property. So he persuaded Author Ferber to become his production partner for a percentage of the profits—if there were any. At this point it looks as if Novelist Ferber has made a good bargain too."

A George Stevens trademark was that his pictures ran over budget, over time, and over years. Young George Stevens, Jr., worked on the film, went into the Air Force in July of '53, got out of the Air Force in July of '55, and resumed work on the film. It was still in production. The cost of making *Giant* was $5,400,000. Stevens, a stickler for authenticity in his special effects, never skimped. There was a scene in the shooting script which called for a massive herd of Longhorn cattle—which particular breed was almost extinct. Stevens' scouts somehow managed to find enough of them, and to ship them all into Marfa, Texas. Not a shoestring endeavor. Then the cattle had to be trained to do certain stunts—parlor tricks. For instance, there was a scene where they had to gather around a huge body of water and slurp it dry. They did it—after innumerable takes.

The running time of the first cut was three hours and fifty-six minutes, which is endless compared to the final cut of a mere three hours and eighteen minutes. To those who berated Stevens for its length, he replied calmly, "The film is well constructed, the way the old tworeel comedies used to be. Everything in it has a place. We analyzed it very carefully in advance. I am the first one to agree that length is a problem. But, with GIANT, no theatregoer has been conscious of any imposition. In fact, many people came back to see it again."

Ferber had one of her better business relationships with George Stevens. It worked because she allowed him to be dominant and herself recessive. It was a friendly female-male encounter with no role reversal. George Stevens, Jr., remembers about them a sense of fun; they kept it light. The middleman, the heavyweight, was Henry Ginsberg, the third partner. He dealt with any tempers that the two giants might have had.

The only time that Ferber got testy was during the writing of the screenplay—of which she had no part other than to read it in installments. It was written by Ivan Moffat and Fred Guiol, and although George Stevens, Jr., vouches for her pleasure with it, her diary vouches for her despair:

"Reading GIANT movie script. Find it illiterate. Much of the dialogue crude and dreadful. Deeply upset. Opening Bick scene impossible."

Ferber, never known to be an underreactor, was probably accurate when she cried illiterate. A goodly portion of the film script was written during the McCarthy hearings with Moffat, Guiol, and Stevens posted around the television set, pencils poised for commercial breaks.

Eventually, she liked what she saw, and so, surprisingly enough, did the state of Texas. When *Giant* was filming in Marfa, Rock Hudson remembers that there were threats of shooting holes in the screen—or worse—if the film was ever distributed in that state. But by the time it was released, either the Texans had mellowed or had gotten curious; they turned out in droves. John Rosenfield, film critic for the Dallas *Morning News,* wrote a piece discussing the unexpected turnabout called "Texans Can Take It":

"Two years ago a Hollywood syndicate columnist spoke in Beaumont while on a lecture tour. She discussed GIANT. Whereupon a sturdy Southeast Texan hauled himself afoot and shouted, 'If you make and show that damn picture, we'll shoot the screen full of holes.' GIANT hasn't reached Beaumont yet and the screen is intact. . . . All that has happened has been business. Our estimate of the first week's earnings in six situations is the colossal gross of $171,000 . . . Not one Texas theatre reports abnormal audience behavior, other than youngsters ripping all pictures of James Dean out of the lobby display frames. Anticipated difficulties were resentment over the flamboyant behavior of the cattle and oil big rich, especially a character who stays drunk and builds hotels; some nauseating examples of anti-Mexican race discrimination along the Texas boarder; the picture's frank statement of a 27½ per cent depletion allowance enjoyed by oil tycoons. . .

"All the fears now seem groundless. The George Stevens picturization of Edna Ferber's critical novel of Texas is accepted for what it is, mighty entertainment . . .

"'I might explain the Texans' patronage of GIANT as local interest,' said R. J. O'Donnell, vice-president and general manager of the Interstate Circuit, 'were it not for the fact that GIANT is doing famously out of the state too. The Texas population, especially in the large cities, has grown so phenomenally that half of it must have come from elsewhere . . . The public is not as touchy . . . as you might expect. I haven't heard anybody say that GIANT misrepresents Texas. It tells of a class and of situations that are part of our life, our politics, our emotional tangents and our jokes and humor. A valid controversy never hurt movie business . . . but I guess we won't have one. And it doesn't look as if we will need one either.' "

It's difficult to think of Texas without thinking of *Giant*—film, book, or both. Ferber was its first and most famous muckraker. She cornered the market. She also exposed the market to the point where one would assume that every single Texan had a personal vendetta. There was one who didn't, one who loved Ferber very much in a nonromantic yet passionate way. His name was Joe Linz and he was about thirty years her junior. Their first meeting, he recalls, "was in February, 1940. I was the film and drama critic of the old Dallas Journal, and when I was tipped off that she was in town I beat it over to the Baker Hotel for an interview. She was having a solitary lunch in the dining room and one of her first remarks was: 'How in God's name could anyone perpetuate a windowless, murky place like this in the land of wideopen spaces and perpetual sunshine?' I thought it was a good question. I had just finished A PE-

CULIAR TREASURE, and, although I was a long-time Ferber fan, it was that book which made me know she was a great, great woman quite aside from being a fine writer. The two don't always go together.

"Edna took a moment to complain about the indifferent fare on her plate, and, since my mother at that time had a superb cook, I invited her to our house the following day for lunch to ease the monotony of her cross-country eating. She got on famously with my family and they of course were enchanted with her. In my interview I had stated that she had a 'strong face.' She never let me forget it and teased me about it for years afterward. 'Who,' she asked, 'wants a strong face?'

"I took a couple of days off—it wasn't difficult since my father published the paper—to show her around San Antonio. One of my father's close friends was mayor of that city, and when I suggested that she see some of the town's seamier night life he insisted on sending along as escort the Chief of the Vice Squad. It delighted Edna and gave me a sense of security, since I felt I had a very precious 'charge' in tow. I guess the high spot of our evening was ending up in a bordello—a famous one. I wager no one else ever had the audacity to show the impeccably chic, totally elegant Edna Ferber a whorehouse. We had a couple of beers in the parlor and chatted at length with a couple of the girls who weren't occupied. I think Edna loved it.

"That first visit to Texas probably planted the seed for GIANT, even though it didn't come along until about ten years later . . . My copy of GIANT is inscribed: 'Dear Joe, I hope you (and Texas) won't mind my saying that I love you.'

". . . Texas was hideous in its reception of the book. Perhaps it was because 'professional Texans' don't take kindly to criticism, and the book was accurate in its spotlighting so many of the things we should be ashamed of. Must I add that I am not a 'professional' Texan?"

From the moment that she met Joe Linz, Ferber called him David. She'd decided that he didn't remotely resemble a Joe, and therefore would not be a party to calling him by a name that was wrong for him. Hence, David. He was her fondest link to Texas, and she reported to him the machinations that went on in the saga of *Giant*. Descending in sequence, one can see from the letters, her turns of mind about the property.

OCTOBER 29, 1959: ". . . You will be revolted when I tell you that GIANT is being tortured into a musical play. Perhaps it will never come off. I'm doing absolutely nothing about it myself. Burton Lane is doing the music. Kermit Bloomgarden is producing. God knows. Wot a world! . . ." (It never did come off.)

JANUARY 20, 1957: ". . . You seem to have liked the film GIANT better than I. Unnecessarily long; scenes (like the Mexican boy's funeral) that went on interminably; lack of pace; that final scene with the dark baby and the light baby, the black lamb and the white lamb . . ."

AUGUST 26, 1956: ". . . GIANT, after all these years and years of endless work and shooting and picking and turning this way and that is due to be released in October. It will not, I am rather sorry to say, open in Texas. I haven't seen the picture in its entirety. Only many rushes, watching the scenes come and go in the projection room on the Warner lot last year. They have tried to cut as much as possible, but it still will be a long picture. But all this brouhaha has resulted, in my opinion, in a superb picture—rich, vital, humorous and compassionate. There is, really, no star performance. It seems to me that they are all good and dimensional. Poor Jimmy Dean! They are now trying to play him down in the publicity. He has grown into a kind of dreadful cult. But nothing, I should think, can hurt his magnificent performance. Poor crazy boy, you knew when you met him that he was starcrossed. And such brilliant talent, so winning and at the same time so terrible . . ."

JULY 25, 1955: ". . . Tomorrow I'm leaving for trouble and Hollywood. They want me to see some of the GIANT rushes, which are, I'm told, very good. No, dear boy, I've seen absolutely none of the John Rosenfield pieces, I didn't even know he had written them. That's George Stevens for you! I'd love to see them, but I imagine Henry Ginsberg has them filed away, and will send me a set. I have great admiration for Mr. Rosenfield, and I'd be enormously interested in whatever he has to say. A man of taste, intelligence and vitality in writing . . . I suppose they'll open with GIANT somewhere in Texas—Dallas or Houston. I don't know. But as for me—well, I shrink from subjecting myself to the possibilities . . ."

OCTOBER 1, 1952: "David dear, you must know what your letter meant to me. I sent you GIANT because I wanted to . . . I almost never send my books out, even to friends. This book I sent—well—

to the Lunts in London; to George Kaufman and Moss Hart . . . and to four other Texans who had been so kind and generous to me . . . The reviews have ranged from very good to savage. I have developed the hide of a rhinoceros. The book is selling fantastically. For me it is a piece of work finished and that's that. If you had resented my writing it I'd have regretted it all my life . . ."

JULY 7, 1951: ". . . I wish I had your knowledge of Texas. If it weren't so hot I'd come to Stamford for the Cowboy reunion which sounds horrible and then up to Dallas for a day, but I'm not going to. Did they ever build that new million dollar hotel? Dallas is such a good town they really should have a beautiful cool modern hotel, if only to show McCarthy how to combine money with taste . . . The novel with the Texas background goes very slowly indeed. I hope to be finished by the end of September but I don't know . . ."

Joe "David" Linz remained in loving touch with Ferber long after the *Giant* thrust had diminished. He'd been important to her long before it had begun. In fact, he'd been an inextricable part of the Ferber-Fox clan. A large helping of years-ago Ferber had wanted something for him. She'd wanted him to be her nephew-in-law. She'd introduced him to her, at that time, young actress niece Janet Fox, with whom he'd fallen madly in love and had wanted to marry. It was during the Second World War. Life and love were topsy-turvy. Janet had fallen in whirlwind love and had opted to marry a young Berlin-born fellow named Henry Goldschmidt, who was an interrogation officer working for the American side. Joe Linz, crushed by her decision, wrote an anguished letter to Ferber, saying that he'd never, ever get over it. The disappointment of Janet's choice was just as large on Ferber's part, but she managed to comfort Joe as best she could. Her letter shows that she knew something about matters of the heart.

"Joe dear, I've thought about you daily, as you must know, and your letter has been read by me more than once. I needn't tell you that from the day I met you in that murky restaurant where I was having my solitary lunch I thought, well, that's the lad I'd like to have in my family and I wonder if he'd fall for Janet or Mina, maybe. I'm not being unfair to Henry when I say that I hoped it would be you. You know, I never met Henry Goldschmidt until the day before the wedding. He seems to me to be a fine lad, intelligent, amusing, good-looking, possessed of taste and sound sense.

Janet seems to be really happy, so that's that. Henry's people are darlings. But I still wish it had been you.

"Janet has been a terribly mixed-up girl these past two or three years. I think I know the reason for Janet's final decision. I think she was torn with indecision almost to the last. Some day I may be able to tell you something of this. But by that time, dear boy, you'll be married to a terrific girl and when I say Janet you'll say, 'Janet? Oh, yes, of course. And how is Janet?' . . .

". . . My love to you, dear Joe. I am certain that by now you have made an adjustment. If you haven't you will. I have an annoying theory that these blows have a meaning and that, if one just accepts the long view it becomes plain that what seemed to be wrong really was right. If that sounds infuriating I'm sorry. I myself have seen it come to pass so many, many times. My love to you, dear dear Joe."

Ferber had the power of generosity. She would pay for Janet's analysis, the children's school tuitions and summer camps, family trips, abroad and domestic; she would give her sister Fan a gift of fifty thousand dollars from the *Giant* proceeds; she would give Molly Hennessy a trip back to Ireland. On whim, she would buy an entire set of blue airplane luggage for a couple whom she had met in Anchorage, Alaska. And, she would deliver a movie star to a nine-year-old with chicken pox.

It's a vague memory—more dream-like than circumstantial. It was 1955. For a reason unknown, some of the stars of *Giant* had congregated in New York. There was to be some sort of a party, or gathering, at Ferber's, I believe. I was invited along with the adults. A great treat. The day before it was to be, the fever came and then the spots. I was put to bed, too sick to go, and too feverish to understand that I really couldn't. The bitter facts of the pox didn't actually hit me until my parents left for the evening and the front door slammed shut in finality. I lay in the darkened room, with all sorts of empty and full juice glasses around me, and cried. The maid came in and turned on the desk lamp. She said that I had a visitor. Mr. Dean. He must have been right behind her for he was suddenly in the room, mumbling, "Hihowareya?" He dragged over the blue desk chair and sat by my bed. He studied my pocks. "Bad case," he said. I asked him if he'd ever had them. He shrugged and said that he didn't remember. I told him not to get too close or he might catch them. He shrugged again and said that everybody should have chicken pox at least once in their lives. Then he gave a funny little squawk. It sent me into giggles. He asked how many chicken pox I had. I said I didn't know.

"Ya mean ya haven't counted 'em?"

"Uh-uh."

So he counted the ones on my face. He asked me if I'd read *Giant*. I said no, I was only nine. He said, "So?" Then he asked me if I liked Ferber. I told him I loved her. He nodded, as if in approval, and then said, "If ya do, ya better read her stuff."

Then he drank some of my juice and was gone.

Although fairy godmother to me, Ferber was often the Godfather to the rest of her family. And to herself—well, she cast herself in many roles. Her favorite being a breadwinning Mother Courage. Her diaries constantly chronicle how she felt about shouldering her burden—valiant and oppressed at the same time. Entry—March 1, 1956: "Worked. To Ernst office at 3—to 5. arranged additional sum of $1413 each to Fan-Jan-Mina. Fan's doctor bills, house (country) etc. I hope that in one more year of work I may be out from under this avalanche."

Ferber was not a great quotation user; she was more often quoted than quoting. She did, however, have two selections—one from Kipling and one from Maeterlinck—the themes of which she used in her daily life. Both deal with female superiority—male inferiority.

> For the woman that God gave him, every fiber
> of her frame
> Proves her launched for one sole issue, armed and
> engined for the same;
> And to serve that single issue, lest the
> generations fail,
> The female of the species must be deadlier than
> the male.
>
> Rudyard Kipling
> "The Years Between"

And from Maeterlinck's *The Life of the Bee:*

". . . Aware, it would seem, that nature's laws are somewhat wild and extravagant in all that pertains to love, it tolerates, during sum-

Ferber at her most photogenic after having written A Peculiar Treasure, *1938.*
(George Platt Lynes)

Noel Coward and Ferber.

Ferber, Julia Ferber, and Janet Fox going abroad aboard the Kungsholm, *1933.*

Ferber's favorite picture, 1936.

Ferber's darling "Mossie"—Moss Hart, 1932.

Jed Harris, 1927.

Sam Goldwyn and Ferber side by side, but not coming to terms—Hollywood, 1935.

Sinclair "Red" Lewis.

Rhett Bromfield

Scarlett O'Ferber

A dark-haired Ferber (photo by Arthur Muray) and sketch from photo by Ruth Hammond, 1933.

Alexander Woollcott and Ferber as sketched by James Montgomery Flagg.

mer days of abundance, the embarrassing presence in the hive of three or four hundred males, from whose ranks the queen about to be born shall select her lover; three or four hundred foolish, clumsy, useless, noisy creatures, who are pretentious, gluttonous, dirty, coarse, totally and scandalously idle, insatiable, and enormous.

"But after the queen's impregnation, when the flowers begin to close sooner and open later, the spirit one morning will coldly decree the simultaneous and general massacre of every male."

During the fifties, Ferber rather passively contented herself with the companionship of couples such as the Bennett Cerfs, the Richard Rodgerses, the Moss Harts, the Russel Crouses; fine, stimulating widowed women such as Peg Pulitzer and Margalo Gillmore, and, the ubiquitous, subservient Molly Hennessy.

Ferber would go to and give dinners for the couples. There was a certain familiarity of loving contempt among Ferber and all of them. They knew her foibles, and she didn't let them forget theirs.

The Cerfs were invited to Ferber's for dinner one evening. Bennett Cerf demanded in a mock-browbeating way that she serve steak. Ferber announced that she was going to have squab and that was all there was to it. At 3:00 P.M. on the day of the dinner, a large, slightly bloody package was delivered to the Cerfs' apartment. It was five pounds of uncooked steak.

One night at the Rodgerses', after dinner, Richard Rodgers decided to lie down on the floor. Ferber, feeling that his behavior was irresponsible, eyed him coldly and said, "Oh, for God's sake, Dick, get up." It was his house, his floor—but he got up.

Ferber was at the Crouses' for dinner one time. She was grousing about the state of the country and its lack of intelligent leadership. "Well, I'll just have to run for President," she announced.

Lindsay Ann, the Crouses' daughter, spoke up. "Oh, Miss Ferber," she said, "not President. I like to think of you more as an elder statesman."

Ferber drew herself into a false rage. "I am going to remove the emerald stomacher from my will, Lindsay Ann," she snorted.

Ferber didn't believe in going to the theatre alone. "Other than Mad King Ludwig of Bavaria I never have known or heard of anyone who preferred to sit alone at entertainment," she writes in a small, private treatise on the theatre. "Half the enjoyment of a play, a lecture, a picture is what is known as audience participation. Anyone who has ever seen a performance in an empty theatre—or even in a half-filled auditorium—knows the clammy silence that blights full enjoyment. Appreciation, transference of any emotion, is an infectious thing."

Her favorite theatre escort was Noel Coward when he was in town. Often, instead of going to some poshery for dinner, they would have soup and sandwiches at Ferber's, and chat at each other like mad. They shared the same sentiment about the theatre—devotion. Most of their correspondence was taken up with being "mad about the play" or mad at the play—whichever play was in play. In a letter to Coward, Ferber wrote:

". . . My feeling about the theatre is so strong, I am so exhilarated when I am working in it at one moment and so despondent the next that I think I act without caution, like a person in love . . . I have, I suppose, lived the life of a stage-struck Jewish nun: working very hard, occasionally running around doing good deeds: Footloose but the hands tied to the typewriter for hours daily . . ."

Coward wrote back: "Dear Blighted Bernhardt . . ."

When Coward wasn't available to go to the theatre with her, there were always people who were. One of them being her sister Fan—but to no avail. Ferber didn't like to go to the theatre with Fan. She would get Fan all the tickets she wanted but would rarely attend with her. Fan had a deviated septum, resulting in a drip from the tip of her nose over which she had no control. The condition seemed to flare up, for some strange reason, in the theatre. She would sit and drip for three acts. As a further irritant, she would hold her bag in her lap, causing the drip to plop. The whole process created such havoc in Ferber that the play, whatever it was, would be ruined for her. Fan, oblivious to her drippings, would enjoy the thing immensely. Ferber's fury was paved whenever she went to the theatre with Fan. So she didn't. On Fan's side of the fence, she didn't much relish appearing in public with Ferber either. Similar in looks, she used to say that she felt like the twin who didn't have the Tony. They didn't hate each other as much as they were unhappy that they loved each other. It was a conundrum for both.

Ferber, for all her supposedly celebrated life, had a forlorn epitaph for December 31, 1955:

"Not bad, not good, this 1955. The Alaska trips the best part of it, though wearing. But I'm well enough and reasonably happy. Dinner, oddly enough, at chinese restaurant with Molly Hennessy. In bed reading long before 12."

1954 was full of promise. She had yet to be afflicted with The Face, and she was still a young girl in her late sixties. She wrote with zest to Ken McCormick about her latest venture:

"I went to Alaska because (for your private ear) I'm interested in doing a novel whose background is the intensely interesting young purposeful people of that wild and improbable region. Today's Alaska, I mean. It has little to do with the Rex Beach-Jack London-nugget-and-dancehall Alaska. No relation, in fact."

One of the early reasons that she was endeared to Alaska was that she could get a good meal. She writes in her notes: "Alaskans know and like good food. This is almost invariably true of dimensional people. Instinctively I shy away from a person who says food-means-nothing-to-me. Such a one himself is almost certain to lack flavor, variety, and the power of vital communication."

One of the lesser reasons why no romance could have possibly burgeoned between George Kaufman and Ferber was that he couldn't have been less entranced by food. He hardly knew what he was eating, but he knew he didn't like it—most of it. Ferber despaired over him. In a letter to Kitty Hart in 1953—before her feud with Moss Hart—she wrote:

"Moss is a Problem Child about lunch. I didn't know until now that he is a no-vegetable no-fruit boy. I am horrified. He must have learned that from George K., early in their partnership."

Ferber's longtime friends were all aware and respectful of her food tooth. Rebecca West, one of the few female authors whom Ferber liked for herself and her work, sent Ferber a particularly delectable menu from the Dorchester Hotel in London, featuring such sundries as: *Le Saumon Fumé aux Crevettes de Morecambe Bay; Le Faisan d'Écosse Poêlé au Céleri et l'Ananas Voilé à l'Orientale.* She accompanied the menu with a rather taunting note, suggesting that food, marriage, and writing can be a happy blend.

"How I wish dear Edna that you had been with us. How fortunate I am to have a satisfying meal plus marriage! It makes up for everything and gives me hope that I will always deal with the greatest worry I have."

There were also dining stories about Ferber. Fanny Butcher, for years the literary critic for the Chicago Sunday *Tribune,* and a lifelong friend of Ferber, told two of such stories in her column called "The Literary Spotlight." The first is charming; the second is Ferber.

Number One: ON THE BACK OF A MENU:

"The gentleman had invited the lady—the ladies, that is—to dinner one evening in Paris . . . There were, besides me, Edna Ferber and a girl neither of us knew . . . Hendrik Van Loon took us to Voisin, one of the great restaurants of Paris . . . Above the banquettes the walls were lined with mirrors . . . Edna Ferber sat so that her back and half-profile were reflected in the mirror which Mr. Van Loon faced.

"We had a marvelous dinner, Hendrik ordered the best of the vintage wines which the famous cellar offered, out came his fountain pen, and, while he was talking, he began drawing something on the back of the menu . . . We paid no attention to him, for we all knew that what he was drawing he would either show us when it was finished or he wouldn't, and conversation about the matter wouldn't change his intent in the slightest . . . So we went on talking and soon noticed that our waiter was doing an inordinate amount of hovering . . . Soon he was joined by the wine waiter . . . Then a waiter from a neighboring table made a third onlooker . . . When the little box of paints came out and he began coloring the drawing there was great chatter among the waiters . . . It was a miracle what Monsieur was doing . . . but it was not possible, said another . . . The third, not to be outdone, countered with the French equivalent of 'But definitely.'

"Then one of the waiters, before we had a chance to look at it at all, took the menu out of Monsieur's hand and went to summon the head waiter himself . . . When that august gentleman, who had become a past master in magnificently snubbing the great and the rich, the titled and the lowly alike in the grand manner, arrived, he was, to our astonishment, radiating smiles as a fireworks pinwheel radiates sparks . . . We had been wondering if it was some venal crime which Hendrik had committed in maiming the menu . . . The head waiter wanted a largesse which he valued much more than the mere lavish tip which he knew would be his.

". . . He wanted to keep the menu, for on it there was the most beautiful little portrait of Miss Ferber's back and of Voisin's decor.

"In payment for the work of art Mr. Van Loon was personally invited to have dinner the next evening on the house . . . and the half bottle of rare burgundy which we had not consumed would, the head waiter said, be waiting for the maestro . . ."

Number Two: ". . . When I see [Edna Ferber] she always is a surprise—in the same way that Helen Hayes is a surprise. Their presence is memorable and impressive and yet both of them are small women . . . Last winter during one of her bouts of pain, Miss Ferber's weight got down to only a little more than 100 pounds . . . Apparently, she intends to stay on the lean side, for she said, 'I'm a great protein girl.' At dinner she had roast beef . . . When the waiter at the Algonquin (where she is treated like Queen Elizabeth on an official call) brought it he said, 'Roat beef medium, Miss Ferber.' . . . That was the title of one of her most successful books, and when I remarked on the waiter's subtlety she said, with a twinkle in her eye, 'I pay them handsomely for that.'"

Not only did Ferber dwell on food for pleasure, she doted on it for the fuel necessary to do all that she felt she had to. She was an activist author all of her life, but aside from that, she could be called a political activist when she believed in something or against something—believed in someone or against someone. She believed in Adlai Stevenson, and along with Dorothy and Richard Rodgers and several of her other liberal "celebrity" friends, she stumped for him in his Presidential race of 1952. She gave time, money, and deep compassion to the governor of her beloved Illinois, champion of the underdog, and antagonist of Joseph McCarthy. When Stevenson lost the election, he thanked her saying, ". . . You have done me a great honor and if I have your respect and confidence I am both rewarded and challenged . . ."

After all their efforts, Ferber wrote a note of proud defeat to the Rodgerses:

". . . Today I've been thinking of the good things that have emerged from all this, dear Dickie and Dorothy, such as the selflessness, devotion and courage with which you both fought to bring about the greatest possible good for the greatest number of people. It has somehow helped me to know that with only one or two exceptions my friends were the people who were working for no material gain, no reduction in taxes, no cheaper prices, no accumulation of possessions. The volunteers for Stevenson did a superb job. The Democratic party deliberately killed them. Well sir, I'm proud to know you."

Ferber shied away from appearing or speaking in public unless it was toward a cause. She agreed to speak about Stevenson, the day of election eve, on the Mary Margaret McBride radio program. The speech is pure Ferberese—powerful, communicative, and ruthlessly honest.

"Right now I may as well break down and confess to you that I'm not on this program today because I wanted to talk about my novel GIANT. People seem to be reading this book and finding it interesting and that's wonderful for me. I wrote it because I wanted to write it, and I wrote it as honestly as I knew how. It took me years because it was a difficult and complicated book to write.

"What I really want to say is so much more important to you and to me than any book written by me for your reading. There's a subject about which we're all talking and thinking and debating in our minds and souls. I've lived through a lot of presidential campaigns but I've never witnessed anything like this one. The men and women of the United States are searching the very spirit within them to decide who shall be the next President of the United States. We know that these next four years will not only be important in the history of our country. They may decide the fate of the world. What you decide is vital to billions of people. Not millions. Billions. It will be vital to the people of India. Of China. England. The captive countries of Poland, Hungary, Czechoslovakia. It may be the test of the survival of civilization itself.

"There is a saying that when a great man is needed in time of crisis in the United States he always somehow, miraculously, appears. And he has appeared. This man, Adlai Stevenson, fits the period in which we live. Here is a man of compassion, courage, wisdom and deep integrity. He doesn't even faintly resemble those old boys who are vainly trying to turn back the clock, and who don't even know what time it is. Here is a man who is a practical diplomat. Here is a man who is a politician in the best sense of the word. Here is a worldly man, and by that I mean a man who knows his world. Here is a quiet, highly intelligent, modern debunked man with a firsthand knowledge of the United States and Europe. Here is a man who knows civil affairs because for years he has worked in them and who knows foreign affairs because he has worked in them too as an emissary from the United States.

"In these past five months Adlai Stevenson has spoken a lot of words and every one of them has made sense. You must have noticed that he has promised no party, no state, no group anything. He has stood before powerful organizations and he has promised them nothing. He has said 'I do not own you and you do not own me. I promise you nothing as a group. When and if I am elected President of the United States I shall think and work only in terms of the greatest good for the greatest number of men, women and children in this country, regardless of pressure groups.'

"It takes courage to talk like that on the eve of a presidential election. There are two kinds of men who come courting the woman they hope to marry. The one is a rather romantic figure. Sort of sweeps you off your feet. He promises you the sun and the moon and the stars. He promises you the diamonds the furs and the cars. He hasn't got them. But he promises them. The other fellow says, look, I'll work and live for you the very best I know how. I won't promise you dazzling things but if ever I can honestly get them they'll be yours. But I won't promise what I haven't got. Maybe he isn't such a romantic figure, that one. But he wears awfully well in the long run.

"Then there's the fellow who says, honey, I know you don't think much of the fellows I'm running around with and I don't think much of them, either, and after we're married I'll reform, I won't see them anymore. But you know that the man who doesn't reform before marriage isn't going to reform after he's got his girl. He'll always be asking what the boys in the back room will have. It's the boys in the back room who'll have him roped and tied and who'll be running his life. You'll be hearing the boys in the back room, loud and reviling. Weigh well what they are trying to sell you, for it is loaded with hate and self-seeking and fear. And the worst of these is fear.

"They tell me that women more than men listen to the program of Mary Margaret McBride. I'm not talking to you as women, or as wives or mothers or sweethearts of men, because I know that the woman of today votes not merely as a woman but as an intelligent civilized human being, a prideful and grateful citizen of a free country."

Ferber never underestimated the value of free speech; she used it for all it was worth. She admired others who spoke out, who had convictions, whether she agreed with them or not. During the HUAC (House Un-American Activities Committee) hearings, for instance, Lillian Hellman was at one of Ferber's dinner parties.

Ferber wasn't in accord with many of Hellman's beliefs. She certainly wasn't supportive of the fact the Hellman had taken the Fifth Amendment, but she believed in Hellman's right to do so. Anna Crouse remembers that it was a particularly stimulating evening. "Edna was always open for disagreement," she said.

Ferber provoked her enemies and stimulated her friends. Frank Sullivan, in a letter to her corresponding with the Stevenson-Eisenhower Presidential race, opens fire on the same issues which bothered Ferber. Would that his pen had been his sword.

". . . I wish that I had been with you on election night . . . From your account all the angels were there; all the people on whose side I am, and whom I'd want to have on my side. I turned off my own radio pretty early as I saw no good depressing myself with what was obviously going to be a steady stream of bad news. But all we can do is keep our fingers crossed, or more constructively, to get right down on our knees and pray that it won't be as bad as it looks. I wrote Swope I thought a Rep[ublican] victory would be the worst thing to happen in this country since Harding's election. I hope I'm wrong. Eisenhower is certainly going to be surrounded by a choice collection of pratts but-silver lining-some of them will be missing. Then I can always think back to the most comical thing, if any, that happened during the campaign—the ineffable Walter Lippmann's column whose theme was that if the Democrats (though don't misunderstand Walter, he liked Stevenson, but On The Other Hand) would only be good sports and let the Republicans win this time everything would be all right but it would be awful if the Reps didn't win, because then they'd have a tantrum. You may have seen the column. So help me, that was his theme, in essence.

"And I can't remember when we have had a phenomenon in this country like this victory-in-defeat of Stevenson . . . From the time of Stevenson's acceptance speech—even from the time of the short welcome speech he made at the opening of the convention—I was his man. At first I kept thinking 'It's Woodrow Wilson. He's another Woodrow Wilson' and then as I read those magnificent speeches and saw him and listened to him on the air, I thought also of Lincoln. I believe the man has caught something from that spirit at Springfield. He is a great man and I say, God give him health until he does whatever he is destined to do for this country.

"I am also praying for Ike's health, the harder whenever I think of that hard-eyed, tight-mouthed, mean little phony huckster Nixon. I think it would set back the cause of American democracy to the time of the French and Indian wars if ever he slid into the White House with Pat and Towser. (Her name is not Pat and she was not born on March 17, as he stated in an attempt to grab the Boston vote). Now if I may permit myself the luxury of some more good out-and-out malice, may I say that another prominent poop in a campaign that was certainly well stocked with poops was La Stevenson, the ex-wife, although I must admit that in my Poop Stakes it was a photo finish with her and John Roosevelt and that Joan of Arc of the new Republicanism, Al Smith's daughter Emily. The least that the unattractive ex-Mrs. Stevenson could have done in the interests of good taste and good sportsmanship would have been to keep her trap shut. No matter how she may feel about Gov. Stevenson she might have taken a little trouble to avoid embarrassing those nice kids, her sons, who obviously worship their father. And, Edna, why didn't the Roosevelts drown John and Elliott years ago, while there was yet time?

"Most of the lace curtain Irish seem to have gone Republican but I am only bog Irish (and a lot of THEM like McCarthy) and I still think the old-fashioned word loyalty is a pretty good word. I was thrilled way back in 1912 by what Wilson had to say when he was campaigning against the colorless Taft and the blustering, humorless Teddy, but I couldn't vote that year. In 1916 I could, and between Hughes and Wilson, guess who I picked. And I have voted for the Democratic Presidential nominee every time since, except this time when I couldn't get to the polls. Without, I hope being a bigoted, closed-mind Democrat I believe any, or at least most, progress we have seen has been accomplished by that party.

"What is this, a sermon? Lay off, Sullivan! I was delighted to see GIANT on top in the Herald Tribune last Sunday and you are to stay there as long as Herman Wouk did. Eighty weeks or so, I believe. Love, Frank."

In these years, when Ferber wanted to get away from it all, she often went abroad instead of just to Arden's. She would make meticulous plans beforehand so that nothing—not reservations, not plane connections, not climate, not even fate—could possibly go awry. Things always went wrong anyway. *Giant* had finally been completed, and in 1952, before its release, Ferber took off for Paris,

London, and Switzerland. She wrote diligently to her family, like a semihomesick child away at summer camp. Snippets from the following letters give an idea of what she was like when she was off alone on vacation without her typewriter. On the top of one of the letters she writes, "I can't make words without a typewriter." She manages.

JUNE 8, 1952: "Dear Fan and any Kleins or Goldsmiths who happen to be in the vicinity:—I'm just now beginning to see out of one eye, and a small part of my mind now seems to be functioning partly. I suppose I was about as nearly exhausted as one can be without actually falling down. When I tell you that I slept eleven hours last night, straight through, you'll get a rough idea. The plane left at eight instead of six. Idlewild was a shambles. We had dinner at 9:30. We stopped at Gander instead of coming through to Paris non-stop. A dull French gent sat beside me. He slept peacefully. Instead of 28 passengers there were 45. At 2 a.m. I took a sleeping pill, woke up at 5:30 and stayed awake. As there were five hours gained between west and east it was three o'clock Paris time when we landed at Orly. Prices are simply fantastic. Compared to Paris, New York is Macy's basement. So far I've been nowhere and seen no one. I walked a mile or so along the Champs Elysees, swarming with Sunday crowds, but I didn't want to do anything more energetic or far-flung . . ."

JUNE 11, 1952: "This is just a sort of town telephone call to tell you all how I am (who asks!). Just today I began to feel a tiny bit rested. I've really done so little here because I just didn't want to put one foot in front of the other. . . . Something is wrong with Paris or with me—probably me . . . Strange objects roam the streets . . . I am longing to get away to a cool and quiet spot. Most people are going to Austria, mainly because its cheap and Switzerland expensive. But I don't think I could take it, or want to. I'm reading the final chunk of page-proofs which arrived air mail yesterday. I'll try to get them off today . . ."

JUNE 13, 1952: ". . . I am just beginning to come out of a fog. Really I haven't cared to find out if there was anyone here I knew. Then Monday night I went to dinner at the apartment of Francis Price who is Doubleday's representative in France and met Jack Laurence and Mrs. L. and a dear English (Scotch really) couple Major and Mrs. Stuart Chant. We had an evening of the most exhilarating talk. They're all connected with SHAPE. Laurence is

Eisenhower's head of Public Relations. Yesterday I ran into Danny Kaye, who is stopping here. He came up and we sat talking for two hours. The night before he had been at Maxim's and the Duchess of Windsor (knowing he's a favorite of the English Royal Family) said, 'Are you still being funny?' So Danny from Brooklyn said, 'Yes. Are you?'

"Today I drove out to SHAPE with Mr. Price and lunched there with six British and American officers. And it was sort of unbelievable because there in the dining room were the uniformed officers of France, Belgium, Italy, Britain, the United States, Greece, Turkey, Norway, Holland, Portugal. God knows if it will work, but I do hope so."

JUNE 17, 1952: ". . . I'm to leave here June 18 for the Montreux-Palace Hotel, Montreux Switzerland. I decided on it because it isn't high (in altitude at least) and it's quiet and beautiful and I can take little side trips to a dozen lovely places from there. I hope to be there about two weeks for a real rest. London July 5 but NOT Claridges. There was confusion about the reservation and I shall be at the Savoy Hotel . . . Yesterday . . . Jennifer Goldwyn, young Sam Goldwyn's wife, (Sidney Howard's daughter) called for me in her car, with a young television director named Norris Houghton. We drove to their place at Chateau Fort for lunch. It's the other side of Versailles. He is with SHAPE. They live in an incredible old French tower that looks like a stone silo. It once was a watch tower, incredible and, I should think, awfully uncomfortable . . ."

JUNE 22, 1952: "Yesterday I started out to rent a typewriter. This new-fangled writing with a pen is strange to me. I can't get the hang of it. But the typewriter turned out to be the size of a Mack Truck. And then, too, I decided that with a typewriter I'd probably go in for those long travel talks. So I gave it up . . . I have that balcony overlooking the Works but since I first knew it over a quarter of a century ago it also overlooks and over-hears a thousand motor-cycles, trucks, street cars, automobiles, motor boats. But I'm feeling better every day. I do nothing really. I sleep nine or ten hours every night. Yesterday I ambled down to the little pier and took the lake steamer to Vevey and lunched there on the lovely terrace . . . Europe is frightfully expensive but here I'm having a real bargain. For my room, bath, balcony, perfect service and three beautiful meals a day I pay only ten dollars. The meals are massive and delicious, full of huge strawberries and rich sauces and meat and fish. There is absolutely nothing to see in the shops. Even the Swiss linens are more expensive than at home. All this week there has been an annual fair in the town's main drag, with roller coaster, ferris wheels, hot dogs and howling noise. Fortunately it isn't in this direction, and it ends today . . . The hotel is full of Americans, and the things they say and do can't be believed . . . I hope you're rested and that Peter has got his reading in hand. Fan, your letter sounded very householdy. The hell with that."

JUNE 23, 1952: "Dear Fan, it came to me that you may have misconstrued the last line of my last letter, so I'm writing again (next day). When I spoke of a 'householdy letter and the hell with that' I meant that you seemed to be doing more household worrying and scurrying than you really liked. Of course, if that's what you want most to do, that's different. Still, I suppose in the final analysis we really do what we want to do, even if the doing is caused by an inner compulsion . . . I came to Switzerland because I was bored with Paris and maybe that was due to weariness . . . Here I set and I amble a little and I ride and ride and ride on the big fat white lake steamboat, a side-wheeler that just moves silently like a huge swan. I go to the next town or the one after that, and amble and look in the shop windows and have lunch on a terrace, and set, and take the steamer back. The lake and the mountains and sky are incredibly beautiful. This hotel is of a day that is gone—yet here it is, full of deep red carpets and hundreds of servants and linen sheets and the most massive meals. Lobster flown from Ostend, salmon flown from the Rhine, strawberries the size of apples, whipped cream on everything . . . A lovely letter from Henry. I think that he is a really dimensional person . . ."

JUNE 29, 1952: "Dear Fan & Mina & Bill & Janet & Henry!— . . . It was so pleasant to find your letter, among others, at my door this morning. I loved the part about Peter. He is an engaging baby and will, I think, look like Mina. Did he really keep time to your singing by waggling his foot! Good God, I hope we haven't a musician in the family. One (poor frustrated fellow) was enough. I sometimes wonder what Uncle Julius might have done with his life if he had been understood and helped. Nothing, probably. A real schizo, I'm afraid. [Note: Uncle Julius was Julius Neumann, brother of Ferber's mother Julia. The strange one of the family.]

"I am having a heavenly time here—by my standards . . . Today I'm staying in Montreux all day, which I haven't done at all, scarcely.

I make trips up and down and everywhere, especially on the lake boat which I call my private yacht. It isn't considered chic and I think most of the stuffy Montreux-Palace guests wouldn't dream of taking it. Yesterday I went to Evian, which is of course France, across the lake and beyond Lausanne. Up the mountain (but not too high of course) on the finicular to Glion . . . I know no one here but the owners of this marvelous hotel . . . and two dreadful elderly (more than me) people simply unbearable . . . I am not for a moment lonely or bored. Yesterday on my yacht I met two American school teachers who are teaching in Germany and have been for two years. Teaching the children of American officers. Their stories would curl your hair like Astrakhan. I'm sitting up on my little balcony overlooking the lovely park, the lake and the Alps. Lots of noise below but I don't seem to mind."

Ferber was a fanatic about cleanliness. To her, it sat on the lap of godliness. Anything that wasn't spanking clean was germ-ridden filth. Switzerland, known to be surgically clean, must have turned her head, for when she got home to New York, she publicly condemned it as being one of the filthiest cities in the country—perhaps in the world. Coming off the ship at the Forty-second Street pier, she told a handful of reporters that New York should be ashamed of itself—what with air pollution, noise pollution, and garbage pollution—it was an unfit environment to live in and certainly to bring children up in. She blasted the Mayor, the sanitation workers, and private citizens who just didn't care. Her rampage carried onto the front page of the New York *Times* and other leading city newspapers the next day. It caused a furor. "'Central Park is unfit for a self-respecting goat,' she thundered. 'New York is a scab on the face of our country,' she roared." City officials were embarrassed; and members of the Sanitation Department picketed outside her Park Avenue building. She didn't go out the next day—not even for her ritual walk—and didn't receive any phone calls. She felt a victim of her own outspokenness. Kate Steichen, still with Doubleday at that time, cooked up a scheme to bring her around:

"Miss Ferber had certainly spoken her piece, which was short and not too sweet, as was her wont. When we got into the office the next morning, we began to get phone calls, repercussions and all that sort of thing. Miss Ferber wasn't taking any phone calls or anything. She could not be reached. I went in to Ken McCormick and said, 'Do you think we would dare send one of the mail boys up to Miss Ferber's this morning with one of those tremendous street cleaner brooms with a bouquet of brilliant pink roses tied to it?' I knew it was a calculated risk, that she might blow her top, but we had to get through to her somehow. So Ken thought about it and shortly after lunch he said, 'Go ahead. Do it, do it.' So I sent one of the kids out, and she came back with this big old broom, and the florist sent up a sheef of brilliant pink roses, and I got a hold of pink ribbon and tied it. Then I sent this sweet, gentle little mail boy in a cab up to her apartment. He rang the bell and the maid answered the door, and there he was just standing there with the broom. The maid called out, 'Oh, Miss Ferber, come quick! Come and see!' So Miss Ferber did because the maid didn't call out to her that often. When she saw it, she burst into laughter—as the mail boy described to us later. But the picture of that gentle little mail boy standing there with his broom—I thought maybe she'd chop his head off—but no, she loved it."

Ferber singlehandedly launched the antilitter campaign that goes on in New York today.

New York knew what Edna Ferber thought of it, as did Alaska and Texas. She could make states—and break them. Rock Hudson gives her stature in the name of the property which gave him his: "She was a giant lady, truly."

GIANT YEARS
1952-1938

FERBER HAD never meant to write *Giant*. She told everybody so. She shouldn't do it. She wouldn't do it. She couldn't do it. For the only time in her life she applied to it feminine illogic. Writing a novel about Texas was a man's job. "Let Michener write it," she said rather sulkily. When she finally conquered it, she felt the need to explain how and why she had.

"GIANT, the novel, was the result of a haunt. Like any other specter it had to be exorcised by the customary mumbo-jumbo before its victim could be free of it. There is only one method by which a writer can be rid of a haunting subject, no matter how stubbornly resistant. The ghostly nuisance must be trapped and firmly pinned down on paper so that its wails and moans concerning neglect are forever stilled, its clammy touch on the consciousness banished. Many a woman has married an importunate childhood sweetheart in her later years just to be rid of his beguiling memory.

"GIANT, in the guise of Texas, haunted me for a decade or more. I shrank from it, I shuddered to contemplate the grim task of wrestling with this vast subject. Finally I wrote it to be rid of it.

"Texas of the 1930's and 1940's was constantly leaping out at one from the pages of books, plays, magazines, newspapers. Motion pictures of Texas background were all cowboys and bang-bang. Texas oil, Texas jokes, Texas money billowed out of that enormous southwest commonwealth . . ."

(Ferber made effective use of the word commonwealth in the novel. It's Rock Hudson's favorite passage, and it occurs when

Leslie Benedict, the heroine, a new bride brought to Texas, looks around at the vastness and says, "Commonwealth, commonwealth, common wealth.")

"The rest of the United States regarded it with a sort of fond consternation. It was the overgrown spoiled brat, it was Peck's Bad Boy of today, it was the crude uncle who had struck it rich. In a brief interval of semi-idleness and mental vacuity that occurs now and then in the life of all writers I decided to go down and have a look at this southwest phenomenon as one might travel to gaze upon the Grand Canyon. This Texas represented a convulsion of nature, strange, dramatic, stupifying.

"That first visit was in April, and it was accomplished by train, not air travel. Unbelievably now, air travel at that time was not casual as it is today. The journey from New York on the Atlantic seaboard to Houston so near the Gulf of Mexico was arduous and tedious even for a traveler who used to enjoy watching America slide past a train window. The temperature in Houston was in the high nineties, the old Rice Hotel was a mass of gigantic beef-fed men in ten-gallon hats and high-heeled boots and dun-colored clothes. In the residence section of the oil-rich there were the most glorious azalea gardens; and in practically every city and town one encountered the worst food to be found anywhere in the United States. Tough beef and fried everything. Houston, Dallas, San Antonio, all interesting, somewhat improbable; brash, overwhelming, hospitable, larger than life. No visitor, casual though he might be, could fail to feel the almost fierce vitality that rocked the whole vast region. Here was something that was being built and enjoyed at the same time; here were arrogance and hard work, and almost stupifying riches spurting out of the earth in the form of oil, cattle, crops.

"But I'll have nothing to do with all this, I said to myself. No, thank you. Nothing could ever induce me to try to pin this giant down on paper. This Gulliver would require a whole army of Liliputians, this Goliath needs a David. I want none of it.

"Years passed. I wrote an autobiography, three or four novels, two plays. I could not put Texas out of my mind. Improbable events, incredible people, fantastic incidents boiled up out of Texas. The effluvia penetrated every corner of the United States. The inner urge to try to pin down on paper this incredible form of civilization called Texas became irresistible. Ten years after my first visit I returned to Texas, this time by air. Brownsville on the Mexican border; Dallas, the north Texas fashion center; the Panhandle; little cow-towns; colonies of wetbacks living in wretchedness. Oil wells, ranches, shacks; fiestas, frijoles, champagne, tequila; the college professor, the grease-monkey, the rancher; the old city of San Antonio, the overnight oil town just rearing its frowsy head above the desert. Texas. Exhilarating, violent, charming, horrible, fascinating, shocking, Texas alive. A giant."

Alternative: The second version of how she came to write *Giant*. It's more dense, more flavorful, but perhaps too much.

"For many years I, together with millions of residents of the United States, had read and heard incredible accounts of the goings-on in a somewhat mythical area called Texas. This was during the 1920's and 1930's, that falsely quiescent period between two World Wars. One heard fantastic stories of million-acre ranches; of oil wells spurting where only desert had held barren reign; vaqueros complete with silver spurs and chin-straps; strange new breeds of cattle, humped and creamy-coated, like creatures out of mythology; bizarre palaces rearing their turrets on the prairies; million-a-week incomes; privately owned planes; huge men in great roll-brimmed Stetson hats that cost fifty dollars; bejeweled women whose fingertips had only recently lost their washtub puckers. Oil fortunes that ran not only into millions but into hundreds of millions.

"Often, in these many years of my life as a writer, I've been drawn to this or that section of the United States by a compulsion that was stronger than mere curiosity. It was, unreasonable, an urge to return to something I never actually had known. Reincarnationists may have an explanation for this. The places to which I travel with a pleasant excitement born of eager anticipation I invariably enjoy—and with a double enjoyment of inexplicable recognition. The cities or countries in which I reluctantly find myself I dislike on sight, and I am wretched until I leave them. This was true of my first visit to Germany in 1914, just before the onslaught of World War I. It was true of the few days spent in Egypt in the '30's. The fields of that flat land were, in my imagination, fertilized with the dried blood of centuries; the smell of decay seemed all pervasive. My departure seemed more in the nature of escape. Perhaps, two thousand years ago, I was a little Jewish slave girl on the Nile.

"In 1939, for no discernible reason, with no definite plan, a vague itinerary and knowing no one in the entire State of Texas, I boarded a train headed for that dramatic commonwealth. Dallas was my first stop. No reason. I knew nothing of Dallas except that it boasted a fabulous shop in which one could buy pigeon-blood rubies, gossamer lingerie, rich rare furs, Paris gowns, or almost any luxury beyond the means of those who were not oil-rich Texans. Dallas's boast was well-founded, but as I had little interest in pigeon-blood rubies I moved on to less effete regions. Houston. Galveston. San Antonio. Even Brownsville on the Mexican border. It was rather hard going, especially in various smaller towns in between. Texas food is probably the worst in the present fifty states of the United States and Texas steaks are a tooth test. In that day Houston had no Shamrock Hotel, there was no omnipresent Hilton holstelry in Dallas, air-conditioning did not exist, the thermometer and the prevailing humidity hovered cosily between ninety and one hundred. Sometimes, if you were lucky, an unwieldy four-armed fan attached to the ceiling above your bed languidly muddled the hot air from one side of the room to the other.

"Yet the whole region was as virile and fascinating as it was vast. It was all drawn on a scale larger than life. There was about it a tremendous vitality. It was incredible that a whole people could possess such energy, such self-complacency, such enthusiasm for living in the midst of this hurly-burly of heat, dust, glare, great distances and much discomfort. I was interested in every minute of the trip. I was confused by it, startled, and frequently shocked by it. And I rejected it.

"Not for you, Miss F., I said. Thank you very much, but this is a man's job. Let some two-fisted hemingwayish novelist write this book of modern Texas. Compared to what you'd have to do on this in the way of research and work, the job you had to do on Cimarron in '28 was a bit of china-painting.

"So I left Texas to its sun and winds and ten-gallon hats and illimitable distances and went straight and for the first time to New Orleans. No reason for that, either, and no previous plan. Perhaps no city in the United States could have presented a more stunning contrast to the Texas towns I had just seen. Raptureously I ate the delectable food at Antoine's, strolled past miles of iron lacework and heavy-scented gardens, gay swarming food markets and incense-haunted churches. I then went home and wrote a novel called Saratoga Trunk.

"Years went by. There were novels, plays, short stories. To Europe as a correspondent briefly in the second World War. Paris on V.E. Day. Yet through the pandemonium of horror, exhilaration, work and travel the Texas experience and the Texas idea never ceased to prick my mind with sharp needles of interest, remembrance and imagined scenes, characters, situations. Wisps of possible book material would float into my consciousness, Texas-tinged, but I would shoo it out and slam the door on it. I had resolved that I definitely would not put myself through the gigantic task of familiarizing myself with this region, these people, the violent and dramatic background of this vast section of the United States. But the needling and the nudging persisted, it could not be ignored. Finally, vanquished, I gave up. There was only one way to rid myself of the Texas novel and that was to write it. So then, back to Texas. Back again, and again and again and again. Research and writing, weaving to and fro between Texas and New York, Texas and Connecticut, spinning the intricate web that makes up a book of fiction that must read like reality.

"Thirteen years after I first had thought of Texas as a background for possible novel material (and had discarded the thought) the book was finished and published in 1952. It was called GIANT.* Various other names had briefly been considered and, luckily, rejected: JILLION; BIG RICH; THUMBNAIL OF A GIANT; NO MAN IS AN ISLAND. Pretentious names, rather cheap titles.

"The novel turned out to be what is known as a controversial book—to put it mildly. But having unwittingly created such a whirlpool of praise and villification; approval and rejection, disclaimer and admiration and shouts of wrath, the writer sits as tranquil as may be. This work is finished. Nothing now can be added or subtracted. With a strange mixture of trepidation and confidence the next book, as yet unwritten, begins its nudging and needling in the writer's creative mind."

To say that in 1952 the impact of *Giant* created a tumult not only in the book world but in the real world of the United States would not be an exaggeration. It was a much-talked-about book not

* Although *Giant* was an impressive title, it didn't seem to read clearly on the dust jacket. The designer had to go through scores of changes before the word emerged as Giant instead of Ghee-ant with a hard G.

only from the standpoint of readability but of libel-ity. The entire state of Texas felt impugned by it, and it created in displaced Texans a surge of nationalistic nastiness. The reviews were some of the best Ferber ever received, and even the ones that were condemning were money reviews. Orville Prescott, who reviewed it in the New York *Times,* must have gotten a flinty smile out of her, for he knew solid reportage when he came across it. His review reads:

"Those screams of rage and anguish emanating from Texas are ridiculously exaggerated. Edna Ferber's new novel 'Giant,' is not just a vicious attack on the beauty and chivalry of our largest state. But the outraged protests certainly have been wonderful publicity. Miss Ferber might write a polite note of thanks to Carl Victor Little, book reviewer of The Houston Press, who wrote, long before its publication day, that '"Giant" is the most gargantuan hunk of monsterous, ill informed, hokum-laden hocus-pocus ever turned out about Texas.'

"Miss Ferber has always displayed an admirable knack for extremely readable narrative and a wonderful enthusiasm for soaking up the atmosphere of a particular American region and era. In 'Giant' she has paid her respects to Texas and the fabulous plutocracy of that fabulous land. She is satirical and sarcastic about certain phases of Texas life, but she is by no means always on the attack. She is fascinated by Texas as well as appalled by Texas. She likes and respects the vigor and vitality and appetite for life of many Texans. Texans with a sense of humor will be amused by 'Giant' and will readily admit that some of its barbs are aimed at thoroughly vulnerable targets . . .

". . . Its social reporting is interesting also with its detailed descriptions of customs and traditions, of skyscraper hotels surrounded by desert, of food and fashions, of ranch operations and of oil money. It is entertaining as a brisk, slick, clever, constantly moving story."

Ferber had a healthy if somewhat shy way of dealing with momentous events in her life. She played them down, behaving as though nothing unusual was happening. During the storm of *Giant's* publication, she marched herself to almost every grand New York department store and purchased things—mostly gifts for others—a hat at John Fredrick's for herself. When she was writing, she never had time to haunt the stores, which she loved to do.

When she had no time to buy, she was an avid window-shopper—especially at night, walking home after dinner. Harriet Pilpel remembers how they would stroll along, in rain or sleet or hail, they would STROLL. Ferber would "wing" Harriet and propel her to each and every brightly lit Madison Avenue window. She would always have a salient comment about the display. "That would be dazzling on a heifer," she would say, or, "I would only wear that fetching thing if I had absolutely nowhere to go."

Harriet would be asked whether she liked this or that, and in the beginning made the mistake of commenting positively on various apparel. "I think this or that is divine," she would say. Presto. The next day "this or that" would be delivered to Harriet Pilpel compliments of Edna Ferber. Soon enough, Harriet learned the subtlety of saying, "Umm," when asked.

So, with the advent of *Giant*, with Ferber's part of the work finished, there were gifts galore. She felt good—better than she ever had about completing a book, and somehow feeling better brought on the bountiful side of her. For me there was a doll's bed, for Irving Lazar and his new bride Mary there was a lavish set of Baccarat glasses, for Fan a new coat, etc. And what did Ferber the giver like to receive? Praise when at all possible and, when not possible, flowers. Praise from the friends she respected was invaluable to her, as she states in a letter to George Oppenheimer, dated September 28, 1952.

"On with your wrestling trunks, then, my hearty, for nobody knows the trouble I've seen—and am seeing—with Texas. It isn't just plain cosy villification. It is everything but actual physical bludgeoning.

"How I loved your letter, dear George. And what a good and friendly impulse it was that caused you to write it. One of the trends that I like is that letters (like your own) say that the book has held the reader. Frank Sullivan writes 'I finished it at four in the morning.' Pat Klopfer, on the Liberte Europe-bound, wrote, 'It is now 6:20 A.M., and I've just finished, etc.' I didn't know that any of them had even seen the book. It isn't published until tomorrow . . ."

Praise was fine with Ferber—as long as it was the right kind of praise. You never knew with her. The late Dan Longwell, her "publisher" during her early years at Doubleday and subsequently an editor at *Life* magazine, wrote what he thought to be a laudatory note about *Giant:*

"I read the sweep of GIANT at a lolling. I mean to say, it rained up in the country Saturday, so I simply lolled around the house and finished the manuscript in one lolling. It is enormously good. Someone should really write an adequate piece about you sometime as the great story teller that you are . . ."

Well! Not good enough. Ferber must have blasted at Longwell, for he answered her promptly with an apology—and, knowing his Edna, he lavished praises:

"I am sorry my letter about GIANT upset you. I think it is the best book you have done, but you must remember that I have long-time affections—Show Boat, for one—that are hard to minimize. I think it is the most decisive thing you have done and will create a great deal of attention and bring you great pride.

"I am sorry, too, about the 'story teller.' I happen to admire people who can write stories. So few people can. You refer to the English understanding you as a novelist perhaps better than we do. I remember Barrie's note to F.N.D.* about So Big, and you forget that I am old enough to have spent a day with Kipling at Burwash and heard him speak enthusiastically about you and Show Boat.

"In any case, won't you have lunch with me next week . . . ? I would like to do something about GIANT, whether in the pages of LIFE or not. Besides, I would like to see you . . .

"Did you ever know that I collect first editions of your books and that I do not have an autograph in any of your books on my shelves? I have always been too shy to ask for one, but I am going to be just like any other reader now and am sending you a copy of the first edition of Show Boat, which I hope you will sign for me."

He apparently knew what she wanted to hear. And people didn't seem to mind bending over backwards—although, when one could steer clear of it, one did. Moss Hart was once asked by Ferber to write a foreword to one of her books. He declined and said to Dorothy Rodgers, "I couldn't possibly do it. I might say Edna Ferber is a wonderful woman, and she would say, 'What do you mean wonderful. Of all the words in the English language, the word I most dislike is wonderful.'"

The word "whimsical" sent Ferber into a frenzy when Norman

* F.N.D. stood for Frank Nelson Doubleday, who, along with other members of his family, owned Doubleday, Page & Company.

Cousins, editor of *The Saturday Review,* applied it in defense of a book review of *Giant* he had run in the magazine, to which Ferber had taken great umbrage. It was a satirical piece, written by what Ferber termed "a Texas peanut grower and press-clipping agent." Upon reading it, Ferber sent a letter protesting the fatuous and whimsical piece, and demanded that her letter be published. Cousins refused, brushing off her fury by saying that the intent of the piece was to amuse—that nobody had taken it seriously. Ferber knew the real reason of Cousins' refusal and felt it despicable enough to upbraid him once again:

"For a long time, Norman, I've wanted to write an article entitled I ONLY WORK HERE. This is not only a phrase. It is a state of mind, a degradation of the spirit, an indication of cracked morale. The waiter who gives you soiled table utensils. I only work here. Eisenhower who clasps the hand of McCarthy and stands, a captive, while Jenner throws an arm about his shoulder. I only work here. The saleswoman who shrugs off her responsibility for an error. I only work here. Norman Cousins, whose name tops the list of editors on the Saturday Review editorial page but who has a 'hands off' policy in the matter of book reviews and who doesn't think the financial backer of his magazine—a rich Texas oil man—should be mentioned in a letter of protest. I only work here.

". . . There is nothing in my novel GIANT that would call for 'whimsicality' in a review. I have said to you—and I repeat—a book review may properly be good or bad, but its tone should fit the tenor of the book. GIANT, which represents many years of intensive work, is a novel of power, purpose, and high readability, among other excellent qualifications. It does not rate whimsical treatment. Your reviewer, incidentally, is as whimsical as a bowl of oatmeal.

"It is incredible that an incident would at once be as boring and as revolting as this one has been to me. I am certain you share my feelings. In more than forty years of creative writing it is the first in my experience.

"Also, incidentally, your reviewer misspells the name of the book's leading character, points to an explorer whose name is not mentioned in the book, refutes as untrue a hideous barbecue which I myself witnessed and endured as a guest, and which was in no way considered as unusual by the local residents; and takes it upon himself to name living characters to fit the fictional characters in my book.

"Whimsical, eh?

"I now don't care whether you run a note of correction or not. No one cares—except you. And your reason for caring should be deep and clear and considered."

Needless to say Norman Cousins was not a frequent guest at Ferber's.

Whenever Ferber was repelled by something, she was also fascinated; the two sensations were synonymous within her. She went with Marc Connelly, the playwright, down to Greenwich Village one evening to see a production of *Uncle Vanya*. Ferber was definitely not an habitué of the Village, so that to make her way down there was considered a journey of exotic proportions. Although she knew some eccentric types, she knew no beatniks—nor did she want to. She had a disconcerting habit when she saw something arresting; she would stand stock still and stare—almost like a child who knows no better. She stared a good deal in the Village that night, went home and assessed what she'd seen. Since she had no one to talk to, she always wrote out her thoughts.

THE BEATS

"They are only a throwback. When first I came to New York, back in 1913 or thereabouts, they flourished for the next fifteen or more years. They were known as Greenwich Villagers and their resemblance to the present-day beatniks, as I now recall them, was striking. They were a sort of western Road Company of the Paris Left Bank. Girls in that day didn't wear men's attire, or approximately that, on the street or, for that matter, indoors. Pants were for men. Pants, for women, were strictly underclothing articles. Women in pants on the street were subject to arrest. The girls were the same stringy-haired, spotty-skinned and painstakingly dishevelled sprites that one sees today stumbling along hand in hand with a more or less masculine replica of themselves, wending their way into some public place that was even dimmer, dirtier and more airless than their own lairs. They wrote books, plays, short stories, poetry, but spasmodically, and they talked about this and sex, exclusively. They didn't sit, they sprawled; they may have bathed but they didn't look it; they were Free Souls. They drank a lot and ate whatever messes were available. Some few of them turned out to be greatly talented whereupon they moved out of Greenwich Village, washed their hair, dressed up and ate steak.

"Then along came the Marquands, the Hemingways, the Sinclair Lewises, Steinbecks, Faulkners and the ladylike daughter of the missionaries, Mrs. Pearl Buck. Well, Brooks Brothers and scotch and white pillared mansions and 'Twenty-One.' The Greenwich Villagers vanished, were comic valentines as obsolete as the old-time comic valentines (which now, too, seem to have been revived in postcard form).

"Now, born of fear and insecurity and rebellion against who-knows-what, here they are again, in their spotted clothes, with their spotted faces, the girls in pants, tight, the boys in jeans or black legging-tight sheaths, talking the same jargon. It's like the revival of an old play that wasn't very charming when it was new."

The antithesis of a beatnik was Helen Keller, whom Ferber had more admiration for, perhaps, than fondness, and whom she saw sporadically throughout the years. They had met through Eleanor Roosevelt, and because of her each believed their acquaintance to be sacred. After a day spent together, which Ferber wrote in her diary was "rewarding," Helen Keller sent a kindly note to Ferber:

"Dear Edna Ferber, Words cannot express the pleasure Polly and I felt in having you with us Wednesday evening. My only regret was that I had not had a chance to read your 'The Giants,' knowing as I do the 'high and mighty' attitude of many Texans.

"It was enlightening to hear you talk on delinquency. Often I brood on this fundamental problem, and I confess that it bewilders and saddens me unutterably, but I never lose my faith that good men and women everywhere will work together for solutions of our fearful social problems that will bring safety and peace to future generations.

"What a sweet thought your gifts to Polly and me were! As we taste the caviar, the candies, the cheese and other delicacies, we smile gratefully to think that you should remember our little, yet important delights which lend charm to a day's routine. We thank you ever so much. With warmest greetings from both, I am, Helen Keller."

Ferber shared a somewhat livelier relationship with the rapier-sharp humor columnist Franklin P. Adams, who had his seventieth birthday on November 15, 1951. In his honor, an all-male Pipe Night was given at the famed Players in New York, and, in special homage, Adams' friends made up a program that was a take-off on his newspaper column "The Conning Tower"—to which each contributed some sally or other. The flavor of the thing harks back to what was known as "the wit of the Algonquin crowd"—clever, cunning, slightly archaic and terribly sophisticated. A sampling of what good fun they had at Adams' expanse rather than his expense:

To know F. P. Adams
Is worth ten Call Me Madams
HOWARD LINDSAY AND RUSSEL CROUSE

WHEN FRANK WAS ONE-and-FORTY

When Frank was one-and-forty
And Smeed was in the Tower
The morns were fair and lusty—
This was our finest hour.
We wrote with endless patience
And seldom paid with rue,
And I was two-and-twenty,
And, Baby, so were you.

Now I am two-and-fifty
And Frank is God knows what;
The morns are dark and empty,
The press has gone to pot.
So let us toast the master,
And build again the Tower
Where Frank was in his heaven
And Muse was in her bower!
E. B. WHITE

AaRONS

His mood was not portentous,
His strength was rhymes, not reams,
He shunned the lads momentous,
For Flaccus, Woollcott, Deems.

The colyum was a showcase
For Kaufman, Marc, and Bob,
And definitely no place
For fool or heel or snob.

The quip or mot pedestrian
Could never win a Stet!
These verses then, sans question
Would rate the oubliette.

EDNA (FERBER)

FROM the LADIES

Dear FPA, your natal day
Fills us with feelings tender,
Though we deplore, as oft of yore,
Our inconvenient gender.

Do gals not smoke, enjoy a joke,
And hold their own as bibbers?
Why segregate on this glad date
Us feminine contribbers?

Fain would we raise a glass in praise
Of one whose rare acumen
Welcomed to print a virtual mint
Of verse from man AND woman.

We'd planned to bake a gala cake
Of seventy luscious layers
Had we been bid to join you, Kid—
And heaven help the Players!

Included out, not ours to pout,
But, whether miss or missus,
We join to send to you, old friend,
Our birthday love and kisses.

SQUIDGE
(better known as Dorothy Parker)

Ferber and her friends believed that plenty was in a name and they were playful with each other's monikers. It was a form of expressing affection, and, when they jousted with their own names, a form of self-esteem. Ferber was a great doler-out of, and often the butt of name-calling. In the early days, her salutation on letters to her family was "Dear Foxies," to her sister Fan it was "Dear Orrea" (origin?), to Janet it was "Jan-Face," to Mina "Dear Minnow." As time went on, the "Jan-Face" and to me "Jewel-Face" simply became "Face." "Dear Face," she would begin her letters. With friends such as Noel Coward, Dorothy Rodgers, Frank Sullivan, and Alexander Woollcott she would sign off as "Schleppe" or "E. Feldman."

Dorothy Rodgers and Ferber had a special name-calling repartee that they used as a code of endearment. "You could get away with a lot with Edna if you kidded her," says Mrs. Rodgers. "I used to call her Fannie all the time because she hated Fannie Hurst, and she used to call me Bertha or Bella. My middle name is Belle and she found that out. A great deal of my letters (from her) were addressed to Bella."

Of all the "name-tinkerers" Frank Sullivan was probably the most expert, with Alexander Woollcott a close, if more venomous, second. Sullivan, in one of his letters to Ferber, writes:

"Miss Ferber, alanna, Correct me if I'm wrong but I believe alanna means honey in Gaelic, and you called me spalpeen. I am going to look that up and if it's a crack, I'll sue you. I think it's all right, though, because if you scorned me or anything you'd have called me omadhaun, pronounced omathawn, and it means schlemmiel. Okay, alanna . . ." And he signs off with, "The Man You Adore. Frankel Solomon."

And in another Sullivan letter: "I think of you always, with fervor. Well it's time I thought of Edna Fervor, is what I say to myself daily . . ."

Alexander Woollcott, during the time when he and Ferber were still friends, signed off with many amusing aliases in his letters to her—his pet one being "Amoeba W." Another was "Emmy Lou." In a letter of 1920, he addressed her as "Darling Egg-beater," and ended with, "Yours to toy with and cast aside like a broken doll—Nicholas Murray Butler." His P.S. in yet another letter read:

"The enclosed nosegay is not an artificial flower made of Carleton flannel but a sprig of Edelweiss, which withers never. Henry W. Longfellow."

Then there was a small boy who went so far as to name an inanimate object Edna Ferber.

Ruth Hammond, a well-known stage actress during the "Algonquin Age" and a friend of Ferber's, recalls that Ferber was always terribly generous toward other people's children. Always gifts —and elaborate ones. Once she sent the son of Ruth Hammond and her husband, Donald McDonald, a china bulldog from Harrods department store in London. The child was entranced with it, taking it everywhere—even out on the street for a walk. One summer's evening, the boy was out on the street a few paces away from the brownstone house where he lived, accompanied by his bulldog. Alexander Woollcott was happening down the same street on his way to the McDonalds'. A casual friend of theirs, he had not met their child, and therefore thought he was a neighborhood kid—anybody's kid. "What a nice doggie you have there," he said avuncularly to the child. "Thank you," the McDonald boy replied solemnly, stroking the toy dog. Woollcott bent down with all his girth. "And what's your doggie's name?" The boy looked squarely at the florid man who was trying to make nice. "Edna Ferber," he said. Woollcott reeled back, and only later upon finding out who the child belonged to, did he think the name somewhat fitting.

Ferber, being a controversial figure, was used to—if never inured to—being criticized and called names. However, sticks and stones thrown and threats made were a new and bewildering experience for her. Immediately after *Giant* was written, Texas was out for her hide. What with her quote of, "Texas is as big as the Texans minds are small," the State of Texas shore didn't want to call her pardner. They wanted to lynch her, or at least Carl Victor Little, who reviewed the novel for *The Houston Press*, suggested that scaffold tactics might be a good idea. And a man named Lon Tinkle,* who was the book editor of the Dallas *Morning News*, reviewed the book, slicing Ferber up as though she was a steer ready for the kill:

"FERBER GOES BOTH NATIVE AND BERSERK: PARODY, NOT PORTRAIT, OF TEXAS LIFE.

"Writing about Texas (or a fragment of it) in her latest novel 'Giant,' Miss Edna Ferber has gone native. Trouble is she has spoiled it by also going berserk.

"This 'native' streak appropriated by Miss Ferber is the passion

* Lon Tinkle was a powerful figure around Dallas. Although he wrote a scathing review of *Giant*, there is no evidence that Ferber held a personal vendetta against him. He also wrote a book called *Mr. D*, which was about a Dallas man named Everett DeGolyer, who was an incredibly wealthy oil geologist and who bought the original failing *Saturday Review* simply because he enjoyed it and didn't want it to fold.

for hilarious exaggeration, the irresistible impulse to turn everything into a 'tall tale.' For sheer embroidery of fact—an art at which Texans are rarely surpassed—Miss Ferber takes the cottonseed cake. She has us all riding around in our own DC-6's. At first blush, you might call it, her book on ranch and oil empires of South Texas reads like a parody of that grand old melodrama, 'A Texas Steer.'

"But Miss Ferber's is a bum steer . . .

"What Miss Ferber finds wrong with Texas is precisely what is wrong with the rest of the world. But having gone native, she reduces our Texan braggadocio to absurdity: she gives us a monopoly on everything. Texas, first in oil, in cotton, in cattle, in size—and first in villainy. Now, now, Miss Ferber, you aren't writing 'Uncle Tom's Cabin.'

"But part of Miss Ferber's confusion is that she doesn't seem really to know what she's trying to write. Her novel sounds off about Texans in general, but obviously this is a 'key' novel written out of hatred. As in all 'key' novels, all novels that present actual living persons and gossip about them in transparent disguise, imagination goes overboard and what you have is a sort of mongrel biography, neither flesh nor fish but indisputably foul.

"Many readers will buy 'Giant' because of the quick identity of many conspicuous and prominent Texas names, some mentioned directly—such as Glenn McCarthy, the Klebergs, King Ranch, Neiman-Marcus and others disguised but as recognizable as your pastor playing Moses in the church pageant this National Bible Week.

"All we can tell you about that is that the chief villain, one Jett Rink who built the famous hotel Conquistador on the outskirts of the big city of Hermosa from his oil profits, is clearly Simon Legree. Not since the days of Little Eva has American literature harbored such a ruthless heel.

"Then, in addition to being a key novel, 'Giant' is meant to be a novel. This is where it fails most conspicuously . . . Third, it is a catalogue of what's wrong with Texas.

"Here are a few items in that catalogue:

"Item one: Texas women are spoiled and exhibitionistic. They all wear 'overbred furs', refuse to fly to parties in tacky little old two-motor jobs, they all shrill instead of speak, their voices are high-pitched and unpleasant, they waste most of the day in gossip and they know nothing about the art of cooking.

"Item two: All Texas men are outsize and outgrown, they resent having anyone prying into their private lives, they are all 'beef-fed' (Miss Ferber has a positive fixation on 'beef-fed' but still her vegetarianism doesn't make us think of her in the same breath with George Bernard Shaw), Texas men invariably withdraw from the women at parties and prefer to talk among themselves.

"Item three: All Texans down absurd quantities of hot coffee and waste a good portion of the day in its consumption. And yet Miss Ferber constantly compares Texas crudity with the leisurely and charming life of Virginia. What do they drink there in their leisure?

"But there are too many to enumerate. These items mentioned, of course, concern primarily Texas mores and manners. In general, Miss Ferber presents examples of these traits on a comic-strip level, with her characters (including some trained at Harvard and Wellesley) talking the same hillbilly argot as Li'l Abner and Daisy Mae.

"On a deeper level, Miss Ferber scores two direct hits. What she says about voting practices and political combines in South Texas is almost daily verified in the news; and her resentment of the exploitation of Latin-Americans will find an echo in most Texas minds. But it is deplorable that Miss Ferber has made of race discrimination a sensational and implausible factor in her plot, dragged in by the neck and not organic to her story. This is sentimental cheating.

"As a novel, indeed, 'Giant' is a triumphant parade of platitudes, with almost no real sensitivity to people as such.

"Miss Ferber's whole problem as a novelist has been that she is powerfully responsive to situations (wife versus jealous sister-in-law, say) and insensitive to the people in the situation.

"This weakness is appalling in 'Giant.'"

Lon Tinkle's review not only is incisive but carries a good deal of insight into Ferber's frailties of her craft in general. Had she taken a course in creative writing, some professor might have told her to curb the platitudes and probe her characters at the outset of her career. But since she prided herself in being self-made, nobody ever had told her or could tell her much of a corrective nature. Mediocre to bad reviews were as much a way of life as was her success. Her best and most instinctive barometer was to write for the people. It seemed to have paid off. But with *Giant,* the people of Texas reared up, and in a man-on-the-street format, their quarrels with her were printed in the Dallas *Morning News* as a contingent to Lon Tinkle's review:

"Sam Nugent, Austin: 'I read with deep interest your excellent review of Edna Ferber's opus about Texas, "Giant." My only comment is that you did not emphasize her bias in favor of Woman, and covered this basis doctrine in one scant paragraph of your review in which you imply that Miss Ferber may be provoked because Texas is not a "womaned" state.

"'By this time the warped thinking of Miss Ferber on the feebleness of the male animal should be obvious. Her books retread the same ground to a degree that even a casual reader can predict the outcome in advance. In "Show Boat" the gambler Ravenal was glamorous and weak and sneaked out on his wife when the going got rugged. In "Cimarron" Yancey Cravat was also glamorous—and unstable; he also disappeared and it was the wife who became congresswoman (if I remember right). In "So Big," not only did Selina, the heroine, carry on after her loutish and unprogressive farmer husband died, but her son is left, at the book's close, a sophisticated failure.

"'Only the women are worth their salt! It is obvious that Miss Ferber's contention is that men may be attractive, but only in the sense that children are attractive. She seems to feel men are only excess baggage in her tidy little feministic world. Thus in her books, without exception, women are the builders, men are picturesque—but really useless.'"

"Betty Jorgenson, Dallas: 'The review of "Giant" is rather vehement . . .

"'The book is not all caricature or a contrast in cultures. She does write of one economic group, but so do some eighteenth century novelists. Miss Ferber is a garish craftsman. It is in her writing that she is so bad.'"

"Inez Nathen, Bonham: 'After reading, or rather wading through, Edna Ferber's ridiculous story about Texas and its natives, I find it conscientiously necessary to thank you for your very fine and just review. I only wish your criticism could be read by natives of other states so that we, when traveling, wouldn't have to listen to the many trite and unfair remarks about fabulous Texas. It sort of wears one's sense of humor down.

"'I have been associated for many years with people who owned and operated huge ranches in West Texas, but they worked hard, lived as well and as graciously as any people I've known anywhere in the world. Miss Ferber probably just didn't meet the right people.'"

Janet has an unsettling memory about Ferber and her public. She and Ferber were promenading down the boardwalk in Atlantic City. Occasionally people would interrupt their stroll, gleefully recognizing Ferber and stopping her to tell her how much her work meant to them. They tended to chatter nervously, but their praise was certainly heartfelt. Ferber was less than gracious and slightly more than curt. Her attitude was that of old-fashioned royalty, annoyed at having to deal directly with commoners. The more effusive the compliments were, the more she shriveled from them, as though, somehow, they were smirching her "art." At one point, an overdressed, rather noisy woman stopped them and declared that she just adored *So Big.* Ferber observed her glacially. "And just what did you adore about it?" she asked. The poor woman squawked out something and sped off, leaving her adoration well behind her.

Janet, although more outspoken than her sister Mina, was usually aware of keeping her lip buttoned in Ferber's presence, but this time it came unbuttoned.

"Oh, Aunt Edna! How could you be so intolerant! Who do you think reads you? These people are your public. They buy your books. They make your living. How can you afford to mistreat them?"

Ferber was too quiet. Then, as though she were chewing each word before spitting it out, she said, "I can write for them. And I can write about them. But I don't have to talk to them."

It was senseless to continue, and Janet didn't, but she remembers thinking how ironic it was that Ferber had the greatest contempt for her most ardent supporters. She would deliberately sink the egos of the "little" people who kept her afloat.

Now, with *Giant,* she was taking her licks—at least from the people and press of Texas. The newspapers were full of "git Ferber" items, such as:

"George Fuermann of the Houston Post turns up a 1940 comment of Miss Edna Ferber in an interview for his paper. Seems the author, on a visit to Houston, was asked if she were gathering material for a Texas book.

"'Texas is too big,' she answered. 'A book about it would be an impertinence.'"

Then there was a choice item entitled "Next-To-Worst Book Of The Year."

"Edna Ferber's 'Giant.' Hah! Miss Ferber's novel about South Texas is written out of spite, instead of deriving from a strong emotion like hatred; it is manufactured from gossip, not organized from basic insight into people. It is No. 1 on the best seller lists and way down at the bottom of our esthetic scales. It is still a major mystery to us, provincial that we are, how the New York critics could hail 'Giant' as a masterly bit of yarn spinning, when for us it is not even good Ferber. Still more of a mystery is the New York critical welcome extended to a light and superficial book, when good and serious and long-pondered true novels about Texas ('Sironia, Texas' and 'The Wonderful Country') were subjected to grudging scrutiny. We have a theory. What's yours?"

And then, when *Giant* was printed in paperback, there was a mean, silly little scrap titled "SHRINKING GIANT" that read: "At last Edna Ferber has been cut down to proper size: that diatribe against Texas, 'Giant,' is now in a 35¢ Pocket Books edition. Who's 'So Big' now?"

Margaret Cousins, author in her own right, and at that time managing editor of *Good Housekeeping* magazine, was a business friend of Ferber's, and a Texan. But, being a transplant to New York, and being in a position to desire any works of Ferber for her magazine, she wrote a very civilized note about *Giant:*

". . . I wasn't upset by GIANT. Of course, I'll be a Texan until I die, but I have more quarrels with them than you do. I was just down there, got off the plane with my dukes up and never stopped scrapping the whole trip. I had a wonderful time. Nobody is as good to fight with as a Texan. They are so violent and naive. I think this characteristic was excellently reflected in Giant, and it's basic . . ."

Despite all the brouhaha about *Giant*, there were those who were not reading current Ferber but discovering vintage Ferber. Margaret Sanger, the great pioneer of planned parenthood, and a gutsy,

Ferber type of woman, came upon *A Peculiar Treasure,* and in 1952 wrote a fascinating fan letter to Ferber:

"Dear Miss Ferber, I have just finished reading your autobiography 'A Peculiar Treasure.' It is one of the most beautiful, frank, uninhibited autobiographies that I have had the pleasure of reading.

"The reason I am writing to you is to ask a very personal psychological question. This question is based upon my own experience after writing my autobiography. The first book which poured out of my being, going and returning on the Europa, was 'My Fight for Birth Control.' It came out at a bad time as far as sales were concerned, and some people thought a bad title.

". . . Writing an autobiography and expressing the deep feelings of childhood and of the early experiences of the birth control movement did something to me which made it difficult for me to rewrite the second autobiography, but nevertheless it was done and the prying went deeper and deeper into my experiences.

"The result left me with rather an empty creativeness if I may describe the feeling as such. Previously I would arise at four in the morning to construct and to write material for lectures, for new essays, a possible new book, all of which seemed to end after I had emptied my being in writing the escapades and experiences of my life.

"I have watched this happen to many writers, and even those that continued to write after they had written the penetrating story of their lives, they themselves felt that the past had been finished and they were sort of marking time for some new creative spark, which in the majority of cases never took.

"As I knew H. G. Wells fairly well I talked this over with him. He didn't entirely agree with me, but he thought it was worth watching.

"I never had the pleasure of meeting you, but we have many friends in common. I think I never clicked with any book in the maternal sense as I did with your 'So Big.' Such beauty, such understanding of the maternal shows that you do not have to be a physical mother to understand the poignancy and love between a mother and child.

"I hope you will forgive this intrusion, but I just wanted to tell you that I loved the story of your life, the richness, the joyful friendships, your constant love of good food, and again I note that over and over again you told of what everyone had done for you, both family and friends, but not one little inkling of what you had done for others.

"The question I wish to ask is, have you felt that after you had written the experiences of your childhood and adult life that you were left creatively empty for any special period, and how long did it take to fill up that battery again? I realize you have written much since that time, but the question is did you feel the lowering of your battery psychologically speaking? Most Cordially Yours, Margaret Sanger."

Praise from a celebrated stranger appealed to Ferber more than any other kind. She had already been an ally of Margaret Sanger, and with this letter became an immediate correspondent and, later, a friendly acquaintance—visiting Sanger at her home in Tucson, Arizona. Mrs. Sanger's letter must have touched many responsive chords in Ferber. First of all, it singled out to compliment two of her favorite works; secondly, it was sensitive toward the fragility of a writer's psyche—about which Ferber knew all too well. But most of all, it bestowed on Ferber the adjective, maternal—a particularly glowing term for a barren woman. There is no record of Ferber's answer, but it must have instigated a lovely feeling between the two women.

Not everything during the time of *Giant* was as massive in impact. No matter what Ferber was working on or what she'd just produced, problems with old properties surfaced continually, and, of course, she had to deal with them. There were always appeals to convert one of her properties into another form—to which she usually responded by being indignant, feeling her personal integrity threatened. She behaved like a lioness with her cubs; she could cuff them, but she'd be damned if anyone else would even look at them—unless it was Richard Rodgers or Noel Coward, or someone whose reputation, she felt, paralleled her own.

There was a young woman who wished to obtain the rights to *Stage Door*—the 1936 George S. Kaufman-Ferber play—and to produce it as a musical for television. Apparently, when the woman had first proposed this, Ferber had deferred to Kaufman. One can see her sighing and saying, "How tiresome. Whatever George thinks best." Kaufman, not known as an unkind man, must have given the woman an "iffy" yes, for she went ahead with her plans for the project. When she had an outline—about six months later—she presented it along with her financial offer to the two original playwrights. Kaufman, in a letter to Ferber, was disenchanted:

". . . [She] had offered $1,000 option money, and then $200 for each episode if daytime, or $500 if night-time. I thought this quite inadequate—I am so bored with the word 'budget'—TV has all the money in the world . . ."

To Ferber, the price was unthinkable and the girl had some mettle even to suggest it and of course she would have to put a stop to the thing immediately, which she did. The woman wrote Ferber a revealing letter—not so much from the woman's angle, but because it lets one glance at the Ferber who could not have cared less about an unknown someone's aspirations.

"Dear Miss Ferber: . . . I do not resent the fact that you did not want me to do this musical, regardless of what names I might have been able to secure for the production. It is your property and Mr. Kaufman's, and if I were talented enough to have written such a play I too would protect it to the utmost and feel that if anything further were to be done with it I would want to have my say as to whom would be involved.

"However, it is the way in which you protected it that I feel is so inhuman and unforgivable. When I first approached you through Mrs. Pilpel six months ago you could have stated 'no'—very definitely—and that would have been the end of it. But to state instead that I was to inform Mr. Kaufman that 'you had no desire to pursue the matter any further but were willing to go along with Mr. Kaufman's decision'—and then, six months later forget that you ever made such a statement, amazes me.

"I have always had a tremendous admiration for you. Had I ever been the sort to have an idol you would have been my choice—but it is beyond me to understand how one who can write with the warmth you do can behave in such a way.

". . . I cannot understand your objections to new blood in the theater, Miss Ferber. Mr. Kaufman's record of aiding newcomers is legend. How could you decide that I was incompetent to produce a musical well, without ever even speaking to me? Did you base this conclusion on the sound of my name? Feuer and Martin, Robert Fryer and the young men who produced 'Pajama Game' are all newcomers to the theater. Has their being newcomers impaired in any way the quality of their productions?

"I am terribly sorry that all this occurred. I am not in the habit of writing impertinent letters—but I think that in the future you would be doing people a kindness if you would state exactly what you mean at the onset and not allow them to have dreams and hopes, only to smash them so thoroughly."

What Ferber thought of this episode will forever be bygone. That she kept this letter in her files is a relevant clue.

There was yet another intrusion into Ferber's peace of mind, when in 1953 the third remake of the film *So Big* was to open in New York. As was her custom, Ferber had nothing whatsoever to do with the film besides sniff in recognition of its title. What she did have to do with was a small piece run in the New York *Times* and the *Herald Tribune* that read:

"BRING FERBER BOOK AND SEE FREE FILM: The Paramount Theater in Times Square is offering free admission to anyone bringing a hard-covered copy of any Edna Ferber novel to the theater any weekday before 5 p.m. during the engagement of 'So Big.' The Warner drama made from the Ferber novel of the same name stars Jane Wyman, Sterling Hayden and Nancy Olson.

"All books collected during the engagement of 'So Big,' which opens at the Paramount tomorrow, will be presented to the libraries of New York City hospitals. The Pulitzer Prize-winning 'So Big' is one of nine of Miss Ferber's works that have been translated into motion pictures."

Ferber replied in what was for her a muted and rather lady-like way. She sent one letter to Bosley Crowther of the *Times* and one to Otis Guernsey of the *Tribune*.

"It is somewhat embarrassing for me to write this letter. But it would be more painful not to.

"I happen to think that books written with integrity are much more than merchandise. They are one of the highest tangible evidences of civilization.

"Please believe me when I say that this has nothing to do with whatever weakness or strength may be found in the motion picture SO BIG now being shown at the Paramount Theater in New York. This picture and all rights in it have long long ago passed out of my hands. I did not even know that this latest version of the picture had been made from my novel until the picture had been finished and was ready for release. This is the third version of the picture made from the novel SO BIG.

"I feel I must, however, register my indignation at the method of the admission that has been announced by the New York picture theatre in which SO BIG is being shown. No matter how worthy the object of the theatre's alleged charity, I find it objectionable and disgraceful and vulgar that the entrance fee be advertised as free to anyone who will present at the gate any one of my novels, regardless of its title or date. I feel that this is a new low in motion picture publicity. I feel certain that any writer of integrity would feel as I do.

"It may be that this unfortunate occurrence already is a thing of the past. I just wanted you to know how I felt about it. Without seeming too stuffy. Sincerely, Edna Ferber."

Only Mr. Otis Guernsey, the motion picture critic for the *Herald Tribune*, responded with very nice lip service:

". . . Your complaint seems to me to be entirely justified . . . There is nothing I can do about it specifically except sympathize with you and pass snide remarks around with the Broadway circle. If I ever get the opportunity to refer to it in print I will certainly do so, as it strikes me as an indignity against books in general and your fine works in particular."

Aside from her work, Ferber had one other magnificent obsession —her mother, Julia Ferber. In 1952, three years after Julia's death, her estate was finally settled and closed, and with that finality Ferber's grief seemed to have been exhumed. Ferber used this monetary event as a springboard to summarize her mother to Fan, Mina, and Janet. The following letter is a rather stilted tribute to Julia. It has a holy tone to it. The reason being that Ferber could never—not three years after her death—not ever—deal with her hatred toward her mother.

"By this time, dear Fan and Mina and Janet, you probably have had a final letter from William Wolff Jr., of the Ernst office, in the closing of mother's estate. Though I was named executor, together with Morris Ernst, I took no active part in the settling of the estate . . .

"There never was a clearer and less involved estate. Highly negotiable stocks and bonds made up the bulk of it, as you know, together with thirteen thousand or more in cash. It seems to me that the jewelry, furs, etc., need not have been listed in the assets. They could have been handled as personal belongings, but legally Wolff was correct. I note that he did not, however, list the dime found in a scuffed little leather purse which he took with him as an item in effects. A plodding and dull fellow.

". . . The entire estate ran to about $157,000, as you will see . . . During the months of mother's illness I had deposited all her incoming dividends, etc., and I paid out of my own income all hospital, doctors' and other expenses, such as hotel, rent, nurses, etc. This I wanted to do and took some comfort in so doing. The funeral costs . . . were left as estate charges because taxes were somewhat reduced by this. Mother left no other debts or obligations of any description whatever. She had left everything in order—her bank accounts, her investments, her correspondence, her few belongings. A miracle of order and clear-headedness and intelligence in any human being, not to speak of one who was eighty-nine, and very nearly ninety when she died.

"So here, for you, ends the story of Julia Ferber. Because of circumstance I knew her better than any of you. I knew the faults and the virtues. The virtues far outbalanced the faults. I always have regretted that, by some mischance of judgement or understanding, you never appreciated the actual dimensions of this unusual woman. I never spoke to you about her to any extent because the mention of her was always met with disparagement. Psychologically, there are certain facts in her life that are clear and explanatory as a chart. She married in her very early twenties. She married a man she did not love. She didn't mean to. She didn't know how not to. She married Jacob Ferber, a decent dull rather handsome man because her mother said she must. She was in love with a man named Will English, and he wanted to marry her. He was not a Jew, there was the most terrible brouhaha, she was bullied and threatened and browbeaten. Will English became a nationally known figure of his day, wealthy and distinguished. Mother would have made a wonderful wife for him, high-spirited, intelligent, quick to learn and evaluate. Jacob Ferber failed in his business, became blind, lost everything, his life insurance and his shop goods were mortgaged, there were two small daughters. Julia Ferber took over somehow, there was no one to whom she could turn for help. Her life, from the time she was twenty until she was about fifty-seven, was a tragic thing. How she emerged from it fun-loving, life-loving and high-spirited I cannot imagine. But she did.

"The qualities Julia Ferber possessed were admirable ones. She had self reliance, courage, fortitude, humor, intelligence, and a sense of values that was almost too keen. She knew values all the way from Meissen china to human beings, and her judgements often were harsher than they need have been, but she hated shoddy. At an age when all her contemporary friends were being properly pampered by maids, companions and the like, she 'did for herself,' as the old saying used to go. I want to help myself, she said repeatedly. I call this a spirited thing in a woman of almost ninety. An admirable character. Very often families know less about each other than outsiders know about them. It's a case, usually, of not being able to see the woods for the trees.

"This, then, is just my little obituary to Julia Foster who is very much alive to me."

It has been said that Julia died too late—meaning that, had she not lived to be so venerable, Ferber would have had a better chance of being vulnerable to a love life, or for that matter, any life of her own. In lieu of Oscar Hammerstein's lyric in *Show Boat,* "Tote that barge," for Ferber it was always "Tote that Julia." True, Julia was an indomitable, eccentric, and provocative woman, but she was not—perhaps as Ferber had brainwashed herself into believing—a great woman. She was certainly not just "a big Jewish Mama," as playwright Marc Connelly said of her. She was more pivotal than a mere stereotype could render. She may have been a courageous and amazing young woman, but those qualities don't necessarily make for a nice old lady—which she was not. She was destructive—almost Shakespearean in the scale and execution of that destruction. Always, she had to have her way—even to the extent of my name, or what she thought was my name.

My parents had named me Julie—partly because they thought it was pretty, and partly after the character of Julie in *Show Boat.* Julia was honored. She had somehow tacked an "a" onto the end of her daughter Edna's first-born great-niece—not considering for a moment that that vowel wasn't intended to be there. And so Julia Goldsmith it was to Julia Ferber, until I was three and she died.

When I was brought to her to be observed, I remember, in a child's wash of image, that there was something nasty and liverish about her. She also more resembled a frail old man than a woman, as if her femininity had receded with her increasing infirmity. She was nice to me, but she really wasn't nice at all. It was that simple. Later, Ferber used to say to me, "If only you could have known your great-grandmother. What a woooonderful woman she was." It was the only time I didn't believe her—for both of us.

Fan disliked her mother, Julia Ferber, with the kind of intensity that could only cause guilt. Of the two sisters, Fan most resembled Julia in mannerism and looks, which helped to sponsor the rage. That Ferber was Julia's favorite, and that Ferber took it upon herself to be saddled with Julia for the rest of her life—never letting Fan forget her sacrifice—put the tail on Fan's tornado. But Fan seemed to have no outlet, or perhaps allowed herself none, for in a strange, subconscious bloodletting she went and married the same sort of man who had ruined her hateful mother's life. Even the initials were the same: J.F. Even the first name was the same: Jacob, although he was referred to as Jack. Jack Fox—a dear, gentle, weak man, who was in the jewelry box trade, in which he eked out a just decent living. Ferber was the one who kept the jewelry boxes brimming. She knew her capacity for ownership-generosity, and states it in a letter to Ken McCormick:

"My life is still (more than ever) fantastically complicated and I must find a way out soon. It is frightful to be unable to have just the few hours of quiet and necessary peace each day to put down the words of a book. Perhaps it is largely my fault. I have spoiled every member of my family and that was a sort of vanity on my part."

After Julia died, all of Ferber's pent-up rage against her was released on Fan. Psychiatrists pet name for it is transference, but since Ferber felt that she was her own best analyst, she had no idea of the cruelty that she was directing toward her sister. And, since she couldn't face the motive, she reversed the intent: Fan was the one who loathed her, and Fan was the one who was vindictive toward her. It was all very complicated. A sibling shambles.

Henry, always slightly regarded as "the foreigner," and coming from a closely knit German-Jewish family, was continually appalled by the Edna-Fan goings-ons. He thought it the saddest, most crippled interaction he'd ever seen. He remembers Ferber telling him once that she was afraid to stay alone with Fan in the Westport house. She thought that Fan might murder her.

Margalo Gillmore, the actress, has a theory about one of the things that might have deeply rankled Ferber about Fan. It had to do with vocal tone. Fan had an unfortunate voice—flat, harsh, Middle Western. It was very distinctive and called attention to itself—

on the street, in a restaurant, at the theatre, etc. Ferber's voice was pitched low; her tone could be velvet, could be acid, could be dulcet, could be anything she wanted it to be. She was queen of her voice box. The two voices together were like oil and water. One could see where Fan's voice could have driven Ferber to distraction.

Ferber was house-proud and servant-proud. Her homes were always showplaces, kept just so by the people who worked for her. She was particularly proud of Miss Molly Hennessy, who was pint-sized, like herself, and had a tremendous capacity to please. Ferber never bragged about her own work—unless threatened—but she did brag about Molly, often to the extent of embarrassment. It was as though she herself had given birth to the perfect little *hausfrau*. "Miss Molly Hennessy," she would say, always elevating the name to its utmost importance, "made the greenest of beans last night," or, "Who do you think was at the airport to meet me? Why, it was Miss Molly Hennessy. What a dear girl."

After Ferber had a hernia operation, for postoperative care the doctor advised taking home a nurse. Ferber nodded toward Molly. "I have my nurse," she said. And during the two weeks of recuperation, Molly changed Ferber's dressings as properly as, and probably more tenderly than, any registered nurse that the hospital could have dispatched.

Among her many virtues, Molly had a way with Ferber's friends:

Margalo Gillmore threw out her arms while Molly was serving and said, "Molly, let me kiss you!"

Rock Hudson—so tall that Molly thought she'd have to do a back flip—kindly compensated by stooping way down to her when he gave her his hat.

Noel Coward, who used to come glittering in, often remarked, "Molly, I think you've grown."

Madeline Sherwood, former wife of Marc Connelly, and not one of Molly's favorites, used to sail through the door without even glancing at Molly. "Who did she think held it open for her? No one?" Molly retorts.

Peg Pulitzer, who also drank more than she ate, but who would unfailingly compliment Molly on the food.

And Molly remembers that Truman Capote used to come to dinner frequently and then tapered off. (Perhaps he stopped because of what Ferber thought of him: "He seemed to me to be a half-portion Woollcott—but without Woollcott's bite or flavor," she said in a letter to Ken McCormick.)

There were a host of others who thought Molly was a treasure, and whom Molly, in her quiet way, had the goods on. But more than any, Ferber was her greatest fan. So in 1951, when Miss Molly Hennessy decided to take her leave of Miss Edna Ferber, it was a severe blow. Molly's reasons were vague: she wanted to go back to Ireland; she didn't want to be "in service" anymore . . . But she stuck to them. She'd given notice and had begun to pack. Although Ferber seems nonplussed in her diary: "Molly said leaving. Perhaps all for best. Will wait for new maid," she was beside herself. How could she manage without the indispensable Molly? She couldn't. For two days she beseeched and coaxed. What she offered in terms of remuneration for Molly's change of mind is unrecorded. At the end of two days, Molly unpacked her bags and went into the kitchen to plan seventeen more years of tempting dinners for Miss Ferber.

On December 29, 1927, a play called *The Royal Family,* by George S. Kaufman and Edna Ferber, opened at the Selwyn Theatre in New York City. Brooks Atkinson, the influential New York *Times* reviewer, wrote:

"Their play is one of the most enjoyable of the season. Nothing could make for a completer exploitation of its theme than this collaboration of a fiction writer, primarily concerned with plot and characters, and a satirist, remarkable for his neat, critical dialogue and his skill in play technique."

On January 11, 1951, *The Royal Family* opened at the City Center in New York City for its first major revival. Brooks Atkinson, still the theatre critic on the New York *Times,* revived his review:

"Last evening was not the best time to take an objective view of 'The Royal Family.' At the end of the first act, John Emery who was playing the part of a flamboyant actor, injured an ankle as he came running down a flight of stairs. Naturally horrified at the prospect of refunding negotiable currency, Mr. Emery insisted on finishing the performance. While the physician was binding his ankle and shooting his leg full of novocaine, Ethel Griffies who was playing the part of a veteran trouper, came before the curtain as an authentic trouper and entertained the audience with humorous stories. 'The Royal Family' is a play about a family of indomitable actors. Mr. Emery and Miss Griffies attached their seals of authenticity to the legend George S. Kaufman and Edna Ferber first put on paper in 1927 . . . Here and there 'The Royal Family' may look a little creaky in the joints. But at heart it is a fond and knowing portrait of the fascination of the theatre."

Ferber did not attend that opening night. She sat home with her dinner on a tray. She'd had quite enough of *The Royal Family*.

FLASHBACK: "George, how 'bout me?" Ferber asked it with a certain middle-aged wistfulness. She watched as Kaufman peered over his glasses and smiled benignly. Her suggestion that she play the role of Julie Cavendish in their brand-new sure-to-be-a-hit collaboration *The Royal Family* did not even warrant one of his pungent comments. She couldn't mean it. They had written only one other play together, *Minick*, in 1924, so their collaboration and friendship had yet to reach their full stride. But it was common knowledge that Ferber was one of the most disciplined and dedicated writers around. "Works like a man—almost," Kaufman, the immaculate technician and stingy complimenter, had said. This woman to whom he had chosen to be wed in collaborative bliss should not have flights of fancy. After all, she was a devout spinster to whom work meant all; he was a devout philanderer to whom work meant all—when he was working. It was for both of them a perfect meeting of the muse, and for Ferber to want to drop the muse to walk the boards was sheer folly—unthinkable—she couldn't mean it.

She did and she didn't. Ferber was stage-struck—she always had been. She loved the theatre passionately yet she understood it with the flintiness of a stagehand. She was also actor-struck, saying of them, "There was born in me the most enormous respect and admiration for actors. I admire their courage and their love of their work; their vanity and their humility and their angelic hopefulness. When they work they work harder than any craft, trade or profession I've ever known, under the most maddening and idiotic of circumstances, and they almost never complain." This particular ode was meant specifically, if indirectly, for Miss Ethel Barrymore, who, in 1915, was the leading lady in Ferber's first play, *Our Mrs. McChesney*, and with whom Ferber was deeply smitten—in the strictly professional sense.

"At rehearsals Ethel Barrymore behaved like an angel. She was tireless, uncomplaining, never demanding. She never tried to steal a line or a scene. She never tried to play upstage. Everyone in the company adored her. I had heard stories of her brilliant wit, and they were true. She took direction gratefully." Forget about the Divine Sarah—for Ferber, it was the Divine Ethel.

Twelve years later, when it came time to cast *The Royal Family*, which was less than loosely based on the stage-faring Barrymores, it occurred to Ferber and Kaufman, who would be better to play herself (in the guise of Julie Cavendish) than Ethel Barrymore? The Divine Ethel became less than that when she rancorously turned the role down flat and even threatened to sue. The first lady of the first family of the American stage did not feel very "patriotic."

During the writing of *The Royal Family*, something new and strange stirred in Ferber. Her hankering for stage legs grew stronger with each new difficulty that she, Kaufman, and producer Jed Harris encountered in casting the leading lady—Ethel's intended part. Most star actresses who were approached felt that playing a character based on the Divine Ethel could only jeopardize and even diminish their own stature. Also, the role of Julie Cavendish entailed being just slightly over the hill. No one was eager for that suggestion either, so Ferber, Kaufman, and Harris auditioned and turned down—approached and were turned down—until the whole thing became more discouraging than a good play and a meaty part deserved. After weeks of agony, after they'd said, "Thank you," to the last actress they didn't want, Ferber, somewhat ruefully, popped the question to Kaufman.

Although an actress named Ann Andrews was finally cast, and turned in a workwoman-like performance, perhaps Ferber should have been taken more seriously. *The Royal Family*, which opened on December 29, 1927 (following by one night Ferber's, Kern's, and Hammerstein's smash hit classic *Show Boat* at the Ziegfeld Theatre), was a hit, but a qualified one. It was not a critic's darling, the way Kaufman-Ferber's *Dinner at Eight* would be five years later. But a successful dramatic partnership was established with this play and the critics bowed to the new pair of dazzlers.

Ferber attended neither the opening of *Show Boat* nor the opening of *The Royal Family*. Both nights she had dinner at home on a tray. The doubleheader was too much for her. The twin victory sent her into a social and professional spin. She felt like Miss America, crowned by her hit reviews. Alexander Woollcott, her at that time dear and acerbic friend and the not so dear and acid critic, simply glowed over *The Royal Family,* clapping his pudgy hands like a happy baby over good Pablum:

" 'The Royal Family' gave me the most thoroughly enjoyable first night I had experienced in many and many a week . . . The audience that sits down before 'The Royal Family' is often weak with laughter at the unbelievable preposterousness of the great tribe that frets and struts through the turmoil of the House of Cavendish. And if at times the eyes in that audience seem to glisten it may be only a reflection, for the play does shine with the ancient and still untarnished glamour of the stage."

The Royal Family had solid competition that Broadway season of 1927. It was running neck and neck with *A Connecticut Yankee, The Doctor's Dilemma, Paris Bound, The Taming of the Shrew, Hamlet,* and other shows popular at that time such as, *Coquette,* that have since been forgotten. *The Royal Family* weathered well, had a good solid run, and then went on tour to please the rest of America.

There was enough substance in the play to warrant several revivals, the most provocative of which occurred in Maplewood, New Jersey, on August 13, 1940. It was on that infamous summer's night that Edna Ferber hit the stage literally with a bang. Cheryl Crawford, the noted producer and, in this case, fairy godmother, granted Ferber her heart's desire by casting her, for a one-week run, in the role of Fanny Cavendish, described by Woollcott as the "snorting, sardonic, magnificent old war horse" grandmother of *The Royal Family.*

Ferber was not prepared for the attention that her debut received. First of all the telegrams—and marvelous ones they were:

> "GAYLORD RAVELSTEIN WISHES FANNEY CAVENBERG GREAT SUCCESS—MOSS HART"
>
> "LOVE AND BEST WISHES TO BLOSSOM GIRL SEE YOU AND HOW TOMORROW NIGHT—PEG [Pulitzer]"
>
> "WELL YOU WROTE IT. FOND LOVE—PEGGY WOOD"
>
> "IT IS A LAUNDRY STOP BEST WISHES FOR TOMORROW NIGHT. HOPE YOU CAN LIVE UP

TO THE AUTHOR'S EXPECTATION OF HOW THAT PART SHALL BE PLAYED. SHE'S VERY PARTICULAR. LOVE FROM US BOTH–HERBERT BAYARD SWOPE"

"LOVE AND KISSES TO THE CONNECTICUT DUSE–ALISON AND RUSSEL [Crouse]"

"I NEVER THOUGHT I'D SEE THE DAY–GEORGE [Kaufman]"

After George Kaufman had seen the performance, he cabled Ferber, and in what was very flowery speech for him said:

"EDNA DEAR I THOUGHT YOU WERE REALLY REMARKABLE IN THE PLAY AND SO DID ALL OF YOUR FRIENDS WHO WERE THERE THAT NIGHT. YOU KNOW I MEAN IT AND I WAS VERY PROUD OF YOU. MY LOVE, GEORGE."

Ferber viewed her debut with less frills and more jaundice:

"The drama critics of the New York daily newspapers–the Times, the Tribune–all of them journeyed out to Maplewood, to my consternation. George Kaufman and Beatrice [Mrs. Kaufman], many other friends and a wholesome leavening of enemies showed up; not only showed up, but the Kaufmans and a sprinkling of other theater-wise ones actually came backstage to see me BEFORE THE PERFORMANCE, when I was making up. This was, naturally, in order to evade the awful moment when they might otherwise be obliged to go back after a probably disastrous performance to tell me how dazzlingly I had carried the whole thing off." She recounts how she carried and then dropped her acting glory:

"After a terrific bravura speech all about the theater and the Cavendish clan and the art of acting, I was supposed to faint; and then to be carried by Louis Calhern up the stairs and ostensibly into a second floor offstage bedroom; no mean feat. Halfway up the stairs he dropped me. As I thumped to the steps the audience sat petrified. So did I. I toyed with idea of fainting in reality but the Ferbers are not a fainting family. Louis Calhern and I managed, by a mish-mash of scrambles, hobbles, and a second herculean effort of lugging on his part, to get me through the upstairs exit and presumably into an offstage bed. At the end of this accomplished feat there issued from the audience a burst of hysterical applause interspersed with helpless shrieks of laughter."

Brooks Atkinson, in his review of the performance, was more courtly about her accident by never mentioning it, but less than kind about her histrionics:

". . . As an amateur actress, in the tradition of Charles Dickens, who also wrote novels, Miss Ferber ranks about half-way between Sinclair Lewis and Alexander Woollcott . . . She settled down into a workman-like performance that did not disturb the drama very much . . . After she gets this whim out of her system she can settle down to the writing of a novel which we can all enjoy without reservations."

Ferber's system was presumably cleansed of the "whim"—she never actively sought to take to the stage again. She had stretched her stage legs and was content to continue her ten-finger exercise for the rest of her days.

Treasure Hill, situated in Stepney Depot, Connecticut, was Ferbers' middle-aged fling. She herself referred to it as a "love affair," and anyone who saw the wedding-cake house high on the hill with acres and acres of land on every side could understand why Ferber felt no need for a "summertime" or a Rossano Brazzi. It was complete indulgent sublimation without a tad of practicality. It was the best bromide for whatever ailed her, and during the years that she lived there her real physical ailments were few. She built it, furnished it, farmed on its land, was productive in its study, was gay and entertaining in its parlor, cleared her lungs in its good countryside air, and walked and walked and walked its fertile grounds. She loved it dearly. The house that Ferb built housed her better than any relationship ever could have. She convinced herself that its atmosphere was her "work oxygen," and that none other had ever given her more impetus.

"You see, I'm the mountain type," she said once. "Them as likes the ocean can have the whole wet mess. I suppose my reason for having bought this big hilltop was that it gave me the feeling of being on a little mountain. I used to go to the Rockies every year. It was like going on a drunk. Being a low blood pressure person it had the effect of making me feel as though I'd had two dry martinis. Curiously enough, always in that altitude I wrote things like THE AFTERNOON OF A FAUN and NOBODY'S IN TOWN. Rather fey things such as I didn't write at sea level."

Even a factual description of the house in the Easton *News* when it was finally sold lends itself to extravagance:

"The two-story stone residence is built on long low lines. The floor plan includes a large center hall extending through to a rear court. On one side is a 34-foot living room with French doors to a broad terrace, an enclosed sun room, and a windowed library. The opposite wing contains the dining room, utility rooms and an attached three-car garage. On the second floor are four master bedrooms, each with bath, a balcony, a study and servant's quarters.

"A 50-foot swimming pool and a two-section stone pool house are on the residence grounds. A four-room guest house is of white clapboard in farmhouse style. Estate buildings include a barn with horse stalls and cattle pens. There also are provisions for sheep, pigs and chickens, a hay barn, equipment shed and a tool house.

"From Maple road, on which the property fronts, a private road winds for a quarter of a mile to the residence. The surrounding 140 acres are in fields, pastures and woodland."

Whenever she talked or wrote about Treasure Hill, Ferber lost her urban sting and acquired a sort of a James Whitcomb Riley—"frost is on the punkin" rhetoric—apparent in her description of the seasons:

"The four seasons are a perpetual adventure, a dramatic entertainment assured yet unpredictable. The brilliance of the gold and scarlet in every shade blazing away to the sound from the top of Treasure Hill was indescribable and it will not be attempted here. Sometimes in the winter when the trees were coated with transparent ice and the sun shone off of them, you were living in a fairy land. Sometimes the snow plow made its way through my road up to the house and there are photographs of C. Harold Curtiss, a tall man, leaning with a triumphant grin against a snow drift nine feet high. Spring came late to Easton. The new green had already burst into life in Westport just twelve miles distant.

"In a way it was like beholding Spring in three separate acts. The season came to New York early and was soon over. The trees in Central Park showed a pale yellow-green in March, and the Japanese cherry blossoms around the reservoir were in bloom. Westport reached, there was spring again, almost three weeks later. And at Treasure Hill it came in full beauty in another two or three weeks so that one had the delight of this magic three times over. The same was true of autumn and the riot of color."

Ferber put Treasure Hill on the market in 1950—recording in her diary: "No qualms of regret about the house." On November 30, 1949, Julia Ferber died. There is significance between the two events; her mother's death and her subsequent ridding herself of her prize. Treasure Hill was the reality of Ferber's tremendous success. It was also used as scarlet evidence to her mother of her achievements. The building of that house was the first thing she had truly done on her own without the meddling of Julia Ferber, and in doing so it was tantamount to saying, "I'm going to run away with this house [man], Mamma, and there's not a thing you can do to stop me!" That house was the most symbolic factor in Ferber's fairly literal life; she knew it and she flaunted it. There would always be a room for Julia Ferber, but it was her house, had been her seed, her creation. It was husband, children, responsibility—the whole ball of wax—and Julia Ferber, like a jealous mother-in-law, resented it. With Julia's death, the proof of the house turned into dust. There was no need for it anymore; it's time was over.

At the age of, as Ferber put it, "almost ninety," Julia Ferber died of cancer of the pancreas in her home at the Surrey Hotel. Since she was a devout Christian Scientist—although, as Ferber would say of her, "She was neither Christian nor scientific—" she saw death as not so much of a tragedy as an inevitability. The act of dying, however, was its usual painful, moving and desperate transition. Ferber and Fan were posted around her deathbed, waiting. She reached out to Ferber. "Edna," she cried, "Oh, Edna, I ruined your life—didn't I?—I did. I ruined your life."

Fan remembered that the irony was that Ferber turned away from her mother's confession, walked over to the window and stood, with her back very erect to the room, while she, Fan, was left to hold Julia's dying hand. Ferber never turned around, and Julia Ferber died holding the wrong daughter's hand.

Julia's death was a milestone in the unclogging of an unhealthy relationship. She would have gone sooner had Ferber not given her a seven-month reprieve. Dr. Alvan Barach told Ferber that her mother would die in a matter of weeks unless she underwent a very complex operation in which the gall bladder would be connected to the intestine, preventing bile from entering the blood stream. Ferber gave the go-ahead for this expensive, intricate, and dangerous surgery in order to give her mother the possibility of seven months more of life. Julia sailed through the operation and claimed her extra helping. Ferber recorded those last months with Julia in a reporter-like, documentary style:

"The operation then, and a kind of miraculous false recovery. There was Julia up at Treasure Hill again, dressed in cool summer garb against the glowing Indian summer days, being driven about the Connecticut countryside . . . But October saw the end of all that temporary bravado.

"During these past months the writing of the novel GIANT had been put aside, perforce. With the approach of late autumn the ambulance carried her back to her New York apartment, high up and sunny.

"She did not once speak during that seventy-five mile drive. I thought she was in a semi-coma induced by the pain-reducing drugs. We drew up at the entrance. The men prepared to carry the stretcher. She spoke, clearly.

" 'Edna, cover my face.'

"She always had had a wholesome pride and proper vanity in her own good looks. Her arrival today was expected, her apartment had been made ready, the hotel staff and perhaps some resident friends might be waiting there in the foyer through which she had passed so many times with a little rustle of silk and a discreet breath of perfume; her step firm, her handsome head held high. 'Edna, cover my face.'

"So I untied the scarf that I wore and with it I covered the noble face, now reduced to a parchment-yellow mask.

"After it was over and winter had come and gone, and the spring of 1950 found me again at Treasure Hill and hard at work on GIANT with my back to the view and my face in the typewriter the decision that must unconsciously have been forming for months in my mind came to a final resolution."

That decision was to leave Treasure Hill—so inextricably evocative of Julia—behind her. There is a thoughtful little postscript tucked in her diary that reads:

"J.—It is difficult to say whether she was a help or an obstacle in my life as a writer. Probably a good deal of both. Full of small faults. Possessed of almost all the great human virtues."

Ferber didn't make false moves. She would stay at Treasure Hill until she found exactly what she wanted in New York. Dorothy Rodgers worked the miracle:

"She was looking for a six-room apartment and it had to be in the seventies and it had to be within two blocks of Central Park and it had to be up high and it had to have sunlight and it had to have a wood-burning fireplace and it shouldn't cost more than a certain amount. Well, I found it in our building at 730 Park, and she bought it and she lived there until she died."

Dorothy Rodgers has wry memories of that time during Ferber's bereavement. She hadn't known Julia well but admitted that the term "hellion" was not an unfamiliar one in connection with her. Julia also had a strong sense of humor. At one point she'd said to Dorothy, "Oh, there's a wonderful dry goods store in Texas. It's called Neiman Marcus."

Dorothy Rodgers had more than an inkling of how rough Ferber's life had been with Julia, how rough it would be without her, and how rough Ferber could make life for others. But she had the key to Ferber which kept their friendship locked for so many years. She kidded her, teased her, was playful with her.

"When she built the house in the country, it was during the depression. One night in 1939, we took her out to dinner at the World's Fair. She was building the house, or had just built it, and we never let her off the hook. For years we used to kid her about it because it was such a staggering thing for anybody to do in the middle of the depression—for anybody to be able to build that kind of house.

"Then one time she took me around the house and said, 'Peg gave me this, and the Lunts gave me that and Noel gave me this . . .' and I said 'My God, didn't you buy anything? Did your friends furnish the whole house?' Well, you could do that with Edna and she would be amused by it. But you never knew what moment you would hit the wrong button. That was what kept you on your toes."

Dorothy Rodgers was aware of Ferber's vulnerable quality—that people often "hit and ran" with her:

"You know, people took advantage of her because she expected them to. I mean people who worked for her. For instance, I remember during the war we kept chickens and so did Edna. One day Edna called me and she said, 'How many chickens do you have?' I said about one hundred. Then she asked how many eggs I got and I said, 'I don't know exactly, Edna. I know that most of the year we have all the eggs we need and enough sometimes to put "down in water glass," and other times of the year we have to buy some.' 'Well,' she said, 'I have twenty-five chickens and I get sixteen eggs and I think the caretaker is holding out.' I said to her, 'Edna, I have a word of advice for you: Either stop counting, or get rid of the chickens.'"

Dorothy Rodgers has a trilogy of "hoodwinking Ferber" stories:

"She put in every bloody tree on that place [Treasure Hill], and one day she was at a nursery looking at a tree that she needed to buy and she found it and she said to the man who owned the nursery, 'Now, I'll tell you how to find my house.' And he said, 'Oh, Miss Ferber, I know how to find your house. I've been there. When you had a tree to sell I went to look at it.' Whereupon Edna said, 'You've never been to my place. I have no trees to sell. You're thinking of someone else.' She gave him the directions anyway, dismissing what he'd said as a mistake.

"When he arrived, she said, 'Now, you've never been here before, have you?' 'Yes,' he said, 'The tree that was for sale was just back of that barn.'

"Well, her caretaker had been selling the trees as fast as she was putting them in."

"Then, she had a prize ram that was going to be shown at the Danbury Fair. The day before he was to be sent to the fair, the caretaker gave him a bath in sheep dip to clean him up and kill whatever insects and brush him out and make him look beautiful. Well, he was very careless and he left the sheep dip there and the cow came along and drank it. The cow became very ill. The caretaker was afraid to go up and tell Edna, and was afraid to call the vet because then he would have had to tell her. So he thought he'd try and handle it himself and the cow died."

"When she was trying to sell the house a family appeared to look at it. Parents and child—a small child and a huge dog. They brought the dog and the child right into the house. The entrance was circular and it had a linoleum or rubber floor that was always polished so beautifully that you could really see yourself in it. It was a great point of pride. So this big dog came in with muddy paws, and Edna suggested that he be kept out of the house. The people agreed, put the dog out and the dog promptly went swimming in the pool, which Edna didn't like a lot. In the meantime, the child saw a bowl of candy in the living room, took a handful of it, got nice sticky hands, and when they walked upstairs the kid smeared it all over the wall. Well, Edna was going out of her mind

—besides, the woman was making remarks like, 'The closets aren't big enough,' etc. Not only was it obvious that they weren't going to buy the house, but on the way out, as a final shaft, they tried to persuade the couple who worked for Edna to go and work for them."

There is a little-known story that is the best example of Ferber's tendency to contract freakish incidents:

Aside from Ferber, and many others, a celebrated doctor's patient list included a well-known pianist. Ferber and the pianist had met socially, but close friendship certainly escaped them. The pianist's proclivities were more prurient than prudent; Ferber's were the opposite. What they had in common was the doctor. One day Ferber had a checkup, which included, among the other fundamentals, her leaving a specimen. Now, Ferber was fastidious to the point of fanaticism about her hygiene, so when the results were reported over the telephone, Ferber couldn't fathom them. At first she was imperious, then incredulous, and finally furious. "WHAT DO YOU MEAN?" she roared. The report meant what it said. The specimen showed evidence of various venereals that Ferber had contracted. What had happened, of course, was straightened out almost immediately. Someone at the office had filed badly, and the pianist's folder had been placed under F. The rightful specimens were returned to their rightful owners.

In 1948, George S. Kaufman's and Edna Ferber's last play written together was produced on Broadway. It was called *Bravo!* and elicited a somewhat lesser response. Although a new Kaufman-Ferber play was always an event, they had rugged competition that particular season. Elmer Rice was readying a revised version of *Not for Children* for the Playwright's Company; Marc Connelly had a new play called *A Story for Strangers;* Maxwell Anderson was bringing his *Anne of the Thousand Days* to town; Moss Hart was presenting his *Light Up the Sky;* and Philip Barry was adapting Jean Pierre Aumont's play *The Emperor of China* to be produced by the Theatre Guild.

Ferber gave evidence of trouble with the play beforehand in mentions of it in letters to Ken McCormick:

FEBRUARY 7, 1948: "I'm writing a play with George Kaufman. We'll be finished about April 1. I don't know whether it's good or not."

AUGUST 12, 1948: "Finished the play, and now it's in that slippery seat, the lap of the gods. We don't go into rehearsal until September 27."

OCTOBER 28, 1948: "We've had rather a tough time. Changed horses in midstream. Stradner. [At the last moment they had to fire their leading lady, Rosa Stradner, a well-known German actress. They replaced her with an equally known Hungarian actress named Lili Darvas, wife of the playwright Ferenc Molnár. The episode was painful and unsettling to cast and crew.] But I hope we have a play. I don't really know."

Ward Morehouse, drama critic on the New York *Sun*, seemed to know when he wrote:

"Edna Ferber and George S. Kaufman, who have given the theater valiant service as collaborators, are teamed together again, which is all to the drama's good, but their new 'Bravo!' is considerably less than a satisfactory play . . . 'Bravo!' has gusto and some vehemence. It has some good incidental detail, but it is weak in its main story. The theater's best dramatists continue to turn in indifferent work."

John Lardner of the New York *Star* seemed to know in a somewhat testier manner:

"Oscar Homolka is a fine actor, and a lot of the other performers who shared the stage with him Thursday night when a comedy called 'Bravo!' opened are pretty fair too, but my goodness, friends, what a suit for non-support all those people have got against Edna Ferber and George S. Kaufman, who set them up in housekeeping with two-tenths of a play and left them there to make due for a whole night while they, the authors, slipped around the corner for a quick one or something . . ."

Brooks Atkinson, always the collaborators' severest critic, did not write a money review for the New York *Times*, but at least he knew the play was a drama.

"Since Edna Ferber and George S. Kaufman wear their hearts in the right place, 'Bravo!' . . . is warm and sympathetic . . . They have written a drama about the poignant plight of some eastern Europeans in New York . . . and a number of other famous Europeans, now living in what are politely known as reduced circumstances . . . Having considerable respect for those civilized victims of a great cultural disaster, Miss Ferber and Mr. Kaufman have written a number of rueful scenes that are haunted by wistful memories of a Europe that is gone and blocked by the impatient realities of America . . . 'Bravo!' skips quickly over the surface of a subject that needs greater insight and profounder convictions . . ."

Then there came a wonderful defense of the play written by a journalist named George E. Sokolsky. It was the kind of editorial tactic that Woollcott used to employ when he believed in a play that all the other critics had buried. It is a gentle piece about a gentle play by an obvious gentleman:

"The theater this year has been so inadequate that I have read the reviews of the professional critics more regularly than heretofore. Most of them hit down a play by George S. Kaufman and Edna Ferber entitled 'Bravo!' . . .

"I wondered whether I had lost all sense of joy and could be amused by anything, or whether the critics had gone collective and had eaten tainted crabmeat together on the same night. Therefore, between the acts, I meandered about the lobby . . . and found a general agreement that this 'Bravo!' is a good play, that the audience is amused, interested, stirred to laughter and to pity, absorbed by interest in how it will work out in the end . . .

"Well, I could not help wondering what happened to my confreres, the critics when they saw this play. Of course they will say that I should stick to my last and write of dull economics and disappointing politics. Still, man and boy, I have been going to the theater regularly now for a matter of more than 40 years.

"So, no one can deny my experience as a spectator—and it is as a spectator, who buys tickets because he wants a relaxing evening, that I write. And as such I say that 'Bravo!' is a good play, interesting, amusing, stirring a nostalgia for other days when Galsworthy wrote gently of human problems and Barrie stirred the imagination by the softness of his characterizations."

Alexander Woollcott could save plays. George E. Sokolsky could not. Even after the actors accepted salary cuts, and even after Ferber gave a financial transfusion of $6,000 (at that time not a sum to be snorted at), *Bravo!* lived only a scant two months. There is always a bit of melancholy levity in the theatre when it comes to flops, as Max Gordon, producer of the venture, displays in a letter to Ferber:

"My dear Edna, Here's the report on 'Bravo' and the check for

$5,935.80 which represents the return on the $6,000 you advanced to defray any additional losses.

"Now, the next time you have boiled beef, please give a man like myself, who respects boiled beef, a few days' notice. All best. As ever, Max."

Bravo! saw the end of an era for three creative people. Not only was it Ferber's and Kaufman's last effort together, it was the last Ferber-Kaufman play that Janet Fox, Ferber's actress niece, would ever be written into. Janet, who had played a small part, had even managed to get a positive mention from Brooks Atkinson, who in his review said of her: "And there is some authentic American poison in Janet Fox's acting of a lethal Polish dancer."

Up until that point in her career, Janet had been a privileged newcomer—a talented niece, but a niece. That tag had been on her since she had graduated from the American Academy of Dramatic Arts in 1932, and had been inducted that same year into her first Broadway play, Ferber-Kaufman's *Dinner at Eight*, and later, in 1936, into Ferber-Kaufman's *Stage Door*. In fact, one of the only times that Kaufman praised her work was in *Dinner at Eight*, when he came up to her and rather offhandedly said, "You know you're pretty good—for a niece."

Ferber tended toward hyperbole when speaking of those she loved. Janet was good, but she was young and relatively untried in the ranks of the theatre. To hear Ferber rave and carry on about her was to feel your collar too tight—especially if you were a producer. "This girl"—Ferber would put it on a pedestal—"could well be one of the most gifted comediennes of our time. She has quality; she has looks; her timing is superb. She has a real future in the theater."

When Ferber and Kaufman were going strong, it looked like Ferber had quite a future as a "stage mamma." Phyllis Cerf Wagner recalls how Ferber plagued every theatre person about Janet, how they all expected her to come around at casting time.

Janet got parts on her own in between Ferber-Kaufman plays, and began to develop a small reputation for herself. But mainly, among the *crème de la crème* of the theatre world, she was still known and stuck with being "Ferber's niece, who acts." There were aspects of it that she didn't mind: it got her through the door and it was glamorous by proxy. Ferber's parties were dazzling; the guest list was like a fabulous marquee: Katharine Cornell, Moss Hart,

Alfred Lunt, Lynn Fontanne, Ina Claire, Danny Kaye, Noel Coward, Constance Collier, Leland Hayward, Margaret Sullavan, the Robert Sherwoods, the George Kaufmans, the Richard Rodgerses, Marc Connelly, Frank Sullivan—not a bit player in the bunch.

Janet, much like a debutante, was "brought out" at these parties. There was one in particular where she remembers that her whole dress was wet from her nerves. She had two drinks to stabilize herself, and, unused to drinking, they were her undoing. At table, she was seated next to Noel Coward, who was polite but certainly not devoting himself to her. On her other side was someone equally notable who also didn't lavish attention on her. She was left to smile, listen, watch, and eat.

The main course was squab. Slippery things, squabs. The serving platter came around to Janet. She grasped the succulent but tiny bird, lifted it, and then watched in horror as it flew out from the silver servers, plopped once on the fine damask tablecloth, once on Noel Coward's thigh, and reached its final rest on the floor. Everybody noticed. Everybody pretended not to. Conversation became more animated. Janet wanted to lie quietly under the table with the squab, but was forced by the prodding of the waitress to be a good sport and take another helping, which she succeeded to do without incident. The tray was passed to Noel Coward, and, deep in conversation with Kitty or Leland or Peg, he feigned not paying attention to what he was doing. The silver servers slipped again. One more squab under the table. When Janet looked at him with sparkling eyes, all he said was, "Don't bother about it." Janet considered it not only a kindness but an act of true heroism.

The supper of the squab was never mentioned by Ferber or by anyone else ever again, but Janet wouldn't have given up dropping it for anything in the world. After all, as a young actress, she had stolen a scene.

Scene stealers ran in the family. Julia Ferber could upstage anything—even a crap game. In the late twenties, Ferber and Julia had moved from Chicago to New York, where they resided together in a large apartment at 50 Central Park West. Marc Connelly had just been given a one-thousand-dollar bill from the War Department. He pocketed it and, because it was after banking hours, sauntered up to Ferber's, where he knew that she and several friends were shooting craps. He sat down, threw the bill in the pot, and joined the game. Julia, who was lurking nearby, as was her wont, saw the bill and removed it from the pot—goggle-eyed.

"Edna," she gasped. "EDNA! Look what Mr. Connelly threw away."

Connelly blithely waved vamoose at her and the bill.

"Go buy a box of candy, Julia. Buy yourself a dress. Go way, go way. Can't you see we're playing?"

Julia finally did go way—with the bill. She hid the bill and left the apartment. Connelly calmly left a bit later, assured that she and his money would turn up at his door. Well, when she came home and found him gone she was frantic and phoned him. Connelly, living only a few blocks away and, in that instance, not the most gallant, said, "All you have to do is just walk yourself over here, Julia, and walk my money with you."

Julia refused to do exactly as directed. Instead, she had Ferber write a check for a thousand dollars, which she brought over to him. She wasn't going to walk the streets with that kind of money. No fool she.

Ferber inherited the mantle of upstaging. Never a docile woman, around a theatre she was voluble to the point of chewing scenery—which she literally came close to doing during the early rehearsals of *Bravo!*

Garson Kanin, author, playwright, director, raconteur for all seasons and many decades, tells the tale with his usual sangfroid:

"I think she was passionately stage-struck, and even when a play wasn't going well and clearly wasn't going to make it, it was still something very, very important to her.

"There was a man named Leo Kerz, who was the designer of 'Bravo!'. The show was just a few days in rehearsal and Leo Kerz came around with the scale drawing of the set. Kaufman was busy with the actors doing something, and out in back of the theater Kerz was showing the design to Edna. George is the one who told me this—that he heard all at once the most outraged scream and yell, then he heard a man's voice, then Edna's voice, and then he heard what wasn't so much an altercation as an assault. He couldn't imagine what was happening so he went back and there in the lobby poor little Leo Kerz was practically backed-up against the wall with Edna, brandishing this rolled-up drawing, saying to him, 'You are the most incompetent fool that I have ever encountered in the theater. I wouldn't dream of having you in the same theater that I am in . . .' George did his best to calm things down. (Leo Kerz was a perfectly sound and experienced designer with an excellent reputation.) Well, she was absolutely bawling the living bejesus out of him and George said, 'What seems to be the trouble?' She said, 'Have you seen this?!?'

"George said, 'Well, yes, I've looked at it.'

"Edna said, 'Look at it again!'

"So he opened it up and he said, 'Edna, the thing takes place in the sitting room of an uptown rooming house on the West Side. It's just a room. I don't see anything faulty with it.'

"Edna said, 'Are you looking at it? You're not really looking at it.'

"George said, 'Yes, Edna, I am.'

"Edna said, 'Well, look at that.'

"She pointed to something, and George, who was a little myopic anyway, couldn't make out what it was.

"Edna bellowed, 'THAT is a gold fish bowl. A GOLD FISH BOWL! Can you imagine a gold fish bowl in this room! What sort of an idiot would put a gold fish bowl in here!' She went on and on.

"Finally, George said, 'Edna, we'll take it out. There won't be any gold fish bowl.'

"Leo Kerz said, 'That's what I've been trying to tell Miss Ferber.'

"Edna said, 'Just be quiet. That's not the point. The point is that anyone who would put a gold fish bowl into this set doesn't understand the play.'

"Finally, she simmered down; Leo Kerz went home and probably went to bed for two or three days, and the production continued.

"George recalled that about ten days later Edna came in to see a run-through. Oscar Homolka had a rather long speech where he simply sat in a chair and delivered it—with no movement whatsoever.

"Edna came up to George after it was over and said, 'Is that how he's going to do that? He's just going to sit there?'

"George said, patiently, 'Edna, he kind of likes to do it that way. It works for him.'

"Edna retaliated, impatiently. 'But it's so boring. He's just sitting there and we're just sitting here watching him just sitting there. Boring.'

"George said, compromisingly, 'Well, I don't know. What could he possibly do?'

"And Edna said, 'Well, couldn't he go over and feed the gold fish?'"

Garson Kanin pegged it when he said that Ferber liked to be in charge. She was generous that way; she had so much command of her own life that she could afford leftover orders and suggestions about other people's lives. For her friends, there were mostly kind suggestions—especially friends with children. She would play the role of the wry but doting maiden aunt, asserting herself and inserting herself every other month or so. Not having a family of her own affected her in her middle years more than at any other time. She was used to standing on the sidelines watching marriages, but it seemed that watching familial events was more painful to her, particularly during her years at Treasure Hill, where childern could have played and thrived. She had made her choice, made her substitutions, but occasionally there is evidence of longing. When Kitty and Moss Hart were going to have a baby, somehow they neglected to tell Ferber about it. Her letter to them about it is fascinating. She does about six emotional things in it: she compliments them; she criticizes them; she passes on information to them; she reminds them that she's sought after; she reminds them that she expects to see them soon; and she reminds them that she's hurt by them.

"It was so lovely to open the big formidable-looking envelope and find myself being greeted by you both, dearest Moss and Kitty. I shall whip over to Pocker for a fitting frame. In the meantime you're on the piano in a makeshift. Myself, I don't think the picture is as handsome as the subjects. The photographer hasn't caught the spirit of either of you. Do you know a photographer named Halsman? He's in West 67th, or thereabouts, and I think he's the best. He did one of me for ONE BASKET. It's the best I've ever had.

"I'm counting on your coming August first. At Saks a few days ago a friend of yours announced to the various sales-people and customers, in ringing tones, that you are having a baby. Also, about nine people told me. I'm the girl who is The Last To Know. Just why you didn't want to tell me when I was at New Hope is one of the things I'll never understand.

"Mike Todd and his bride, in Hollywood country clothes, appeared unannounced at the front door on Friday at 7 p.m. They are looking for a house in Connecticut, preferably one costing between $100,000 and $150,000. I now do not feel the resentment I once had for the possibility of destruction by the atomic bomb. I'll call you for details about your arrival time, etc. My love to you. Edna."

Ferber took it upon herself to think she might contribute name ideas for the Harts' child. They beat her to it, had their child, and named it promptly without consultation. Ferber's letter:

"Dear Harts, I came across this tucked away in a note-book. You'll remember I spoke to you about it not so long ago, Kitty. I must have been brooding about a name for Miss Kathy before she was born, and after. I think Kathy Hart is lovely though I've never seen the lady of that name." Alongside the note is Ferber's name list—just in case they wanted to change their minds.

"Deborah Hart, Hannah Hart, Gay Hart, Valerie Hart, Leslie Hart, Letitia Hart, Lisa Hart, Carole Hart, Emanie Hart. I love you. Edna."

Even though their lives were younger and different, the Harts saw Ferber socially and enjoyed her immensely. There was always a current give and take, which allowed her to feel more part of a threesome than the third one of a twosome. There were other old friends, however, who were rendered, through circumstance, part of her past. Every five years or so they would resurrect themselves in a "newsletter" to Ferber—telling of children and grandchildren and investments and recalling the good old days. One of these was Louis Bromfield, author of *The Green Bay Tree* and popular novelist during the twenties, thirties and forties. Bromfield was handsome, charming, intelligent, married and just a good friend. A farmer at heart, he appealed to Ferber's Middle Western ideals. Janet sketches him quickly:

"He was very handsome, but he had funny teeth—and his wife had awful teeth; they protruded straight out. Louis wore a beret a lot to hide his thinning hair. He was very lean and sinewy and brown. He had a farm in Sont Lis—outside of Paris."

In 1935, to regress for a while, Louis Bromfield felt that he knew Ferber as well as anyone, and vouched for it in a portrait he did of her for the *Saturday Review* that was titled simply: "Edna Ferber." Not only does it explain their friendship, but it illuminates the best of Edna Ferber. In the language of journalism, it is a love letter:

"She is one of the personalities of our time and in order to know her you must be her friend, because toward strangers she has a manner which is at once a mixture of shyness and hostility and because she shuns publicity as much as most novelists court it. She is difficult to write about, not only because I am very fond of her but also because she is a curious and complicated mixture of tastes, of impulses and emotions. The truth is, I think, that when America gained a fine chronicle novelist, an excellent playwright, and a writer of short stories of the first order, it lost a great actress.

"If, as one sometimes does in playing parlor games, one was to give Edna Ferber mythical parents, I should at once choose Sarah Bernhardt as her mother and the Prophet Jeremiah as her father. This strange parentage is one of the elements which makes her character difficult and sometimes a little confusing. And I think that possibly among her parents and grandparents one would find that she is somehow related to Werther. She is an incorrigible romantic in the good nineteenth century sense. I myself understand perfectly the essence of the romantic's soul. It is born of the profound belief, never abandoned in the face of the most disillusioning experiences, that people, especially one's friends, should always be nobler, finer, more virtuous, more glamourous, and more beautiful than it is possible for any poor mortal ever to be.

"If the stars had been in a different position on the night she was born she would have been a great actress, something which at the moment the world has need of. For myself I am satisfied with the novelist and playwright, more satisfied than Miss Ferber herself, for she is always in a state of distress over her shortcomings, sometimes real and more often imaginary, as a novelist. I know that at times she has a great yearning to emerge from the wings and play a great role, and frequently, at the rehearsals of one of her own plays, she is seized with a violent longing to climb over the orchestra pit and play a role as it should be played. Blocked at its source, all her instinct for acting has been sublimated into a talent for writing for the theater, for the perfect sense of drama which is in her novels and made Showboat on the stage one of the greatest events of our troubled times; and sometimes it has been sublimated into a talent for poking life itself into something as fine and as exciting as the things which happen behind the footlights . . .

"Life is rarely as exciting as that, so Miss Ferber is likely at moments of baffled irritation to take it by the scruff of the neck and slap it into shape. Now and again, without any warning, you find yourself caught up in a terrific situation and there you are suddenly, trembling and frightened, playing opposite a great actress in a role and a scene which you never quite understand. At first all this is baffling but with a little experience you begin to understand that you are simply an instrument in the hands of Miss Ferber, being used to poke and prod life into being more exciting. After three or four weeks of hard work in some hideaway, she has begun to find life very dull and so, after going over one of the largest lists of sincere and devoted friends possessed by any individual alive today, she selects you at random and sallies forth to invent a little drama.

"After a really satisfactory performance, Miss Ferber's instinct for drama will be appeased for days and even weeks and she will get a lot of work done. She has had an extremely distinguished list of leading men which includes Noel Coward, Jed Harris, Marc Connelly, George Kaufman, Harold Ross, Alexander Woollcott, and many others. As heavy women she has employed Margaret Pulitzer, Dorothy Parker, Beatrice Kaufman, and others equally well known. All of them love her.

". . . A good deal of it is a simple matter of vitality. It is impossible to write of Edna Ferber without writing as well of her mother. Known simply as Julia to her friends of all ages, she is ageless, indefatigable, handsome, entertaining, and the best company in the world. And she has character. She is always as young as the youngest person in the room. She loves good food, and the best food in New York (and I say this as one whose only vanities in life are gardening and food) is to be had at her flat and that of her daughter Edna. In Miss Ferber's flat the food is concocted by a fabulous and handsome colored woman called Rebecca Henry who herself deserves a whole article. It is concocted with strong hints from both Miss Ferber and her mother because they 'know.' The walnut cake and the lobster and fish salad to be had at their small dinners are only two items on a long list in a household so hospitable that I am tempted to list it among the five best restaurants in the world.

"Her dinners and her parties are always small and are, I may add, handpicked. There is no shoving, pushing crowd, guzzling cocktails; there is never any screaming or yelling to make one's self heard. Miss Ferber understands the very great art of entertaining, and when one sits down to dinner, the guests are as good as the food. Thus her flat is virtually an oasis in New York. Somehow or other she has managed to isolate her own modest apartment against the New York disease.

"Sometimes her mother is present at the parties, and on such occasions she is, when she will permit it, my chosen companion. There is about her a Greco-French sense of reality and truth, and if ever the conversation becomes a little high-falutin and arty, it is likely to be deflated at once by a tart, well-aimed remark from Julia Ferber. She has had a magnificent life, and I might add is still having one, for she is one of the fortunate who never lose their zest, and out of her life she has learned (if she did not always have them) wisdom, truth and taste. Much that appears in her daughter's books and plays and stories has been learned from her; much of it is reality. Both mother and daughter have the blessed gifts of vitality and friendliness.

"One of Miss Ferber's great qualities is her sincerity. I have known many writers who were sincere either as writers or as people, but not many who were sincere in both roles. As a rule the literary temperament is unstable, changeable, and even cynical. She is none of these things; you know exactly where to find her both as a writer and woman. She attempts neither to deceive others nor, what is far worse, to deceive herself. She is one of the most successful writers of our times, and she deserves her success because she has worked for it with all her spirit and body. She has never pretended that writing is all inspiration, that novel writing is done by some spirit control which pours out words for you. She has always done her best and whether it has been excellent or indifferent, each thing she has written, each word she has put on paper, is put there through belief.

"I have seen her work and I know that sometimes it is for her as it is for any good writer, pure, unadulterated agony. I have seen her resisting the most terrific temptations, to remain at her desk and do the thing she has to do. For two or three summers we lived in houses, side by side, writing, each doing a novel. Of the two she was by far the more conscientious, for to her what she was doing was the most important thing in the world. By that test I failed because I could not resist the sunlight of the Basque coast and the sight of the blue-green sea rolling up on a white beach, or the prospects of fishing in the surf which was churning like champagne over the rocks at the end of my garden. I gave in, but Miss Ferber stuck to her guns.

"Like any good artist she respects her craft knowing that no writer can say all of what he means to say until he has learned the craft, forgotten it, and thrown it away. You never hear from her arty, adolescent talk on the subject of writing, but no one I know is more appreciative of the work of others when it is good; and there are few people I know whose judgement I would trust as profoundly. She knows a good book when she sees one, and she is not to be hypnotized by tricks or by the fashions of the moment. That is, I think, because she knows her craft.

"She is, too, an extraordinarily modest woman, far more modest about her own work than is just to it, but there is no hypocrisy in her attitude nor any false modesty. She is proud of her work and at the same time she is never quite satisfied with it. She is aware always that there is something just beyond which somehow has escaped her. I have heard her say again and again, 'This is the last novel I will ever write!' but there is always another and there always will be, because she does not think that she has attained perfection. Knowing her very well, I know that she never will, for she is much too intelligent. It is impossible to imagine a smug, a complacent, Edna Ferber.

"Like her mother, she is the best company in the world, not only because she is witty and intelligent but because nothing ever escapes her and if, even for a moment she is deceived, the deception does not endure and when it is gone she is the first to admit it and to laugh at herself. I have been with her in Sweden, in London, in the Basque country, in New York, and never once under any circumstances has she failed. She has, as every writer should have, a fine sense of the spectacle and her presence at table in a restaurant or at a party raises the whole level of gaiety and amusement. And she is just as good company on a beach or the edge of a cliff above the sea. I think the reason is . . . indeed the reason for everything about her, the very reason for Edna Ferber—is that she loves life and people, and that is a supreme gift from the gods.

"We have one bond at least in common and that is our strange and unbalanced passion for and detestation for travel. She hates traveling and is uncomfortable and grumbling most of the time she is on her way. None the less she is one of the most restless souls I know. I have seen her planning trips which she does not in the least want to take. I have seen her departures and her arrivals and can testify that she is likely to be ill-humored both before and after the event. And I think I know the reasons for this strange dementia. If she has escaped the New York disease, she had no such luck with what I call the Middle Western fever.

"Middle Westerners are incorrigible travelers, and I have a suspicion that it has something to do with a hunger for a sight of the sea, for variety, for the excitement which somehow or other none of us was able to find there as children. Born in the center of a vast rich country, one grows up infected with the idea that excitement, color, and fascinating people all live just beyond that infinitely remote horizen. You have to travel no matter how much you hate it. Some of Miss Ferber's journeys are made conscientiously, in search for authenticity of background, but most of them are, I think, the result simply of a kind of cantankerous restlessness and of that old romantic trouble of trying to discover a world as fascinating as it should be.

"She has been almost everywhere. Only last winter she made a flying trip to Egypt. It was not, I imagine, the ideal country to interest her. In any case I got the impression that Miss Ferber did not much care for it and that she had not particularly enjoyed all the trouble of journeying there. She has seen a large part of the world and before she has finished, I imagine, she will have seen very nearly everything there is to see, grumbling all the while. What she likes best is America, and by that I do not mean the America of the crowded cities or even the small stuffy towns but the America of the Rocky Mountains and the desert of Arizona and New Mexico.

"The superficial biographical details of her life are, I should think, well known to practically everyone in the United States who is literate. She has had what seems to me the best possible education for life in this modern America. Having been born in the Middle West, she came before she was twenty-one to know in detail the life of two or three small towns, each one a laboratory in which to study American life, and she made the most of her opportunities. She has worked for her living and knows how to make one dollar go as far as five, if that were still necessary. She has known a large share of the distinguished and clever people of the world and as many of the worldly ones as she chose, but has no great liking for the worldly and the fashionable, either in life or in letters. She prefers to write about those solid, sometimes humble people who are the very essence of American life and she knows profoundly the difference between what is American and what is imitation European. She will never be one of those American writers who espouse the cause of the Left Wing or one of those who are influenced by the decadence of Europe. About everything she writes there is an atmosphere, a treatment, a penetration which is profoundly authentic and American.

"I may have given the impression that Miss Ferber is a simple and direct person and if I have done so, I have failed completely. She is as feminine, as intricate, as contradictory as it is well possible for a woman to be. She is a good many people rolled into one. It is not only Sarah Bernhardt and Jeremiah and Werther whom I have discovered but several other people less well defined. But then Goethe himself once said something very profound about genius being born of what we should call in these times a divided personality. If you are only one person, it is quite likely that you will be dull and not accomplish much of interest to the rest of the world.

"There is much more to be said on the subject of Miss Ferber. One could indeed write an entire book with no trouble at all. But I must add that she is the soul of generosity and that she is a demon shopper. I have seen her in many parts of the world engaged in what is one of her favorite pastimes—buying lace, glass, porcelain, and Heaven knows what. It is virtually impossible for her to pass the window of an attractive shop without going in, and once inside she rarely escapes without buying. A good many of the things go to her friends but no one in the world could have enough friends to care for the shopping urge of our leading American chronicler. I am convinced that somewhere, hidden away, there is a vast room filled with packing cases and packages which bear the labels of Stockholm, Prague, London, Cairo, Biarritz, and Timbuctu, which have not yet been opened because she has been unable to think up a place for the contents. Someday I hope to see a large Edna Ferber Auction which will empty that mysterious storeroom so that she may begin all over again. Or perhaps she will only take another room.

"If you have never met Miss Ferber you have lost much for she is one of the persons to know in our time. If you have her for a friend, you are more than lucky, for not only is she a stalwart friend but she has the gift of making life exciting."

Fourteen years and one war later, Louis Bromfield did not know Ferber at all anymore. They had gone their separate lives. He tries to bridge the gap in a letter full of distance:

"Edna, I should have answered your letter long before now but I have been swamped with work of every kind including the proofs on the new novel 'Mr. Smith' which comes out in August. It is rather grim—about all the middle class well to do Americans with cars, radios, television, plumbing and God knows what in material things . . . and in the end nothing. It will probably be pretty controversial but that never hurt the sale of any book.

"Just in addition to writing let me list a few of my activities . . . the whole running of this place which is in itself a business, a ranch in Texas, twenty to twenty five thousand visitors during the year . . . mostly farmers with some scientists, editors, agricultural authorities and what not, about 150 speeches a year, a weekly newspaper column that goes to eighty more or less key papers, articles, and personal troubles of a whole army of people. So you see I don't have much leisure time and literally have not had a holiday in eleven years . . .

"But you must come out. In spite of everything, it is a busy merry, friendly life full of fun and accomplishment and satisfaction. At times it gets like 'You Can't Take It With You' but it has its laughs.

"I did not know about Julia and can certainly appreciate the hole she has left in your life. There was certainly a vital character. It is impossible to think of her as being gone but we must admit that she got a kick out of life and didn't miss much and that's about the best epitaph anyone can have. She always seemed to me as young as anyone I ever knew and as full of gaiety and laughs . . .

". . . I will certainly get together with you when I come to New York. I don't get there very often and when I do come it is usually for not more than forty-eight hours. The armed forces have taken my farm manager, my assistant herdsman and my son-in-law who could have taken over, so I have every small detail on my shoulders. Now they're trying to take a fourth key man. I'm fighting this. But it's all so idiotic and unecessary . . . If we had a decent president and state department none of it would have happened or be happening now. My old home town barber Mr. Kip would make as good or better President than the one we've got. At least he'd have some moral sense and integrity.

". . . Do plan to come out and spend at least a week-end here. I think you would like it and get some laughs. I think you were right to get rid of the farm. Nobody today in his right mind wants an estate and a farm is the most difficult and complicated operation in the world. It was a beautiful place but, I am sure, not worth all the time and trouble.

". . . Incidentally I forgot to mention that the household includes nine dogs . . . four boxers, a mastiff, a collie and three cockers. They have their own dog's door so you don't have to get up to let them in and out.

". . . Now do fix a date to come out. It's an easy trip . . . just overnight on luxurious trains."

Ferber never went to Louis Bromfield's farm in Lucas, Ohio, for "some laughs," and he in turn kept postponing that forty-eight-hour trip to New York. They continued to correspond, however, with Ferber usually being the one to reach out first, and Bromfield being the one to apologize for negligence. Almost like an ex-sorority girl, she would try to get the "good old days" back together again in New York at one of the good old haunts like "21" or the Algonquin or Voisin or The Colony. Her dear friends Alfred Lunt and Lynn Fontanne, who had semiretired to their farm in Genesee Depot, Wisconsin, were better about reunions than Bromfield. They came to New York infrequently, but when they did Ferber was always on their agenda. One time she tried to get Bromfield to New York with the lure of seeing the Lunts, but he passed, making it clear that he lived in and preferred the present.

"As to Twenty One and lunch, I feel less and less myself every time I come to New York. Actually the ties I have with it today are few and pretty far between and places like Twenty One etc. and the people in them are likely to turn my stomach. I get so tired of everyone having an angle and everybody working at it and I must say that by any standard New York is not what it used to be.

"There is nothing I would rather do than have dinner with you and the Lunts whom I have always loved. The only thing is that you might get fed up with Alfred's and my agricultural talk. I will certainly let you know in advance when we are coming to New York, but I doubt that it will be before Xmas."

Christmas came and went without Louis Bromfield.

"Although she often pretended to be very airy-fairy about business matters," says Garson Kanin, "I suspect that Edna was very hard-nosed about them—very shrewd—as were G. B. Shaw and Mark Twain."

Not only does he put her in good company, but he's right. During the first act of business transactions Ferber might have played "the little woman," but by second-act curtain everybody knew who wore the pants. She also had immaculate business taste, never stooping to sideshow display—often part of a best-selling author's reticule.

In 1951, Doubleday republished three of Ferber's biggest books: *Cimarron, So Big,* and *Show Boat.* The following correspondence to Ken McCormick points up not only her taste but her mettle, muscle, and almost frightening pride.

"Did I, when we spoke of the books Friday night . . . really convey to you how happy I am about them? I was afraid they would turn out to be those limp and tasteless jobs that one so often sees in reprints. These aren't reprints at all, physically at least. The jackets are arresting, the type and paper clear and good, the books have style and a look of substance and dignity.

"I opened SO BIG and read the first chapter, and then the ending of the night in the market place. Ken, they're still good, after a quarter of a century. Without false modesty I say lovely writing, Mr. M.

". . . Anybody going to buy them at three dollars? After all these years. I hope so. I wish we could announce that they are back in print in the regular editions. I don't mean advertising, in the commercial sense. I mean through columns, book news, etc. . . .

"I've just had a letter from Germany signed by twenty German students. They seem to be adults, as one is a Dr. Somebody-or-other. They had read SO BIG in their class work. The comments are fascinating. They say this is a United States whose existence they didn't know. What harm the motion pictures have done to this country these past years. Most of the world has formed its opinion of us through these idiotic films.

". . . I suppose that, like Scott Fitzgerald, you have to be dead to be good. I'll oblige, sooner or later. But my story is that Fitzgerald wasn't so very good as a writer, dead or alive."

"I had a beautiful time Tuesday evening. I recall, however, in a moment of hilarious spirits (I'd only had one drink so it couldn't have been that) saying that I'd autograph books. You know, of course, that autographing seems to me just about the shoddiest thing an author can do. It has a medicine-show connotation that cheapens both book and writer. If, after more than thirty-five years of good and successful writing I must write my name in my books in order to sell them I am willing to concede that I am through. But, honeh, I'm not through."

"These books are still alive after a quarter of a century. There must be a reason for that. The reason is that they have vitality; they have color and movement; they have a feeling for life and for living and for the emotions of human beings which somehow communicates itself to the reader. If this were not true they would have died the year after they were born. But they didn't."

"Thanks, dear Ken, for the check. I find it rather unsettling to know that the books didn't catch on as well as expected in the cheap edition. Morris Ernst says that this is true of all books (or almost all) other than the bosom-and-crime type. I'm thinking of doing one in which May West murders Dean Acheson. That ought to have about everything."

Franklin P. Adams crowned Ferber with the moniker of "The Jewish Cinderella." In terms of achieving the American Dream for a little Jewish girl, indeed her pumkins had turned. She had wealth and she had position—what more could be asked out of life? Well-known fellow Jews took great pride in her. Two show business veterans—Billy Rose and George Jessel—discussed her in rather holy tones:

Billy Rose wrote of her: "What with one thing and another, I know you fellows are finding it difficult these days to select books for your overseas libraries which will give our friends abroad a sympathetic picture of what we're like and what makes our wheels go round. Well . . . I'd like to make a specific suggestion. Namely, to stock your library shelves with the collected works of a little lady named Edna Ferber. Miss Ferber, now a gracious and gray-haired lady, has been carrying on a love affair with the 48 states ever since Wilson was president. Her string of novels includes 'Show Boat,' 'Cimarron,' 'Come and Get It,' 'So Big' and 'Saratoga Trunk'—every one a thank-you hymn to the land which welcomed her emigrant parents.

"For a roundup of life in these United States during the past 100 years—how we lived, loved, dressed, fought, thought and ate—I doubt whether any of the conventional historians can touch, tie or top Miss Ferber. It's all there and 3,000 miles wide—the saga of our country from Cape Cod to Puget Sound with stopoffs in New Orleans, Oklahoma, Chicago, New York and dozens of other places.

"If you have read her books, you, of course know that Miss Ferber, despite her crush on this country, has never compromised with her compulsion to tell the truth about it. As a result, her novels are an exciting blend of brag and brabble.

"This combination of romance and solid reporting, easy to read and easier to remember, may well give the people you're trying to influence a more appealing picture of America than the hopped-up jingosism which has become so popular of late."

George Jessel's lauding is somewhat simpler: "The most forceful women I've ever met and capable of filling almost any man's job are: Madame Chiang Kai-shek, Mrs. F.D.R., Edna Ferber and Sister Kenny."

Ferber the lover of life; Ferber the compass spinner; Ferber the Jewish Cinderella intones like a Greek chorus in her diary of 1949:

"A really dull life. Wot a dull, dull life., but perhaps the book [*Giant*] is growing in which case dullness doesn't matter."

The "Stage Mamma" surfaced again in 1948, when Henry Goldsmith was out of the Army, with wife and small child, and out of a job. He had suffered loss and shock from the war. There was something deep-seated in Ferber that empathized with his problems more than she could ever identify with the other family members' problems. Henry was a survivor. She honord him for that. In a letter to Ken McCormick, she introduces Henry Goldsmith:

"In your audience listening to the forum or debate on publishing a few nights ago was a brilliant young man whom you do not know. He is my nephew-in-law, Henry Goldsmith, who is the husband of my niece, Janet Fox.

"Here's the situation: He isn't looking for a job with Doubleday, so I may talk freely to you . . . I needn't hesitate to ask you if you'll see him briefly, if you can possibly manage the time.

"Henry Goldsmith is more interested in the publishing business than in any other type of profession or work. But he feels that he should ally himself, if possible with a small publishing house so that he may get experience in all departments if possible. I think he particularly wants to ask you if you know a smallish and intelligent firm in which he may perhaps later invest some small capital. This he will be able to explain to you better than I can.

"He was in the Intelligence during the war, spent almost all the war years in England, handled the top-boy German officer cases in many instances. He speaks French and German fluently, as well as English of course.

"He is steamed up about publishing and isn't deterred by the fact that the publishing business is having a bumpy ride just now. He's a brilliant young fellow, well read, knows books, wants to be a publisher, isn't (I repeat) looking for a job with you folks . . ."

Like a filled prescription, Henry got the exact job he was seeking with a small publishing firm, and has been there to this day. Ferber took care of her own.

Being taken care of and being happy are two different animals, as Henry well knew. One day he and Ferber rode to Philadelphia in a limousine she had hired, to see Janet open in a play. Ferber turned to Henry and got personal. "What would you have done," she asked, "if there had been no Hitler? What would you have wanted for your life?"

Henry could feel the God-tentacles reaching out. "I would have been a doctor," he replied. "I always wanted to be a doctor."

If Ferber could have smiled down on him she would have. "Do you still?" she asked with the soft voice of power.

He was tempted. For a moment he was tempted. "No," he said. "Nonsense," he said. "Absolutely not."

And had he answered yes? "It would have proved embarrassing very quickly. I would have been over fifty when I graduated medical school."

Ferber never recovered from World War II. It was an atrocity that she recollected over and over again like a necessary liturgy. She tended to be a zealot about things that were morally corrupt—expressing herself boldly on paper or in a drawing room. She used to say about Hitler's reign of terror that there were no words for such a horror. She always managed to find some. She felt that anywhere and at any time people could be subject to a dictator. A few years after the war she delved back into her past, found an apt parallel, and put it down on paper. She titled it *The Bad Old Days*. To my knowledge it has never been published.

"Over the moldy crusts of our past we oldsters have a trick of spreading a thick and palatable layer of nostalgic butter. We babble quite a lot about good old this and do you remember wonderful old that. The grimmer memories of our youthful days are stuffed into the trash can of forgotten things. Only the gay, the dramatic, are cherished. A fine healthy process, really. Nature's way of healing our early wounds (the psychiatrists probably would fight me on this statement).

". . . When I wrote A PECULIAR TREASURE, a sort of autobiographical book whose underlying purpose was not at all autobiographical, I devoted pages to fond recollections of my only alma mater, Ryan High School, of Appleton, Wisconsin. In those pages the crumbling dated old edifice emerged as a unique seat of learning, staffed by wise, tolerant and companionable teachers; full of skylarking but brainy students; victorious in school contests, whether football, dramatics, oratory or track meets.

"Well, strangely enough, so it actually was. We loved it. Saturdays, often as not, we'd sort of amble over there to sit and talk on the side porch steps in the spring or to play tennis on the gravelly court in the summer, or clatter through the halls or the manual training room on non-existent errands. As a reporter loves the sounds and smell of a newspaper office, as a stage-struck actor loves the feel of a theater, full or empty, so we were somehow reassured and content to know the worn wooden boards beneath our feet; the dim halls, the battered classrooms, the shabby desks within our vision. Architecturally and practically the old Ryan High School was a mess. Spiritually it was a Taj Mahal of splendor.

"Don't ask me why—unless it was Prof. Pringle, the Principal. But even before his time the school had had a reputation for certain items never formally named in the curriculum of this or any other school. Self reliance. Fair play. Self respect. Self expression. Freedom of speech and thought. Fun. Never listed, certainly, they somehow existed and flourished. The spirit of this shabby little high school was strangely like that of a free and noble university. Perhaps this seems absurd, for we were fourteen, fifteen, sixteen, seventeen, eighteen years of age. But it was true.

"The teaching staff was not composed of Platos and Minervas, by any means. Among them could be found the crotchety, the pedantic, the vague. We frequently misbehaved and got our come-uppance for it. The ruling hand was velvet-gloved but firm. These men and women had our respect and they respected us. Perhaps the regime could have been called the honor system, but it never was. Prof. Pringle, the head, simply gave us credit for reasonable intelligence, taste, a sense of decency. Those who failed this assumption knew punishment. Talking, laughing, studying; learning to speak on our feet extemporaneously at the Forum Debating Society; reciting, arguing, playing, working, we were a fine little democracy there at Ryan High.

"Then, one autumn, at the beginning of the term, there came into the school faculty a new teacher to take the place of an elderly one who had died suddenly during the summer vacation. He was younger than the other members of the staff—years younger than Prof. Pringle. Handsome in a vulpine way.

"We learned to hate him. Agile, crafty, treading, oh, so swiftly and furtively, he brought fear into the free corridors and class rooms of Ryan High. Between classes we students always went to the big general assembly room, where each had a desk and where we studied in preparation for the next class. For each hour of each study period a teacher sat in charge at the desk facing the room and the students. Usually he, too, had his nose in a book. If we became too restless, too talkative, too peripatetic, he might rap smartly for order with the tip of a pencil or a ruler on his desk. But that was all. Sometimes a gentle hum pervaded the half-filled room, sometimes it was silent, sometimes there was the clatter of heels on the way to the cosy privacy of the reference table in the corner, its book-laden shelves forming a fine cover for whispered confidences.

"The new teacher did not seat himself at that desk facing us. He always took a pupil's vacant seat in the last row at the back of the room. We could feel his eyes raking the back of our heads. We never knew when his soundless swift step would bring him, menacing, beside our desk. An accustomed freedom of thought and action and speech was somehow, mysteriously, gone. If, according to established custom, we rose to fetch a needed book from a fellow student's desk, if we went to the reference table, if, work finished we lolled in relaxation before the bell sounded for the next class, we were barked at as a sadistic top sergeant blasts at a raw recruit. Doubt, fear, suspicion, apprehension suddenly became spectres haunting our halls. Now, for the first time, we knew the rule of the hostile eye, the iron hand, the pounce, the ambitious vindictive mind. The air of our free rooms was vitiated by an insidious poison. Student was turned against student. Teacher against teacher.

Slowly it dawned on us that this new one had in mind not only our subjugation; that cold bold eye was on Prof. Pringle; it was the chair of the Principal toward which his feral glance was directed. He planned, not only to rule us; he planned to rule the staff, the Principal. Prof. Pringle, the gentle, the humane, the somewhat bewildered, must have sensed this astounding fact.

"Now the time has come to present a dramatic finale. An uprising of indignant and rebellious students; reports (dignified but definite in tone) from the Principal to the School Board. Nothing of the kind happened. We sulked. We became rather sly, we did hold occasional private meetings during which we voiced our bewildered resentment. We complained to our parents about this new atmosphere of suspicion, distrust and dictatorial arrogance. They said, 'He's new and feels his own importance. Just give him enough rope, he'll hang himself.' Or, 'Maybe a little discipline for a change won't hurt you kids.'

"Those of us who were nearing the end of our high school years thought, well, we'll be out of this pretty soon. The lower classmen, squirming under the new regime, said, 'I'm not going to be the one to squawk, get him on my neck and I might as well be dead.'

"Graduated, I went to work as a reporter on the Appleton Daily Crescent at $3 a week. Grandly this sum mounted to $5, then $8. Crazed with success I went to Milwaukee and the Milwaukee Journal at $15. My thoughts were no longer with the grubby halls of Ryan High, but turned now to the starlit realms of journalism. Ryan High! Kid stuff.

"But in this past year or two my thoughts have traveled back to the lovely town of Appleton, Wisconsin, in the Fox River Valley, and to those prideful boys and girls whose freedom and intelligence were, almost before they were aware of it, degraded.

"Lately I've wondered how things really came out, there at Ryan. Through bewilderment or carelessness or fear did our school democracy degenerate, perhaps, into a hated dictatorship? If it did, each of us was as guilty as the rest."

Ferber did not do her best work in the recovery years after the war. She was distracted, disillusioned, irritable, and very social without seeming to want to be. Her diary reads like a disgruntled debutante's—weary of the names that she drops. There is a blasé tone that is unfamiliar for Ferber.

Entry: "Dinner for Hugh Beaumont, god knows why. Not bad. Lillian Hellman, Janet, Moss, Warburgs, Helen Hayes, Charles MacArthur, Neysa, Dick, Dorothy."

Entry: "Too much champagne and caviar last night. Didn't fall asleep until five a.m."

Entry: "Moss Hart to dinner. With him to see Lunts opening in 'O Mistress Mine.' To Stork Club with Moss, Marches [the actors Fredric and Florence], Terry Helburn. Not as amusing as it should have been."

Entry: "Dinner 7:45—Marches, Dorothy Rodgers, Stan Griffis, Gordons, Creens, Janet, Danny Kaye. Not bad. Stayed until 1:30."

Then there is an entry that brings one up short. It concerns a good time that she did manage to have. It is self-explanatory:

"Party at Neysa McMein's for fliers who dropped bomb on Nagasaki and Hiroshima. Very gay and pleasant. Bing Crosby sang."

Her behavior during this time—'46-'47—was erratic. Her usual discipline seemed to have sprouted wings. She lunched and cocktailed and time-killed. She was, as the penny novellas used to put it, not herself.

She left Doubleday—for the second time in ten years—in 1947. Simon & Schuster published a collection of her short stories under the umbrella title of *One Basket*. None of them were new; they had been published in *Woman's Home Companion* and various other magazines years before. They were merely old work in a new volume. She tried to make an event of it, and even consented to record one of the stories, "The Gay Old Dog," for Goddard Lieberson at Columbia Records. In her introduction to the recording, she plays the sage old short story dog:

"Only a very young writer, lavish and wasteful with ideas and vitality, could have been so foolish as to compress into a single short story the materials that should have made a full length novel. Into the short story entitled THE GAY OLD DOG are jammed twenty-five years of a man's adult life. The story begins when he is twenty-seven and ends in his middle fifties, yet it totals perhaps less than eight thousand words. In it we follow the years of an unselfish, rather sentimental and mistaken bachelor; his family life, his hopes, his emotions, his disappointments, his tragedy. But this is material for a book of one hundred thousand words. Its use in the short story form was like trying to cram a trunkful of clothes into a suitcase. If the receptacle doesn't burst it certainly will bulge in places, and perhaps odds and ends will stick out or have to be discarded.

"THE GAY OLD DOG was written in 1917. That is a long time ago, reckoned in the life of a short story. Yet this one has somehow survived, and it frequently is used in anthologies and in text books as an example of the use of the time element in the short story form. The theme had interested me long before I began to write the story. I had known men like Joe Hertz; patient, imposed upon, bewildered, desperate. For weeks, for months, for a year I had had the story in mind, the process of planning and construction and characterization went on until the structure was really complete, though no more than rough notes had been put on paper. Finally, in 1917, I began to write the story and finished it in a few days, the final draught being the third.

"The short story of today is a different matter. It catches a mood, an incident only. It moves with the tempo of our day. This particular short story and others of its kind were written before I had even thought of novels such as SO BIG, SHOW BOAT, CIMARRON, SARATOGA TRUNK, GIANT. It is, perhaps, interesting to the reader or writer who comes upon it because it plainly marks the transition process—the emergence of the short story writer into the novelist."

One Basket did respectable business for a revival, but nobody carried on about it—except for dear supportive Noel Coward, who instinctively knew when she needed hyperbole:

"I haven't said a word about 'One Basket.' They are brilliant. Some I had read before and some are new to me. Every one I enjoyed. Oh Darling, what a very satisfying writer you are. All my love and thanks for giving me so much pleasure."

As old a saw as it might be, for Ferber it truly was "meanwhile, back at the farm." She poured her energies into tending Treasure Hill. In a strange way she came close to taking on the personna of Selina Peake, her heroine of *So Big* who farmed so well without a man.

Garson Kanin recalls that the house was furnished in "Park Avenue" rather than country style. But the grounds were strictly rural and the livestock Old MacDonald. Ferber managed a record book that was in keeping with her; it was thorough, accurate and legible —in other words, a man's way of doing things. Excerpts:

FARM LABOR—1946

June 6—George Hitchcock—5 days-$25.00
June 6—two boys digging septic ditch-$4.50
June 16—Fred Candee-mowing lawn-$2.50

LIVE STOCK—1946

cow-grade Jersey-Thomas—$200.00
chickens-allen Prior Pullets—$28.75
14 hens—$25.00
Ram-paid to C.T. Maxham—$50.00
sold grade Jersey Cow ($50 loss)—$150.00

She really got carried away with blights on trees and so forth—this lady who loved Poiret and Chanel, Meissen china and Aubusson rugs. Yet though she bought fertilizer and even laid it, inside the house she was the lady of the manor. No flour-dabbed fingers dusted off on aprons for her; no potluck; no "come anytime you get here"; no informality whatsoever. She ran her house—country or town—like she ran her mind—with total control. Her regimen for weekend guests was as amusing as it was precise. All of her friends concur on the drill: one arrived on Saturday in time for lunch, bearing a gift, which she would pretend to be surprised at but would have been surprised if there wasn't one. The afternoon would be spent around the pool. There would always be a game of croquet—the favorite sport of that set. Then the guests would retire to their rooms to nap, bathe, and dress for dinner. Semiformal evening clothes were a requisite. The guests would then descend the long broad staircase, much like fashion show manikins, to be greeted and complimented by Ferber. She would usually have invited several members of the surrounding gentry to join her out-of-town houseguests for the evening. After cocktails—one or two apiece, no more—Ferber loathed big drinkers—they would have a meal fit for royalty (which they rather considered themselves anyway) prepared and served by Ferber's French couple, Jean and Alice. After dinner they would adjourn to the living room, or, if it was a hot night, to the terrace for stimulating conversation, a spot of brandy, and perhaps a game of charades. Then the local guests would leave, usually en masse—taking the cue from each other, and the houseguests, taking the cue from the departing ones, would make their good-night murmurs and thank-yous and retire upstairs. They could do nothing but have a blissful country sleep; as an unnamed source has said, "You just didn't do it at Ferber's." They would be awakened by dream-like breakfast smells of buttery biscuits, chickory coffee, smoky bacon, and occasionally they could hear the tap of far-off typewriter keys. If they were smart they would dress in their traveling clothes, for after a jolly breakfast they would go upstairs to find their beds stripped. If that wasn't enough of a hint, Ferber would ask them when they reached the city to post some letters so that they would go out on the Sunday night special. There was no Sunday night special. Any guest worth his salt would know that and beat it out of Treasure Hill right smack after his farewell breakfast, which, to be fair was more like brunch and ample enough to fortify him for the day. If he should fail to heed the signal of the stripped bed and the Sunday special, he would be—as they say in Hollywood today—on the D list. A weekend at Ferber's could be velvet if one followed the iron-fisted rules.

Ferber was fairly predictable in her eccentricities of etiquette. Her friends tended to have fun with her behind her back. Kitty Hart tells a story about going for a weekend at Treasure Hill. She remembers that she and Moss were both chewing great wads of gum while driving up to Connecticut. Moss predicted everything Ferber would say and do from asking them to dispose of the gum to apologizing for the pink guest room, to having their beds stripped on Sunday morning, to handing them the mail after brunch on Sunday as the clue to get out and go home. As soon as they got out of the car, he was right on the die from gum to mail.

Garson Kanin tells a story parallel in nature. He and Ruth Gordon, his wife, were the weekend houseguests of Fredric and Florence March, who had a home in Weston, Connecticut. Upon inviting them, Florence March had told Ruth Gordon to bring one formal dress in case they should go to a party or have one. As Ruth Gordon packed her party dress, she also decided to bring a marvelous and gigantic emerald ring that Garson Kanin had given her shortly before. When they arrived at the Marches', Florence March told them that they'd all been invited to Ferber's for dinner, and hoped that they didn't mind. They minded slightly; they didn't feel up to Ferber, but it was a *fait accompli* and there was nothing they could do.

As they were dressing, Ruth Gordon debated about wearing the ring. "Oh, I don't know if I can stand Edna's comments," she said to her husband. "She'll probably take one look at it and say, 'My God! That is the most pretentious thing I've ever seen in my whole born days.'" Kanin told her to wear it anyway—that it would be fun to hear what Ferber would actually say.

In the car en route to Ferber's, the two couples began to play let's-guess-what-Ferber-will-say-about the-ring. Each put in his bid from, "My God, it's the rock of Gibraltar," to "Tell me, do you have anymore at home like that?" Ruth Gordon stuck to her original version; she was sure that it sounded like Ferber dialogue.

As they approached Treasure Hill, they were all giggly and eager for the verdict on the ring. They piled out of the car, guffaws stuffed down their throats, and were greeted at the door by a warm and gracious Ferber:

"Darling Freddy . . ."

"Dear Florence . . ."

"Sweet Gar . . ."

"Dear, dear Ru . . ." And then she saw it, and said it. "Oh, my Gawd! That is the most pretentious thing I have ever seen in my whole born days!"

Whereupon, as Kanin tells it, they all doubled up and rolled on the floor. Ruth Gordon had called every syllable correctly. So as not to be completely rude, they told Ferber about their guessing game, toward which she showed amusement. What she might have felt about being the butt was something else again.

In May of 1947, all was not pastoral at Treasure Hill. Ferber was named in, of all unlikely things, a divorce case. In her diary she gives it brief mention and dismissal saying: "Divorce case on at Bridgeport. I was in the witness chair for over an hour. Not pleasant." Perhaps she gave it such short emotional shrift because it was preposterous. The couple who were involving her in the aforementioned happened to be her caretaker and his wife. Ferber probably didn't want to dignify the whole mess by being upset.

The "whole mess" was simply a case of mistaken emphasis. Ferber was always terribly demanding of the people who worked for her, and although she paid them amply, their time was often not their own. Janet puts the episode in perspective:

"Aunt Edna was a demanding person, who demanded more than

equal time. She would talk endlessly about land and about what she wanted done, and anything she asked about, she wanted to know more than just an answer. She had a researcher's mind. So, if her caretaker would say, 'Miss Ferber, there's a blight on the oak tree,' she would not only ask him all about it, she'd go to the library and look up blight and study up on it and go back and bend the caretaker's ear about her findings. Well, his wife felt that Aunt Edna was taking up too much of her husband's time. She was a small town, simplistic, small minded lady who thought that Edna Ferber was trying to woo her man. She had no idea that you could talk that much about blight on trees. So she took it to court, naming alienation of affections as her complaint. As I remember nothing much came of it, except that Ferber had to fire him. She'd been upset about that because he'd been such a good caretaker—and a good listener."

Ferber prided herself on having a *raison d'être* for all of her novels' existences. In the case of *Great Son*, her novel about Seattle, published in 1945, the *raison d'être* was better than the novel:

"It seemed much farther away than Europe. There it was, that prodigious corner of the United States known as the Northwest. For years I'd tucked it away in my mind as a region fantastic, improbable and magnificent. I longed to see it. But then, weary after a long job of work, it always was so much easier to take a taxi over to the North River docks (which isn't north at all) and board an ocean liner. At the end of five heavenly days and nights of rest you found yourself trying to tell a customs inspector at Havre or Cherbourg, in your execrable French, that, no, you had no phonograph records, perfumes, tobacco or silks.

"Though I had bounded about in Oklahoma, California, Texas, Maine, Louisiana, Michigan, Illinois, Arizona and most of the other forty-eight States, somehow the States of Washington and Oregon seemed mythically far away and inaccessible. You heard them spoken of—somewhat undemocratically—as the Northwest Empire. To one who is not quite bright on the subject of geographical boundaries they sounded vaguely Canadian and were sort of mixed up with Vancouver and red-coated Mounties. Then, too, there were those Chamber of Commerce pictures showing fishermen standing hip-deep in rushing torrents, huntsmen drawing a bead on a velvet-eyed deer, or skiers twisting themselves into bow-knots down a snowy mountain slope. Fishing bores me, I wouldn't shoot any furred or feathered thing, and I still bear the scars of my one ski performance.

"Still, the thought of the region fascinated me. The people and the background sounded high, wide and handsome. They sounded American. Fresh, vital, unspoiled and wondrously American. Also roses, they said, bloomed the year round, the salmon and rock-crab were a gourmet's dream, and the scenery would knock your eye out.

"But the years went by. Then, a few winters ago, I found myself in Arizona. After a month of desert and the star-spangled sky I motored to California (those were the days!). It turned out to be cold, rainy and bleak, no matter what the Los Angeles Chamber of Commerce may say to the contrary.

"Roses all the year round in the Northwest. Later I recalled a strange look in the ticket agent's eye when I said I wanted a Streamliner reservation to Seattle, Washington, where I intended to spend two or three days. I neglected to look at a map or a time-table, both of which documents always have baffled me. The railroad fare seemed to be a trifle high. En route I discovered that the distance from Los Angeles, California to Seattle, Washington embraces one entire side of the map of the United States. Perhaps I should have continued my formal education after graduating from the Ryan High Schook, Appleton Wisconsin.

"Tucked away in a Streamliner compartment I traveled a night and a day and a night and a day and the hours piled upon hours but mile after mile the sights outside my train window became more unbelievable more breath-taking. This was another world.

"Portland. Another change of trains and then Seattle with its Japanese and Filipino and Hawaiian porters giving the railway station itself an exotic touch. On foot, by automobile, by boat I explored this dramatic region. To the trained and professional writer any region, any experience, any human being encountered is automatically put through the test tubes of the writer's chemistry. Is this a play, a novel, a short story, an article? Good or bad, pleasant or unpleasant, everything is possible material to the writer.

"After a week of surveying this gigantic region and its dynamic people I told myself that it couldn't be done in a novel a play or any written form other than a massive factual history—and I'm no writer of history. There was too much, it was all too improbable, though true. There were the pioneers of 1851. There were the Mercer Girls. Indians. Chinese riots. Early Spanish English Russian and French explorers. The Alaskan Gold Rush with Seattle as its jumping-off point. Gigantic mountain ranges. Incredible bodies of water. Primeval forests. Towering skyscrapers. And over all the region a sort of dream-like quality that made it unreal in spite of its vital reality.

"No. It couldn't be done. Too stupendous. So I came away full of salt air and tremendous mental pictures and fresh salmon and rock crab and with new friends from whom I parted regretfully and with a handful of hard bright blue zircons as trophies.

"No book, though.

"In the years that followed I wrote a novel and a play and some short stories and articles. But this region and its people stayed in my mind. Again, somewhat to my surprise, I found myself on a Streamliner bound for Seattle. This time it was no accident. I wanted definitely to see this region. But again I saw and departed and put the whole thing out of my mind and slammed the door on it. This time I flew from Seattle to New York as though to get away from it before it could again pursue me. Its wistful face kept peering in at my memory's window. And when I pulled down the shades I could hear its voice saying, 'Let me in! Let me in!'

"Then came Pearl Harbor. The writing of fiction in novels or plays or short stories—my occupation for many years—now seemed to be a silly process indeed. Together with most of the professional writers of the United States I began to write propaganda. That which was ordered or requested or that which seemed to me to have constructive value in our war program I wrote. Writers toured the country in War Loan Drives and other war causes.

"And now there emerged a magnificent and wonderful race of people. They were Americans, and their ages ranged from about eighteen to twenty-five or even thirty. Boys and girls. They were, perhaps, the fruit of the past ten years. Evidently they had not spent those ten years idly. These boys and girls were possessed of great dignity for their years. They were quiet and resourceful. They talked little but seriously and well. They had risen out of the gaudy 1920s and the desperate 1930s. They were, I thought, the best generation that America had produced since the old covered wagon pioneer days.

"Well, here was something that cried aloud to be written and would not be denied. I struggled against writing it. This was no time for books of fiction. Then the Northwest crowded again into my mind, reared itself indomitably as the background for a book about the Bearded Boys of America—the Bearded Boys of Seattle, perhaps, all the way from 1851 to 1941. Adventurous, bold, nerveless, courageous. These new bearded boys whom we saw smiling out at us from the news reels and the magazines and the newspapers were the new pioneers, freezing in the Aleutians, sweating in the jungles, expecting no material gain and receiving none. Fighting and dying for an intangible thing, a spiritual thing, a thing called freedom. A line presented itself as a book title—a line from Shakespeare, as there always is a line from Shakespeare, though this was taken from the worst play, perhaps, that he ever wrote.

"'Thou know'st, great son,' the line went, 'the end of war's uncertain.'"

Ferber liked Mike Todd the producer. She called him "the dashing masher." She wrote of him with her usual knowing adjectives:

"This ebullient man's memory probably will vanish after his Jovian death in the skies . . . as a public figure. But no one who knew him will forget him in a lifetime. Restless, dynamic, improbable and highly amusing, preposterous and handsome. A disarming showman. Vitality, but somehow exhausting, too, like being in the company of a ten million volt electric wire. You can't let go, but you realize you'll be destroyed if you don't."

There were a few men whom Ferber couldn't penetrate deeply enough to castrate. Their charm was greater than hers; their will to get their own way was stronger. They were either big virile babies or real men—whichever way one chose to observe them. To Ferber, they were the closest thing to the "male animal" that she could perceive yet not understand. She was excited by their naughtiness, their cheekiness, their different species-ness. They were the kind she never wrote about in her novels. They were too dominant. What they did was to provide her with stirrings of sexuality, and she never wrote about that. Mike Todd was one of these men. There was speculation that she liked him a great deal more than met his eye. What did meet his eye was the property of *Great Son*, which he bought for $400,000 and never made. The deal was as unconsummated as their relationship.

Although *Great Son* was only fair Ferber, it was, as always, beautifully researched. Her notes read like reporter's poetry. Nothing escaped her; she enhanced everything.

"MODERN SEATTLE MARKET: Phonograph records. Old ones, new ones. Swedish—Scandinavian records. Norwegian. A favorite was Den Norske Fiskermann.

"Zircons in a grubby little jewelry case, their hard blue eyes like Katie's [Katharine Hepburn]. Simple names were the fashion in the early Nineteen Hundreds. Dusty diamonds, too, and bits of silver and junk jewelry.

"Tiny coral shrimps that you bought and ate out of a paper sack, like candy. They were as sweet as candy, too.

"There was no competing with the Japs at the vegetable stalls in the market. They sprayed their produce and weighed it with the water dripping from every leaf and branch. But the lettuce heads, the carrots the beets the radishes the rhubarb were brilliant with their scarlet and green and orange and plum color. The red was redder, the green more vivid. Only forty years ago the Japanese gardeners had started their little truck gardens and they had delivered the vegetables, peddling them from door to door.

"Fish market. Columbia River salmon. Fresh Alaska King salmon. Columbia River Sturgeon. Columbia River Smelts. Home cured black cod. Red snapper—orange colored and Indian red.

ALASKA—GRAMPA—ALASKA GOLD RUSH

"Ships were pressed into service. Atlantic liners racing around the Horn. Seattle stopped wailing about the depression of '93. Crates and bales piled up on the Seattle waterfront. Men in plug hats, girls in trailing skirts. Clerks and lawyers, teachers, grocers, printers, doctors yelling back promises from the deck—promises to bring back gold, sacks of it.

"These knew nothing of the horrors of Chilkoot Pass. Miles of snow. Feet had tramped a trench in the earth and snow.

"The saloons were the most imposing buildings in the towns. They looked down like vultures on a huddle of tents, shacks. They were the clubs, the home, they meant sociability, love, warmth, relaxation. Dark Indian faces, painted faces of women, bearded gaunt faces that had looked upon death and horror. They had heard the howling of the grey wolf-pack and the answering snarl of the malamutes.

"A hamburger was $2 but caviar was $1. Oyster stew was $15. Eggs $1 each. Bread $1.50 a loaf baked by a woman who had come in with the first rush. She sold tickets for the day's baking, the loaves came out of the oven hot and fragrant and the men stood sniffing in the doorway like hungry little boys.

"Women in sun bonnets, leg-o'-mutton sleeves and heavy boots.

"The Marchons! of the French-Canadian sledgers became mush on! mush on!

Ferber saved exceptional fan mail and hate mail, occasionally answering the former. Most of the adult letters came from women whose lives, through her novels, Ferber had deeply affected. There was a letter from a woman from Seattle, Washington. It is an example of the best of fan mail. Ferber thought so too and wrote on the top of it, "Superb letter. Moving informative intelligent. Answer personally." The letter:

"My dear Miss Ferber: I trust that I am not taking the liberty of slamming my mind in your face but I have just read your 'Great Son' which reminded me that I had wanted to write you after finishing your 'A Peculiar Treasure.' I hesitated doing so because I thought you probably were deluged with letters from strangers. You must feel we express ourselves rather poorly.

"Having lived in Seattle twenty-five years, operated a fire insurance business there and lived on Queen Anne Hill, I know you have done a splendid piece of work in 'Great Son.' I enjoyed every bit of it and so did my friends. Have read 'Show Boat' and 'Cimarron' but to my mind the most useful book at this time is 'Peculiar Treasure.' When anyone asks me to loan them a good book, the first one I suggest is 'A Peculiar Treasure.' They invariably bring it back with the remark that their understanding has been helped immeasurably thereby . . .

"It has been said that if you wish to know a man's ideas, ask him what injustices and humiliations he endured in youth. Here we have something in common for I too have had difficulties because of the prejudice against women . . .

"Your remark about the completely feminine woman being abysmally dull, is certainly true. Most married women never quite leave their children at home even when they do not bring them along. Neither am I one of those creatures so strongly pro bono publico. It simply means that we prefer to live independently and are able to assume responsibility for ourselves. There seem to be two things to aim at in life: first to get what you want; and after that, to enjoy it. That much at least, we do have in common, I believe . . .

"Conventionally it is not proper to extend an invitation to one whom you have never had the pleasure of meeting, but if in your travels you come this way, there is an airy comfortable guest room at your disposal . . . The help may not provide cordon-bleu cookery—the nation has to feed Goering—but there are always Scotch and sodas.

"So may the skin of a gooseberry make an umbrella large enough to cover all your enemies and do write another book soon."

Unfortunately, that rather quaint homily didn't serve Ferber during the descending years. No skin of no gooseberry could cover Adolf Schicklgruber, the former house painter and his band of virulent men.

My father Henry has often used a Hebrew term called a *"mitzvah."* It means to perform a blessed thing—usually of a sacrificial nature; taking upon oneself something that makes the heart heavy but cleanses the soul. A blessed burden, then.

Ferber's mitzvah was to give American birth to a family of German refugees by the name of Hollander. There were four children: Gerhard, Kurt, Eva, and Gunther. Their father, a prominent Berlin judge, and their mother, an attorney, were, from all silences, extinguished in a Nazi concentration camp. That Ferber brought the children over and financed them was an accident of bloodlines. It so happened that the Hollander children's grandmother was a cousin of Julia Ferber. Therein the motive for the mitzvah, which turned out for Ferber to be a not so blessed burden.

It all started at the beginning of what Ferber calls "the Hitler horror." There was a lady living in Chicago named Mrs. Louis Asher, nee Ines Neumann, who was a niece of Julia Ferber. The precarious situation of the Hollander children and their parents' incarceration came to Mrs. Asher's attention, whereupon she contacted Julia for sanction in order to appeal to the higher, wealthier court of Ferber. Julia said that she was sure her daughter could and would be pleased to give her all. Before she even knew it, Ferber had been committed.

Ines Neumann Asher moved in on Ferber, asking her to sign and send affidavits for all of the children. Gerhard's was the first; and since it was in the early stages of the persecution of the Jews in Germany, he was able to come to the United States very quickly. Then Ferber sent affidavits for the three other children and, after many machinations, succeeded in having them flown out of Germany into England. They were her wards during the five years of their stay in England, and she was entirely responsible for their financial and educational well-being. Their repayment with literally thousands of "Dear Aunt Edna-thank you" letters could not possibly appease the tremendous financial drain on Ferber. Then, after countless trips to Washington and numerous letters and cables to England, she performed the feat of bringing them to America—financing their trip over and seeing that they arrived safely in Chicago and into the hands of Ines Neumann Asher. After six years of *Sturm und Drang* with the Hollander children, she felt that Mrs. Asher could now do her part. Mrs. Asher received her sentence but could not uphold it—either emotionally or financially. So Ferber, morally trapped, continued the transfusions.

The two older boys displayed a certain amount of initiative. Gerhard (Gary) became a radio technician with the Navy in San Francisco; Kurt enrolled in the Canadian Air Force. The girl, Eva, a student at Hyde Park High School, began to display grave emotional instability that was worrisome to all involved. It was the youngest boy, Gunther, who was the wunderkind—balancing out the averageness of the others. With integrity, charm, and mathematical genius, Gunther became one of radio's favorite "Quiz Kids," winning scores of hundred-dollar war bonds to go toward the furthering of his education. Gunther Hollander was the special one; the one who had pride in himself; the one who earned Ferber's pride. He repaid her with achievement and with constant good news—as is evident in a letter to her dated June 4, 1945:

"Dear Aunt Edna, I just heard you had come back from Europe and so I wanted to write you how much I liked your articles, and they were the first things I turned to in the paper. [Ferber was a war correspondent for the War Department. When overseas, she issued a series of articles for the American press.] I was very surprised to hear that you had gone, but as I afterwards heard you were too—deciding overnight.

"I have been such a bad boy for not writing you so long that for a change I have something to write you about.

"Yesterday I received notice that I have won an honor entrance scholarship to the College of the University of Chicago, for which I took an examination April 21. This scholarship is for one of the four years (value $330), but if I make satisfactory progress at the college it will be renewed until I get my first degree.

"I suppose I wrote you many times that I am a Boy Scout, but now something new has come up there too. I have collected 1,000 pounds of waste paper for the General Eisenhower drive and so I am going to get a special medal. This summer I am going to a scout camp in Michigan for a couple of weeks.

"Last month I attended a production of 'Philadelphia Story' given at the U. of C. by the Office of Dramatic Production. I thought it was very well acted, and I liked the story very well, I had never read it before.

"At school last quarter my grades were:

English: S	Geometry: S	
Biology: E–	French E–	Music E
S equals 96–100%	E equals 88–95%	

"I guess that's just about all so I have to close. Many regards to Aunt Julia, Aunt Fanny, etc. and to yourself. Gunther Hollander."

On November 15, 1945, Gunther Hollander made tragic headlines:

"QUIZ KID CRUSHED TO DEATH UNDER BUS":

"The short but brilliant life of a youngster who became known to millions of radio listeners as a 'Quiz Kid,' was at an end today—crushed out under the heavy wheels of a Chicago Motor Coach Co. bus.

"Gunther Hollander got away from the Nazis and worked dangerously but unharmed through the London blitz only to meet death in his 15th year in a Chicago street accident.

"Such were the ironical twists of fate attending the brief career of this gifted youngster mourned today by his youthful colleagues on the 'Quiz Kids' panel and by thousands of radio listeners who can recall Quizmaster Joe Kelly saying: 'Yes, that's right, Gunther.'

"A boy with blue eyes, black curly hair, an engaging grin and a quick trigger mind, Gunther was crossing the street late yesterday near his home . . . when he was struck by the bus . . . His skull was fractured and he died 20 minutes later . . ."

When the United States entered the war, Ferber called George S. Kaufman on the telephone–in the morning–a most illicit act for her.

"George, I must do something for my country–some sort of war work. What do you think I can do?" were her approximate words.

Kaufman, having no idea, said, "Well, I really have no idea, Edna."

Ferber persisted. "I have got to do something! What are you going to do?"

Kaufman, pitting reason against emotion, replied with something to the effect of, "Well, I'm going to wait to be asked to do something and then I'll do it."

Annoyed, Ferber bulldozed with: "Well, I for one can't wait. I won't wait. Tell me, George, what do you think I can do?"

Kaufman, who understood so well her need for an answer, applied his humor to tone down her need. "Well, Edna," he said thoughtfully, "you could be a tank."

Ferber had wanted to serve the war effort during World War I. Her dear friend William Allen White had tried to deter her saying, "There's nothing humorous about war. War is a dirty, deadly, brutal stinking business. Don't go." She paid him no heed, and when asked by the American Red Cross to go to Europe and send back articles for the American press, she accepted. However, things didn't work out very smoothly, and Europe didn't accept her.

"We were to land in France. I went down to the French consul's office to have my passport visaed. The place was bedlam; I waited my turn amidst an unbelievable clamor of English and French exclamations and expostulations. My time came. I handed over my passport. The young clerk looked at it, disappeared with it, there then appeared a tall harassed and haggard-looking man of middle age, grayish, with a grizzled mustache. Vice-consul, or something official like that. He regarded me with a lackluster eye.

" 'Madame, you cannot go to France.'

"I said, 'What?'

"He repeated it, very precisely, with a French accent: 'Madame, you cannot go to France.'

"My heart stopped beating, but I didn't die. I spoke, trying to be as precise and distinct as he had been: 'I'm afraid there has been a mistake. This is my passport. I am sailing tomorrow. My name is Edna Ferber. I am a writer. I have been chosen by the Red Cross to go to Europe to write a series of articles. There has been some mistake.'

"He only repeated it in a fatigued way; and I suppose he was fatigued, poor overworked man. 'Madame, you cannot go to France.'

"Well, then all my fine calm was swept away, my heart began to beat again, it hammered, it pounded, it thundered, it shook me with its terrible blows.

"'But why?' I shouted. 'Why! Why! Why!' Faces began to turn toward me.

"He turned. He conferred a moment with another weary face behind the enclosure. He turned back to me. 'There has been found to be many spies in France working under the guise of the Red Cross and other similar organizations. The French government has just this week made a rule that no one may go to the zone of war except under strict surveillance and as part of a unit under command. This passport allows you to go anywhere you please. The government will not allow it. It will not allow you to go to France. Your father was born in Hungary.'

"The room whirled and whirled and whirled. I thought it never would come right again, but I clung to the edge of the counter and it did stop revolving. 'My father! My father came to America when he was a boy. He lived here all his life after that. He never left it. He has been dead for ten years. My mother was born in Milwaukee. I was born in Kalamazoo, Michigan (his right eyebrow went up, ever so slightly), I am an American. You can't do a thing like this to me. You can't! You can't!' It must have sounded comic. He seemed hardly to hear.

"He bowed a little, in finality. 'Madame, I am sorry. You cannot go to France.' He turned away."

This time out, Ferber was indeed tank-like in her determination to be sent overseas. But there were inner doubts; she was older and fearful of her heart's acting up (what Dr. Alvan Barach called her "hysterical angina"). In the months before she actually did go overseas as a war correspondent, she went through not so much a malaise of the physique as of the spirit. One can feel it through her diary entries:

JANUARY 1945: "To Washington at 1:30. Mayflower Hotel a shambles of politicians, clubs, orchids, and badly dressed women. Snowing. Dinner in my room. Out for a walk but felt considerable discomfort in the heart region. Probably partly due to apprehension. A dreary evening, really. Why didn't I go to the Stage Door Canteen or some such thing? Decided that rest might make some difference in my heart tests tomorrow."

"To Navy Building—had cardiogram (electro). Showed no heart ailment. Went to Bethesda Naval Hospital, Maryland for air tests. Drove with Admiral. All officers very charming. Took test called 'The Two-Step' running up and down two steps twenty-one times. Spent 20 minutes in test equal to 15000 ft. altitude. Chart showed cones depressed. Heart artery not wide enough. To White House reception. Seven o'clock train to N.Y."

"The first fine day in weeks. Reviews of Great Son in Sunday Times, Herald Tribune, Saturday Review of Literature. Not all bad, not all good. On the whole perhaps deserved. A two-mile walk, called for mother at Science Church, Fan there. Mother to lunch, behaving in the eccentric and trying manner that always precedes an impending birthday. Cross and upset myself. I behaved impatiently and, like a little girl, regretted it afterward. Janet in. Looks well, exhilarated by her plans for U.S.O tour. Very depressed myself. To bed at eleven. Read life of Madame de Stael. The Clare Luce of her day."

"Mixed reviews in morning daily papers on 'Great Son.' The Times (Orville Prescott) violently bad."

"Extremely depressed. To Dr. Barach for a shot. Told him of Washington trip, Navy cardiac tests. Asked about possibility of April European air trip. He said no. Todd telephoned asking if I'd see Jeanette McDonald and him. I arranged for them to come to dinner on Wednesday. Dinner guests—Dick and Dorothy Rodgers, Kip and Polly Fadiman, Adrienne and Bill Whitney, Marc Connelly to dinner. Rather pleasant."

"To Dr. Kerman's office because of clogged right ear. Ears washed out, feel quite clear. There had been a queer muffled sensation in the right side. Moss telephoned. Just returned from trip to Panama on plane carrier Shangri-la. A thrilling experience. Talked to Jeanette McDonald. Todd had told her I would write a play for her. An incredible character, he."

FEBRUARY 1945: "Awoke feeling ill. Swollen throat and aching bones. Acidity, and probably partly psychic, too, because of disappointing reviews on the book Great Son."

"Ill, laryngitis—no temperature. Mother's 85th birthday. A remarkable record and an amazing human being. She hates the thought of her age and consequently this day too. To see 'I Remember Mama,' a lovely play with a performance by Oscar Homolka as Uncle Chris that is as fine as anything I've ever seen in the theater. Mother upset. Too much of a day for her. Dr. Barach in to see me. More concern with himself than with me."

"Dinner with Max and Millie Gordon and Moss Hart at Voisin's and to opening of 'One Man Show,' Jed Harris's production. A psychological dish—father daughter angle—rather pretentious and very blurred. Should have been interesting but wasn't. To the Stork Club, a nice evening. Moss very amusing."

"Awoke feeling awful—too much hamburger at noon, steak and red wine at night. Upset by Janet's telephone behavior about Mitchell Field. Fan's doings, evidently. A lot of talk about my going with 'The Man Who Came to Dinner.' Fan called me and put her oar in. A mess. Too much family. Too little sense. Fan has no sense of human dignity." (Translation: Ferber is referring to the fact that Janet was cast to play in Moss Hart's U.S.O. tour of *The Man Who Came to Dinner*. Hart thought it might be interesting for Ferber to go along on the tour as a sort of a side attraction. Obviously, in finding out about the possibility of her aunt coming along, Janet had been most undone. Ferber declined Hart's offer, but not until after everyone had hated each other for a while. Mitchel Field was an air base, which Hart did convince Ferber to visit.)

"To Mitchel Field with Moss Hart and 'The Man Who Came To Dinner' company. By train. With Col. Hildreth and Mrs. Hildreth to the hospital. Saw the boys in the psychopathic wards, much more dead-seeming than those just brought in badly wounded from overseas. Wounded with legs off, faces off, but somehow more real and vital than the psychically sick."

"Shocked to have Janet say on telephone that she wouldn't go to say goodbye to Grandma but would merely telephone. I told her that she needn't come here in that case. Janet came in at about ten. A tragic girl, now almost ruined by her mother."

"Janet left by train (I suppose) for Seattle and the South Pacific with Moss Hart's U.S.O. company. Seems utterly fantastic, and is. Haunted by Janet's stricken face. A wonderful girl poisoned by her mother."

MARCH 1945: "Not feeling very well when awoke but much better during day. Pain almost gone from back but now located in left ovary. Telegram from Moss Hart, Seattle. Says too much of everything in Seattle but not as I said and that I am a liar. No clear news from Janet. A cryptic telegram."

"Janet's telegram evidently intended for Fan's birthday which isn't until next month."

"Guests to dinner—Quentin and Virginia Reynolds, Morris and Margaret Ernst, Billy and Eleanor Rose. Mike Todd back from Hollywood looking superb having lost a lot of weight. A rather nice evening. I felt pretty well."

"A beautiful sunny day. To the farm. A long tedious talk with Curtiss about deep freezer; about buying and butchering a steer; building a chicken house, etc."

"Lee Barker in at 5:30. New advertising copy. Bad. Said 'Great Son' first place best seller Herald Tribune list for March 25. Mother to dinner. With her to see Tallulah Bankhead in Phillip Barry's 'Foolish Notion.' A showy performance, superficial. A bad play. Talked telephone Mike Todd. He left for San Francisco. Decided against buying deep freezer."

"A lovely day. A brief walk. Called for mother at church. Mother to lunch. Margaret Case Harriman in to talk about Todd for New Yorker profile. Rather absurd to take time for that."

"Looked at luggage at Saks. Blue canvas bags. To Dr. Barach for typhoid shot. My arm sore and feverish from shot."

In April of 1945, Ferber and Mina—both looking snappy in uniform—were in Washington for their briefing before taking off for overseas. Ferber recalls that day in her notes from her war journal:

"Washington . . . 1945 . . . Briefed . . . Elaborate instructions on what to do if the plane ditched. Reading matter detailed. Trying to catch up on one's reading, adjusting your glasses, getting everything in orderly shape while the water gurgled over your mouth your nose your eyes your head. Also, it said, sagely, no matter how crazed with thirst do not drink urine. In this blithe spirit we prepared to board the plane. From Washington. Two unmilitary figures in American Army uniforms.

"We were to fly the next day. That evening there seemed to be a strange commotion in the streets. Groups of people. We went into a shoe repair shop a little neighborhood place to have Mina's shoe fixed—a minor bit of repair—a nail or a little bump in the lining. We went into the shop and the door was open—the tools lay as though they had been deserted in a panic. No one. We waited. We left. Little knots of people on the streets. Oddly enough, no news stands and no newsboys crying extra editions of the papers. We saw these clusters of people. A man passed, his face oddly tense and strained. I stopped him.

"'Excuse me . . . uh . . . a stranger here in Washington . . . (as though everyone wasn't a stranger here in Washington!) . . . will you please tell me . . . is something wrong . . . I mean, has something happened . . .'

"The man said, without looking at me, 'Roosevelt's dead.' And hurried on.

"It was like a physical blow that sent one reeling. I remember saying aloud as I stared after the stranger's hurrying back, 'No! No!'

"That night the big dining room of the Mayflower Hotel was packed elbow to elbow with what was, perhaps, the most macabre roomful of people that any hotel has ever sheltered. Franklin D. Roosevelt was one of most beloved and revered men in the world; Franklin D. Roosevelt was one of the most hated men by a small group. Both factions were represented in this noisy feverish room. There were the silent ones, their faces drawn and lined with shock and sorrow and apprehension; there were next to them at adjoining tables the exuberant and articulate ones who were actually celebrating the death of the man, these Americans were actually celebrating the death of the President of the United States.

"They held high their glasses and there in the dining room of a hotel in the Capital of the United States they shouted: 'To Roosevelt. Dead! To the death of F.D.R.!'

"It was the most savage exhibition I have seen in my lifetime.

"In a lifetime of having seen strange sights, gruesome exhibitions, savage manifestations of the human race at its best and at its most gruesome, I never had seen anything that for savagery and putrid hate, equalled this moment in the history of a great and civilized country."

Ferber believed that mourning necessitated action. Luckily she got it. On April 14, 1945, two days after Roosevelt's death, Ferber's and Mina's itinerary read:

"Departed National Airport, Washington, D.C., by 'plush' C-54 (or Douglas Aircraft DC-4), stopping New Foundland or Greenland and arriving at Bovingdon Airport, London. Hotel Savoy, London, with trips to fighter and heavy bomber bases of Eighth Air Force."

Although it wasn't a luxury trip, the War Department made sure that Miss Edna Ferber and niece had the very best in accommodations, guides, jeeps, food, and sights. In other words, they saw what the war had wrought, but through the eyes of VIPs. There were two Ferbers who went on this junket: the foremost one was the reporter, filing pungent stories to be sent back home; the other was Julia's daughter, writing rather girlish newsletters. A sampling of the latter:

APRIL 24, 1945: "Dear Mom, I'm sure you've been wondering why you haven't had long letters from me. It's impossible to try to make plain to you how difficult it is to write letters or anything else. The days are crammed full, I go to bed late at night and get up early in the morning, but for all that I feel better than I have in years, I am not as tired as I was in New York when I was doing practically nothing all winter.

"Mina and I have seen such wonderful and unbelievable sights that I don't think I can even begin to tell you about them. Our trip over from Washington to London—it seems months ago—was a beautiful one, and I was as comfortable as could be. A magnificent plane. On it was Lewis Douglas, President of the Mutual Life Insurance Company. I had met him years ago, he took us under his wing and when the plane stopped at Newfoundland and at the Azores we were his guests at the officer's club for dinner and for breakfast. Instead of going to Scotland as our landing stop we were fortunate enough to come into an airport just outside of London. Our rooms were ready at the Savoy and we had a night's sleep and BACON for breakfast. The five days in London were too rushed. I can scarcely remember them in any kind of sequence. We had Monday in which to establish contacts with the Air Force Public

Relations, the North American Newspaper Alliance, etc. Early Tuesday morning we were taken out by car to a bomber base and a fighter base (American Air Force) and spent the night in a tiny hospital room, as there is no provisions for women otherwise, except the Red Cross, etc. We were shown everything, it was a thrilling and marvelous two days. It's no good trying to write you about it, I'll just have to tell you when I see you. I saw Lynn and Alfred [Lunt] in London and they were darling, sent us seats for their play and gave a dinner for me. I went to a largish party on Wednesday of that week at the Savoy, given by Hugh Beaumont, and saw most of my friends there—Noel Coward, Lady Colefax, Gladys Calthrop, Sybil Thorndike, Emlyn Williams, John Gielgud and lots of others. Mina probably wrote Fan that we had a wild goose chase after Henry [Goldsmith], were told that he had gone to France, and then quite by accident he telephoned Gar Kanin from his station to London and Gar asked him if he had seen me. That was the first Henry knew about us. He took the train down, spent the night at the Savoy and all the next day. He looks wonderful, is a darling, is enormously interested in his work, but of course wants terribly to come home as do all the other millions of boys, but of course it's no good thinking of that. This is something that will take years to settle, even after Germany and Japan are defeated. If only the people back home could get used to the idea that the boys are going to be sent right over to Japan, and that's all there is to it. I know.

"We left London last Saturday, flying in a bucket-seat plane in one hour and ten minutes. And here we are at the Ritz in Paris, living in lovely rooms, quiet, clean, beautifully furnished, with huge bathrooms and every convenience. We eat downstairs in the officer's mess the best food you can possibly want. Soups, meat, fresh vegetables, cheese, salad, dessert, coffee. No one in all of Europe eats as well as the American soldier . . . Mina has had a delirious time, with hundreds of handsome young fliers whirling around her. I've seen quite a lot of people I know—William Paley, Major Warburg, even Leigh Dannenburg of Easton Connecticut—remember, Mom? He is on the Bridgeport Herald. I had lunch today with Major Warburg, General Hughes and Major General Smith and went with them to the Gare D'Orsay to see the tragic and terrible spectacle of the slave prisoners (French) returning from the German camps and towns where they had been deported to work for years. Some of them couldn't even stand . . . We have all our packing to do, as we leave tomorrow (April 25) for about two weeks in Germany. If you don't get letters don't worry. I think the mail out there is bad. Everyone goes, and everyone says it is very comfortable. We probably shall be two days in Belgium, then to Wiesbaden, Weimar, etc., with a visit to the horrible camp at Buchenwald if it hasn't been evacuated entirely.

"We are coming back to Paris from Germany, and I'd like to stay here for a few days to rest up . . . I'll keep you informed as best I can, but don't be worried or disappointed if you don't get letters. We're both well and we're having an incredibly fascinating time. It's no use trying to put it into a letter. Much love. I think of you so much and hope that you are well and comfortable. Ed."

Chatty, thoughtful, but diverted. She was saving it. For when she filed her piece from Paris for the North American Newspaper Alliance, her words are like laser beams:

"Uncle Joe is top of the heap. Uncle Joe is cock of the walk. There can be witnessed in Europe today the sight of a great nation known as the United States of America standing, hat in hand, in the outer office waiting for permission to walk into Berlin. I am reliably informed (trite phrase, but true) that America's military, economic and diplomatic heads have long failed to receive a reply to their requests, made to Joseph Stalin of Russia, that American war correspondents be permitted to enter Berlin. I myself have tried every available source by which one might gain entry. As for Uncle Joe, he certainly received these requests coming, as they have, from high military, economic, and diplomatic quarters. And what does he do? Like the character in the song, he doesn't say yes, he doesn't say no. He just sits tight and says absolutely nothing. All requests have been ignored.

"Being a civilian, a free citizen of the United States and an intelligent human being I should like to say that I think this state of affairs is the most dangerous I've heard since Mr. Chamberlain and his umbrella returned from Munich. Appeasement is appeasement in any language, and one would hope that the lesson of the failure of appeasement as a policy had long ago been learned, and bitterly. I would like to suggest that someone speak firmly to Uncle Joe. Into this little curly head there has crept the muddled thought that Uncle Joe, the poker-faced, is slightly crazed with success.

"No one outside Berlin knows what is going on in Berlin. It may well be that the Russians are doing a fine job of housecleaning there and that when the place is scrubbed and aired and the dust swept out—or perhaps just swept under the rug—they'll invite the neighbors in. But that kind of procedure is a trifle high-handed when directed toward the country that furnished the utensils for cleaning in the first place—not to speak of some millions of young men of the Army, the Navy, and the Air Forces.

"Every now and then some optimistic correspondent takes off in a jeep or a plane toward Berlin, but always he is stopped this side of the gates, usually some seventy or more kilometers this side.

"Homely midwest similes are sometimes a bit overworked, but as I sit here in Paris together with dozens of other correspondents I am reminded of my Appleton Wisconsin girlhood days. To that pretty Wisconsin town in the Fox River Valley there occasionally came a visiting girl from another and perhaps a larger nearby town. She had new ways and her clothes were perhaps a little different from ours. We would accept her in our midst, we would give in her honor small-town luncheons of home-made chicken salad and hot biscuits and ice cream and coffee, we would have get-togethers in which we home girls would let down our hair and Tell All. We would confide to this newcomer our girlish secrets, give her our favorite recipes for fudge and nougat, feed her up, take her buggy riding, ask her to write her name in our autograph album and reveal our feelings about our town boys, including their characteristics, financial state, and general desirability. And now, we would say naively, tell us all about yourself, huh? Whereupon the visiting girl would rise up, brush the cake crumbs off her lap, regard us with the chill stare of utter contempt and sail out, taking our beaux away from us, one by one, in cold blood.

"Take it or leave it for a parable.

"As a quick change of subject it is to be hoped that wives mothers and sweethearts and sisters back home are not entertaining high hopes in the way of gifts from returning warriors. In all Europe there is nothing to buy. Nothing. Here in France bottles of perfume are displayed in every shop from grocers to hardware, but most of these can better be bought at your home-town drugstore. In all the shop windows throughout Europe nothing beautiful or rare or desirable meets the would-be purchaser's eye. Perhaps these bits and pieces are what remains of stuff made originally for the less critical taste of the German trade, but it certainly is awful. Most of it resembles the souvenirs one sees for sale at Coney Island. Unfortunately, as the GIs all have money and are bent on spending it for the womenfolks back home they are seen in droves buying these atrocities. It is hoped that American women, viewing the proffered junk, will hide their real emotions realizing that it is the best that Europe now offers.

"Paris itself appears to be the gathering point for all nations. In the next three months this probably will turn into the ten-dollar tour. At least, indications point that way. Every small-time politician or everyone who has done a favor for a small-time politician will doubtless be filing by to view the Remains. They are a grisly enough sight, heaven knows. But one has the rather dreadful premonition that the Remains may not remain remains.

"In the Place Vendome, on the Champs Elysees, swirling around the Scribe, up and down the Rue Rivoli you encounter the most surprising Americans in and out of uniform. Amon Carter with his young son who has just been released after two years in a German prison camp. Mrs. Anna (The Brain) Rosenberg just back from a week in Germany, talking none too optimistically of what she has seen. Michael Todd of all people smoking a large dark cigar and wearing a vague uniform that resembles a skiing costume. George Backer in from London on his way to Germany. Gertrude Stein trudging the boulevard accompanied by her very dressy large white French poodle. Everyone stares at her. She has a formula for preserving peace forever. She holds forth about this in the Tuilleries Gardens and on any chance street corner, she likes to speak to groups of soldiers. Just let every nation flatter every other nation, she says solemnly, let everyone flatter everyone else and everyone will love everyone and there will be no more wars. A pose is a pose is a pose, say I."

When Ferber and Mina hit Naples on May 13, 1945, Ferber sent another "Dear-Mom-and-apple-pie" letter:

"Dear Mom, you must by now have put me down as a selfish and thoughtless person. Please believe me when I say that from morning till night there has scarcely been a minute when I could have written you. And my mind has been so crowded with the incredible things I've seen and done that any letter (such as this) would be either a jumble or a blank. I now can understand why the GI's letters aren't very descriptive or revealing. You just can't write about this incredible war world.

"After Germany (and THAT was something!) we came back to Paris for four days. I did two pieces, but as VE Day came along the day after we arrived in Paris and lasted for three days with everything closed I didn't even have a chance to do anything or see anything but the insane crowds celebrating. We were again at the Ritz which is entirely occupied by high Army officials and we were incredibly lucky to have been billeted there.

"Yesterday morning Mike Todd appeared at the Ritz announcing that he had the rank of General but his uniform had no brass and its general effect was more like a street cleaner's uniform. But he was very nice, though exhausted from his plane trip, and took everybody to dinner (dinner, by the way, costs 50 cents for us and nothing for Army. Very very good food, all GI).

"Yesterday at 9 a.m. we took the plane for Naples, stopping at Marseilles to be picked up by another plane for the remainder of the trip. The first plane was of the bucket-seat variety, very uncomfortable for a long trip, but from Marseilles to Naples it was again plush seat and we slept for over an hour we were so weary. Naples isn't very badly bombed—nothing at all compared to the cities we've seen in other countries. Mom, the Grand Hotel and the Excelsior were bombed and out of use, but probably will be rebuilt or repaired. The city and the people are all very dirty. This noon we're going in a special boat to Capri to stay overnight. It's a big rest and recuperation center for officers and enlisted men both, and I'm very keen to see it. Then we're going to Rome, Florence, back to Paris and then home . . . How glad I am that I came, and that I paid no attention to doctors. I haven't been ill a minute, thank God. See you soon. Ed."

Ferber may have simplified the aftermath of the war for Julia (who, after all, was more concerned about the welfare of the Excelsior Hotel), but for the American people she darkened her colors, telling them what they should be concerned about, what they should expect from the returning soldiers. Her observations and research on the soldier's displaced habitat and his survival therein is touching and timeless.

"The American boys all want two things above all else. For the most part they want, possibly demand, wangle or scrounge, these two things at the moment. This frustration they accept with the most engaging grace and fortitude and a minimum of griping.

"It may sound sissy, but it most definitely isn't. From the generals living in chateau or villas to privates billeted in tents or Nissen huts, they long to come back home and they crave a long cool glass of fresh milk. In the bases, villages towns and cities of Europe one can drink available water chlorinated, wine, beer, cocktails and cognac.

"Incidentally, the liberated Russian slave workers around Nordhausen were blithely drinking the V-2 juice out of the liberated V-2 bombs and let no one confuse that with the American V-8 product. It's a mixture of alchohol and high octane gasoline and one wonders why under its potent influence, the Russian can't take off right from the ground where he stands under his own steam, straight for Kiev or wherever his home town happens to be.

"Naturally point-counting among the enlisted men is the favorite indoor and outdoor sport but millions of them know that this will be for them just a bit of mathematical exercise and no more. Amazingly enough, though they hate war, they complain very little. A dirty job is still to be done and they'll do it, but in a shirt or pants pocket, on every desk, in every wallet, above every cot there is that picture of the wife and kids. It outnumbers the famed pin-up girl by the millions.

"Not that they aren't having a pleasant time of it now with the European war at an end and the South Pacific still looming in the future, but after you've admired that snapshot of the very young girl holding that very rugged little replica of the lad you're talking to, you inquire as tactfully as possible about their future plans.

"What's the first thing you want to do or have when you arrive home? 'I want to peel this off and put on green pants and a yellow coat and a purple tie and a pink shirt if I feel like it. I want all the milk I can drink.' 'I'm going to get me a blushing bride. That's what I'm going to do.' 'I want a great big cool glass of fresh milk about this high.' 'I don't ever want to see a jeep or powdered eggs or a Nissen hut as long as I live.' 'I want a glass of cool fresh milk. That's what I want.' 'I just want to sit still somewhere and do nothing for a month but just sit.' 'I want a great big glass of milk.'

"Perhaps it would be fair to warn the dairy companies of the United States that milk bars are going to be the favorite hangouts of American returned fighting men of every age and rank.

"Perhaps the most interesting form of extra-martial activity that now has blossomed into a fine art is the technique of scrounging.

This deserves not only a book but a manual. Its intricacies never can be polished off in an article or extra chapter. Some of the more hard-bitten branches of the service call it ghouling, but this is an exaggeration of the whole. So far as I have been able to ascertain by observation and questioning and personal experience, the American soldier has behaved very well indeed in the matter of appropriating articles which do not strictly belong to him.

"A really smart GI can start with six cigarets and wind up as the owner of a nice little liberated Benz or Fiat car. On the way up he will have traded eggs, knives, guns, swords, fur-collared blouses, not to mention cameras, SS daggers and walking sticks. Most of this is stuff that has been left in scrap heaps. Most of the parts come from old airplane graveyards; the wood is a ration box; the speaker is an old-fashioned ear phone, the dial is a piece of cardboard with stations indicated on a scrap of paper. Three lads in uniform in Naples flash past at 50 miles an hour on bright scarlet scooters. The tires are tail wheels off small discarded planes. The frames are welded fuselage parts, the engines are air compressors, the seats are old parachute sheathes, the handlebars are bent pieces of fuselage frames, the gas tanks are four or five GI No. 10 tanks.

"In any pond, lake or pool in camp or base you can see a boat devised from abandoned belly tanks that have carried the extra gas in a medium bomber. These are 150-gallon belly tanks welded together by the boys so as to form a pontoon arrangement. This prevents the rounded bottom from tipping. A motor made from an old motorcycle or a generator is rigged up between the pontoons and the whole effect is much like the boats one sees in Hawaiian waters.

"Any farm boy who has run a tractor at home can make himself mechanically comfortable, given an old airplane scrap heap in which to rummage. Traveling by plane and by motor through the countrysides of England, France, Belgium, Germany and Italy, I have not seen one single tractor or piece of motor-driven farm equipment of any kind, though it was the spring plowing season and all Europe was trying frantically to supply itself with food for the coming year.

"A lowly jeep can be transformed into the elegance of a Long Island station wagon by wooded sides built from old ammunition crates with windows of cello glass from an abandoned plane, the whole varnished and waxed, rainproof and warm. A young captain who has spent the winter in a tent defeated the elements by remembering his college chemistry and devising therefrom a gas vapor stove made on the blow torch principle from a 10-gallon gasoline drum.

"This ingenious milk-drinking, home-loving fighting force has come out of this war hating war as they hated it when they went into it."

In 1944, when Ferber was still sitting atop Treasure Hill, writing War Bond speeches and feeling desolate, she received a letter from a "GI Joe" stationed in England that pointed out just exactly how she was helping the war effort and the morale of the boys. It is moving without being maudlin; I found it pressed in her diary like an old corsage. It said that the writer was trying not to write a mere fan letter—one from a soldier overseas who wished to express his appreciation to one he had long admired. But as a "camouflaged civilian," he supposed that it would be received by Ferber as just another letter of the "You must be tired of having people say they like your books, but I just want to tell you" variety.

He pointed out how many of her novels and collected short stories had been read by the American serviceman, both at home and overseas. In all the camp libraries in the States where he had been stationed—from Florida to New York, Missouri to South Carolina—he had found worn-looking copies of *Show Boat* and *Cimarron* with an occasional *The Girls* or *Buttered Side Down* for good measure. He was sure that she must be exceedingly proud of the fact that her books always appeared on shelves soiled and dog-eared, covers slightly dilapidated and conversations underlined, evidence of enjoyment the author had given mankind.

He mentioned an evening, when he had hitchhiked to a very small village of thatched roofs and a weary-looking Norman church to get coffee and doughnuts from the Red Cross. In their Victory Book Library, next to *The Collected Essays of Ralph Waldo Emerson,* he had spotted *A Peculiar Treasure* and had grabbed it quickly, to carry back to camp. He was halfway through it and three of his friends were almost as far along. Some of them had read it before, but that was part of the fun, the writer suggested. It reminded him of all the freedom and privileges he and his friends had once enjoyed as United States citizens in a peaceful land.

He concluded by saying that she had reminded him of his own mother. He thanked her for writing the kind of stories he could pass on to a stranger and foreigner with pride and confidence. He was particularly appreciative for the hours of pleasure he and his friends had had in reading her books.

During the war years, the realization crept into Ferber that the course of human events was occasionally more important than her work. Once she'd decided this, anyone who fell short of that realization was not living up to his humanity. The owner of the New York *Times* was one who she felt was wasting his time. In an entry in her 1944 diary she writes: "Worked, but scarcely two pages written. Foolishly to see Arthur Sulzberger at N.Y. Times office. Wanted to talk to him about the critical Anti-Semitic condition growing here, but he babbled on and on about himself for an hour and it all came to nothing."

Ferber never babbled. Ever. And although the thought of the slaughter of six million Jews caused her spasms of hysteria, it was an articulated, constructive hysteria. When applying to Ferber the cliché of "Boy, was she pretty when she was angry," it would be converted to "Boy, could she write when she was angry." She was angry *for* the Jews that heinous persecution had been done and done and done to them, and, in her stubborn originality, she was angry *at* the Jews for letting it be done and done and done to them. She exploded and exploited her anger in War Bond speeches and articles; she became known as somewhat of an expert on rage. A rage sample:

"As the so-called civilized world looked on—no, as it cast down its eyes and looked the other way—the Jews of Germany and of all Europe went through a pageant of unspeakable horror and degradation and death which never has been equaled in the history of mankind, and which the imagination rejects as being too fantastic to be true. Six million men, women and children of the Jewish religion were carefully and deliberately murdered.

"But it is true. It's rather a dull old story now, for the sensibilities of the world are blunted by horror. The world has seen the pictures. Many of us have seen the reality as we surveyed Buchenwald or Dachau or Oranienburg. We have seen human flesh heaped like humus. We have seen men and women and children piled any whichway, lumped and mashed and disintegrating like heaps of garbage. These were men. This exquisite mechanism, the beautiful edifice which housed the soul and the spirit of man, was degraded. For the first time in the history of the world the dignity of man was flouted with complete contempt. Man, other than the Nazi German, was garbage.

"Almost every nation, in the past two thousand years, has tried its hand at destroying the people of the Jewish religion. Hitler has come the nearest to success. One more good try should, I think, do it.

"There now has crept into my mind the suspicion that the Jew himself is responsible for this. He expects it. He even invites it. Since Biblical days he has been a breast beater, a garment render and an ash head-heaper. Usually he writes about himself. Christians don't write about Jews very much. The Jew writes about himself, he seems fascinated by his own image, Narcicus-like. And when he writes he is gloomy and long-suffering. This is unfortunate, for the Jew himself is likely to be sprightly, witty and vivacious in conversation, with a wry salty wisdom. What is known as good company. But once he begins to write about himself or preach about himself he feels sorry for himself. This trait is one which the world does not find endearing. If he would delete the letter R from his habitual attitude and become a beast-beater instead of a breast-beater he would do much better for himself.

". . . Before this war there were, according to accepted statistics, about fifteen million Jews in the entire world. This amounts to about twice the population of New York City. Of these fifteen million, millions have been murdered. Unless help comes, and quickly, millions more will be murdered. Even in this country we hear from the rabble-rousers—the White Shirts, the America Firsters, the Father Coughlins, the Lindberghs, the Joe McWilliams, the Henry Fords—that if jobs are scarce and people are depressed and frightened after the war, and the weary world wants that old familiar scapegoat for bad temper and fear and frustration, why, blandly, of course they'll take it out on the Jew.

"What insolence! What savagery! Certainly the bully always beats up the smallest boy first. Hitler did it successfully. But if that smallest boy, handicapped though he may be by size and inexperience, decides to surprise his fat lumbering opponent by thumbing his eye out, for example, perhaps the fat boy will think better of it the next time. He may even think better of it this time.

"That Jews should be admitted into the free lands of all countries including Palestine, and quickly, is or should be the opinion of every civilized human being of any or of no religion. That the free countries should provide a haven for all desperate and dying people of any faith should be a truth that needs no stating.

"That Peace Table of which we speak so hopefully will have as one of its most gigantic and pressing problems the welfare and settlement of millions of dazed and desperate and homeless people of every faith. Among these will be some millions of Jews . . . Those who sit at the Peace Table should hear representatives of all minorities, including in the Jewish field Zionists and non-Zionists. Any enduring peace must make clear that the Jew must be given the same rights accorded any other civilized human being of any religion—the right to live and worship and speak and think where he pleases and how he pleases in accordance with the laws and customs of the country of which he is a citizen.

"I quote . . . from a writer I know well, the lines being taken from a book written in 1938: It irks me to hear people say that Jews are wonderful people or that Jews are terrible people. Jews are wonderful and terrible and good and bad and brilliant and stupid and evil and spiritual and vulgar and cultured and rich and poor and beautiful and ugly and gifted and commonplace. Jews, in short, are people."

The "writer I know well" was herself, and the quote was taken from her autobiography, *A Peculiar Treasure*, which launched her publicly as a Jew.

For all of her heavy duty moral fronts, Ferber could be bitchy behind her fan. In a 1943 letter to Julia she wrote:

"I had dinner Wednesday night at Lynn and Alfred's [Lunt]. They are waiting to go overseas. Their apartment has been rented to a Brazilian couple and they'll have to get out and go to a hotel if they don't leave by Wednesday . . . Lynn told a wonderful story about your friend Gertrude Lawrence (of whom she is somewhat jealous, I imagine). Lynn met her in Saks' and said, sweetly, 'You know Alfred and I are going overseas to play in London and to the soldiers in the camps over there.'

"Gertie said, 'I'm going over in June.'

"Lynn said, rather bewildered, 'Uh, this is August, isn't it?'

"'I mean next June. I have committments all this winter that will keep me in this country,' said Miss L.

"Lynn said, 'Next June! The war will be over by then, surely.'

"And Gertrude said, 'Oh, dear, I hope not!'
"She's really a terrible fool. I can't wait until I tell Moss."

And to Samuel Hopkins Adams, who was preparing a biography on Alexander Woollcott and who requested her aid, she replied:
"Dear Samuel Hopkins Adams:—Yes, I'm in New York, but I want no part of Woollcott, alive or dead. Sorry. Sincerely, Edna Ferber."

And after having dinner at "21" with George and Beatrice Kaufman she wrote in her diary: "Talked for awhile with Ruth Gordon and Gar Kanin. Ruth at forty-seven or more looked younger than Gar who is scarcely thirty."

And her comment about Lillian Hellman: "I always know how to vote on any board that Lillian Hellman is on. Whichever way she votes, I simply vote the opposite."

And toward her friend Katharine Hepburn she puts out rather oblique claws when she writes in her diary: "Saw Kate Hepburn in Philip Barry's 'Without Love.' Kate pretty good; touching and rather believable; the play bad. Back to see her afterward, but she was showering or something. Didn't see her. Strange behavior."

The relationship between Ferber and Hepburn was not without its feline elements. During F.D.R.'s second term as President, Ferber and Hepburn were both invited to lunch with him at Hyde Park. Ferber said that she was going to drive from Easton, Connecticut, and would Hepburn like to join her. Hepburn declined, saying that she would fly from Saybrook, Connecticut, where she had a country home. Ferber said something mock-huffy like, "Oh, well pardon me," and drove alone, arriving ahead of Hepburn. Hepburn flew and was surprised at being met at the airport by F.D.R. himself. He drove her into Hyde Park, and Ferber, seeing them arrive together and thinking it was a setup, said with great huff, "Oh, well pardon me. I was born yesterday."
"Underneath all that," says Katharine Hepburn of Edna Ferber, "was a suffering human being. I feel she was greatly injured by the fact that she wasn't fascinating looking—in terms of beauty—to men."
Hepburn and Ferber met through Leland Hayward, the agent, about 1934. Hepburn was Hayward's girl cum fiancée at the time;

Hayward was Ferber's movie agent and possible secret male interest. (A secret to everybody but Ferber. Later there was some speculation about it.) Hepburn was twenty-four years Ferber's junior. She was not the big star she would become. Ferber was the big star of the two. Since Hepburn was so much younger than Ferber, it never occurred to her that Ferber might have turmoil. She thought Ferber was a completely solved lady. Now, in retrospect, she realized how emotionally fallible Ferber probably was.

"Edna had great simpatico. I could discuss problems I was having at the time with her. She was like a well as far as receiving. She was very, very generous of spirit."

And they had their upsets, these two bruiser ladies.

"She was definitely a violent person. I watched my P's & Q's with Edna," says Hepburn concerning the Ferber Fury. "I wasn't exempt from it. She called me a dithering idiot many times, but I was strong enough not to let it get to me. I could take it."

The two women had dinner together quite often at one or the other's home. Hepburn remembers one time she had invited Ferber to dinner at her brownstone in New York. She had told Ferber that she would dispatch her chauffeur, Charles, to pick her up. The time was set for seven o'clock. Hepburn had invited a friend for cocktails whom she knew Ferber didn't like and whom she realized wasn't about to leave until good and ready. She didn't want the two to clash, so she told Charles to stall Ferber—to drive her around the Park a few times—anything. Finally, at about 7:45, Charles appeared with a very shaken and ruffled Ferber. She took a taxi home. Early.

"Edna was tactful only when she wanted to be," says Hepburn wryly of her friend.

The success of their enduring friendship was that each recognized the unicorn quality of the other; each gave the nod to the other as a person who stood up, habitually, even if it meant standing alone.

"We were dangerous women," Hepburn says of the era that bred strong women. "There aren't any more of us around. Now it's pretense and anger. Before it was that we just were."

Hepburn acknowledges that in all their years of closeness Ferber never once let down her hair, confided anything of a personal nature. But according to Hepburn, that was not so odd. She brings up the point that women of those days—people for that matter—didn't reveal their emotions. "It was nobody's business," she says. She remembers that, as a child growing up, if she didn't feel well, her mother would say briskly, "Well, don't talk about it. Get up to bed."

It seemed that the bromide to living was common sense, a sense of humor, and a minimum of emotions. Getting on with the business of life was the ticket. Hepburn credits Ferber with this ability: "Edna never hid her opinions, but she hid her emotions."

Not where her work was concerned, she didn't. With her sentiments about the war running high, she wrote an inflamed letter to Malcolm Johnson, her Doubleday editor at that time. Along with others, he had questioned the popular merits of *A Peculiar Treasure.*

"You'll be interested, I'm sure, to know that A PECULIAR TREASURE brought $5200 at auction in the small city of Meriden, Connecticut, at the War Bond rally at which four writers, including myself,* spoke. The other three books were by well-known male writers. A PECULIAR TREASURE brought more than double the sum bid for any other book, and ten times the sum bid for two of them. It seems to me this might be slight proof against the statement by the committee on Books For The Armed Services to the effect that A PECULIAR TREASURE is essentially a book for women. (My book) was written and published in 1938. The other three books were published in 1943 and 1944."

When Ferber's emotions did rise to the surface they were apt to be the childish ones of, "Nah, nah," "So there," and "I win."

It is Henry's opinion that Ferber practiced a no-lose policy all of her life—that if she'd had a few bona fide failures thrown into her career she would have been a different woman—perhaps better adjusted to the world at large. As it was, she was a surprisingly well-adjusted megalomaniac.

Alexander Woollcott, who also had a penchant for megalomania, died on January 23, 1943. At the time, Ferber was recovering from the removal of her gall bladder and appendix and was generally laid low. Whatever love had been lost between her and Woollcott was irrelevant for the moment. She paid him the courtesy of acknowledging his death as a major one, and railed against his disrespectful obituaries. She wrote in her diary: "The Herald Tribune

* Christopher la Farge, S. J. Perelman, Henry S. Canby.

Sunday obituary a scathing and vitriolic piece—the most vindictive thing I've ever read in a newspaper. The Times pretty bad, but not as frightful as the Herald Tribune."

Only by virtue of death was their feud of long standing absolved—or at least softened. The Feud (recorded earlier on) not only caused them to not speak for nine years, but provoked Woollcott into making slurs about Ferber whenever he could. They had a certain viciousness about them that was not so much sexual as sibling. He was known to have sent such nosegays as: "Why would anyone call a dog a bitch when there's Edna Ferber around."

In a series of letters to mutual friends he would flag-wave their feud—almost in a childish attempt to make them drop her. In a letter to the Lunts he wrote:

"Edna Ferber has just unnerved Jack Wilson by renting his Connecticut house for the summer."

In a letter to Beatrice Kaufman: "You ought to have some kind of flag by which Ferber . . . could be warned, just the way a passer-by at Buckingham Palace can tell at a glance whether the King is in town."

In a letter to Lynn Fontanne: "Indeed, it was presented to me just before one of your less successful dinner parties—the one when you thought you could insure a relaxed and digestive evening by limiting the guest list to me and Edna."

In a letter to Thornton Wilder: "I was staying at the White House for a week, living in the Lincoln Room but sleeping in a little ante-chamber because, unlike Edna Ferber [who had been a previous occupant] I felt unequal to the strain of lying in his bed."

Ferber was not exactly passive when it came to the subject of Woollcott. She did her share of backbiting as a portion of a letter to the Rodgerses indicates:

"I'm delighted about July 15th, dear Dorothy and Dick. I'll write you about clothes. Save your bathing suits, if only it will be warm and sunny. Croquet I hope. Anyone you're dying to spend a weekend with? I'll ask them if you say so. Unless it's maybe Woollcott . . . or some such flotsam."

Possibly it was a no-fault feud. Possibly it was a Ferber-fault feud. She did so relish feuds. And possibly, upon Woollcott's death, she remembered a letter that he had sent to her so long ago that came as close to being hat-in-hand as Woollcott would ever get:

"Dear Edna Ferber, This episode seems like a nightmare to me—

possibly because you are quite unrecognizable and because I cannot (from your ghoulish description) recognize either myself or my frolicsome fellow defendants. If you were to dip your pen in a bottle of red ink and it thereupon wrote a vivid green, you could not be more bewildered than I am.

"There is something sick and monstrous about it. To behave with utter absence of intent to offend and even without consciousness of having offended and then to be excommunicated with the language and feeling usually reserved for deeds of evil thought and mean purpose—that is a nightmare.

"When in the past I have been excommunicated for what seemed insufficient cause, I have gone happily on my way and said 'To hell with him.' Or her as the case may be. It has been both, at one time or another. I haven't cared two straws, feeling that the papistical parties didn't matter. This agreeable attitude is difficult to preserve now, for you do matter, obviously.

"In as much as something I had thought would grow into a great friendship has been miserably and contemptuously scrapped, it would be silly not to confess a sense of real impoverishment. But it would be false and insufferably condescending to express an atom of unfelt contrition . . .

"There can't be even acquaintance between two adults, A and B. when B thinks of A. as a deliberately rotten, insulting and humiliating fellow and A regards B as an alarming explosive, likely to blow his head off when he is most innocent. I don't see quite how one who writes with so much wisdom and tolerance and humor can bear such a strong family resemblance to nitro-glycerine. B., by the way, stands for Bomb.

"I am sorry to make a Jane Cowl exit. Not weeping my lady, and don't you think it, but rather shouting and struggling and enunciating 'They're sending me to prison for something I didn't do!' However, that's my story.

"I hope you spend some very pleasant conventions this summer. Yours respectfully, Alexander Woollcott."

Whatever the case, Ferber was a loyal friend to Woollcott—when he died.

Financial loyalty toward the living ran high with Ferber; emotional loyalty was less easy for her to maintain. She fluctuated between love and hate the way some do in choosing between the flavors chocolate or vanilla. She played games of favoritism between the Fox daughters, Janet and Mina—one week preferring Mina's goodness, the next, Janet's spunk and individuality. No doubt Mina pleased her more, but of the two, it is common consensus that her emotional and goal investment lay in Janet. In fact, Janet has often said that when she was young she secretly thought that she was Ferber's illegitimate child, given over to the more capable upbringing of Fan.

Ferber understood all too well Janet's longing to be free and unfettered by family, yet she cloaked the girl with disapproval whenever she slipped out from under the reins. For instance, when Janet, still living with her parents at too old an age, needed a breather and holed up in a hotel for a while, Ferber chastised the behavior in her diary and yet she slipped Janet a little something to foster her independence. The recorded events also bring Mina in as a go-between:

"Janet left home to go to Algonquin. Wrote her and sent $300 check. Terribly upset about Janet. Telephoned her but she didn't want to hear from her family. Lunch with Mina. Poor dear girl. Thought of Janet constantly. The talk with Mina was upsetting.

"Feeling ill. Lunch with Mina. Talked of Janet. Poor darling Mina so unhappy. What to do!

"Found message from Janet. Dinner with her at Algonquin. Talked. Not much good."

The touching point was that when Janet did run away it wasn't to Boise, Idaho, or Los Angeles or anywhere with miles between. It was to the Algonquin Hotel—so very associated with Edna Ferber.

Janet created another sore spot for Ferber, for she, like her mother Fan did not particularly cotton to Julia, and refused to pay filial piety to the old woman. Any combination in a room of Julia, Fan, Janet, and Ferber was bound to be a combustible one.

When Ferber was recovering from her gall bladder operation, there was a typical familial three-car accident:

"Didn't go out today. Mother in at three. Fan in and immediately the atmosphere became poisonous. After she [Fan] left I was horrified to find myself having the first attack of hysterics of my lifetime. Screeched like a locomotive and couldn't stop. Poor Julia. Perhaps it was good for me, though."

For the "Jewish Cinderella," Julia was always depicted as the prince/mother charming, and Fan as the wicked, ungrateful stepsister.

Once, when Fan tried to extricate herself from Ferber's financial grasp, Ferber chalked it up to an aberration:

"A depressing talk with Fan who seems to grow queerer and queerer. Says now that she doesn't want any money from me. God knows why or how she means to live."

Fan was not without her own set of talents. She was deft with a needle, exemplary in the kitchen, and she wrote well. Much to Ferber's not very well hidden chagrin, Fan's first novel, *I Know a Little Milliner,* was published in 1941 under the name of Fannie Ferber Fox. Earlier, Ferber had written in her diary:

"Talked to Fan. She is upset about failure to sell "I Know A Little Milliner." The fact is, it isn't well done. Diffuse, not clear, no attack."

The fact was, Ferber was riddled with jealousy. The fact was, the novel was decent. No *So Big,* but so acceptable that it was published. Earlier, Fan had had a cookbook out, but Ferber had put that safely in the domestic achievement category. For Fan to write a novel was as though she had gone and built a house on Ferber's land. It was trespassing, territorial invasion; it was an assault. Ferber struck back.

Fan had written a short story that she hoped to sell to *Cosmopolitan* magazine. She made the mistake of showing it to Ferber, who said that it was all very well, but to change the ending if she wanted a sale. Against her grain, Fan did so and submitted the story. It was rejected. Upon its return, Fan put in the original ending and resubmitted it. *Cosmopolitan* bought the story.

Just prior to her death, Fan talked about that episode:

"I hope Edna believed she was doing the right thing for me. I was certainly no threat to her. I don't know why she hated me so. It spoiled so many things."

Sometimes the very simple can become, with years, an emotional logarithm. Ferber had always subtracted her looks from her sister's, which might well have been the square root of her animosity. As late as 1941, she mentions it in a letter to Malcolm Johnson, concerning a photographic window display on her latest novel, *Saratoga Trunk:*

". . . I spoke to them about those photographs they had used in their S.T. window display. Did you furnish those pictures? I assume that you did. I'd love to have the one showing my sister Fan and me. She is the pretty little great-eyed girl and I am the baby with the egg-shaped head like a Mongolian idiot."

Even death, when associated with Fan, couldn't move Ferber. Jacob Fox died in November of 1941. Ferber woodenly records the proceedings:

"To Peg Pulitzer's for dinner Dick and Dorothy there. Called by Fan. Jack had died at Eisner's while they were playing gin. After the game was over, they noticed. Typical. Campbells Funeral Co. in charge. Home with Fan at about one."

Ferber's main concern was Julia, and that she'd failed her:

"Hadn't told mother about Jack Saturday night. Meant to call her early Sunday morning. She unfortunately awoke early. Read it in Times obituary."

1941, a vintage year. Aside from family irritants and war afflictions, Ferber had a relatively positive time of it. She brought forth a hit book and a play with George Kaufman. The book was *Saratoga Trunk,* which claimed one of the best sets of reviews she'd ever had. She must have been admittedly pleased, for she underlined certain sections of them—as in the New York *Times,* which said:

"The most cautious reviewer can predict skyrocket success for 'Saratoga Trunk'—and not feel that he is getting out on a limb, either. Few of Edna Ferber's vastly popular novels of the past decade have arrived on the book counters with more fanfare."

Better yet was the *Herald Tribune:*

"One closes 'Saratoga Trunk' with the feeling of having lived in a rich and exciting world, peopled by fascinating and exciting characters no less real because they are eccentric and romantic. The secret of Miss Ferber's achievement is rooted in many things—her vitality and belief in the people she creates; her meticulous care with all details of background and characterization; her unfailing sense of drama. Possibly this adds up to genius."

Four months earlier, as a dissonant counterpoint to the glowing reviews, she had written to her editor, Malcolm Johnson:

"Am I right in thinking that you said the deadline was August 15th? I should have easily had the rewrite finished before that time —long before. But this book, as you know, has me stopped. I've loathed every writing minute of it as I've never before hated anything I've written; and now rewriting is a thousand times worse. Nothing can convince me that anyone will ever read this mass of blubber . . .

"Your letter said something wild about 100,000 copies of S.T. Boy, you're going to have an awful lot of waste paper if you order good white paper on that basis . . .

"About George K., and the play. I haven't seen him, but I think his line of reasoning isn't too bad. A play may be an utter failure. Then its appearance in book form is painful. Also, we're rewriting beginning Monday August 4th, at George's house in the country. The book shouldn't be published until we've rewritten. We may do further rewrite up to the very final rehearsal. The book should have the benefit of such changes. Don't you agree? . . . I'm closing up the house about November first. I've been doing all my housework until the past ten days—cooking, cleaning, dish-washing. I now have a tiny colored girl who looks just like a panda, and who is exactly as helpful. I went out and caught her with my bare hands in the jungles of Bridgeport.

"When I've finished the book as best I can, and the play as best I can, and covered the odd jobs that have piled up in the past year, I'm going to run up and down Fifth Avenue ringing doorbells and screaming 'School's out! School's out!' at the top of my lungs."

Margalo Gillmore termed the relationship between Ferber and Kaufman as a "literary roll in the hay." That is as spicy a phrase as anyone could use when discussing the two of them. Together, they were sensory without being sensual; provoking without being provocative; teasing without taunting.

Shortly after the opening of *The Land Is Bright*, George Kaufman wrote a piece for the New York *Times* about their collaboration which has an adjusted-fond-resigned-remote husband quality about it:

"Walk around the reservoir any morning—any reservoir, for that matter—and it's an even bet that you will run into Edna Ferber. Miss Ferber is a walker. That daily walk, she says, is essential to her physical and mental well-being. Me, I'm different. In the words of Ring Lardner, the only exercise I get is when I take the studs out of one shirt and put them in another.

"Miss Ferber also has a preference for height. Her home in Connecticut . . . stands on top of a great hill, and she is never happier than when briskly ascending a mountain. Height clears and stimulates her mind, she will tell you. Here again I have to enter a demurrer. I have tried out the theory in miniature by getting up on a chair when I had a knotty problem to solve, and I can testify that it isn't worth a nickel.

"But I am not adamant on either subject—I should say that a certain sweet reasonableness is one of my outstanding characteristics. So, looking around for a place to work last March, and wanting both hills and open spaces, we ran a finger over the map and hit upon White Sulphur Springs. Neither of us had ever been there, but somebody's cousin had gone down the year before and she reported that it was wonderful. Just far enough South to be warm without being uncomfortable, marvelous food, everything.

"We had a great idea for a play. Refugees. Not just ordinary refugees, mind you, but the great figures of the artistic and scientific world. Molnar, Fritzi Massary, Einstein. It was to be a play that was both serious and gay, a play with compassion and gallantry in it. Looking back, I don't know what made us think that that would be a good idea. Bits and pieces of it had already been used in several plays, and Dorothy Thompson* and Fritz Kortner had written exactly such a play, and got nowhere with it. I suppose it was our eagerness to write a play, any play, that misled us. We had written just three plays together in fourteen years.

"So we went to White Sulphur . . . A splendid cold greeted us as we came down the [train] steps; the car had been pulled off into a siding, and there wasn't a porter in sight. It was at that precise moment that the refugee idea began to slip. As days passed it was destined to get worse and worse, but I should say that the instant of our descent of those car steps was when it first started to go.

"We stayed in White Sulphur for ten days, and it rained and was cold for nine of them. Whenever the downpour slowed to a drizzle Edna was into her stout boots and off into the hills.

"We started out with a strict working schedule. We would meet for lunch at 1 o'clock—that was my breakfast, of course—and we would discuss the play until 5, when we were off for our sulphur baths. (A very trying goings-on, those sulphur baths, by the way, and I strongly suspect the ensuing massage of being nothing but

* Ferber diary entry: "Took Fan to opening of Dorothy Thompson's play 'Another Sun'. A bad play about Viennese refugees. No action. It will close, surely.

Julia Ferber and E.F. in Paris, 1932.

Ferber in Mexico with Marc and Madeline Connelly—1932. Fourth from right: E. Ferber; second from right and far right: Madeline and Marc Connelly.

Ferber, Julia Ferber, and Fannie Ferber Fox not exactly kicking up their heels in Mexico City.

The equestrians: Janet Fox (standing) and Mina Fox, 1925.

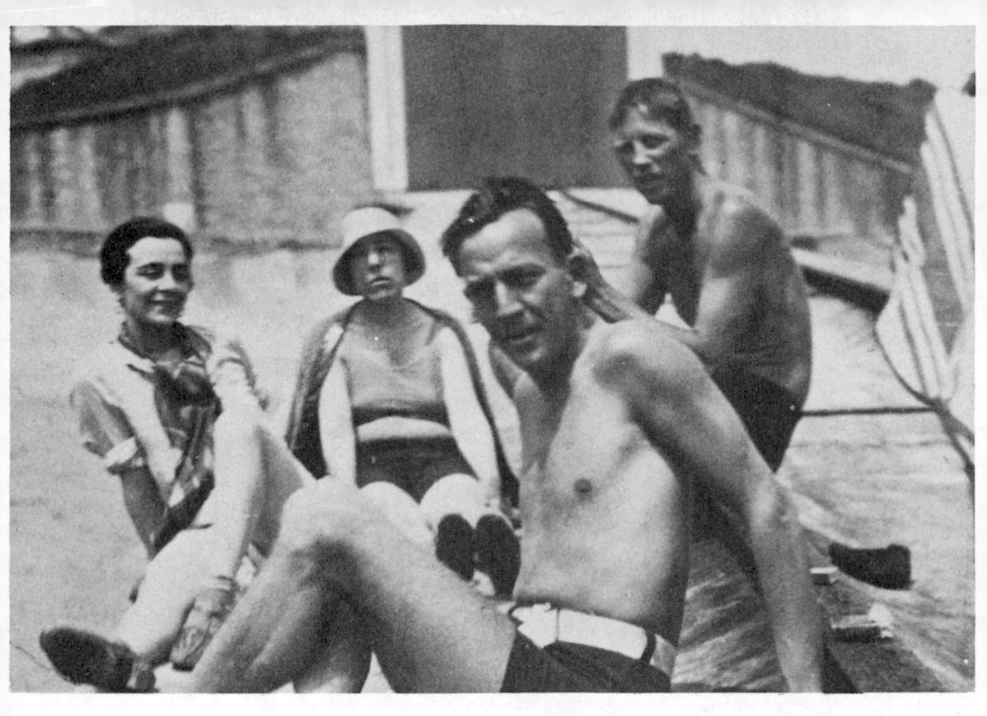

By the beautiful sea on the beach in Socoa, France—Basses-Pyrénées, home of Louis Bromfield. Left to right: Gladys Calthrop, Ferber, Noel Coward, Louis Bromfield, 1924.

Ferber and Louis Bromfield cutting up in Socoa, 1934.

William Allen White and Ferber at White's home in Emporia, Kansas, 1930.

The way they were. Identifiable are: top row second from left: William Allen White; bottom row, second from right: E. Ferber; far right: Julia Ferber, 1924.

Back from France in the latest Paris style, 1924.

dna with her given nose, 1920. (photo by Nickolas Muray)

The nieces Janet Fox and Mina Fox, 1917.

Early Edna, 19

Edna and Julia Ferber in their finery in Chicago, 1913.

Edna strolling in Chicago's Hyde Park, 1912.

The Democratic and Republican conventions of 1912 in Chicago. Edna and friends.

disguised exercise.) Then at 8 again for dinner—we agreed to talk play all through dinner, and as far into the night as we could stay awake. In this way we would not only come back to town with a complete scenerio but probably two or three other plays as well.

"The first day's session started in businesslike fashion . . . Now! I should say the scene should be Molnar's apartment—he's more or less the leader of the group—the others would all flock around him, come to visit . . . Fine! How about an old house down in Gramercy Park? There could be a woman who's let them have the house—old New York family . . . Now, these people are all trying to adapt themselves to life in America—of course, over there they were tremendously important and here they just have to take any jobs they can get . . . One of them goes out and discovers ice cream sodas—that'd be good! . . . Oh, yes! And chewing gum! How about a scene where one of them chews gum for the first time! . . . Fine! And I know! Texas! Somebody tells them they ought to leave New York—go to Texas! So they look up Texas in the encyclopedia—there could be a wonderful scene . . .

"Along about the third day Edna discovered a climbable mountain somewhere in the vicinage, and then she was happier. She started climbing it every day, and staying up there longer and longer, until I felt sure she was coming down with another Ten Commandments. We got to seeing the movie every night, no matter what it was. 'The Three Mesquiteers,' 'Hopalong Cassidy,' anything . . .

"Occasionally we would get a break. Leland Hayward got to calling up from California—he was in the middle of selling Edna's 'Saratoga Trunk' to the movies for twelve million dollars or something—and when Leland gets on long-distance, time is but water. An hour would pass, two hours . . . Jack Warner says . . . Cary Grant, Irene Dunne . . . I would sit happily waiting, doing nothing. But eventually even Leland would hang up, and there we would be again . . . Einstein, Fritz Thyssen . . .

"In desperation we began joining the old ladies in the lounge at 4 o'clock every day. Tea and organ music. 'Drink To Me Only With Thine Eyes.' . . . I even kibitzed a bridge game one evening, with the players averaging seventy-six years. There were three revokes in one hand, but nobody noticed. I kept right on kibitzing, too—it was the only game in town, as the old joke goes . . . Losing my mind completely, I even took a walk one day. It was a terrible experience but better than Einstein and Fritz Thyssen.

"On the tenth day we faced each other and had it out. Each started out to convince the other, but it was evident in two seconds that neither needed any convincing . . . I'm so glad! I feel as though a weight had fallen off me! We don't know those people—how can we write them! The only person we know in the whole play is that American woman who comes in—you know, old New York family . . . Yes, we could write her . . . Hold on, there! Old New York family! Why not? Those are people we can write! We know them, or know about them? . . .

"Atlantic City—Edna was through with height—she wanted sea level. The train reached North Philadelphia at 7:14 in the morning, as usual, and 7:20 found us breakfasting in the railroad station, wondering what we were doing there. After all, there was a handsome empty house in Connecticut, to say nothing of my own in Bucks County. In heaven's name, then, what were we doing in a railway station in North Philadelphia at 7:20 in the morning trying to write a play? But dismal though the setting, we were happy. The first act had fallen into place almost over night, and already there were bits and pieces of the second.

"The boardwalk, of course, was made to order for Edna. She walked and walked and walked. I sat. We had our palms read, played bingo, dropped in at auction rooms . . . 'Worn by Marie Dressler in the celebrated movie Dinner At Eight!' boomed the voice of the auctioneer . . . Strange that we should happen to enter just at that moment.

"Peculiarly enough, I have no recollection of the actual writing. That seems to be true with most plays, so far as I'm concerned. The whole business of getting ready to write, finding the actors, rehearsals, out of town—bits and pieces of all that linger in the mind. But all I can tell you about the weeks of writing is that the meals at Ferber's house were elegant."

Recently the John F. Kennedy Center in Washington, D.C., mounted a revival production of Kaufman's and Ferber's *The Royal Family*. I was privileged to have spoken at a seminar there whose theme was the playwrights' collaboration. One of the questions from the audience was what did Ferber write and what did Kaufman write and was there any way of telling? Instinct led me to speak up. "One can almost be dead sure," I said, "that any line concerning food was Ferber's. Also, the names of the characters—especially the women—were most likely given by Ferber." Then the Kaufman expert, a Dr. Malcolm Goldstein, reported what he felt Kaufman had contributed. It was a good question.

Although I had winged it, I now stand by my answer, for later I found a series of Ferber's notes for *The Land Is Bright* that included a smattering of characters' names that were eventually used: Matt Carlock, Lacey Kincaid, Blake, Ollie Pritchard, Jesse Andrews, Tana Kincaid, Deborah Hawks, Dan Frawley, Letty Hollister, Count Waldemar Czarniko, etc.

As far as the food lines go, George Kaufman was notorious for not caring about what he ate, so for him to write a line like "little curls of crips bacon"* would seem highly unlikely.

The Land Is Bright lost about $20,000. Needless to say it was not a smash. John Mason Brown, a friend of both Ferber and Kaufman, helped inter it in his review for the New York *World-Telegram:*

". . . Both Mr. Kaufman and Miss Ferber have long been fascinated by a through-the-generations story of this sort. Miss Ferber, in particular, has found it in fiction to be a reliable device. In the past she has brought her richest talents to developing it.

"Although Mr. Kaufman and Miss Ferber are far from their best when they now re-employ the trick, The Land Is Bright is one of those productions at which you do listen and listen attentively (often out of sheer incredulity).

"Most decidedly you are not bored. There is far, far too much to keep you wondering. And you do laugh gratefully at the lines which gleam as pure Kaufman. The story, too, with all its complications, may have a fatal fascination for you. Yet in spite of the brilliance of the settings, the smoothness of the direction and the competence of the acting, it is impossible not to realize that as dramatic literature The Land Is Bright is something to be taken about as seriously as a comic strip serial, which it closely resembles . . ."

Eleanor Roosevelt liked it better and in keeping with her generosity of spirit, saw real social significance in it. In her Washington newspaper column, "My Day," she wrote:

"In the evening a few of us were the guests of Mr. Max Gordon†

* From *The Royal Family.*

† Max Gordon was the producer of *Bravo!*

at his new play, The Land Is Bright . . . It is certainly a very interesting production, building up to the climax in a way which leaves you no moment when you are not tensely held by the action on the stage.

"The play is well acted, and I came away with one great sense of satisfaction, for the youth of today are more serious and more purposeful than the youth portrayed in the first two acts of the play. The honesty of the younger generation, as it looks back on its ancestors, is like a breath of fresh air. It points the moral that the whole level of public responsibility and integrity has gone up over the period of the last 50 years."

In 1940, Ferber was not only at war with The War but with everyone else. Treasure Hill was finally totally built and livable, but had built-in problems—mainly its upkeep. What to do about servants, caretakers, etc. How to find people responsible for making the place run smoothly. Ferber could never just get decent help; it had to be exquisite help. A big upset at this time was that a woman named Rebecca Henry, who had been Ferber's "retainer" for many years, was not up to the work the big house involved and was taking her leave. According to Dorothy Rodgers: "Rebecca had a kind of serenity that is very hard to come by, and that you do often see in black women. She had a strength, an inner strength that was absolutely superb."

The departure of Rebecca marked the invasion of menopause. Ferber had always regarded menstruation as her personal enemy, saying that the week before and the week during she was suicidal, but now this—this deprivation was worse. Perhaps she felt it so keenly because indeed she was keening for all that she had missed during her fertile time. She was disconsolate about everything. She lost her sense of proportion—equating in one breath in her diary the treachery of world affairs with personal ones:

"At ten the ghastly news of the Nazi German occupation of Paris. All France's population streaming along the Southern roads to nowhere. Impossible for me to write a line. To Danbury with Mother. A hideous town. Mother behaved like a maniac on the way home. Took full charge of the trip, orders, etc. Too maddening to be endured. The thing piles up and up. A nightmare trying to support all my people. It is making me terribly nervous."

With the purchase of Treasure Hill, Ferber had learned to drive—badly. Night driving was her bête noire; day driving was certainly no frolic. She was the sort of maniacally cautious driver who blames everyone else for recklessness.

A favorite part of George Kaufman's repertoire was telling about being in a car with Ferber. They would start out for an amiable little spin that would rapidly become, for Ferber, a surreal Grand Prix course. They would be going—at about 20 mph—on a completely deserted back road, when way in the distance Ferber would spot a speck of another car. She would employ emergency tactics—slowing her brakes, hunching over the wheel, ready to swerve or stop dead at any moment, and she would say in an outraged voice, "WHAT does he think he's doing! Just WHAT does he think he's up to!"

But the most hideous infringement of all was when another car passed her. She would say, "Did you see that!?! Why, that driver is a menace! How dare he get so close to me!"

Kaufman would just smile benignly, perspire profusely, and think that someday, in some play, he'd use it.

One would have thought that Ferber was playing in Sartre's *No Exit* instead of in her own *The Royal Family* at the Maplewood Playhouse in August of 1940. It was that much of a hell for her. All her life she'd ached to put on greasepaint, to play to the gallery, to hear immediate applause, and when she finally did she said of it:

"Too scared to eat. Opened. Very frightened. Was told couldn't hear me in first act, but better later. Didn't enjoy playing. Myself only depressed by the whole thing. Too bad that this should be so."

If living out her fantasy couldn't buoy her spirits, nothing could—nor did it. Weariness seemed a way of life—probably to combat the anger, which spurts out of her diary:

Entry: "With Mother, Fan and Jack to lunch at Old Hundred. Most unpleasant all around. Fan's behavior indicates such deep frustration and resentment toward life as to make me fear a physical or mental breakdown for her."

Entry: "Very weary, very hot, very humid, very upset, and generally in a mess, what with Mother, Rebecca's sudden decision not to return, and Fan's telephone nagging. A dreary deadly evening with Mother. Won't be able to take much more of this. A nightmare month. I tell myself that I only have to hold on until tomorrow morning, and tomorrow and tomorrow and tomorrow."

Entry: "Foxes anniversary. Not, I should say, an event for rejoicing. A check to them for $1000. This makes a little more than $10,500 to Foxes so far this year. Horribly weary almost beyond bearing. Mother continues to take her summer beauty rest. Fan, perhaps unconsciously, makes her so uncomfortable when with her that naturally Mother refuses to go to her house to stay. It works out splendidly for Fan."

Entry: "Fan, Jack, Janet to dinner. John and Elizabeth the new couple did very well. Surprise! His strawberry meringues delicious. The delphinium in the walled garden is so lovely. The world outside is so horrible, today."

Ferber's angst spread out onto her friends, who, en masse, she found quarrelsome. Everybody was out of step.

Entry: "Peg Pulitzer, Dick and Dorothy Rodgers here at 3. Played croquet for three hideous hours in the broiling sun. All because the Rodgers are entering the Long Island croquet tournament."

Entry: "The Malcolm Johnsons arrived at about 12:40. Had lost their way. Morris Ernst telephoned from Nantucket asking to bring Connie here for the night, and to meet them at Bridgeport airport. Whee! How I long for a little decent peace and quiet. Waters Turpin (Rebecca's son) appeared and had to be called for and sent back. Then the Ernsts had to be called for. All very trying and hopeless, somehow."

Entry: "A shattering and hideous day. Fan and Mother quarreled early in the morning. The bickering grew out of nothing until I found myself, as usual, involved. Mother silent throughout lunch. At 11:30 with Fan, Jack, Mina to look at houses for their summer rental. They took one in River Lane at $880 including agent's fee—all which I pay for. They left at 4:30 leaving me heavy-hearted and resentful. At 5 Noel, Lynn and Alfred. Noel talked bitterly about America. I made an unfortunate joke about the Norwegian campaign. Lynn as bitter as he [Noel]. Pretty disconcerting, all of it."

Entry: "Not feeling well. News of further German advance in Norway. Dinner at Hotel Lafayette for William Allen Whites' 47th wedding anniversary. Pretty awful. Noisy, bad food. Frank Adams came in briefly. Said he had sent me $500 check for $1000 owed me.

Seemed disgruntled. I shall therefore return it. An unprincipled man."

There was definitely a gypsy in Ferber's soul, for the only time all year that things picked up was when she took her first trip to Texas and then on to New Orleans. The breaking of routine and the absence of Julia and Fan always seemed to refresh her. She almost prided herself on not becoming enthusiastic, but through her diary entries there creeps a note of glee at a new experience and the glimmer, perhaps, of a novel.

Entry: "Dallas at 9:30. A dusty hotel called the Baker. My room not made up, and very dirty. Gave the Topsy maid a dollar to clean it up. Walked a bit around town. At lunch interviewed by a charming young fellow named Joe Linz, Dallas Journal. Peter Molyneaux, friend of Will White called. Stuffy. Drove with Linz and Molyneaux and a friend of theirs around Dallas. Saw old Linz house, absurdly Victorian. Dallas has a certain spirit and worldliness. I like the people. The city and surroundings flat and dull."

Entry: "A walk. Nieman-Marcus store. Very smart and Saks-ish; an astonishing place for this sort of town. All the rich new Texas oil women buy their clothes there. Lunch with Mrs. Linz (Joe's mother), Joe and the Journal's managing editor, at the Linz's house. I like the Linzes. Easy to be with. Dinner at the Becks. Very bad, dull and dirty talk."

Entry: "Left for Houston on the Rocket—a bad steamliner. Ninety degrees in Houston. Rice Hotel terrible. Noisy, hot, lobby full of oil men. Dinner in the stuffy dining room, bad, dirty, noisy. Saw the new shipping canal."

Entry: "Motored to Galveston after a rather uncomfortable interview with two reporters. A girl and a man. A nasty gleam in their eyes, I'd say. Galveston a ghost town. The crumbling Victorian houses seem built of ashes. Lunch (bad) at the Buccaneer. A dreary lunch room with the ocean successfully blotted out of view. A walk along ocean front, lovely, cool."

Entry: The train to San Antonio. Very hot in San Antonio. Met at station by reporter who looked like Thomas Wolfe. Another reporter, a girl, very silly, who said she wanted to get acquainted first and have a good visit. The Linzes and Joe motored here. Dinner with them at a dusty little road-house outside of town. Awful food, service. The Linzes dear people. Picked up a vice squad cop and toured a rather dreary red-light district."

Entry: "Mayor Maury Maverick in at 10:30. With him and the Linzes to see La Villita, an old section of San Antonio now being reclaimed by Mayor Maverick. Visited the old governor's palace with him. Maverick an original—forceful, an actor, courageous, not at all smooth. Liked him. Saw the Missions. Climbed a lot of winding stairs. Felt fine. Pooh to Barach. Drove with Joe Linz and Red the cop. A dull business."

Entry: "Drove to the country with Holland McCombs . . . a cottage on Lake McQueeney. Horses, trap-shooting, a barbeque lunch, all the things that bore me, including very dull people indeed. Lots of snap-shots and vacant laughter."

Entry: "Lunch with Mrs. Maury Maverick and five of her friends. Pleasant intelligent women. Lunch edible, but no decent food in Texas!"

Entry: "By plane to New Orleans. Lunch at Roosevelt Hotel—attractive sitting room and bedroom. Sitting room presented me by the management. Interviewed by reporter. He took me to Royal Street, just the other side of Canal, where the old French Quarter (Vieux Carre) begins. Walked a lot. Shabby, fascinating. Enchanting iron balconies."

Entry: "Louis B. [Bromfield] arrives late. Lunch with him at Antoines. At last savory stuff. Photographs by publicity man for Roosevelt Hotel. He is nephew of Weiss, owner of hotel who is out of the penitentiary on appeal. Deeply involved in long political scandals."

Entry: "At noon motored with Louis to see Oak Allee, old restored plantation in bayou country. Ferried across Mississippi. Small plantations, sugar factories, negro cabins. The levee dotted with negros in their bright Sunday clothes. Stewarts, who now own Oak Allee pleasant, chatty, etc. A horrible lunch at a noisy tavern. The drive back too long. Louis not well on drive home. Bad fried oysters, probably.

This sort of day would most likely end up as a paragraph somewhere in a Ferber novel. One can smell the fictional fuel. For example, in the phrase "levee dotted with negros."

Entry: "Walked about in the French Quarter. Met Louis at hotel, with him for 2½ hour boat ride on Mississippi stern-wheeler. Louis and I to dinner at the Roark Bradfords.* Excellent New

* Marc Connelly's *The Green Pastures* was derived from author Bradford's *Ol' Man Adam an' His Chillun.*

Orleans dinner, pleasant talk. Terribly warm, though. Everyone sits indoors, no air. Odd."

Entry: "Home. Well, New York. Not so very glittering to my eye."

There are four high points of interest about Ferber's trip: 1. There is not a mention of being weary; 2. She thought she'd found the correct husband for Janet in Joe Linz; 3. The solo appearance of the married Louis Bromfield; 4. Ferber's fixation about food.

There are hardly ten pages of any of Ferber's work that don't mention vittles of some drooling sort or other. In a sense these passages substitute for more prurient ones. In a small succulent pamphlet, Ferber defends her food "writes."

"Dickens did it. If, in the old walnut bookcase back in Appleton, Wisconsin, we had had a complete set of, say, Jane Austen instead of Charles Dickens, I probably should not now be accused by our more spiritual book reviewers of being vulgarly lavish in the amount of food and clothing that I bestow upon my fictional characters. One midwest critic of somewhat anemic cast devoted two columns to the expression of his overwhelming repulsion at the amount of food spread over the pages of 'So Big,' and his delicate shrinking from the sordid paragraphs that describe the clothes of the people who move through the chapters of that, in his opinion, all too earthy novel.

"It all comes, I suppose, of having been brought up on Dickens and Thackeray—but mostly Dickens. There weren't many books in that walnut bookcase; so I read and reread what there was. Veal and ham pies, hot pineapple toddies, succulent oysters, great joints of beef and mutton, stews of tripe, and rashers of bacon oozed and sizzled in the volumes that made Sairey Gamp and Mr. Micawber, Bill Sikes and Fanny Squeers, real and living persons to me. Daniel Quilp could never have been so delightfully horrible in my eyes if I hadn't seen him drink his boiling hot tea without batting his mean little eyes. Imagine a Miss Havisham without a description of her age-yellowed and withered satin wedding gown, her shroudlike veil, and her tattered stocking of finest silk. I knew these people; not only what they said and thought, but what they ate and drank and wore. They were real. They were human beings.

"I like to know what people eat and wear. I enjoy writing about food and clothes. But apparently it isn't done. Ever since the discovery of sex by our younger set of fictionists (. . . they just stumbled upon it as is so often the way in the revelation of a great truth) all other appetites have been barred from the fictional page. It has got so now that mention of meat and drink is looked upon as being downright indelicate. Of course some upstart claimants have come forward recently with the contention that sex was an acknowledged fact way back in 1911, but the Younger Fictionists soon made short work of these. One poor fool even had the effrontery to mumble something about the Book of Genesis, but he was quickly shouted down.

"In time they will probably have their way, these new purists. Of course it will make a lot of difference in some old stories of which the fogies among us have grown fond. The story of Adam and Eve, for example. Eliminate the apple and the fig leaf and it loses something. I don't know what—but something. And that one about the loaves and fishes. Somehow, it would seem so different with all that vulgar food left out. The whole school of what has been called gefullte fiction will, in time, be stamped out. The new generation will never be subjected to the degrading glimpses of Jos Sedley and his top boots. They will know nothing of the crass details of what Jos and Becky Sharp and Amelia and her young man—Whatshisname—had to eat at Vauxhall Gardens. Take food and drink and raiment away from Joseph Hergesheimer's* novels—banish the Bacardi rum, the rose-pink clams, the chiffon, the perfume, the silver girdled girls—and you have—well—what have you?

"Give these Nice Nellies of fiction another twenty-five years and we shall have a whole new set of moral standards. Food will be something not to be mentioned in polite society. The offspring of two decades hence, dashing in upon a roomful of people with his shameless, 'I want a piece of bread and butter and jelly,' will find himself hustled from the room by an embarrassed and irate parent and treated to a lecture such as:

"'Melville, hasn't Mama told you that you mustn't say a thing like that in company! It isn't nice. Those are things we don't speak of. You can come and talk to Mama about them, but not anyone else. What will the ladies and gentlemen think!'

"But in another fifty years the revolution will come. Slowly it will dawn upon a narrow world that it is, after all, wisest to be Open

* A *Saturday Evening Post* writer very much in vogue. He wrote *The Three Black Pennys* as well as many other books.

and Honest about the Facts of Life like Food and Clothes. The child will find it all out one way or another. Why not teach him, frankly and intelligently, in the home or in the school? We shall have modernists who will advocate taking the child out into the fields and woods to let him behold how the mother bird feeds the angleworm to her young. And then, very gently, his maternal teacher can say, 'Melville, dear, that is why your dear father works in the great big office downtown, and why Mother goes to market and buys chopped beef and turnips and magel wurzel and bread pudding and all the delicious things you like so much. It is because they want their little Melville to grow up to be a strong, sturdy, clean limbed young American.'

"But before that day of freedom dawns, the drama, too, will no doubt be writhing under the cruel thongs of bondage. Instead of the big seduction scene as we have known it, the real thrill of the new-school play of daring will come when tea is served in the second act. And there's little doubt as things are shaping themselves now, that when the heroine utters the almost unspeakable line, 'Lemon or cream?' the minions of the law, armed with right and power, will rush in and close the show."

There is a rather frightening story about Ferber and Julia and luxury items. Its prologue is a 1939 diary entry: "With Mother to order linens at Broadway Linen Shop. Lovely embroidered sheets, etc."

Ferber adored linen sheets, which crumple easily. She told Rebecca that because they did so she'd like them changed twice a week. Soon, she realized that her orders weren't being carried out and demanded to know why. Rebecca confessed that Julia had contradicted Ferber's wish, insisting that it was too, too extravagant. Ferber, livid at having been overidden by her mother in her own home, tore one of the linen sheets into shreds and stormed into Julia, dumping it before her on the floor.

"This cost a great deal more than having them laundered," she spat out.

Hence, the sheets were changed twice a week–sometimes three.

Ferber had had a young girlhood friend named Edith Brown, to whom Ferber gave the rather startling nickname of "Putz." When Edith Brown married and began to have children, their friendship dwindled. She can't remember why but has an inkling that it might have been that she didn't want to be a drag on the celebrated Edna Ferber. She speaks of herself as "just an ordinary, non-famous person." She is sure there was no quarrel with Ferber—it was just that life intervened. She had the impression that Ferber, clothes, food, and Julia were all somewhat pathologically tied up. She feels that, since Ferber never had an allure for men, she tended to show off for Julia by dressing beautifully. There was a period when Ferber loved to throw money around—partly to prove she could, and partly to thumb at Julia.

Edith Brown remembers that one night she and Ferber took a walk and landed at Reubens (the late Reubens was an extravaganza delicatessen) for a late snack. Ferber, very cavalier, ordered two caviar sandwiches and two splits of champagne:

Edith: "Edna, did you have a fight with Julia?"

Ferber: "Edith, how did you know?"

On New Year's Eve of 1939, Ferber was home with a dinner of scrambled eggs, reading a book and turning in at eleven. On New Year's Eve of 1938, she wrote to Malcolm Johnson:

"I am sitting up at Treasure Hill in front of a typewriter. It's very pleasant."

As Ferber would say, "Pretty dull stuff." But in between, there had been a wondrous event. Edna Ferber, popular novelist, hidden behind states of the Union, had taken a chance. She'd come out as Edna Ferber, a peculiar treasure.

TREASURE YEARS
1938-1927

FERBER'S AUTOBIOGRAPHY, *A Peculiar Treasure*, has two dedications. The first, public and sensible, reads "To Janet Fox and Mina Fox with the hope that my reason for having written this book may soon seem an anachronism. E.F." The second, found among her notes, is private and fierce: "To Adolf Hitler who has made of me a better Jew and a more understanding and tolerant human being, as he has of millions of other Jews, this book is dedicated in loathing and contempt."

Ferber had once said: "Autobiographies and confessions usually leave me cold. It's what people won't tell and wouldn't for the world show that fascinates me. A bandage can be so mysterious. Removed, it so often reveals only a hang-nail."

For Doubleday, as far as promotion and sales were concerned, the book was more than a hangnail. It was a sore spot. A story about a Jewish girl with an abundance of chutzpa and talent written at a time when Jews were being persecuted, when being a Jew, even in America, was touchy, was a story that Doubleday deemed as being "special"—"not for wide appeal."

Ferber had once mused that if there was a fire and she could only rescue one book it would be *A Peculiar Treasure*. The fire of being ignored hurt and threatened Ferber when she wrote to Nelson Doubleday:

"I think that you and your advertising staff and your publicity staff and your selling staff should cease to think of this book as an autobiography purely. The hundreds of letters I have received almost without exception stress the fact that the book had (for the reader) the march and tempo of a novel. I don't know why this is found to be the case. There was no such intention when the book was written. If it is so, however, why not capitalize on it. You yourself have said to me on a number of occasions, 'But this is an autobiography. It's doing well for an autobiography.'

"That's out. When a book sells (or has printed, rather) over 35,000 in less than three months I think we can wake up sufficiently to realize that we have here still a potential seller of major dimensions. Just pretend, will you, that you are selling something that has wide appeal. If it hasn't then why do I get letters from University professors and housewives; from Christians and Jews; from boys of 18, bewildered and resentful of the world in which they find themselves; from men and women in their seventies!

"Pretend this is a great masterpiece like REBECCA, see. Pretend it's Campbell's Soup. Pretend it's SHOW BOAT. Pretend you believe in it. Stop thinking of it as a bit of very special nonsense that I now have got out of my system. Stop thinking of it as an autobiography. It's a story of a middle-class Jewish woman and her family in America, and it is readable and moving and, in my opinion, important. And if you don't believe that then let me hire someone on your staff who does. Or let me buy it from you, and turn it over to a publisher who does believe in it sufficiently to want to advertise it. For I believe in advertising. I'm pretty tired of that special brand of Doubleday selling argument which is, in a nutshell: 1. It's an autobiography. 2. People won't spend three dollars. 3. The rental libraries are afraid of a $3 book. 4. There are only 1200 book stores in the U.S. 5. Business is bad. 6. How about letting us put it into our Dollar Book Club. 7. I don't believe in advertising.

"I can't believe that the book publishing business is so dead on its feet that the only method it knows by which to push a book is to take space in the New York Times and the New York Tribune to tell a palpitating world what the St. Louis Post-Dispatch thought of a book that was published almost three months ago. If that's the publishing business than I'm through writing books. Sorry. E.F."

Not only was she not through writing books; she was not, nor never would be, through writing missiles of outrage. When Malcolm Johnson, via Doubleday, took her up on her pro-advertising stand and suggested that she stump for her book, speaking in department stores and autographing copies, she sent him a letter that boxed his ears:

". . . The thing that baffles me is that an intelligent publisher should expect a writer of some standing to go through that kind of cheap sordid pushing around. Suppose that I were to use my time, energy and nervous force in visiting and signing autographs at ten or even twenty stores. Suppose that by doing so there should be sold 200 books at each store—a large number, I should think. That would mean 2,000 (if ten) or 4,000 (if twenty) copies. How absurd, how ridiculous, how truly sordid. It is the cheapest kind of motion picture publicity technique applied to the writer. And decent writing depends on serenity, quiet, and freedom from just that kind of shoving around."

Writer vs. publisher. Age old. Always before she had pretty well understood her minimum bargaining position. She was the fury, but they were the fates, and if a book didn't do so well in Des Moines, Iowa—then how tiresome, but not much more. This was personal; this was her guts made into sentences; if this was ignored it was a crime against her total nature. In her early middle age, this book was her chrysalis—new and unprotected. Sweet Jesus, did she want it to fly.

The reviews were admirable but not airborne. Most of them were so surprised at her departure from her usual that they gave her rather dull plaudits—as though they were secretly grudging not being able to attack her rich sap prose.

The New York *Times*—a woman reviewer—came close to a somewhat obscure rave, ending the review with:

"To her own amazement, Edna Ferber burst into a speech in Union Square once, smashing down with hard facts and clear thinking upon an oratory which was shrieking of Russian 'freedom.' She has the same weapons against Nazism and anti-Semitism. But what she leaves with her readers here is something subtler and more pervasive than argument: the far stronger thing which is simple memory; not hers alone, but theirs as well. The small town which is the American background; the pioneer spirit which has been building America for 300 years—which of us has not such traditions, such pride? At its worst that spirit was ruthless and greedy; at its best it sought a real Promised Land. Pilgrim, Huguenot, Catholic, Quaker, Jew—here are our memories; here is the spirit of a nation; here is our peculiar treasure of democracy and freedom, to be guarded by us all."

To Malcolm Johnson—who got the grumblings that Ken McCormick was later to inherit—Ferber took the review and reviewer to task, and then herself for doing so:

"It [the review] definitely is favorable and most kind, and I hope you won't think I am an ungrateful wench when I say it lacks the compelling quality which would make a reader want to go out and buy that book. I wish the review could have been written by a man. Any review should contain some adverse criticism. This contained really none. I was rather amazed to see that Miss Woods almost completely ignored the fact that I wrote this book for a reason which had nothing to do with autobiography. Still, I am ungrateful in voicing all this . . ."

Occasionally, in the thick of book dealings, Ferber would send Johnson (or McCormick or Dan Longwell) a non sequitur note—charming, airy, and slightly daffy. She would suddenly treat them like suitors—her words batting their lashes—as in the one she sent to Johnson when she had the flu:

"I'm feeling better than before I was hit by the flu. I used some sense, for once. Called the doctor first thing in the morning, he bounced in and gave me some mysterious powders to be taken every three hours for the ache and the headache and chills.

"AND (this is important) he told me to drink HOT fruit juices all day—hot orange juice, hot grapefruit juice, hot tea and hot lemonade if I liked it. I'd never heard of hot orange and grapefruit, but it is wonderful.

"And so are you. E.F."

Ferber, quick to cite others' mistakes, was meticulous in catching her own; she proofed and reproofed, trying never to leave anything to Doubleday's oversight. When she was fallible, did make a mistake, she was always the first to claim it.

"There are in 'A Peculiar Treasure' two additional errors which I have only recently caught, and which I regret very much, particularly as they will doubtless appear in the Literary Guild edition. I assume that that has already been printed, if not distributed. Listing composers I named Rachmaninoff who is a notorious anti-Semite, instead of Horowitz* who is the man I had in mind. I don't see how I could have pulled a boner like that except that I was writing under pressure. If this can be caught in another edition, if

* In correcting her mistake, she pulled another musical boner. Vladimir Horowitz is a performer, not a composer. Akin to Somerset Maugham, she had no knowledge of or any particular feeling about music.

any, I shall be very grateful. Maybe this has been caught, and, if in that case, will you please substitute Horowitz who is a fine musician.

"Also I find that I have attributed the Morality Play, 'Every Woman,' to George V. Hobart. 'Every Woman' was written by the late Walter Browne. Hobart's play was entitled 'Experience.'"

Ferber was selfish and generous and always angry at herself for being both. She gaveth and she tooketh away simultaneously—as in the case of Waters Turpin. He was Rebecca's son and a bright boy. Ferber, who appreciated nothing better than a good mind, had volunteered to sponsor him through college if he followed the strings attached. She'd presented the offer to Rebecca thus:

"I'll put him through college if he has something to do there. Otherwise he's wasting my money and his time."

He did neither. In fact he utilized both to try and become what his patroness was—a writer. Janet remembers a twist to the thing. One of the ways he was to return Ferber's favor was that during the summer he would help out at Treasure Hill doing odd jobs—pruning when pruning was needed; chauffeuring when that was needed. He would be at beck and call, at step 'n' fetch it. Waters Turpin would have none of it. Ironically, with Ferber's gift of higher education he had risen above the station that she wanted him at during the summer. He lounged around and acted like lord of the manor until Ferber realized that it was useless. She agreed with him that it wasn't working out, but not without thinking—and probably letting him know—that he was an ungrateful so-and-so.

By 1938, Waters Turpin was writing prodigiously, and had sent one of his manuscripts to Malcolm Johnson at Doubleday. In a letter to Johnson, Ferber expresses mixed feelings about Turpin's initiative and possible talent:

"I am startled to learn that Waters Turpin's new manuscript was sent in to your office. I didn't know that he was going to send it to you, though I remember that you spoke of being interested in his work . . . I sincerely hope that you will not consider this manuscript with any thought of me to balance your decision one way or the other. I have helped Waters Turpin through many years. He must now stand completely on his own. What I have done I have done because of his mother, Rebecca Henry, who, as you know, has been with me for fifteen or more years. Waters is now married; he has a good job teaching in a college. I have tried to get a Guggenheim for him on next year's list. Altogether, I must ask you to look at this book with a cold and unbiased eye. I do not want to be a factor in it."

In 1939 she was of a different mind about Waters Turpin. This time, the letter was to the chieftain, Nelson Doubleday:

"I just received a completely unsolicited line from William Allen White which I am sending on to you. It began his letter to me, thus: 'Dear Edna, I have finished "Oh, Canaan." It is a beautiful book. The boy can write and he has got something on the ball. If you know any place I can write a review for it I shall be glad to do it.'

"I hope you'll take advantage of that offer. And I hope you'll do something to present and push this new novel properly.

"From a brief talk with him I have learned from Waters Turpin that he is planning three more novels, making a group of five in all. One of these, entitled THESE LOW GROUNDS was, as you know, published by Harper. When the group of five is finished I think that they should be done in a set, for they will constitute the first thoughtful series of intelligent and arresting novels written about the negro in America, taken as a comprehensive study. This is something for your consideration, I think. And I think, too, that you cannot toss this boy off as just another beginning writer. I know that you have little or no interest in nursing a writer along. Well, you're wrong." And then, signing off with her wonderful whimsy, "Can you use your influence to get me some rain? Edna."

Writing about herself unbottled Ferber. There was a passion about it that rarely shows up in her prose. Again, the outtakes of the book are special; some seem a little tremulous, which allows one to perceive her as more vulnerable than usual:

"I never wanted to be a writer. I never even thought of being a writer. I wanted only to be an actress."

"I am afraid that middle age has made me tolerant. I have very few active hates. I hate tomato preserves, and Hitler and knitted underwear and injustice and spite and extreme piety."

"All the bright young men are resentful. They have what used to be called neither salt nor pepper. No flavor or body. They are vaguely for the working man as though he were a special kind of pet dog. I was brought up in the kind of community in which there was practically no discrimination. My school chum was Belle Harris, whose father was janitor of the school. He drove the dray, passed the contribution box and was a grave black-broad clothed suher [?] at the Congregational church. Week-days he stood in his blue overalls driving his team and wagon past the house up North street to his noonday dinner. There was a college clique; and a paper mill millionaire group but it was not exclusive.

"They peter out, the bright young men. They don't seem to have much stamina, once their little rather feminine malice is weakened. They have a little tale to tell about themselves. The Scott Fitzgeralds, the Floyd Dells, the Clifton Fadimans. You will hear them tell what's wrong with William Allen White and Teddy Roosevelt. Twenty, thirty years roll by, and there is William Allen White a national figure of strength, wisdom, achievement. And where are all those Bright Young Men!

"You really don't have to bother about the Bright Young Men. Time takes care of them."

"NATIONAL CONVENTION: Chicago Armory. Harding nominated. Wept. [The first reference to Ferber ever weeping.] I knew that the post-war talk had all been words, and that we were in for years of sordid materialism. I remember looking hard at a little window high up—one of those absurd windows they put in armories—and crying with my eyes wide open and the tears running down my cheeks, and thinking meanwhile of the cobwebs that festooned the window. The shouts, the false and built-up cheers. My end of belief in human beings' purpose after the War."

"WRITING: Romantic writers are likely to be discredited in America during their lifetime."

"LADY ASTOR: This is the woman who is agitating the removal of the Jews of England, and threatening the Jews of America. This expatriate."

"WRITING: Don't tear up your stuff. I have written page after page through the day in a kind of agony of ineffectualness, weary, limp and unvital, only to find, on reading it bright and fresh next morning, that it has a freshness, meaning and pace. Never tear up your stuff until you've slept on it."

"WRITING: Good or bad, it always has been the best I could do at the time. People who may think that I could have written better are flattering me. I worked like a horse, and wrote the best I could. Never have I written a line except to please myself. I never have written to order. I never dreamed of being a best-seller."

"In the second year of the 1929 depression saying that this was not a mere economical depression but a collapse of the soul and spirit of the civilized world. To this statement no one paid the slightest attention other than a contemptuous snicker."

"Those of us who came into the spotlight twenty or twenty-five years ago, are still young enough to march with the new crowd or drop behind with the old. We are men and women in our thirties and forties and early fifties. It is silly to pretend that we haven't been brilliantly successful in our day. Whether or not we live is really rather unimportant. We have lived. I don't think any group of people ever had so much fun."

One of Ferber's glossy friends was Beatrice (Bea) Kaufman. She was one of the few women whom Ferber did lunch with on occasion. On the most sophisticated level they were girlfriends—gossiping, theatregoing, party arranging. On a more basic level they were natural enemies, although neither would have admitted it for the world. Anne Kaufman Schneider, daughter of Beatrice and George, puts the antagonism into place:

"Mother had the trappings of a kind of glamourous thing that Edna didn't have. She was married to a very successful man. She was very successful in the department of other gentlemen. She was very popular, very social, and ran a very socially popular salon. Edna had none of that whirlwind around her, but she had something that Mother didn't. She had her work that made her famous, and she had work with Daddy that made them famous as a pair.

"They were not unlike, the two women. Both were not really what we would call attractive today. Both were not tall enough to be modish; they were too thick, sort of chunky. Both had big heads with mane-like hair.

"Edna made jealous associations with my mother, who was a terribly important part of my father's life—much more so than Edna was. My parents were totally involved with each other to the extent where Edna might have felt excluded."

Wifely Bea apparently gave literary mistress Ferber the kind of nourishment she needed to plunge ahead with *A Peculiar Treasure*. In Beatrice's copy Ferber wrote:

"You know, dear Beatrice, that you ought to take your share of the blame for this book. You were, I think, the first person to whom I talked about doing it. I shrank from writing it, somehow. And you said, that day at Barley Sheaf Farm, 'Go on, do it! Do it!' So I did. Affectionately, Edna."

The allegations that Beatrice Kaufman called Edna Ferber a "money virgin," and that during the opening of the Kaufman-Ferber play *The Royal Family* she sat in a nearby bar with Heywood Broun drinking to its failure, seems unreasonably apocryphal. But when one considers that Beatrice Kaufman was one of the lights of Alexander Woollcott's life, that they conferred and conspired about everything, and, that Woollcott was always falling out with Ferber, it's suddenly not so unseemly that Beatrice Kaufman caught some of Woollcott's venom by proxy.

With the Kaufmans, like the Harts, Ferber had her nose pressed against their familial glass. She used her work as a protection against bursting through—against wanting more than her share of their companionship. For young Anne Kaufman, she gave the best gift she could think of—her work. Ten books of it, and in the hope that Anne would appreciate them someday, she dedicated them in an amusing manner:

> "Dear Anne, I really don't think you'll like these books very much. E.F."
> To tell you the flat truth—I hope you won't because
> They weren't written for young ladies of eleven.
> Even if they happened to be extremely interesting young
> ladies of eleven, like you. I'd much rather have
> you like them five years from now—or even
> Ten! Because they are quite good and all about
> people in the United States. Still, if you should accidentally
> happen to like 'Fanny Herself' (the first half, that is) or 'So Big' or
> 'Show Boat' or 'Cimarron,' why, I'll love you just as well.
> Edna Ferber."

Although the sales of *A Peculiar Treasure* were not as staggering as those of her novels, the mail on it was more overpowering, more controversial than any she'd ever received. Outraged letters, hallelujah letters, crackpot letters, VIP letters; the range of sentiment was vast. Carl Sandburg was one of the book's biggest supporters—to the point of carrying it around with him on his lecture circuit. Known as one of the literary heartbeats of America, he hailed Ferber as being one also.

The book worked as an antidote to despair for such diverse people as Adela Rogers St. Johns, the author, and Mary Martin, the actress. Each read it at a low point in her life, and each advocated it as a health tonic.

Ferber, especially as she portrays herself in *A Peculiar Treasure,* brings to mind the story of the great and healing psychiatrist whose personal life is less than noble, always painful, and often more than he can deal with. *A Peculiar Treasure* is a peculiar sort of mining for a life. Never once does Ferber reveal anything emotionally dishonorable. There is no mention of the ambivalent, crippling feeling she had toward her mother; there is not a glimmer of the bitterness between herself and Fan. There is not, sadly, any mention of any large love, lost or found, in her life. How much richer the broth would have been with some insight into what caused her pain as well as what supplied her with her supposedly lusty love of life. Honesty should come before a falling into an autobiography, but Ferber could never allow herself to fall from her own esteem. In a sense writing her autobiography was a way of getting around herself—of avoiding herself—yet being able to say to the world, "There! I did it. That's me."

There are hints in her diaries of rather prissy romantic feelings. One in particular is interesting.

Occasionally Ferber would pick up and go to Chicago, which she considered to be her early literary proving ground and was also a watering hole of old friends. On one such trip, she was on the Century bound for Chicago, when:

"A man named Lewis Ruskin turned up, astonishingly—a friend of Victor Cazalet—Chicago man—deeply interested in Refugee work."

That was not that. Three months later she had a visitor at Treasure Hill:

"Lewis Ruskin arrived, having come on the Normandie. Looking young and gay and thinner than when I last (and first) saw him . . . Dancing on the terrace with Ruskin. He sprained his ankle.

Behaved splendidly about it—very quiet and game. Called Dr. Friedman of Bridgeport. Bound it."

The next day:

"Lewis Ruskin's ankle quite swollen. Sent for a crutch. With him to lunch at Cobb's Mill. Very very hot. To Tammy Ryan's, with William driving. Got lost. Left Lewis there, after a rather astonishing farewell kiss."

And that was very much that with Lewis Ruskin. One begins to think that Ferber dosed herself up with preventative medicine against romance—when it did come along.

Treasure Hill, in its way, was like a late marriage. It represented commitment and security. Before she took the plunge and bought the land and started to build, she had terrible premarital jitters. As far as living quarters were concerned, she'd always been a bachelor—footloose and migratory—depositing herself and her furniture in various cushy flats and hotel-apartment suites all over New York. She wrote a flippant piece about her habitual unrest prior to her Treasure Hill settling.

"Whether I find myself (God forbid!) at the Osage Hotel, Pawhuska, Oklahoma; or at the George V in Paris, the Ritz in Boston, the Stephanie in Baden-Baden or Miss Tuttle's boarding house, New Milford, Connecticut, the same madness grips me. Before unpacking my bag, before turning back the covers for sheet inspection, before glancing out of the window to see if I face an all night garage, I go through a mildly insane ritual. The form it takes is this: I move the bed to the place where the dresser stands, the dresser where the table-desk is, the table-desk where the chair is placed . . .

"This means that I have the soul of an interior decorator. There are, however, other and less flattering explanations of this overwhelming compulsion to arrange furniture to suit my own taste the instant I enter a room. The Vienna boys probably would say that is my desire to impress my will on something—anything—if it's only a helpless little hotel bedroom. My enemies (members of the well-known Legion family) say that it is perversity, showing a wish to change or contradict whatever my confront me. There may even be still more sinister meanings attached to this particular frenzy. Somewhere in it the analysts may find Sex rearing its ugly head.

". . . For something like thirteen years . . . I lived in hotels, surrounded by hotel furniture. That was before the day when hotels had begun to take on the Home Atmosphere. Red plush or green plush was the thing, with an imitation mahogany table, round, in the center of the sitting room. No serving pantry, no kitchenette. You cooked your egg and heated your canned tomato soup in the bathroom.

"If ever I moved into an apartment of my own, I said, emphatically, I'd have exactly what I wanted, as I wanted it. And I got it. The nineteenth floor, east. Every window facing south, and the New York sun is the south sun. A wood burning fireplace. A great outdoor terrace overlooking the Western Hemisphere, and big enough to play tennis on. Plenty of closets. Gay English chintzes; gold and apple green for the bedroom; greens and lemon yellows and flame color for the living room. Colors, line, grouping, light, just as I wanted them at last. So I'm thinking of moving again."

The building of Treasure Hill and *A Peculiar Treasure* was simultaneous. Releasing past life; building rooms for new life; metaphorically therapeutic.

Although the book was the most personal work Ferber had ever offered, she was more aware than ever that it had to go public. However, she tussled about it with herself:

"In putting down these things about myself I say that I do not mean to have them published, and as much as a writer can mean this I suppose I mean it. But writers write to be read. Only amateurs say that they write for their own amusement. Writing is not an amusing occupation, any more than is childbirth, ditch-digging or toiling up a mountain top. It may be interesting, even absorbing. But when I hear anyone say he writes for his own amusement I know there is the congenital amateur."

The now defunct *Woman's Home Companion* magazine was accustomed to serializing Ferber's novels, offering vast sums of money to support their eagerness. A woman named Gertrude Lane had a great deal to do with these transactions, for she was editor-in-chief of the magazine—a position of sublime peerage for a woman at that time. She and Ferber had first met back in 1920, when Ferber had pitched her novel *The Girls* to the magazine for a possible serial. Ferber waxed jaundice more than ecstatic, but for sleek and brainy women she gave astute appraisal and limitless praise. Her first impression of Gertrude Lane was like that of a young girl in the first throes of a crush:

"We met for lunch at the Cosmopolitan Club. It was the beginning of a friendship that has lasted eighteen years. I saw a sturdy quiet alert woman. You sensed her power and intuitive understanding. She looked New England—with a glint in the eye. Dressed very quietly as she was, it was only after you had talked with her for half an hour or so that you began to note certain details. As you talked, you thought with one corner of your mind, 'H'm, those look like real sables.' Then, a moment later, 'Moses! They are!' A single fine emerald on her right hand. Line and fabric had been cunningly contrived in that sedate blue dress. She ordered lunch, and there obviously was a woman who knew and appreciated good food. Here was a grand combination of Maine saltiness and Latin temperment. Somewhere, surely, far, far back, a great-great-great-grandma or -grandpa in the Lane line must have stepped out to have produced a Gertrude in this century."

So, by rote, Ferber sent *A Peculiar Treasure* along to Gertrude Lane, who bought it out of fidelity but didn't like it. She was not quite that blunt, but in excerpts from her letters to Ferber dealing with its presentation, one can follow the blue pencil trail of disapproval.

She said that she liked the first lot of the manuscript very much and that there was no doubt whatever of wanting to use it. It would have to be rather heavily cut for the magazine, and a little more heavily than would ordinarily be the case because of the steadily decreasing size of the magazine owing to the falling off of advertising. Since their readers were more interested in Edna Ferber than her parents and grandparents, quite a bit out of the part which dealt with her forebears would have to be cut. She would not be able to use the photographs themselves but they would be helpful to the artist in making drawings of the characters in the book.

Gertrude Lane's tepid reactions did not sit well with Ferber and she blamed it, in a rather twisted way, on the fact that Miss Lane was not a Jew and therefore was either biased or ignorant and certainly reluctant in her objective editing of it. Ferber, the one who always wanted her work to penetrate, embrace, and sell to the widest regions, felt sour toward Gertrude Lane, who only wanted the same—out of pure business ethic—for her magazine. She tried to explain the practicality of a little bit of whitewash to the enraged Ferber.

She wrote that on page 8 she had underlined a few words that would show that they did not eliminate the word Jew from the copy. Until she had received Edna's letter, she had not seen the advertising folder and had nothing whatever to do with its preparation. That was all done by the circulation department. She stated that she hoped that Edna would not be bitterly disappointed in the omission that had been made from her manuscript. Miss Lane always considered in material of this sort that they selected those parts that they thought would be of most interest to their readers.

In the midst of these unfortunate dealings cropped the question of a title, which Ferber was still unsure about. Again Miss Lane tried to be magnanimous toward Ferber yet thoughtful of the average reader.

She said that of all the titles suggested, most of the staff liked "Half a Life" best. She was not sure that she liked it. Her preference was either "A Peculiar Treasure" or "Gusto." If the former was used she thought it would be a little hard for the average reader to understand unless Edna would include with each installment the quotation in which the title occurred. (Ferber's title derives from Exodus: XIX, 5, which reads: "Now, therefore, if ye will obey my voice indeed, and keep my covenant, then ye shall be a peculiar treasure unto me above all people; for all the earth is mine; and ye shall be unto me a kingdom of priests, and an holy nation.")

Ferber's diary indicates her disturbance, which she fronts with righteousness:

"Did only two pages today because I seem temporarily at least to be upset by Gertrude Lane's letter. She wants to do only five installments of the autobiography (I'm glad of that) and doesn't seem to like it much . . . but I don't care because I know it is written pretty much as I feel. No writer of fiction could write (or would want to write) the lively two-fisted sort of thing that she . . . evidently wants."

There was something else that came between the two women, adding political injury to editorial insult. Gertrude Lane was a Herbert Hooverite. Ferber was not. In February of 1938, Hoover made a trip to Europe, one of the purposes being to meet and talk with Mr. Hitler and Mr. Goering. Ferber was more than indignant, she was afflicted. This was a personal atrocity. Because she couldn't prosecute Herbert Hoover, she prosecuted Gertrude Lane, who defended Hoover's motives in a series of letters. It is a *double-entendre* defense.

On March 25, 1938, Miss Lane wrote that before Mr. Hoover left for his European trip she had had a long talk with him and was assured that he had quite as strong a hatred of Hitler and all his ways as Ferber could possibly have. She had a hunch that his purpose in talking with Hitler was merely to get a personal impression of this strange man and that she was willing to bet that when he returned he would denounce him in no uncertain terms. He had already announced that he would give two broadcasts about his European trip after his return, and Miss Lane thought it would be only fair for Ferber to listen to the broadcasts.

Miss Lane assumed that Ferber had seen the statement Mr. Hoover had made after his interview with Hitler, to the effect that Hitler's ideas would never be tolerated in America—Miss Lane felt safe in saying that Hoover was not "hobnobbing with the beasts of Berlin" and that her belief in the man Hoover was unshaken.

Later, on March 31, 1938, she wrote that she had just come from lunching with Mr. Hoover and while there she had read the speech he was to make that night over the radio. She thought it was very fine and hoped that Ferber would be able to listen to it.

In the course of conversation he told Miss Lane that he was very reluctant to call on either Hitler or Goering. He did not seek either interview but as soon as he arrived in Germany he received invitations to call upon Hitler and to lunch with Goering. Mr. Hoover asked the American Ambassador if he could not get out of it, as he had a bad cold and could use that as an excuse. But the Ambassador begged him to go, saying that he had to live with these people and it would make it difficult for him if Hoover refused the invitations.

Again, on April 7, 1938, Miss Lane wrote to say that they must agree to disagree about their friendship and affection for one another. Since Ferber felt so strongly about it, she suggested that Ferber ask her friend, Mr. Roosevelt, to cut off diplomatic relations with Germany and then the American officials would not be subject to the embarrassment that Mr. Hoover must have felt when he thought he was obliged to break bread with Goering.

There is a poignant postscript to the Ferber-Lane scrimmage. It came from Miss Lane, who conceded vulnerability and pleaded understanding for that unpardonable sin—Miss Lane wanted to explain something that might have seemed petty to Ferber. From Ferber's charming paragraphs about their first meeting she had eliminated three words: "approaching middle age." This was perfectly correct and the reason she had cut them out was that their two principal competitors, the *Ladies' Home Journal* and *McCall's,* were edited by very young people and some of the advertising salesmen on these two publications had made a great point of the fact. If they should see in the *Woman's Home Companion* that eighteen years ago Miss Lane was approaching middle age they might have pounced upon those words and declared that the *Woman's Home Companion* was being edited by a woman who must have now been approaching senility.

She explained this to Ferber so she would not think it was personal vanity but merely an attempt to protect her hard-working young men from the dirty digs they might get from competing salesmen. In other words it was business and not personal vanity that caused her to make the elimination. She was sure that Ferber would understand this and not be too disgusted with her.

There was an aura of despotism in the fact that under all circumstances Ferber retained her title as ruler. Everybody she dealt with, at one time or another, deferred to her—with one chronic exception. Julia Ferber.

Before Treasure Hill, and especially during the year and a half that it was being built, Ferber and Julia were almost constant companions. Ferber, with a feverish guilt about turning her attentions toward a house, gave Julia a last fling. Julia took full advantage of the situation. Ferber, by offering her a finger, barely managed to maintain her work schedule in the morning, for Julia would barge in and grab both her hands. Her diary practically sobs with frustration:

"Worked on 'Peculiar Treasure.' Only two pages. Mother in with her auction pieces before I was through and upset me terribly. If only someone could understand the strain of work and house-building and help me to stand it. But no one does."

Julia had a gambler's streak. She would bet on cards, people's professions, what people would order in restaurants—anything. It stands to reason, then, that she was an habitué of auction galleries. She adored them and bought almost every stick of her own and Ferber's furniture through gavel channels. She was inordinately shrewd about knowing the quality of what was up and what to bid for it. She even had a "system." She wouldn't show her hand at first, but would wait until the bidding had gotten well underway, and then like a dark horse would gallop away with the item—or halt if the bidding was overpriced.

In the afternoons she and Ferber would make the rounds like bookie and client, and Ferber would usually come home with a winning horse she hadn't even known she'd wanted until Julia gave the nod. Seventy-five dollars for a Lalique fruit bowl. Sold! Two hundred eighty dollars for the small Aubusson rug. Sold! And that's partially how Treasure Hill was furnished.

Julia assessed Ferber's friends in much the same manner she did items at an auction. If they weren't quality she didn't bother with them. She would become ominously silent, letting them know that to her they were inferior goods.

One of George Oppenheimer's favorite stories concerns his meeting with Julia. He titles it "Julia and the Winstons." It goes like this: In 1934, Ferber was giving Oppenheimer a lift out to his summer home in Manhasset, where she also had a rented summer house. She had to stop and pick up Julia, whom Oppenheimer had never met. Ferber introduced them and Julia, with her shrewd eye, immediately went through all the Oppenheimers, trying to place him socially. The East Oppenheimers, the West Oppenheimers, the North and South ones. He denied blood ties with all of them, leaving her to think the worst. In the ensuing car talk he mentioned a weekend at Green Cove, where he'd previously stayed. Julia asked, "Is that a borscht belt place?" "No, it's the Winstons' home," came the reply. Julia, unabashed, asked whether he went through the main entrance. "No," he answered, politely amused, "I usually go in through the back." Ah, Julia was satisfied. A back-door Oppenheimer, then. Just as she'd suspected.

There is a story that Ruth Hammond, the actress, tells about Julia's decline from snobbish grace. In the thirties it was the vogue to give and receive "kitsch" gifts. It became a passionate pastime for friends of that era to find the ugliest of gifts to bestow on each other. Ruth Hammond and her husband found the most ghastly ashtray in some little Treasures 'n' Trash shop and gave it to Ferber. They all had a good laugh over it, going into ecstasies about its homeliness. Ferber placed it on one of her living-room tables for all to hate. One day it was gone. Julia had secretly coveted it, and finally, not being able to contain herself, had taken it.

Ferber served as Julia's escort in the evenings of 1938. Her diary is laden with what Julia would call "fincy outings." They would go to dinner and the theatre; they would attend the latest movies—most of which Ferber condemned; film was not her medium—Ferber would squire Julia to parties, would have parties for Julia, and, although they lived in separate apartments, there was an invisible Chinese checkers board stretched between the two, for in the evenings when they didn't go out that was their hobby.

Ferber had said about Life with Mamma that it was always stimulating. "We talk man talk," she had said. An odd gender reference for a mother and daughter.

Moss Hart was a frequent and charming third wheel at this time. He found Julia extraordinary; she found him to be more than ordinary. Sold! to the mother and daughter as good company.

Ferber records a couple of their theatre goings—salting them as usual:

"Mother and Moss to dinner and then to the theater to see 'The Sea Gull.' Lynn and Alfred (Lunt) interesting, but the play a dull thing, really, and badly written except for certain scenes."

"Moss Hart and Mother for dinner. A lovely chocolate charlotte for dessert. Mother bought Moss's second helping. To see a revival of 'The Circle,' Maugham's play. Dated I thought. A terrible boner when an actor said, viewing a photograph of Maxine Elliott, 'Her breath would take your beauty away.' The audience died."

It is difficult to establish what Hart was to Ferber and she to him because there were so many wrinkles in the relationship. Earlier on, to be sure, they had had a love for each other, the memory of which, as the years climbed, became too complex to settle down into mere friendship. They were passionately emotionally involved without ever having been passionately involved.

Janet's memory reminds her that when Hart was callow and needy and just being discovered as extraordinarily talented, he asked Ferber—nineteen years his senior—to marry him. She declined the offer as a gallant, impossible, more than slightly Oedipal gesture.

When he traveled, he dutifully wrote, cabled, or phoned her. In one particular letter, written from Miami Beach, he shared with her his horror of the plastic place, and his tender feelings toward her for always understanding his struggles with talent and vulnerability. He condones her for sticking by him no matter how "absolutely nuts" he might appear at times.

Aside from being creatively gifted, Hart was a personality prodigy—possessed with an almost imbalance of charm. Garson Kanin, no slouch in the charm department, allows that "Moss was the most charming man that ever was." Dorothy Rodgers concurs, recalling that he could almost move trees—but not quite. Hart and Ferber were lunching at the Rodgerses', who had an incredible oak tree planted in front of their house. Hart had just treed his Bucks County farm and was very tree conscious.

Hart: "That's the most magnificent tree that could possibly be."

Dorothy Rodgers: "Yes, it is."

Hart: "It certainly is."

Dorothy Rodgers: "It certainly is."

Hart: "How big a ball of earth does it have?"

Dorothy Rodgers: "Well, you really couldn't move it, Moss."

Hart looked crushed. He'd wanted the Rodgerses' tree.

Hart was given to excesses: flamboyance, grandeur, extravagance; moodiness, depression, manic depression. He couldn't seem to assimilate his glittering present with his impoverished boyhood. He had fought to become and panicked to remain. At turns, the pressure made him emotionally ill. Those who were close and cared for him agonized over his agony of confusion and doubt. Ferber was one of the few whom he could approach when he despaired; he trusted that large level head. She solaced him as well as she could, but occasionally she was given to flights of intolerance, and his self-indulgence was one of its propellants. She felt that often Hart indulged himself and she would not indulge him in that act. When she chose not to understand him, involuntarily she became hurt and angry at him. Her jumbled emotions are revealed in her diary:

"Dinner at Voisin's with the Kaufmans, Moss, and George Jessel. Moss behaving more strangely than I could have believed possible. A lot of whiskey. A lot of whispering with Beatrice; he seemed to be someone I had just met. Gravely disturbing."

When she was intolerant of one dear one, she was tolerant of another—for Fan emerges in the 1938 diary as a, "Poor kid, what a marriage—lively, fun-loving, and Jack just a decent pleasant enough vegetable."

Fleeing gaseous air, Ferber went to Arizona in February of 1939, and while there at the Arizona Biltmore over her morning paper she found a new rage-vent. Stanton Griffis, a well-known magnate

—one of his magnate activities being chairman of the board of Madison Square Garden—had allowed a "Bund" meeting to be held there—meaning that Nazis had gathered within its confines. Griffis had been a friend of Ferber. Upon reading the news she stripped him of that title. Ferber's letter flogging Stanton Griffis:

". . . You are, I know, a director and large stock-holder in Madison Square Garden. I, as an American, a Jew, and a civilized human being, object with every fiber of decency and justice in me to your having consented to allow Madison Square Garden to be used for the Nazi meeting last Monday—or for any Nazi meeting. It may be that you agree with their aims and beliefs. I think—I hope—I know you too well to believe that. You may say that the renting of the Garden is outside your jurisdiction. I don't believe that, either.

"I know you are a rich man. It can't be that money would be a consideration in permitting these apes to present in Madison Square Garden the ghastly exhibition of this past week.

"I have known you for years, I have liked and respected you. But this I must say to you, and you must believe that I mean it:

"If ever again Madison Square Garden is rented for the purpose of a Nazi meeting I shall spend my days and my nights talking and writing to every New York Jew who can possibly be reached by my words and my typewriter, asking that they boycott Madison Square Garden. I have attended hockey games, fights, athletic exhibitions —all sorts of occasions—at the Garden. I know what proportion of your audience is made up of Jews. I won't rest until every one of them has pledged himself to stay away from the Garden.

"If this is construed by you as a threat, you're right. It is one. I'm sorry that my feeling of shock, indignation and outraged decency makes it necessary for me to write you in this way."

A hard act of defense to follow. Griffis, in true athletic tradition, donned body padding and presented his.

He wrote that although he resented from the bottom of his heart the things that she had written to him, and the general tone of her letter, his affection for her of many years' standing told him that perhaps, in an hour of excitement and emotional pressure, she had said things that perhaps she would not have said to an old friend had she known any of the circumstances surrounding what he might have done.

First of all, he was fully responsible for anything that was done in or in connection with the Garden. He took full responsibility for permitting the so-called Bund meeting to be held in the Garden.

He pointed out that she must understand the background for this decision. For years the Garden had stood fast to the principle of free speech in America, and the right of any political organization, race, creed, or sect to hire its facilities so long as it was willing to keep the peace and maintain order. In this, the Garden had always believed that it was following a basic American principle, one of the principles the change of which had resulted in the conditions which existed in Germany. It had believed that this freedom was what America meant, and so had rented the Garden to Socialists, Communists, Republicans, Democrats, Jews, and gentiles alike and would continue to do so.

He wrote that as a matter of historical interest, the lease of the Garden to the Bund was made much, much earlier, with no feeling on its part that the general public would be particularly interested in the meeting. When it became evident that there were going to exist a widespread interest in the gathering and possible disorders of a sort, the first thought at the Garden was to consult with those of its directors who were Jews. Those men were firm in their belief that the meeting should take place, that the democratic processes be permitted to work in an orderly way.

They had gone further and consulted men like Mayor LaGuardia, Morris Ernst, and various Jewish organizations. All Jewish friends with whom the matter was discussed felt that the meeting should proceed.

He pleaded that no one in their senses who knew him could possibly believe that he had anything but abhorrence for the aims and beliefs of Nazism, but by the same token he trusted that no one who knew him well, and would have any desire to regard him as fit for the category of their friendship, could feel that he could be either frightened or intimidated by the threats which she was making. This, he wrote, hurt him as much as her feeling that he would evade responsibility, or that for a rental fee he would betray the countless friendships he had with those who like Ferber were proud of the fact that they were Jewish, "both on their mother's and father's side."

Since this famous meeting, he had read many columns of editorial comments and publicity regarding it. He was convinced that more harm was done to the Nazi cause in America by the meeting than had been done by any agency or group of agencies during the entire Hitler regime. From this he hoped she would derive some comfort.

He closed by saying that he trailed along with Voltaire and that he would try to look any man in the face with the quotation which he feared he was butchering. He prayed for better days on earth and signed off.

Three days later Stanton Griffis received this telegram:

> "YOU ARE RIGHT STAN AND I WAS WRONG IT WAS AS YOU SAY AN EMOTIONAL NOT A MENTAL REACTION CAUSED BY THE SICKENING EFFECT ONE GOT ON READING THE REPORTS OF THE MEETING AT THIS DISTANCE. EDNA."

In her early Chicago short-story days, the critics had touted Ferber as the successor to O. Henry, to which she retorted, throwing pique on pleasure, "I'm not here to refresh Mr. O. Henry."

Years later, as a refresher between novels, plays, and shopping for land on which to build, Ferber gratefully returned to the short-story format, producing a volume called *Nobody's in Town*. It consisted of two stories about which Ferber said, with a certain immodesty, to Malcolm Johnson:

"I feel that, light as it is in treatment, the story NOBODY'S IN TOWN is the best piece of writing, as writing, that I've done in ten years. I am saying this because I honestly feel that those two stories, making a smallish book that may seem most unimpressive to the average salesman or buyer, mark a real step forward in my life as a writer. I think they're not novels or novelettes (hideous word) but novelties, with a real meaning hidden in their lightness. A good hard fistful of knuckles—I hope—in the velvet glove.

"It may be that you and your selling staff and the gr-r-reat Amurrican public will never see in those stories the thing that I fondly hope they contain. Maybe they'll never see the woods for the trees. I'm used to that. In CIMARRON I wrote a story whose purpose was to show the triumph of materialism over the spirit in America, and I did show it, but perhaps I was too reticent about it. It emerged, in the minds of most people, as a romantic western or something. It broke my heart, though the thing sold by the tens of thousands. In SO BIG I used the same theme, in a completely different background. Same result. Terrific sales; about nine people knew what I was driving at. Oh, well, maybe when I'm dead——."

After Ferber had finished pecking out her work on the keys, she would then work out by pecking at her editor and the publicity staff in order to get the proper advertising. She even gave Malcolm Johnson a layout of what the ad should say:

"A rather unconventional and arresting advertisement might be made by using two sharply contrasting comments on NOBODY'S IN TOWN. Under the heading such as: It Takes All Kinds To Make A World (or words to that effect).

BOLD AND BITTER AND BRILLIANT.
—Isabel Currier in the Herald-Tribune.
SKILLFUL WARM-HEARTED AND NICE.
—Clifton Fadiman in the New Yorker.

"You know—you pays your money and you takes your choice."

Johnson did as he was bid and was rewarded, but it was still not enough:

"Dear Malcolm Johnson, I wrote you before I had seen the bold-bitter-brilliant ad. Werry nice.

"I see that some one whose initials are K.S. says pleasantly in the Sat. Review of Lit. that I'm this and that and those and these, but isn't it a pity I'm not a first-rate writer. Wouldn't it surprise him (or her) to learn that by God I am!

"What we need with NOBODY'S IN TOWN is a leg up. I wish I knew someone to give it to us. I wish we could get Eleanor,* the Peripatetic Presidentess, to read it and comment in her naive way. I am told that Woollcott liked it very much, but as he and I haven't been seeing each other for about five years I can't quite request him to blast forth on the radio about my deathless prose. If he knew it wasn't going very well he prolly would, though. He is often really magnificent about such things. A strange mixture of malice and generosity."

Ferber took her friends' written work almost as seriously as her own. She evaluated it with truthful finesse and was rarely wrong about its pulse. When in 1938 William Allen White came out with a book about Calvin Coolidge, Ferber wrote her mind:

"Before I saw your book I would have thought it incredible that anyone could make an interesting or dimensional figure out of that

* Eleanor Roosevelt.

meagre Coolidge who is your subject. But then you could make a stuffed gunny sack seem vital. I must confess that Coolidge has always filled me with a kind of distaste which was more than just dislike. Whatever his reason for the inhibitions that made him what he was, I always felt him to be much less an object of respect than even so vulgar a blundering tinhorn sport as Harding. Of all the people in the world I think I dislike most the cool, fish-mouth, slit-eyed negative type, whose sins are those of omission, not commission.

"Maybe from this you gather I don't really love the boy, but I do think your book is a fine piece of work, and my congratulations to you."

If there was an official term called "Patroness of Encouragement," it would have been aptly applied to Ferber. Never having any problem with her commitment to writing, she was pained to see talented colleagues "blocking" or frittering. Such was the case of Robert Sherwood, the playwright. He was having difficulty with his concentration prior to his writing *The Road to Rome*. Ferber stepped in, serving as the liaison officer between him and his creative duty. In a letter to her, he reminds her just what she did for him:

"A year ago last summer I was engaged in conversation with you at the Swopes' summer White House, with crap games to the left of us, chemin-de-fer games to the right of us, Irving Berlin in front of us and the usual jolly round of volleying and thundering from our host. You said to me, 'The best thing that could happen to you would be to have you snatched out of the Algonquin and exiled to Kansas City for two years. At the end of that time, you'd come back with some fine work.' That casual observation so impressed me that I left the Hotel Algonquin, where I had had lunch practically every day for six years. I didn't go to Kansas City, but I did go to work and wrote two plays—'The Road To Rome' and a dramatization of Ring Lardner's 'The Love Nest.' Furthermore, I feel a great deal better because I wrote them. The object of this letter is not, presumptively, to suggest that your glowing prophecy has been fulfilled—but to thank you for giving me a shove in what unquestionably was the right direction."

Sherwood doffed his hat in his description of Ferber: "Edna Ferber with her fine lioness's head, her alert black eyes, her expertly mobilized gifts, her tenderness and sensitivity, and her anger which could erupt so that some wondered if she should not have been named Etna."

He tipped his heart in a letter to her following the 1931 opening of his play *Reunion in Vienna:*

"Due to the stupefaction induced last Monday night by an opening and a lot of beer, I couldn't adequately tell you how grateful I have always been, am, and will continue to be for your affectionate partiality for the results of my labors.

"Though now entirely sober, I still can't approach adequate expression, so I shan't try.

"Anyway, I have a feeling of obligation to you that puts you practically in the awkward position of a reluctant muse."

Ferber's other cheek was ruthless and damning when she felt a work was not up to snuff—as is evidenced in a 1937 diary entry: "George and Moss awarded the Pultizer Prize for 'You Can't Take It With You.' No play of this year deserved it. Certainly not that one."

Ferber had had no play that year, although she'd wanted one. Perhaps a few sour grapes were served in that instance.

Eventually *Saratoga Trunk* was a novel, but the original idea had been invested in a play. A play that Ferber would collaborate on with George Kaufman. A play that neither one wanted to do with the other.

She had found an inspiration spot in Saratoga Springs, New York. She was so keen on it that she wanted to present Julia with its charm. They motored there in the summer of 1937. Ferber's impressions have the heavy scent of infatuation:

"An incredible town, still 1865, its building of a Victorian architecture which has taken on dignity, and a kind of quaint beauty with time. The United States Hotel and the Grand Union are like nothing else in this or any other country . . . The Grand Union Hotel has rope fire escapes, crystal chandeliers, marble-topped tables."

Ferber talked a good Saratoga game to Kaufman, but she couldn't seem to infuse him with her own enthusiasm. He had an innate sense of what project was right for him. This wasn't. All winter long she tried to coerce him into visiting the town with her, and then he'd see. He didn't want to see. Ferber tried to manipulate. If the Lunts agreed to star in the play—if they literally built it for the Lunts—then would he do it? Well, maybe. The Lunts weren't interested. "Lynn very difficult," Ferber notes. Anybody who didn't see eye to eye with Ferber was apt to be "very difficult." She kept at Kaufman, who began to become an expert at hemming and hawing.

Actually, both of them were undergoing an identity crisis as collaborators. Kaufman, so well versed in many areas of the theatre, could exercise his muscles with others or alone—as he did when he directed *Of Mice and Men*, about which Ferber said: "A superb performance, magnificently directed by George. One of the most thrilling evenings I've ever spent in the theater."

Ferber, in an uncharacteristic slant for her, deeply needed Kaufman in order to function as a playwright—although she was ambivalent about this truth and resisted it: "I shrink from another collaboration. Still, I don't feel confident that I can do this one alone—or any alone."

Finally, after cajoling and practically wooing Kaufman with her eagerness about the project, she pulled her trump. If Kaufman didn't want to do it, then perhaps she and Jerome Kern would collaborate on a musical version. So there.

On December 21, 1937, almost a year after the subject had been broached, George Kaufman accompanied Edna Ferber to Saratoga. It didn't work out. She records the event like a conceding candidate who says, "I lost, but I enjoyed the race."

"The 9 o'clock train for Saratoga with George Kaufman. George slept most of the way to Saratoga. Colder there, but not bad. To the Gideon Putnam. Then out to see the United States Hotel, the Grand Union, the Casino, the race track. All pretty dreary in their winter dress. George definitely unimpressed. The closed eye. I rather enjoyed the trip."

Kaufman's eye spotted another possible collaboration with Moss Hart on a play called *The Cracker Barrel*, which never came off. Saratoga went on to become a popular novel. Ferber went on going to the Kaufmans' dinner parties and having them to hers. Those were the days when pleasure outweighed business.

But Ferber couldn't enjoy pleasure; not for its own sake; not as a pastime. Work, in its most pure, most rigorous, most sacrificial form was the lady's pleasure. Only when she could really beat herself up with it was she content. The year 1937 was her year of discontent, for she was self-unemployed. True, she wrote *Nobody's in Town*, but that took only a month, which left her dangling with eleven more to fill. What to do? Never at a loss for neurosis, she contracted a duodenal ulcer (later rediagnosed as gallstones) and went to bed for four weeks with a bland diet. She received roll calls of visitors, took up French with "a queer little rabbit of a Frenchman," gave up smoking, read Virginia Woolf, "vague and deadly dull, certainly over-rated," and Thomas Mann, "slow and dullish," subsisted on puréed vegetables, cream soups, puddings, and bananas, "Whee!" and generally went through the roof at every little thing.

She was living in a penthouse at 791 Park Avenue, which had a terrace with a garden so lush that it caused even the inveterate gardener Alfred Lunt to exclaim, "Peach trees in a New York apartment! I never!"

As recovery therapy, Ferber threw herself into gardening. She hoed and spaded and watered and transplanted; she had awnings put up and new flagstones put down. She carried on as though that little garden were the Tuileries. The preoccupation with it lasted for about two weeks, at which time she felt hail and hearty enough to be at loose ends again.

There used to be a bromide for rich, bored women. They traveled. Ferber, going through a rich, bored stage, did just that. She had reservations about going to Colorado because in her earlier days she had spent some lovely summers there in Estes Park, where she had been the toast. She feared that that aura would be gone, with the era, but planned the trip anyway, arranging on the way home to stop off to visit the Lunts in Genesee Depot, Wisconsin—a guaranteed joy. Her diary, for the most part, reads like an annoyed travel guide:

"Denver at 9:20. Hot and noisy. The Brown Palace Hotel. Indians in full regalia dancing in the lobby to advertise frontier day at Cheyenne. Arranged to motor up to Central City to see Ruth Gordon in 'A Doll's House.' Fifty miles up the mountain roads to the old gold-mining town. The Teller Hotel and the Opera House, built in the '70's, incredible for that region and time. Ruth very good, but too old and sharp-faced for a doll wife. But a fine performance."

"Brown Palace Hotel. Hot and noisy. The Indians working mechanical whoopee in the lobby. Started the drive to Longs Peak at 10:30. Arrived at the Inn at 1:30. Misgivings all along the way as I saw the road lined with new cabins, lunch rooms. The Enos Mills place has been preserved, but it is as dead as Lenin in the tomb at Moscow. The heart and life of the place is gone. It is grisly and deeply depressing. I have the Mills cabin, comfortable but spooky. Never go back. Go forward."

"Longs Peak Inn. Feeling decidedly jumpy in this cabin. Pretty nightmarish, the whole thing. Met two women—middle-aged spinsters living together in Maine. One of them has with her a hundred year old doll for which she is making clothes. Sort of frightening, and very easy Freud. Slept in jerks."

"Climbed Cabin Rock, very briskly in 55 minutes there and back. Drove with Mrs. Mills to Estes Village. Full of girls in awful pants. Feel better but not much energy about writing. I now think it is just laziness and having got out of the habit of writing. I'd no doubt write fast enough if I had no money."

"Cabin Rock climb as usual. Very little discomfort from the region of the supposed ulcer. Esther Mills and Miss Baldwin (a monstrous woman who writes children's stories and a Peoria paper column) in after dinner. We lighted a fire; and caught a mouse in the trap as we sat there. Nuts!"

"The food wretched at lunch, which I had served in my cabin. The flies drove me mad all day. Killed hundreds with swatter and Flit. Walked up Timberline trail for an hour and hated it. A bath, dressed, a miserable dinner. To see the Jean Harlow picture 'Saratoga.' Incredibly bad, dull, stupid. Left after the stand-in who finished the picture following Harlow's death, came on. A dreary little holiday, really."

"Birthday. Let's not go into that. On a picnic in Elk Park with a bonfire and hot soup and trout. A lovely sky, and the stars lavish. Felt ill and feverish."

"To the Broadmoor Hotel at Colorado Springs. The place looks noisy and unattractive. I feel the drop in altitude—from 9000 feet to less than 6000. A nightmarish experience at breakfast—a series of stupid blunders—no coffee cup, no hot milk, no butter. Again and again. Breakfast ordered at 8 and not eaten until ten. A lot of energy wasted screaming at waiters, clerks, manager. The noise of workmen hammering in the hotel made work impossible. And radios bleating, children shouting. No work. An incredibly bad dinner—pot roast and vegetables served in a kind of glass square goldfish bowl—salad of lettuce and red clay—and a sort of mud pie. I didn't mind much. This illness makes food unimportant, which is too bad."

Things picked up a bit when Ferber stopped off in Chicago for one day and one night. This time, only the room was wrong:

"A noisy and impossible room at the Drake Hotel. Changed to a quieter and really charming suite across the hall. Bathed and dressed, met Aunt Jo at the Blackstone for lunch. Poor girl. I feel so touched by her illness and helplessness. Met Lena Elkan, looking stout and middle-aged; she prolly thought the same of me. A massage and facial at Arden's. Dinner at the hotel in my sitting room with Lillian and Gudrun, very pleasant. Moss Hart telephoned me from New York. A long talk with him about his mother's death."

And at last, a respite. The Lunts.

"Met in Milwaukee by Alfred Lunt and drove with him to Genesee Depot, where their dear little house stands. The country side terribly dry and dusty. A lovely day talking with Lynn and Alfred. Their house is enchanting. A swim in the pool. A walk before dinner. Dinner a relief. My appetite miraculously returned."

"Genesee Depot. A wonderful night's sleep. Raining a lovely soft rain. Up at the house on the hill at about 10:30. Lynn was playing solitaire and calmly waiting, she said, for a movement. Alfred cooking creme vichyssoise in the kitchen. A walk up the road and down a pleasant lane. Lunch, and the day slipped by. Listened to some Viennese waltzes on the phonograph in the studio after dinner. Alfred gay and amusing. I shall hate to leave."

In March of 1937, before her ulcer-vapors, Ferber hit the road for the first time that year. Phoenix, Palm Springs, Seattle, Chicago. She seemed to be idly traveling—looking for something to hang her prose on. Much later Seattle took its novel's shape, but for the time being, while there, she settled on discovering a young writer named Michael Foster, who apparently stirred her although she didn't quite know what to make of him:

"Interviewed by a crazy young Irishman named Michael Foster, of the Post-Intelligencer. Brilliant interesting mad, with a handsome weak face. Drink, probably. Invited me to dinner at his house."

"Michael Foster called at 6 to take me to dine with him and his wife. A ghastly incredible evening but interesting, too. An untidy stuffy little apartment; screaming children, nauseous hot rum and butter; a foul dinner in a dirty kitchen. But the man is touched with greatness."

"Michael has given me his new novel 'American Dream,' to be published in June by Morrow. Pam seems to be a good and decent girl, not over-bright, but plucky to stand life with this mad fellow."

"Michael Foster's book is a beautiful and moving thing. I didn't know that he could write like that. It is almost a great book. I read it all day. I was weeping when I finished it."

Ferber was drawn to Michael Foster much in the same way that she was drawn to the young Moss Hart. She wanted to help them, to ensure them of their worth, because they made her feel. Ferber's compassion—not for causes but for someone—was a premium. And, as was often the case when vital, difficult, restless men met up with Ferber, their wives (if they had them) suddenly didn't seem very interesting. Ferber could arouse a cerebral passion that made sex seem amateur. Michael Foster "fell in delight" with Ferber, sending her a letter that is ineffable. The Ferber that he writes to is certainly not the weary Ferber of her diaries. He even renames her:

"Dear Julie Ponsonby: Your letter came—and your telegram: they came within the same hour. Nothing, ever, has so profoundly disturbed me as your magnificence (that isn't the word I want) over work of which I am not proud. Because, Julie, it isn't such a very good book. Not nearly what it should have been. I tried so hard to be popular, changing so many ideas because I wanted to write something people would buy. Don't think I'm arty—there is no notion so hideous as that. But things should have an austerity of outline and color, and a humanity deeper and richer because it is not distorted for effects which, after all, are rather phoney.

"I wish to God (in defiance of your excellent and cauterizing truth) that I had a drink, because then it's easier to remember you as a swell friend we were with for a little while: and not be scared by remembering that you are a great and sure-working artist. Do you know what I mean?: not a fumbler. Don't you dare think that I'm talking about your celebrity. I loathe celebrities as social phenomena. I loathe the mass psychology which makes celebrities possible. Before you, I have invariably avoided—to the point of rudeness, if necessary, making friends with celebrities.

"But don't you see, Julie—I read your letter, over and over, and I read the last line of your telegram: and I have the knowledge: 'This is, after all, Edna Ferber, and she wrote SO BIG and SHOW BOAT and CIMARRON, and the short stories; and her hand never boggled and she never made a frightful ass of herself in her whole life.' It's a bad feeling, and it's ruining this letter, this reply which I had hoped would be satisfactory and even maybe kind of urbane. But let it by—you are a darling, and if I had a drink I could tell you so. And I do keep reading your letter over and over again—it's getting all cottony already in the creases of the paper—and I shall keep it forever.

". . . Now look, Julie. I am getting to the point of this letter. It's about you: Why can't you come out and be with us for a summer of work? The place we have heard about is swell and large—you'd have a little separate house of your own, like a creature of Hans Christian Anderson, in the trees, above the sea. And we'd work like hell all day and meet at dinner: swell dinners, with evenings before a fire of driftwood on the hearth. (You'd work much better there than in New York—no noise, no one even knowing where you were.) And have you ever heard, after you've gone to bed at night between Hudson's Bay Company blankets (twelve feet long, they are, and gorgeously wooly) the long hiss and sigh of the tide in a lonely cove, like time breathing in its sleep?

". . . You will come, won't you Julie? Don't say you won't. Don't be important. Please. Come out and be humble with us, on the beach. You've never seen the stars until you've seen them from a wilderness beach, with one planet glimmering like a lost world in the tide. Damnation, if I had one drink, I could write such a letter as would make you come."

Ferber did go back to the Fosters', but not for the summer. She swept through Seattle, bought them a big lavish dinner, and swept out again. Michael Foster wrote to thank her—mooning, adolescent, and resigned that she would never meet him on his terms:

". . . I am going to feel horrible in the morning: I shall die twice in the bathtub and three times while I am moaning and shivering into my clothes and end up with a loud final death rattle on the street car going down to work at noon. And I know how awfully I shall regret this letter, then, and that is why I am mailing it tonight.

"You can't possibly know how we think of you . . . The lights on the lake are so bleak . . . We were sitting here and remembered that we hadn't even thanked you for that lovely dinner. Somehow, we hadn't thought of it. I'm sorry: but whom, after all, have you ever thanked for a night when you saw the stars so clearly. That sounds frightfully silly but there are things which do not remind you to make smirking gestures of acceptance. Anyway, please don't mind me tonight . . . I am going now to an all night hamburger joint down the street and eat raw onions while Pam sleeps. And talk to taxi drivers who are a wonderful, a compassionate race. God be with you, my good woman."

Even though George Kaufman was with her in 1936 for the writing of their fourth play, *Stage Door,* good reviews were not. Brooks Atkinson wrote hard on them once more:

". . . Mr. Kaufman and Miss Ferber are the kind of authors who know how to put a keen edge on the blade of comedy . . . 'Stage Door' is a taut pattern of related vaudevilles . . . Mr. Kaufman and Miss Ferber have at least one positive notion. They are flying a little bunting in honor of the legitimate theater as a place where acting can be learned and social-minded drama can be practiced with independence . . . Probably it is unethical to stare at a popular comedy through sober eyes . . . To me 'Stage Door' would be funnier if the whole subject of acting were less painful. But in all fairness I should ask the forgiveness of two of our brightest playwrights for dragging another funeral through the midst of their hornpipe."

Behind the scenes of *Stage Door* there lurked a romantic comedy, which began its second act while Ferber and Kaufman were still writing their first act. It had a cast of three: there was the agent Leland Hayward playing a stage-door Johnny; there was Katharine Hepburn, the movie actress about to be thrown over; there was Margaret Sullavan, the young stage actress waiting in the wings.

About the time Ferber and Kaufman had announced their embarkation on their next venture, *Stage Door,* Hepburn and Hayward, who had been courting, announced their engagement to be married. Ferber extended herself to throw them a bash. Hayward overextended himself by telling his bride-to-be that the collaborators wanted her for the leading lady in their new play. Then Hayward went wayward. He turned his affections to the diminutive, husky-voiced Margaret Sullavan and promptly married her, making her heir to the leading part in the Ferber-Kaufman play.

As far as loyalties were concerned, Ferber's were with her friend Hepburn, but as Hayward was also her friend and, more important, her good agent, she was as cordial as could be to Sullavan, who in return was as difficult as could be. In rehearsal her blond personality began to show its dark roots, and by production she was, as Ferber would say, "Really very trying." She had collected from the critics the praise that the play didn't, and therefore felt superior to the whole production. She was aware of, and used, her strategic position: if she left, the play closed. It didn't seem to faze her that she had signed a run of the play contract with a national tour clause attached. After all, her agent was her husband; love was contractually blind.

It became clear that Sullavan wanted out. She would be late to the theater; she would be ill and have to skip a performance, and finally the coup of excuses—she was pregnant. Ferber's diary entries concerning Sullavan sound like something out of Clare Boothe Luce's *The Women.* They are written with talons:

"Home to meet Margaret Sullavan at 5:15. As I feared she announced she was going to have a baby. As I had predicted some such charming trick before 'Stage Door' ever opened I wasn't surprised. But what a miserable little double-crossing wench it is."

"Sullavan's news means that she can't possibly play later than the first of April. She says she will tour after October, but doubt it. We were to have played until July 1."

"The Sullavan situation about 'Stage Door' is now insane. She and Leland evidently will do anything to get out of her touring. I am completely fed up with the whole thing."

The tale did not end there. A short while afterwards, during the filming of the movie based on the play, in which Katharine Hepburn did play the lead, she felt it fitting to thank Ferber for originally wanting her to do the stage play. Ferber knew nothing about it. It had been Leland Hayward's sweet nothing.

The last lick: for a wedding present Ferber bought Hayward and Sullavan a set of Steuben glasses. She usually purchased nothing less than Baccarat.

There were no two people farther apart than Edna Ferber and Bruno Hauptmann, the man who had kidnaped and purportedly murdered Charles and Anne Lindbergh's baby. In January of 1935 Hauptmann was put on trial in the inconspicuous, sleepy town of Flemington, New Jersey, which before its own eyes became a national hotbed. To say that the trial—that the handling of Hauptmann on the witness stand—was undemocratic would not even scratch the surface. To say that it was a witch hunt would put it mildly. There was nothing remotely judicial about the trial. Bruno Hauptmann was guilty before proven innocent. The trial, then, became a sadistic event; a spectator sport; many lions, one Christian. Ferber attended one day of the trial. It made her sick. She felt more in alignment with Bruno Hauptmann than with what was posing as human nature around him. She wrote a piece for the New York *Times* which some consider a classic best of all her outspoken pieces.

"It is considered chic to go to the Hauptmann trial. Though I myself am not chic, and have never been invited to an Elsa Maxwell party, I hope I know what is being done. A mink coat, one of those Cossack hats, the word 'divine' in your vocabulary, and there you are, if a woman, equipped complete for a day at Flemington. It's as easy as that.

"I know, because, stepping out of the motor car in front of the Union Hotel on the snowy main street of the little town, I found all the Maxwell party countersigns and passwords were being cooed back and forth. All the mink coats were saying to the Saville Row topcoats and burgundy mufflers, 'Hel-lo, dar-ling! How are you! Isn't this divine? Isn't it wonderful!'

"Well, it was wonderful. It was wonderful. It was horrible and sickening and depressing and wonderful, and it made you want to resign as a member of the human race and cable Hitler saying, Well Butch, you win.

"The little town of Flemington at noon looked like a frosted picture postcard gone mad. Mobs churning the prim little courthouse steps. Crowds milling in and out of the quaint Union Hotel. A constant stream pouring toward the lunch room in the basement of the church just across from the courthouse. Flemington townspeople. New Jersey politicians. Actors. Theatrical producers. Society. Reporters. Lawyers. Novelists. Playwrights. Hel-lo darling? Isn't it divine! Have you had lunch?

"If some one is to make money on the Hauptmann trial it may as well be the ladies of the church, and it most emphatically is. The church lunch room is the swank place to eat and don't make a mistake. For the duration of the Hauptmann trial that church lunch room is the Algonquin, the Colony Restaurant, the Rainbow Room of Flemington. Seventy-five cents and a very decent meal—clam chowder, roast beef, boiled potatoes, stewed tomatoes, cole slaw, apple pie and coffee—with all the visiting celebrities thrown in. Real apple pie, too. Flaky, juicy, hot.

"You are served by the ladies of the church, and no nonsense. Neat, dowdy, no lipstick, no rouge; black dresses with a collar of homemade tatting fashioned with a round brooch. Did you taste the pie? It's divine! Oh, well, diet tomorrow. Darling, is that Wilentz? Is that Reilly? Is that Winchell? Is that stomach-turning?

"The court room. Through the side entrance, brushing past the fenders of the faded green-gray car which belongs to Bruno Hauptmann. You fight for your seat to which your newspaper card entitles you, only to be thrown out later, but you manage to sneak in again for a two-hour session with Hauptmann in the witness chair.

"I was astonished to see that this Bruno Hauptmann is a distinguished-looking man—distinguished and graceful. The line his body makes from shoulder to ankle as he sits there is fluid, graceful. A painter or a sculptor would be pleased with it. The face. Now I've seen that before. I've seen a thing like that before. It is no color. It is, for that matter, no face. That is, it is no living face. It is not white, or gray or yellow. It is wax. That's it. It is the face of a corpse.

"Curiously enough, it has a sort of dignity which is the dignity of the dead. It has the deadness of the face in the glass box of that marble sepulchre in Red Square in Moscow. As dead as that, except for two small sunken eyes, like dark coals that smoulder dully in the caverns under the brows.

"So there we sit and look and look, hundreds and hundreds of us who have no business there, who should be turned away from there. We sit and stare hungrily like vultures perched on a tree, watching a living thing writhe yet a while. We are like the sansculottes, like the knitting women watching the heads fall at the foot of the guillotine. We have got into the room through cajolery and bribery and trickery and lies and high ups and low downs.

"A good show. Most of them had been there day after day, day after day. I felt like a frosh at a senior brawl. Darling, were you here this morning? What did they do? Are you coming tomorrow? I'm lunching with Reilly. I'm lunching with Fisher. Do you want to meet the Sheriff? Oh, he's sweet.

"I should like to say, as a taxpayer and a human being, and an old busybody, that that courtroom in Flemington, N.J., should be emptied and kept emptied of all except the judge, the jury, the lawyers, witnesses, reporters, special writers and such people as are definitely connected with the trial of Bruno Richard Hauptmann. For the jammed aisles, the crowded corridors, the noise, the buzz, the idiot laughter, the revolting faces of those of us who are watching this trial are an affront to civilization.

"This man Hauptmann, when he speaks, does so in a hollow voice—a voice without a tinge of warmth or life. A voice as dead as his face. I fought, he says in his lifeless voice, I fought in the war when I was 17.

"Guilty or innocent, this man, when he was 17, his bones not yet a man's bones, his mind not yet a man's mind, saw and knew fear, agony, ruthlessness, murder, hunger, cold. He was a German soldier in the war and a product of war. And perhaps this man with the face of the dead and the hollow cold voice like a voice from the grave is the complete and triumphant product of war."

The reactions to the piece were as sensational as the trial itself. Ferber supporters in the issue were not only her compatriots, such as Walter Lippmann, whose telegram read: "Proud of you a noble piece." It was the public who cheered her. The New York *Times* printed two whole columns of letters—all positive—one extremely articulate. It not only praises Ferber but comes close to the nub of the real issues involved—thus furthering Ferber's point:

"Edna Ferber has added to our indebtedness to her. We respond with a heartfelt amen to her piece . . . in which she cries 'Vultures' to the men and women who infest the Hauptmann trial . . . I am at a loss for words to describe my despair and abhorrence of this type of human being. I regret the limitations of the word 'disgusting.'

"A baby was murdered—a man and his wife were stricken with a nameless grief—a man is on trial for his life. And the thrill-seekers at Flemington laugh and wear miniature ladders and exchange pleasantries over their great fun! With greedy eyes they watch the writhings of the accused man in the witness chair. And they feast their sadistic souls on the mute suffering of another man, whose baby wore the little shirt so often displayed in the court room. All this in the name of Justice."

On the distaff side, there were letters like this one, addressed to Ferber personally:

"Have read your article for the Times, concerning the Hauptmann trial. I, as many other Americans, cannot see what this trial has to do with Hitler, the representative of a 67 Million Nation. If you, as a very important person, do not like this man, try and show better taste at least. You are one of the dirty swines, this country has to get rid of."

That type of letter was rare but was wounding in its ignorance. There was a letter from Dorothy Parker to make up for it, especially since Parker and Ferber were often at barbed-tongue points.

"Dear Edna, I can't help it. I can't keep another minute from telling you to your face what I have been saying behind your back—that your piece on the trial in Flemington is the finest and the most powerful and the most blazingly passionate thing you ever wrote in your life (hell, that anyone ever wrote in his or her life!) and as necessary as fire—It was re-printed here in the Los Angeles Herald and Express, the evening version of the Los Angeles Examiner, and God, what it was to come upon it in that mess!

"I wish there were more words—All I can keep saying is 'greatness!' Dorothy Parker."

The word greatness, the surge of admiration that comes with that word, seemed to apply more often to Ferber's character than her work. She was certainly in great company in the Women's Hall of Fame along with: Helen Keller, Marian Anderson, Pearl Buck, Margaret Sanger, Margaret Bourke-White, Margaret Mead, Eleanor Roosevelt, Jane Addams, Ethel Barrymore, Amelia Earhart, Edna St. Vincent Millay, Grandma Moses, Babe Didrikson Zaharias, etc. One can't help feeling that it was her admirable life of work, her commitment to her beliefs, and her ability to articulate them that landed her in the "greatness" category more than her work itself. When praise for women novelists was due she was always a front-runner, grouped with the likes of Edith Wharton, Willa Cather, Dorothy Canfield. But as a novelist per say, she has always taken a back seat. Highbrows would respond to her sterling character; slightly lower brows would respond to her work. Her audience, then, was Everyman, as was well pointed out in Heywood Broun's New York World-Telegram column, "It Seems to Me":

"I rode in a taxicab yesterday with a driver who seemed in the same morose state as myself. We were both suffering from nervous exhaustion. Two or three cars almost took his mudguards away, and he cursed under his breath.

"The swirl of traffic tossed us into a great Sargasso of stalled taxis, and most of the chauffeurs tried to move the car ahead by blowing horns. Once upon a time there must have been a traffic jam which was solved by the simple process of concerted clamor. I have never seen it done. According to my observation, the tooting and the honking only serve to make the black hole of Calcutta a little more torturing. The taxi driver seemed to feel the same way about it.

"'You know,' he said, 'this street is a madhouse.'

"He settled down to ruminate and wait for the green light.

"'You know,' he asked, 'what I do after I've had a couple of good days with the hack?'

"I supposed, of course, that he went on a boat or a bender or a street car, but I made no attempt to guess. I just indicated that I was curious to know.

"'Well,' explained the driver, 'I know a little street in Brooklyn where nobody bothers you. I just drive the taxi over there, get inside and read. I'm set for the day.'

"'Do you know the works of Edna Ferber?' he added.

"I admitted that I did.

"Well, she's my favorite author. Hot stuff! It sort of rests me.'"

Broun was not the only columnist who dabbled in Ferber mentions. Franklin P. Adams was devoted to doing so in his whimsically stylized column, "The Conning Tower." One of the special attractions of the column was that one day a week Adams converted it into an entertainment called "The Diary of Our Own Samuel Pepys," wherein he chatted in the syntax of Pepys about current celebrity doings. Ferber was featured in a great many of these—usually for her dinners:

". . . And so I to Miss Edna Ferber's for a dinner, the best I have had in more than seven weeks, the board fairly sobbing with nutritious provender. Dean Cornwell the artist there, and later L. Bromfield the tayle-writer come in and full of fascinating talk about letters and life, and he pressed Edna to tell about a bull fight she and her mother and her sister Fannie had attended in Spain, which was the drollest recital I ever heard in all my life, and I was weak from laughing thereat."

Occasionally he would plug one of her novels as he did when he wrote:

"Had I million I would bet it
On Edna Ferber's 'Come and Get It."

There were many who would have liked to sue Ferber for a million upon publication of *Come and Get It,* a 1935 novel whose characters were Polish-Americans working the lumber mills of Wisconsin. Ferber, always true to authentic ethnicity, had used the term "dumb Polack girls" in the context of the story. No doubt, in her research of the territory, she had heard it mentioned. To Polish-Americans, it was unmentionable. Fists of outrage came down to pummel Ferber in letters of protest. The book was first serialized in *Woman's Home Companion.* Polish-American subscribers severed their subscriptions, berating the magazine for publishing Ferber's slur. The writers-in may have come from divergent educational backgrounds, but they all made the same point. Some were blunt:

". . . I find that the story written by Edna Ferber is absurd because Polish girls are just as good as any other girls . . . If ever Polish people were driven out of any country they would have good old Poland to go to, and the Jews—what would they do if driven out of every country? When driven out of Germany they begged Poland to take them and Poland kindly did. Therefore what right have the Jews to say such things about the Polish people? And the sayings in the story about Polish girls may be true in some cases but I find the Jewish girls just as bad . . . I am no longer a subscriber of your magazine."

Others were more textured, more informative in their reproof—such as from George G. Sadowski, Congressman for the First District of Michigan.

He wrote that he was of Polish extraction and proud of the heritage. He pointed out that in every nationality there were all classes of people, all types of people, and it would be untrue of any nationality or race to class them all as brilliant or wealthy or of the highest rank socially. He found it just as untrue and farfetched to class all Poles as "dumb Polacks" and inferior mentally.

He went on to say that because Polish people were workers, in fact the most honest, the most capable, and the most dependable workers in America, he saw no reason that they should be classed as dumb. He concluded by saying that they may not have accumulated the wealth that people of other nationalities had who came to this country, but they had made good citizens and were highly respected by all who really knew them.

There were non-Poles living in Wisconsin who also had a beef against Ferber. It was one of ethics and etiquette rather than one of ethnics. When she went to Wisconsin to do research for *Come and Get It,* she enlisted the help of an executive of a large paper mill in Neenah. When Ferber wanted something, she appealed to the origins, the heart, the mind, the vanity of a person. She was fetching. The executive gave her all she needed to know. What he didn't know was that he unwittingly gave her himself to use as the main character in her book—a rather ruthless chap named Barney Glasgow. What stung him was not so much her portrayal of him, but the fact that she never, after their long sessions together, even wrote him a thank-you note. And, as is often the case in tight-knit societies, everyone knew about her rude conduct. The whole town tsked.

After talking to the executive she drew a tentative portrait. In it one can see how she threaded her needle with fact and embellishment:

"His appreciation of luxury. He always over-dressed. Rich soft materials, rich foods. But he liked sometimes plates of the old food of the lumber camps—beans, pork, pies. He sometimes ate a can of cold tomatoes. They knew nothing then of vitamines. They only knew that a can of tomatoes quenched thirst and somehow refreshed them. And he drank quantities of the tea of which the jacks and rivermen drank quarts. He was tall, but so broad shouldered and beautifully proportioned that his height was not unduly noticeable. He used to go to Milwaukee—Chicago for his suits and overcoats. In those days he had hair and mustache so black that he was accused of dying them; red cheeks that looked painted, very blue eyes. From his Scotch mother he probably had his terrible tenacity of purpose and a certain puritanism and self-denial that was constantly to war with his Latin strain. His family had come from Maine to Wisconsin.

"There was about him still something of the pioneer quality. A little ashamed of luxury, and a little afraid of it. They sometimes gingerly took private cars. The private car was considered the height of magnificence. They liked rich foods, duck, pies, thick soups, red wines and whiskey—rye, bourbon. They liked to survey largely their holdings—their mills, their lands, their crops, their families, their employes, keeping a kind of possessive hand on the whole. It was as if they still could hardly believe that this they had wrested, just one generation removed, from the virgin prairie or forest. It was as though a benevolent Goth were to settle down to enjoy the benefits of his ravishments."

Ferber was like a surgeon always risking malpractice suits because she cut into so much. In the early days of preparing a book, however, her tack was akin to a medical student's—studious, exploratory, careful, reverent. The subject of *Come and Get It* is lumber and its "jacks." One of the major distillations of lumber is paper. Hence, it behooved her to know the history of papermaking:

"When the Arabs captured the splendid city of Samarcand from the Chinese, about 704 A.D., they gained something more than material booty, for the art of paper making flourished there, and they carried the secret back with them to their own towns and cities. Western Europe, in turn, learned it from the Arabs, through the Crusaders who visited Byzantium, Palestine and Syria. (Stress here dignity of the paper maker. A respect for his trade, which is like a profession. Their faces have a nobility, clear cut craftsmen. The young men were a handsome lot. The old fellows had faces like cameos, lean, sinewy. You never saw a fat paper maker.) To the Chinese is now generally conceded the discovery of the art of making paper of the sort familiar to us from fibrous matter reduced to a pulp. Chinese saying: Time and patience will change the mulberry leaf into satin. Chinese discovered mulberry might be put to still another use besides silk. The tree they chose for their new manufacture belonged to the mulberry family. From its bark they made, by a process that must have seemed to them something akin to magic a material which, in its developed and improved form, has been of priceless value to the world far exceeding that of the rich and costly stuffs woven from the cocoons of the silk worms."

Ferber was contemptuous of phonies, which, in her book, included Hollywood. There was a line in *Stage Door* which succinctly captured her disdain of the town: ". . . and they have little mink swimming pools up to here," the actress saying the line draws her finger across her throat in a gagging gesture.

When Ferber did go out to Hollywood, which was rare, she felt as though she was being choked—especially around the legs. She could never accept the conditional that when in Hollywood one just didn't walk. The director George Cukor fondly remembers Ferber stalking through Beverly Hills, one of the few sanctioned walking grounds. Another irritant was the weather; she stormed over its constant sunniness:

"Always to have known security and ease and comfort seems to me to be like living in a land where it is always summer. It means never to know the exquisite hope of the first pale lemon green haze of Spring; never to at last relax under the deep ardour of the long-awaited summer sun. Always to have the warm sun—that must be enervating."

She went to Hollywood in 1935 for a series of talks with Samuel Goldwyn about the possibility of writing the screenplay for *Come and Get It*. She found that talking without walking was stifling. A diary entry: "Talked by the pool with Sam Goldwyn. Talked over lunch. Talked over drinks by the pool. Talked over dinner. Not much settled. Told him I had to go home and walk it out."

Ferber went home and walked—not into the arms of Jed Harris. Although she may have wanted to.

Jed Harris: he was a producer, on occasion a director, and on every occasion a heartbreaker. His hits included: *Coquette*, *The Royal Family*, *The Front Page*, *Serena Blandish*, *Uncle Vanya*, *The Green Bay Tree*, *The Lake*, *Our Town*, and others, which today have not much vintage. His women, too numerous to mention all of them, included Margaret Sullavan, and Ruth Gordon. Katharine Hepburn remembers that Harris seemed to have had a case on her for a while but that she would have none of him. He paid her back when he directed her in *The Lake*. "He practically destroyed me. He was perverse and diabolical."

And charming. When Ferber first met him, around 1927, she was bowled over, and in a letter to the "Foxies" wrote:

"Dining down at Luchow's with George [Kaufman] and Jed Harris. I'm crazy about Jed Harris. I think I told you about him. Only 26, and so brilliant and wise and amusing. He merely owns half of Broadway, which means he'll be a millionaire in another year."

That first blush was replaced by a flush and then a sort of a mottling—for eight years later her tone about Harris was quite different—as her diary points out:

Entry: "Jed Harris called up after 12:30. Talked for an hour. A thing that must stop. I can't have that kind of annoyance."

Entry: "Talked to Jed Harris. Fearfully bored by it. Fed up with him and his Sullavan."

What happened in those years? Nobody seems to know. Everybody seems to conjecture. Enough people have hinted that Jed Harris was Ferber's grand passion to make it seem near the truth. Dorothy Rodgers, who was about as amicably close to Ferber as one could get, has said: "Now, I never would have dared ask her about Jed Harris, but the story was that this was a great love."

Ruth Hammond is another who emphasizes the name Jed Harris in connection with the quest for a man in Ferber's life. She feels that during the production of *The Royal Family* Ferber was definitely stuck on Harris. "They sparred like lovers" is Miss Hammond's description. One Christmas Harris sent Ferber a great big heather plant. In her thank-you note to him she complained, "I want frail flowers, Jed, not amazon structures." She signed it, "Etna." A note from him came back saying among other epiphets, "Etna, I salute you the perfect louse."

Margalo Gillmore, another close friend who might have been privy to parts of Ferber's personal life, is skeptical about the Jed Harris possibility: "He was useful to her. He was part of her box of colors—her palette. She was fascinated by him more as an author than as a woman."

Proof is in the eye of the beholder. There is no denying that Ferber was involved with Harris on what was for her quite a large scale. She didn't talk on the telephone into the wee hours with just anyone.

Rumor is in the mouth of the deliverer. From Ferber's mouth to Julia's ear:

"The rumor is that Ruth Gordon has had a baby in Paris, presumably Mr. Harris' and everyone is talking about the Act of God. She will probably come calmly back, announce that she has adopted a baby, and go on acting. What a girl!"

Ruth Gordon did have a child by Jed Harris—presumably illegitimate. That is fact. The rumor was that she was really married to him and that during the time Gordon and Harris were supposedly married Ferber and Harris were having a fling. Ferber was missing from the scene for a while and nobody ever knew why. Ferber never explained it.

Like Rasho-Mon it unfolds. It was nothing; it was more. Just an interlude; a long-term thing. Intellectual; not. Camaraderie; chemistry. Although it is difficult to think of Ferber as having an "unguarded moment," Jed Harris would seem the likeliest of candidates to cause her unbalance.

I had resisted the supposition until I saw a photo of the young Jed Harris. It was a face to cause maximum vulnerability in others. An amazing face—like Pan dressed in Mafia clothes, like Peck's Bad Boy gone worse. The eyes were like acupuncture needles tipped in velvet; the mouth a lemon twist. Malevolent merriment, promises of emotional calisthenics, more demand than supply—all working in his expression. Not a step-right-up face. A lie-right-down face. Irresistible.

The antithesis of Jed Harris was Noel Coward—theatrically and personally. Where Harris was inspired, Coward was inspirational. Where Harris had contempt for actors, Coward had compassion. Harris had success; Coward had successful longevity. Harris was egocentric; Coward was eccentric. Coward was everything Ferber could want in a person—if not a man. Harris was everything that Ferber was drawn to in a man—if not a person. It is interesting, therefore, that these two men—again in opposite ways—stood at the helm of the Ferber-Kaufman play *The Royal Family*. In 1927, Jed Harris produced it on Broadway. In 1934 Noel Coward directed it in London under the title *Theater Royal*. Coward, as courtly in business as in friendship, sent Ferber a blow-by-blow letter about how her play was doing:

"Ferber my little darling, This is just to tell you we have had our last dress rehearsal and it looks pretty good. Larry Olivier is playing Tony for the first two weeks on the road and is marvelous—Then Brian Aherne takes over for London. I think you'd be delighted with the whole cast with one notable exception and that is W. Graham Browne as Oscar Wolfe who, owing to being very old indeed and unable to act at all (combining these assets with complete inaudibility) will present to a resigned public one of the most degraded characterizations of the modern Theater—pardon the word modern.

"This unfortunately is absolutely unavoidable as Marie Tempest will not appear without him and she is beyond words superb as Fanny . . . I think you and George would be pleased with the whole performance and production. Anyhow I hope so as I've worked very hard over it and have been living all through rehearsals in a Nursing Home. I am better now, however, and shall join the play at the end of the week . . . and devote the last two weeks to polishing up. I'll be arriving in New York on the 20th so put the kettle on the nob, there's a dear and please may I tell you, dear Miss Ferber and dear Mr. Kaufman, that I think "The Royal Family" ("Theater Royal") is one of the most superbly written and brilliantly constructed plays that I have ever had anything to do with."

Ferber couldn't say as much about the 1933 George Kaufman-Alexander Woollcott play *The Dark Tower.* In fact, she didn't even come in on it until the middle of the second act. True, it was a mediocre effort, but that was beside the point. The point being that it was a tour de force for Woollcott, who demanded from his friends that attention be paid. Not only was he the co-author; he was the star. An event.

On the evening that Ferber was to attend this event, she had another, prior event: dinner on Stanton Griffis' yacht (situated at the New York Yacht Basin) along with Gary Cooper and his wife. Afterwards, they would all go to the theatre. Apparently nobody had watches and everybody had lots of caviar and champagne, causing Ferber, who usually was so early that anyone arriving on time was considered late, to be late to the theatre. She testily records it:

"Stan Griffis' dinner caused late arrival at Kaufman-Woollcott play. Caused by Gary Cooper's tardiness at dinner. Was slow as he is tall."

For the audience the event was not the play, but to see the immensely popular Gary Cooper stride down the aisle in the middle of it. One can only imagine the swiveling heads and hiss that went through the theatre. One is loath to imagine the expression on Woollcott's face.

It seems fitting that the notorious Ferber-Woollcott feud was inaugurated after the play. Margalo Gillmore, who was the leading lady, received Ferber and her party in her dressing room. Woollcott happened to be visiting Miss Gillmore and lambasting Miss Ferber as Ferber entered. He gave Ferber a stony look. Ferber said that she really couldn't help it, and then quotes Miss Gillmore, "Such pyrotechnics as you never saw."

In front of God and Gary Cooper, Woollcott apparently lit into her with the kind of energetic venom that caused Ferber to summon her most malicious troops. After much brutal badinage, she decked him with, "You New Jersey Nero! You mistake your pinafore for a toga!"

And that was the curtain line on their friendship.

Three evenings later Ferber was invited to a dinner where she was seated next to Woollcott. "He was insufferable," she records. Small wonder.

Actually, their friendship had never been a generous one. Its ingredients were enjoyment, respect, and competition—no wide berth of undying love. They were too much alike in too many ways: both single people, both overachievers, both temperamental, both attempting to put wit before hurt, and both, as was generally speculated, were ambivalent about their sex lives.

Their favorite place to cat and dog it was at the Round Table of the Algonquin Hotel, on West Forty-fourth Street in New York. Much has been written about the cactus children of this secret club where someone was always willing to play verbal patty-cake. Marc Connelly, an entrenched member of the verbiage experts, recalls: "There was no sentiment among that crowd. We had affection and respect. It sufficed." Apparently, in that thorny ambience one had to go through a form of "hazing" every single time. One really had to be up to the potent snuff that wafted around the table. Ferber assesses:

". . . they were actually merciless if they disapproved. I have never encountered a more hard-bitten crew. But if they liked what you had done they did say so, publicly and whole-heartedly. Their standards were high, their vocabulary fluent, fresh, astringent, and very, very tough. Theirs was a tonic influence, one on the other, and all on the world of American letters . . . They were ruthless toward charlatans, toward the pompous, and the mentally and artistically dishonest. Casual, incisive, they had a certain terrible integrity about their work and a boundless ambition."

There are various reports about who were the chosen few at the Round Table, and who did the choosing. It is without dispute that Woollcott was a charter member—never to be deposed because he outlasted everyone, in terms of food consumption and bons mots. He was the czar, the potentate, the big *béarnaise.* As for the others, it varies with sources. There were sitters and there were members. Ferber belonged to the latter. She sat and sparred when she chose —never needing an invitation. She couldn't have gone every day or her body of work would have been "So Small." George Oppenheimer swears that she was never a habitué; Janet heartily supports this, yet Marc Connelly attests to the fact that Ferber was a consummate Round Table sitter. Among the steady women besides Ferber he says were: Peggy Wood, Alice Duer Miller, Peggy Leech Pulitzer, Dorothy Parker, and that Neysa McMein, the artist, who was credited with being a regular, for the most part would take lunch in her studio. Connelly recalls the regimen of the Round Tablers. The group would break up shortly past noon, and after putting in a few creative hours, would meet again around 5 P.M. at someone's apartment—often for an evening of revelry. It doesn't seem as though Ferber could ingest that sort of diet, yet her diary entries of the early thirties and late twenties list the Algonquin as one of her top social priorities.

In 1933, Frank Case, the owner-host of the Algonquin, must have thought she knew her Round Table stuff, for he asked her to write a public relations piece on the hotel. In her notes for the piece she itemized her version of who the regulars were: Robert Sherwood, George Kaufman, Marc Connelly, Brock Pemberton, Margalo Gillmore, Katharine Cornell, Neysa McMein, Deems Taylor, Franklin P. Adams, Herbert Bayard Swope, Louis Bromfield, Kathleen and Charlie Norris. The piece that she eventually wrote was more about Frank Case than the flock. It gives a wonderful feeling about the Algonquin household:

"It is difficult to write of the Algonquin without writing almost entirely about Frank Case, who owns it. And it is practically impossible to write about Frank Case without becoming sentimental. The Algonquin is Frank Case. Without him it is just a hotel. With him, it becomes a club, refuge, free hospital, rendezvous, salon (one o) and mother's knee. A surface description of Frank Case doesn't help. He looks less like mine host than can be imagined. Tall, suave, slim, quiet, keen, there is nothing of the plump ruddy boniface about him.

"The Algonquin food is good enough, but nothing to tempt a gourmet. The rooms are comfortable, but less than dazzling. The lobby is smallish and rather dim. There is no gold, little plush, and the doorman is not a general wandered out of Graustark. The hotel contains one passenger lift, which creaks. In it, ascending or descending, you are likely to pick up, from floor to floor, Ethel Barrymore, Douglas Fairbanks, Henry Mencken, Dorothy Parker, Hendrik Van Loon, Irene Franklin, Ina Claire, the Swedish Ambassador, Constance Collier.

"Perhaps two brief stories, one about a member of the Swedish legation in Washington, and one about Miss Constance Collier, will serve to give a rough idea of the general goings-on at the Algonquin and in the mind of Frank Case. It is difficult to pick and choose among the stories about this hotel and its owner. They are so many, so fantastic, so heartening, that woven together they amount to a saga.

"Miss Constance Collier set fire to the Algonquin Hotel. Her particular New York annoyance is the lunatic shriek of the New York fire department siren. Her English maid has all the cockney's love of the street dramas. At the first sound of the siren she leaps to its mad call. On this occasion Miss Collier, in her hotel apartment sitting room, was awaiting the arrival of Noel Coward, who was coming to lunch. The sound of the fire engines, and in rushes the maid.

"'A fire! Fire! Miss Collier! Fire!'

"'You can't go,' said Miss Collier, firmly. 'I'm expecting Mr. Coward to lunch and besides I can't have you running out every time an engine screams in the—'

"'I don't have to run,' said the maid. 'It's here.'

"And so it was. Curtains ablaze, bed ablaze, smoke pouring out of the windows. The maid, having finished pressing a garment, had gone into the bathroom, leaving the hot iron cosily on the floor near the curtain blowing at the open window. The heat and the draught made a perfect combination. There followed an hour of confusion, noise, water, smoke, flame. In the midst of it Mr. Case ordered Miss Collier's belongings moved quietly to an apartment on another floor. He was very apologetic. He sent her flowers every morning for a week. If she had burned down the hotel he doubtless would have sent her a tiara.

"This member of the Swedish legation. You see, he had come to New York to attend a large low-cut social affair from which he returned to his apartment at the Algonquin late and weary. He turned on the bath water for a sleep-inducing tub, forgot about it, fell asleep on his bed and awoke hours later to find his bed an island and himself marooned on it, surrounded by turbulent waves. The water, finding it was not wanted in the tub, had majestically swept from the bathroom, under the locked door, out into the hall, down the stairs and when discovered in the early morning had reached the breakfast room and, in fact, had taken complete possession there. The flood's source was traced, finally, to the locked door of the sleeping Swedish diplomat.

"With visions of a four-figure bill for damages, and prepared to fight to the last dollar, that damp guest dressed hurriedly and sloshed his way downstairs to be confronted by the suave Frank Case himself.

" 'Good morning,' said Mr. Case.

"The Swedish diplomat squared his shoulders and prepared to make a battle of it. 'Good—uh—g—now see here, it's no use—'

" 'There's been a little accident,' continued Frank Case, very velvety. 'The plumbing. I'm sorry—'

" 'Yes, I know, but look here—'

" 'I'm sorry to say that I'm afraid you'll have to take your breakfast in the large dining room this morning. The breakfast room is flooded. I hope you won't be too much inconvenienced.'

"And that was the last the Swedish diplomat ever heard of that mishap. Maybe it was cannier of Case than meets the eye. For they do say that Swedish diplomat went back to Washington, to Sweden, to Norway, Finland, Denmark, Iceland and the Arctic Circle spreading the praises of Frank Case, the Algonquin, and American generosity and hospitality. And now no Swede of any importance would think of stopping anywhere other than at the Algonquin. It seems they considered it a sort of national debt they owe (and pay) to Frank Case."

There are several interpretations about what the Round Table group meant in terms of historical placement. Were they merely a bratty-chic clique who made good copy, or were they more the counterpart of Bloomsbury or the elite grouping in Paris during the twenties? Was their métier an important artistic statement or just one-liners? Were they witty or vicious? Frivolous or hard-working? Did their careers flourish or flounder while they ate sundries and tossed sallies? Were they important or only influential during that time?

Wit has never been taken seriously, but is appreciated and understood as an entity in America more, perhaps, than in any other country. Whatever the Round Table wasn't, in terms of lasting importance, it was very American and very funny. Its members were qualified witmongers whose rhetoric has been marketed, packaged, sold and resold to this day.

"It was all fun," recounts Katharine Hepburn. "There were individuals in those days. Nobody suffered outwardly. It wasn't cricket."

More tennis than cricket, they volleyed for service and then smacked their opponent with a cry of "love." Ferber did very well at this, remaining poised, alert, and ready to move in for the kill.

One day she and Woollcott, among others, were lunching at the Algonquin. She, just back from Paris, sported a broad-shouldered suit, the *outré* style of the day.

Woollcott commented, "Why Edna, you look almost like a man."

Ferber eyed him levelly. "Why Aleck, so do you."

When the going threatened to get rough, there was always someone to turn the right phrase and set the table back on its course. Often it was George Kaufman who was rather absently present when Ferber and Woollcott got into one of their frequent snares and snarls. Rapid fire—Woollcott, Ferber, Woollcott, Ferber, who seemed to be bettering him. Whereupon Woollcott, never to be outdone or undone when stung, retorted, "You shut up, you Godamn Christ-killer."

Kaufman, with back like a ramrod, said with asperity, "I just want to warn you that that's the last time I'll have my race insulted. The next time I'll walk out. And Mrs. Parker, I trust, will walk halfway with me."

Dorothy Parker happened to be one half Scottish and one half Jewish.

Ferber was popular among the Round Tablers. Her work, perhaps, was less so. Franklin P. Adams' comment was: "She had the habit of industry." Marc Connelly's summation of Ferber's approach to her work was: "It had a certain journalistic ephemerality."

They were a tough bunch.

If given her druthers, Ferber would rather have sat on the front porch of the William Allen Whites in Emporia, Kansas, any day than at the Algonquin's Round Table. William Allen White: statesman, newspaper editor, author, humanitarian, and the one man who made any real romantic sense in Ferber's life. By romance, meaning that during their twenty-two-year friendship he provided her faith, endurance, self-respect, hope, humor, insight, farsight, and, at intervals, peace. My concept of romance. I also think that he was deeply in love with her. There is nothing concrete to point to and say, "There! Ah ha! On the night of October 1 . . ." It wasn't like that. Whether sex entered into it is moot, irrelevant, doubtful. White, Ferber's senior by about twenty years, was already middle-aged and married with children when she met him in 1912 at the Democratic National Convention in Chicago. His countenance was sweet but plain. Her description of him implies that to her he was better than handsome:

"I saw a rotund broad-shouldered man in a pale gray suit and astonishing pale gray kid shoes that he displayed with pride at having been snared from a shoe drummer in Emporia, Kansas . . . He had the smile of a roguish little boy, with dimples complete; the broad noble brow of a philosopher and statesman; the eyes of a poet and the shrewd determined mouth of the politician, businessman, newspaper editor. The eyes dominated. I noticed that ordinarily they were a rather washed-out blue as though the color had drained out of them when he relaxed. When he was stirred, emotionalized, they would darken and deepen and widen until they were blue-black pools in his round pink face. He saw everything; he knew everyone; his wit was pungent, salty, homely and sophisticated at the same time. There was a difference of perhaps twenty years in our ages. We were friends and comrades from the start."

Over twenty-two years "Bill" White, as she called him, preserved her past for her, advised her present, and invested in her heart. When he died she went to bed for three days.

Before the dedication of the William Allen White Memorial Library, Ferber, among other notables, was asked to contribute a short recollection of him. What she wrote is less than her best. It was as though she couldn't grapple with emotion into words:

". . . When I think of him now it is rarely in terms of his better known qualities. It is of the times when we walked along the streets of Chicago or New York or San Francisco or Baltimore or Emporia, laughing. When we sat laughing and talking in my apartment in New York. It was free, wholesome, healthy, tension-relieving laughter. A wonderful sound, and a heartening one, laughter. Where has it gone? . . . It vanished somehow, just about at the start of the Second World War and it never has really come back. I don't know what's become of it, here on earth. Not the big true ringing kind. But wherever the spirit of William Allen White may be, there it is, there I know is that great healer and rejuvenator, lost laughter."

William Allen White's feelings toward the young Ferber were ambivalent. He had a wife, Sallie, who, from all clues that he's left in his letters, fell short of the kind of woman he needed. She was an invalid a great deal of the time, whereas he was robust all of the time. He seemed to have the capability of digging for Ferber's marrow and coming up with the precious stuff. His letters to her are, to my way of sighing, love letters under very little disguise. They are caring, tender, prodding when she could do with some. They are letters that reveal what a tremendous stake he had in her being—with passionate emphasis on her work, for he knew that she knew that that *was* her being, her body and soul. There is subterfuge, but between the lines there is such loving that I should think it would have been hard for either of them to miss. But, then there's this. Perhaps I'm alchemizing a personal electricity into a romantic one. I do want her to have had a great love and to have been greatly loved, however subterranean and undeclared. Perhaps, however, in those days (although people have always had a tendency to remain people) the delicate nuance of feelings was and could be defined and understood. Perhaps, in those days one didn't play around with subtext. But talking myself out of the fact that they were having a love affair through correspondence is pure folly.

And so in 1933 Ferber went to Emporia, Kansas, to laugh. White's telegram to her, just prior to her arrival, is brimming with the amusements that would follow:

"Will have fire department Kansas national guard and Emporia silver coronet band at station with Mayor and city dignitaries. Stop. This is my birthday am sending you loving greetings with a hearty wish for many more of them. Stop. As your shadow grows slim may your income tax grow heavy as your heart grows light."

The last laugh was on Ferber. The episode captures the sweet and wry essences of her. While at the Whites' she was to attend a party they were throwing for some Osage Indian friends of theirs. Bill White knew that this would be right up Ferber's alley. Ferber felt the same. Local color, she said to herself. She didn't deliberate at all while packing. What could she possibly need? Nothing fancy. She would never want to show up the Indian women by flaunting Mainbocher or a Poiret—and it was Kansas not Paris, anyway. A few simple printed cottons would serve. Off she went with her "play it down" wardrobe.

The night of the party the Osage women filed in. Dressed to the nines. On their backs were Poirets and Chanels and other name designers. The men were equally dandified. They were *the* most sophisticated and educated of people. Ferber, with her designer dresses hanging in New York, in her effort to be "just folks," was the frump of the party. But for all their finery, Ferber recalled the women's eyes betraying the acquired sophistication with deep pools of Indian oppression. "Licorice drop eyes," was the way Ferber phrased it.

She also went to the Whites' to eat. She describes a meal there with her usual calorific style:

". . . platters of chicken, and always another platter of chicken. Vegetables of the bouncing Kansas kind. A great salad mixed honestly in a bowl, and turned and tossed until each jade-green leaf and scarlet tomato and blanched spear of endive glistened in its own coating of oil dressing."

White, himself an epicure, wrote affectionately about Ferber's appetite:

". . . Under the stimulation of food she glowed like a steamboat at night. She required no alcoholic torch to light her fireworks. And she loved man's food—steaks, chops, green salads, tasty puddings, and carrots to make her hair curl and spinich to make her grow up into a nice big girl.

". . . I remember one day we went marketing together with a big market basket, down to the Baltimore city market. What a revel it was! We bought crabs and frying chickens and strange tropical fruits. Heaven knows we did not try to resist anything. And the next morning we had a table full of guests—politicians, reporters, editors, writers in the higher brackets of fame. And Edna sat behind the bubbling coffee urn, vastly more brilliant than the amber fountain before her, dispensing a breakfast which began with strawberries, rambled through beaten biscuits, fried chicken, hashed brown potatoes, with an optional detour to crabs, and ended—God have mercy on us—with pancakes and honey and coffee.

". . . The picture I remember best of San Francisco . . . [was] when we two . . . walked down Market Street, buying fruit at the corner fruit stands, eating it out of sacks as we went, throwing skins and seeds in trash cans, abandoning ourselves to the childish joy of breaking all the rules of decorous conduct, popping cherry seeds through thumb and finger at the wide, wicked world, discussing politics and art and life and what it was all about, getting nowhere but happy on the way."

Much farther along the way, Ferber's letters to White still have the sense of fun that he cherished in her as a young girl. For him alone she seems always to remain young, playful, adventurous and constantly seeking advice:

"Dear Mr. White, I have long been an admirer of yours, and what are you going to do about it!

"Would you like to come in at tea time on Tuesday—say five? Object, conversation. Or would you like to come to dinner on Tuesday, and maybe see a play. Money no object.

"I am trying to write a novel, and I seem to want to go away from New York. I should like to be away for January and February at least. Advice. Much love, and hoping this finds you the same. Rspctfly, E. Feldman."

Part of every reason that she ever wanted to get away was Julia —away from Julia. She could stand so much of the proximity and then, figuratively, she would start knotting handkerchiefs to drape out the window for her escape. It usually came at a time when Julia demanded unequal time:

Entry: "A quarrel with mother. She complains that I don't spend enough time with her. God!"

Spiritual adviser and travel agent, White, who had just traveled in Russia, suggested that it was worth a look-see. She booked her passage. The trip fitted in perfectly with her plan to go to London to see their production of the third play she had written with Kaufman, *Dinner at Eight,* which had been produced in New York the previous year. She would also go to Socoa, France, for a month, where Louis Bromfield and his wife had a house, and a standing invitation. And that took care of her getting away.

While away, Ferber was such a chatty letter writer, so full of acres of news that one wonders if her days were as full as the letters imply—or whether a good deal of time was filled with writing home about the gala time she was having.

She found Russia certainly worth seeing and wrote William Allen White to thank him for it:

"Don't you think Russia is beyond anything the most interesting single experience you've ever had? If I could be allowed to wish myself into the city that I'd rather inhabit for two weeks than any other city in the world (that's a mixed sentence, but you know what I mean) it would be Moscow. Zowie! It was like a series of electric shocks . . . Will you tell me, in six words, what you think of the Human Race. Sh-sh-sh-sh! Such langwidge!"

From London she wrote to her "fambly" telling them what-all—throwing choice fish to the seals:

". . . The dress problem in London is incredible. Peggy Morris has made clothes for Gertrude Lawrence and Benita Hume and the things she made for Lynn [Fontanne] and Margalo [Gillmore] last summer were lovely. She made that brown suit and red coat for me, you know. I always loved it . . . Old Irene Vanbrugh, who is to play Ann Andrew's part, has a figure like a pear. She announced that for the last scene (the dinner) she would like to have a black net dress with pink stuff at the top to make it look low. As I wrote Mom, I haven't even heard of a garment like that since the Hammel weddings in Appleton, Wis. Then she said that for the second act she would like lace pajamas. You'd have to see her to realize what she'd look like . . . The play comes on pretty well, but it never will be the New York production . . . Everyone is giving all sorts of parties, to most of which George [Kaufman] and I can't go. I had to cut the luncheon that Freddie Lonsdale was giving for me at the Garrick Club, and Victor Cazalet's lunch at the House of Commons, too . . . Night before last, at halfpast one, my telephone rang and an American male voice at the other end said, 'I represent the Hearst papers in London. I have a cable informing me that you have been barred from Mexico because of a short story you wrote about Mexico.' That was all news to me. I said I didn't know anything about it, and didn't want to go to Mexico anyway, so it was Oke with me . . ."

And dutifully from Paris:

"I'm all packed and ready to go on the de luxe train to Socoa . . . Louis says he will meet me tomorrow morning . . . I hope it will work out all right. I've just heard that the bath tub is in the pantry. But as there is said to be no water anyway, I don't think it matters . . . I bought a new trunk at Vuitton's . . . I engaged a woman to pack me—a job I hate—also from Vuitton's, as they have that service for their customers. She was to come at 4:30 or five. At 4:30 in walked a French gent who looked like a truck driver—enormous smelly red-faced pop-eyed old boy, who announced that he had come to pack my trunk. I said, 'Don't be silly,' or as near as I could come to it in French. But he insisted, and what's more he actually did pack both trunks. I don't know where anything is . . . Jed Harris, who was maniacing around here last week, and whom I didn't see, wrote asking me to motor in his car down to Socoa, but not I . . . Sam Harris [the producer of *Dinner at Eight*] cables that, while every other play in New York has slumped, DINNER continues to sell out. Isn't that fine!"

It wouldn't have been so fine if Ferber had let a minor feud with Kaufman bar her from writing with him again. He wanted another play, and appealed to her better half:

"Dear Edna, I'll be forty-five to-morrow, and in another ten years I'll be middle-aged. These feuds and semi-feuds are silly things, and besides I miss you. In other words, how about writing a play sometime?

"I am chancing your refusal because I would so very much like to do it. If you say 'No' I shall still love you, but I won't like it. George."

The play they built was *Dinner at Eight*. It was a structure of the society of manners; a tongue-in-cheek comedy-drama of the world they both knew so well. It was a hit—both public and critical. An excerpt from one of the reviews reads:

". . . its arrival is an occasion that inspires the cheer leading mood. With crisp, vitalized stage direction, and with a large cast that is rich with distinguished players, this work by George S. Kaufman and Edna Ferber, who practice the craft of letters with the golden touch of invariable success, comes under the well known heading 'a cross section of life.' Its material, moreover, is high life, Park avenue life in the terms of the society magazines, and the juicy scandals that are rumored to lurk behind its glittering curtains . . . It permits its audience to sit as keyhole Olympians, enjoyably observing the private affairs of the upper classes . . ."

Ferber was indeed pleased with it on three counts: profit, that it was good work, and that Janet was in it. "The play is bitter and entertaining," she wrote to William Allen White. "You'll probably not like it a great deal. My darling Niece—her first Broadway job—Janet Fox, plays the tough hard-boiled blackmailing maid who attends Mrs. Packard. I'm very proud of her."

Although Kaufman conceded to an apology in order to get the show on the road, he would not concede to forfeiting his creature comforts while writing it in the summer of 1932. He would bend only so far with Ferber, who often tried to break his bough. This time, she did the compromising—fretting about it to William Allen White:

"I find myself on Long Island for the summer, much to my surprise, and considerably to my discomfort. I started a play with George Kaufman, you know, in April. George won't leave New York (Long Island being practically in New York) and as he and that fearsome wife of his had taken a house here at Manhasset for the summer, I took one too, near theirs, thinking that we'd be working on the play until August. We finished it, in a burst, in June. And here I've been ever since, high and wet (for it's dampish on L.I.) with one of the most enchanting houses you ever saw, but not liking the rest of the Island very much. It's full of Whitneys and things, giving Circus parties and fetes."

When Ferber and Julia traveled together, Julia had the better time. They underwent a role reversal. Julia was the naughty child, always running off; Ferber was the governess, in hot pursuit. One gets the feeling from her letters home that Ferber wished it otherwise—wished to kick up her heels, but was a slave to her duenna duty.

In the summer of 1932, mother and daughter went abroad on the Norddeutscher Lloyd *Bremen*, a German luxury liner. Nothing strange save for the fact that Ferber was rabidly opposed to German anything, and was known to blare her sentiments. Margalo Gillmore remembers that if any of Ferber's friends booked passage on a German ship, they would receive cables from her saying that she'd never speak to them again. Perhaps Ferber's protest went into remission. Perhaps the thought of all that *gemütlich* food won her over. At any rate, they were off.

In those days, before travel was considered routine, an ocean voyage was quite an adventure—the high seas and all that. A terrific, extravagant send-off was mandatory. A gros bon voyage with champagne and streamers and flowers in staterooms was the order of the day. Ferber and Julia had it all. Ferber gloats about it:

"We got a perfect flood of telegrams and letters . . . There came a huge basket of fruit, and all sorts of candy, prunes, dates, figs, white cherries, hot house grapes, mints—everything imaginable, from the Stokes and Morrows; a magnificent corsage of red roses and lilies-of-the-valley; a huge box of roses from Bert Boyden, a lot of candy, books, champagne, etc. A package of books from Frank Adams, and letters galore."

Before she died, my Grandmother Fan handed me a stack of letters saying, "I want you to read these early letters of Edna's. You won't recognize her in them. She was so young and gay and loving."

A great deal of that was a pose, I feel, that she couldn't maintain as she grew older. Anyone with her kind of drive cannot ever relax enough to be gay and loving through and through. But some of the letters—markedly the ones from the *Bremen*—have a patina of well-being, a sort of ironic *joie de vivre*. Their contents also offer a rare glimpse of Ferber trying to flirt—of halfheartedly hoping for a shipboard tryst; and of being humorously thwarted.

". . . In the deck chair at my right, instead of the English polo player I had hoped for, is a very old lady, crippled, whose crutch rests cosily on my knee . . . On Saturday morning I was awakened at 8 o'clock to receive a wireless. I opened it coyly, thinking it might be from a disconsolate beau. It said: Bon Voyage. M. L. Farber. (The furrier) . . . The only drawback to the voyage is the lack of young people. It's really remarkable. The entire passenger list is married, and when they dance on deck, as they threaten to do this evening, I'll have to drag a stoker up from the hold. I have to content myself with resting, which is a pastime that palls, and with flirting with the wireless operators, who are most unsuspecting German youths, and who aren't even aware that I am practicing my deadly wiles on them. At our table sits a frightful Italian doctor, who speaks no English. But he'd make a 'little story for me.' He's a regular old rep-tile, but we're picking up Italian from him like mad. He eats peas with a knife—honest' Gawd! I didn't think it could really be done off the vaudeville stage. Then there is another Italian, a merchant, who looks like a Jew, and I betcha he is. And there is a fledgling from New York, who is going abroad to study architecture for two years. He's harmless, and uninteresting, and much taken with a lanky young lady who is going to study Montessori in Rome.

"(Mr. Hartman, who is standing in the doorway, sends his regards and announces that he will tango with me this evening. He's fat and not particularly dashing, but he seems to be the only available tango material.)

"For the rest, they are human various. A miniature painter, very famous, and very German, who does her hair in a bun, wears no corsets, and runs about in thick flat half-shoes and awful brown stockings. Most of the others from Rockford, Jamestown, and points west. The steerage interests me more than they. There's a tiny baby down there only six weeks old, all tied up like a papoose, so that when you hold him it's like holding a club . . . Gene Tunney and his wife are on board . . . There's a pest named Fraulein Dr. Gertrude Ferber who is the captain's secretary and who pursues me with family trees . . .

". . . I have always wanted to walk before breakfast, but I never get to it. It's the laziest life you can imagine. Mama looks rested and different already . . . It is so lazy and lovely to sit out on deck all the day long, playing, reading, walking, sleeping, listening to the band, eating barrels of candy, exercising in the gym, sitting up on the sun deck, and eating, eating, eating . . . We haven't missed a single meal, though today it was fearfully rough . . . The boat is tossing like mad, but it hasn't seemed to bother us, though a number of people are sick. The service is really wonderful, the food delicious—Fan, you'd revel in the way they load you with appetizers like caviar, and sardl.

". . . The Harriman dinner turned out to be fun, with Gene Tunney, very handsome and, oh, so intellectu-al, and a chap named Knight, crazy, with whom I've crossed lots of times, and a composer who has only one hand, and who plays the piano beautifully . . . We stayed up late—at least, I stayed up until four, which is late for me—but the rest were up until seven, or something. I'm handicapped by not being able to stay awake.

". . . Altogether it has been a wonderful week, and we've both loved it. It's a singularly and most awfully manless boat, with bridal couples galore, but no single gents. However, I'm not so accustomed to being swamped with attention as to miss it now."

With a hit on Broadway, and a well-received novel, *American Beauty,* the year before, Ferber seemed less guilty than usual about not cracking her work whip. She decided to go to Mexico, sans Julia, and wired the Whites with an invitation:

"Would you and Sallie consider going to Mexico for about ten days with me or does that sound slightly insane. I mean it. Edna."

They turned her down for family problems, but Marc and Madeline Connelly agreed to accompany her. It was an odd trio, but nobody seemed to mind except the then Mrs. Connelly, who apparently felt washed out in the company of the two celebrities.

When they stopped briefly in St. Louis en route to Mexico City, they were converged upon by reporters—one of whom picked up on this:

"... Walking with them, a reporter interposed a few questions and asked them to pose for a picture. Although they obligingly consented, the proceeding was held up a bit because Mrs. Connelly did not think she should be in the picture and Miss Ferber had to coax a little to get her to pose ..."

Ferber did not particularly enjoy the Connellys, and wrote home about it.

"Marc and Madeleine are leaving on Saturday for New York. Madeleine hasn't seen one inch of Mexico. What a queer person she is. I can make nothing of her. They were both very nice to me, but I wasn't comfortable traveling with them—or rather, being so much with them. I wouldn't do it again."

She did, however, make the most of Mexico—inspecting and detecting everything.

"... The Connellys ... and I were given an audience with President Ortiz Rubio. The palace is too lovely, situated on Chapultapec (meaning grasshopper) Heights, overlooking the entire city. It was the castle of Maximilian and Carlota, and has the most magnificent terraces and patios and gardens and stairways, and is furnished with such a combination of splendor and horror and junk as I never before saw assembled under one roof. After the audience ... we were shown over the palace ... It is indescribable, including the mass of spots of all colors and sizes covering the once white table cloth of the table which was laid for dinner, and to which we, fortunately, had not been invited. The table was further graced by bottles of Snider's catsup and chile sauce, just as they come from the A & P and by Worcestershire, etc. The room itself is magnificent, full of beautiful leather and old silver and velvet. Senora Rubio looked as if she had just come in from a romp with an elephant ...

"... We drove through the lovely Chapultapec Gardens, had lunch, and went to the bull fight. And such a bull fight! It was like a Weber and Fields imitation of the Spanish one. Two of the bulls refused to fight and had to be literally pulled out of the ring. It was all pretty dull and dirty and clumsy."

Rudyard Kipling gave "twice told" praise to Ferber and to her publisher, Nelson Doubleday, for her 1931 novel *American Beauty*.

James Truslow Adams wrote about it: "[It] is Edna Ferber at her very best. It is an extraordinarily arresting book, splendid in its technique, absorbing in its story and startling in the picture it leaves with us. It is a flaming STOP, LOOK and LISTEN for sixty-mile America at the 1931 grade-crossing. It shook even me, hardened New England historian."

William Lyon Phelps, the erudite professor and lecturer at Yale University, wrote a small lecture on it, including comparisons and similarities between Ferber and Willa Cather, who also had a new book out, called *Shadows on the Rock.* (In a letter to Fan, Ferber's feelings about Willa Cather in general: "I'm enclosing the Times review of Willa Cather's new book. It pans it, which gives me a little feeling of joy for no reason at all except that I'm just that malicious. She's been getting too much of this goddess stuff just because she wrote one good book—My Antonia.") Phelps was more charitable, and discerning:

"Edna Ferber's 'American Beauty' is a novel of high distinction. Her best work has been done within the last ten years . . . She is a sincere and scrupulous artist; who writes only when thought and emotion clamor for release . . . The new book, 'American Beauty,' reveals her style in full mastery; and that smouldering indignation which women of sympathy must feel.

"'Shadows on the Rock' . . . is a novel of an entirely different denomination from previous works by the same author . . . [her] hard brilliance . . . is totally lacking in Willa Cather's latest books —which are written with warm, affectionate sympathy . . . 'Shadows on the Rock' . . . like 'Death Comes for the Archbishop' . . . might so easily in other hands have been a representation of people living in ignorance, superstition and slime, is closer to the truth because the author loves her people.

"Many of our book-reviewers seemed to have missed the significance of these two books just as they missed the meaning of the latest two by Edna Ferber. These distinguished artists seem fated to misunderstanding or at any rate misrepresentation. Many reviewers said that 'Cimarron' and 'American Beauty' were written for the 'pictures'—that 'Cimarron' was a straight romantic story, with the wife held up as the 'purest type of American womanhood'; if they could have only known how Edna Ferber hated her!

"Likewise, the reviewers of 'Shadow on the Rock' complain that they get no 'kick' out of the book; that it is slow, without action, and without excitement.

"Thus Edna Ferber and Willa Cather have been condemned for precisely opposite reasons; the former, because she has thrills and the latter because she hasn't. In both cases the artists are right and the reviewers wrong."

Even though Ferber couldn't often claim good reviews, notoriety was never a problem for her. She was always offending someone, some town, some class of people in her fiction—with *American Beauty* being no exception. This time she used Yale as her soapbox for a sterling defense. Her diary betrays any staunch attitude she might have had: "Talk at Yale. Cold bowels." But the actress in her prevailed—especially since the New York *Times* was covering the event:

"Edna Ferber defended herself . . . at Yale University today from criticisms which she has received over a description of a Connecticut house and characters in her novel, 'American Beauty.'

"She declared that she had drawn these from her imagination, although newspapers had told of persons who were offended by supposed allusions to Brookfield people whom she had visited while writing her novel. Miss Ferber insisted that she planned her characters first and her plots later.

". . . 'After I featured Cimarron, I learned from the people of Oklahoma that I was very unpopular there,' she said. 'One newspaper called me an 'unpleasant personality' and I was quoted as saying to a person who offered to tell me about something of which I inquired 'Say, big boy, I don't want any facts.'

"'This brings up the book American Beauty and the house in Connecticut referred to,' she added. 'The house exists only in my mind. Yet The Boston Transcript recently ran a full page showing a picture of the house, and a lady whose feelings I had hurt and a picture of a farmer described in the book. In writing the book I traveled through New England from Amherst down the entire Connecticut tobacco region to Hartford. I read descriptions of old Connecticut houses from a delightful book whose authors gave me permission to use anything I wished about the houses, taking a fireplace from one, a staircase from another and shifting a partition from still another. From this I built my own house. I wish I could convey in my writing that I am just pretending and that I am just playing.'

"Criticizing George Bernard Shaw for taking the lead in bringing the private views and lives of authors to the fore, Miss Ferber declared that 'authors should be read and not seen or heard.'"

Like a new bride rushing home to Mamma, whenever Ferber had a new book out, she made her way back to Chicago. It was her literary nest, where she felt safe, appreciated, and loved.

In a letter to her, the playwright Thornton Wilder wrote, "As far as I am concerned you are the truest Chicagoan of them all: you conferred an immeasurable gift to that city—you gave it a voice. From square miles of troubled hopeful confused apartment houses you lifted the curse of inarticulateness."

Perhaps. But in terms of geographical literary deposits, the names of, say, Upton Sinclair and Carl Sandburg might come up in conjunction with Chicago sooner than that of Edna Ferber. It bothered her; it created a sense of displacement within her. To Chicago critic and friend Fanny Butcher she would comment sadly that she'd spent most of her early life writing about Chicago, yet critics didn't recognize her as a Chicago writer.

Fanny Butcher did. When Ferber came to town, she would feature her in her column, bugling local-girl-comes-home:

"And one of our own, Edna Ferber, returned to us last week for a few days. She did all of her early work on the south side of Chicago, Ill., and she feels for Chicago a real affection. Unlike most modern realists, she isn't ashamed of saying so. She left the middle west as a source of material in her latest book, 'American Beauty,' for the first time . . . Miss Ferber is looking for a homestead anywhere outside New York, which gives you a mild idea of what it means to be a successful novelist and playwright in that town! She says that she has looked at high buildings so long that she has an 'edifice' complex."

What Ferber did, in her aging youth, was to establish a home outside of Julia. It was an emotional landmark, for they had always lived in tandem. Ever since they had come to New York in 1918 they had shared flats—at 50 Central Park West, at the Hotel Majestic, at the Hotel Lombardy. The only respite Ferber got was when she traveled, or when Julia went back to Chicago for spells, visiting the "Foxies," who were still housed there. In fact, Ferber once wrote to Fan of their early cohabiting days in New York: "As always, while Mama is off the job, I get delightfully mixed up with gents. I'm sure that if it weren't for Mom I'd long ago have wedded a lowlife that I'd have had to support."

The rather late weaning occurred in 1930, not without much *Sturm und Drang.* Several have claimed to have been the sole supports who brought Ferber to her senses, but she attributed her extrication to William Allen White, who, although fond of Julia, had told Ferber bluntly that she was living in an unhealthy environment.

Ferber's declaration of independence was in the form of the new lease that she signed for Julia. Address: the Lombardy Hotel. Apartment: on a different floor. Not a large move, perhaps, but a major one. Ferber was resigned to the premise that you could take the daughter out of the mother but you couldn't take the mother out of the daughter.

While Julia was sojourning in Chicago with relatives, Aunt Jo and Uncle Julius, Ferber was busy making amends for the shock that would follow by decorating Julia's new apartment "something grand." Ferber could be thoughtful to the point where she, and everyone else, wanted to scream. This was one of those times. Everything had to be perfection. The drapes had to hang better than most; the doors had to be louvered just so; the chaise-longue pillows had to be plumper . . . It was an act of ecstatic agony. A labor of very frightened love.

Julia returned. Ferber met her at the airport with a limousine. As they drove into the city, Ferber told her that there was a surprise waiting. Julia was dubious, "What kind of surprise?" Ferber was soothing, "A lovely surprise, Mama."

What went on when Julia was taken to another floor is unrecorded, but in hearing distance of the imagination. If Ferber could have carried her across the threshold, she would have—not that it would have done any good.

As Ferber showed the apartment off, Julia was silent, sulking, all the while casting her auction hawk-eye around. Ferber needed to be condemned out loud.

"Well, Mama, what do you think?"

"Well, Edna, I hate it. I just hate it. I'll be good and miserable here."

She wasn't. After causing a just-right trauma in Ferber, she rallied quickly. In describing the event to Fan, Ferber is puzzled and hurt:

"She has liked nothing, expressed herself as being pleased with nothing; uttered no word of pleasure at being installed painlessly in one of the loveliest apartments in New York. I never saw anything like it, unless it is Aunt Jo when you bring her an expensive birthday present and have her look at it and never so much as thank you for it." (A lack of grace obviously ran on Julia's side of the family.)

Ferber regained her humor about Julia and realized the benefits of the move in writing to William Allen White:

"Mother celebrated the market crash by buying a gorgeous broadtail coat with a sable collar. She goes to two parties daily with almost fanatic regularity, doesn't think her blue moire is as becoming as her gray lace, is having a seventieth birthday February third, and I'm giving her a diamond bracelet. Wot a girl!

"How distressed and really desperate I was that Sunday I talked to you . . . How understanding and beautiful you were, and patient with me. And how much better things are now that I've my own apartment, and mother hers."

In affairs of the family Ferber could never straighten herself out. With Fan and the girls safely tucked away in Chicago, Fan had kept her place, and therefore could be used as an ally against Julia. When Ferber went back she would behave and be treated like visiting royalty. She basked in it. The girls would pop with excitement, Fan would cook sumptuous meals, and the town would turn out. Janet replays the scene:

"I remember in Chicago, when we were kids, and Aunt Edna would come to visit us—this was D Day—this was F Day. We were living on the south side at 5431 Cornell Avenue, and whenever Aunt Edna would come it was everybody down to the station—the whole family. She would come to see Fanny Butcher and Rose Alschuler and I. B. Lipton and Lillian Adler and Newman Levy—she had lots of friends. And, of course, reporters would always be at the station, asking, Miss Ferber this, Miss Ferber that . . . I can just see Aunt Edna—which visit it was I don't know—but she looked so chic. She wore a little hat with a tight veil, and everything she had on her was very pristine. I mean, she wouldn't have put on a suit that had a spot on it for anything in the world. And I remember Gene Markey coming to the apartment. He seemed ten foot nine and very handsome and dashing. Who knew Gene Markey in Chicago? Nobody did, but everybody knew him in New

York and in Hollywood. He was a writer at that time and an awfully handsome young man. I remember they did, to our Midwestern background, that dramatic and romantic thing of, 'Edna, darling'—'Gene, love'—embracing and what-not, and Mina and I took it seriously. We didn't know anything about the hyperbole of the theater and writing world. So we said to each other, with giggles and snickers and awe, 'Do you think they'll get married?' I don't know who Gene Markey was married to then, but he was subsequently married to Hedy Lamarr and Joan Bennett (not in that order) and a string of them. So that was that. I just have a picture of a tall, dark—his hair was full and slicked back—beautifully dressed, handsome man—who seemed to be Aunt Edna's. We'd never seen anybody like that in our house."

In 1930—the year Julia was moved out—the country mice came to the city. Ferber shifted her gears. Julia became her ally against Fan, and it remained so always.

The girls were still at school and would follow later. Mina, with inklings of a scholar, was at the University of Wisconsin. Janet, with yearnings toward the stage, was killing time at something called the LaSelle Seminary for Girls.

Celebrity provided Ferber with superiority, which she often used like a cudgel. There is a myriad of reasons for this, the top one being that as a child in Ottumwa, Iowa, Ferber had confronted anti-Semitic feelings, had been badly discriminated against. As is often the case, when she grew up she used wealth and fame as a shield against discrimination, and as a permit to discriminate. It was poking fun at rather than hard-core hatred, but it was there. An example of it appears in a letter to Fan. She is commenting on having been a weekend guest:

"My week-end at the . . . was just so-so. The truth is I hate week-end visits. They exhaust me. The place itself is lovely. But (and can you imagine us doing this!) after a breakfast of orange juice, toast and coffee at about ten I was confronted, at one-thirty, with a lunch of pancakes, sausage and sauterne and nothing else. It knocked me cold, of course, and I have felt as if I had swallowed a golf ball ever since. Aren't goys comic!"

She was ever watchful of Janet's and Mina's companions and social activities as they were growing up, and when she found something that caused her disdain, she would say to Fan, "A nicer class of people [person] would be more appropriate, doncha think?" She was highly critical—almost ruthless—in evaluating young people, as is evidenced in another letter to Fan, where she recounts a week-end treat that she gave Janet and three school-girl friends. There are several points of interest: she belittles Janet's school; she makes fun of everybody but Janet, whom she extols, and she is delighted when Janet makes fun of something too.

"The school has served its purpose, I think, but it never has impressed me as being interesting or important. But then that would be true of any girls' school, unless it were, perhaps, Vassar, Smith, Wellesley or the like. Janet has got something out of it, [and] has met types of girls she hasn't before encountered . . .

"We went to the Ritz, freshened up a bit, and met the girls downstairs for tea. The room-mate is incredible, but she was a silent little thing, and one couldn't resent her. She looks like a little bath-maid in a hotel, or like a stock-girl in Macy's. I can't imagine how she got into the school . . . They seem to be the best of friends. I think Janet has been very game about making that adjustment . . . The little Trenton girl was a very pretty sweet little thing, well bred and gentle enough. No harm in her. The Spear girl was rather impertinent. She tries to be different, and isn't. The result is that you want to slap her. Janet stood out head and shoulders above them. She has personality, charm and individuality.

". . . Janet's account of her Syracuse visit, by the way, is simply grand. She imitates the great Bronxy Jewish ladies she encountered there. It appears that one of the young ladies was injured in an automobile accident the day of Janet's arrival, and Janet's imitation of the horror and grief of the Syracuse ladies is something to pay admission for. They dragged Janet to the hospital while they visited the young lady, and they all emerged from the hospital room shaking their heads, sobbing, and saying, 'Oi, w'at a gowjous goil! Oi, she was so gowjous! She was so gowjous and now look.' I roared with laughter.

". . . Janet drove back to school with the Spear girl and her beau. The beau, by the way, was the most utterly revolting looking young man I have ever seen. An enormously fat, gross, red-faced lump, with two little pig eyes sunk in a mass of lard. I said he looked like a butcher's assistant, and it turned out he was a grocer."

It wasn't that she meant to be cruel. She was snobbishly motivated, but never intentionally malicious. She was a reporter. She saw the truth, the whole truth, nothing but the truth, and reported it so help her "Gawd."

And when she was kind, she was very very kind. Dorothy and "Dicky" Rodgers had temporarily moved from the Lombardy in order to give their apartment to Dorothy's parents. At the time, her father was suffering from what they used to call "melancholia" and was in the throes of a nervous breakdown. While they were at the theatre one night, her father threw himself out the window. Dorothy Rodgers talks: "And Edna stayed up that whole night making coffee for us, and the next day–she was going away for the weekend–she gave me the key to her apartment, which for anybody else might not have been so remarkable because we were good friends. But Edna was very house-proud; she protected her territorial imperative. And the idea of anyone being in her lair, without her being there, must have been very difficult. But she gave me the key and said, 'Please use it as your own.' That was quite wonderful. I never, never forgot that. I was deeply touched by it."

In the case of Lillian Adler, Ferber's kindness ran to philanthropy. Lillian Adler was a girlhood friend from Chicago days, who had always been rather slavishly adoring of Ferber. Ferber's affections were not as ardent, but she was certainly fond of the woman. In fact, there is a passage from *A Peculiar Treasure* that certifies her feelings:

"It is a curious fact that, with one or two exceptions, the handful of people on whose friendship I know I can count to the last drop are men . . . Among the women of whom I can say it is Lillian Adler. She is now functioning superbly as one of the chiefs in the United Charities of Chicago, a social service organization . . ."

What Ferber chose to delete was that Lillian Adler–through the years–was a bit of a charity case herself, and that Ferber saw to it that her purse and her causes were amply financed.

There are great books, and there are greatly misunderstood books –often one being tantamount to the other. Such was the case of *Cimarron,* according to the gospel of Edna Ferber, Clark Gable, Nelson Doubleday (her publisher), Dan Longwell (her editor), William Allen White (her mentor), Rudyard Kipling (her illustrious and dogged fan), and a handful of others.

Everything about the book was in commercial order. The film rights were sold for a "telephone number" to RKO. Morris Ernst, her lawyer, had worked the deal out. Later, she and Ernst developed a terrific personality clash. She played the grande dame; he played the grand seigneur. The two roles didn't mesh. But at this time she had said that she wouldn't dream of walking across the street without Morris Ernst. So, in the middle of the street, they made quite a profit.

Ferber always equated the selling of film rights with a Faustian exchange. She felt that she had relinquished all artistic value. She often said that if she didn't have to feed so many mouths, there wouldn't be so many film sales—forgetting how much she liked Italian shoes and Devonshire cream and Nova Scotia salmon and sable and freesias. Those who knew her knew her penchant for luxury better than she did. In fact, upon the movie sale, she received a telegram saying, "MAY IT BUY YOU MANY FREESIAS."

Starring two of the most sought after movie names of the day, Richard Dix and Irene Dunne, *Cimarron* was touted as a "classic," a "masterpiece," "one of the most beautiful and dramatic love stories ever witnessed on the screen." Even Ferber gave it a small salute, it being her favorite of the two versions made.

Once again, as in so many instances in her life, the stimulus for the novel came from William Allen White, to whom she gives credit for being the legal father:

"There was no other home in Emporia, Kansas like the William Allen Whites' red brick house that had been reconstructed from plans by Frank Lloyd Wright.

". . . Emporia, back in the late 1920's, was a small Kansas prairie town of perhaps ten thousand people. Straight little streets, neat frame houses, tree-shaded . . . The middle west knew a hundred small towns such as this one. Yet people had been known to travel from New York to California or from California to New York merely as an excuse to stop over on the way to spend a day at the Whites' house in Emporia. I was one of these.

"It was the conversation. It was the stimulating, compassionate, constructive conversation that enriched the mind and heart of everyone who set foot within that house.

"It was on one of those trips in the early Spring of 1927 that I found myself in the big front room at the Whites' in Emporia . . . The talk was of the trip they had made in the autumn of the preceding year. Bill White and Sallie and young Bill, Jr., had motored to and through Oklahoma. Their keen observant eyes, their brilliant humor sense, their trained reportorial noses had missed nothing of the fantastic, the dramatic, the tragic, the absurd in that bizarre commonwealth so newly oil-rich. Their stories stunned me.

"Until that moment I was literally completely ignorant of the history of the State of Oklahoma . . . I knew nothing of the history of the spectacular opening of the Territory; of the discovery of oil; of the Indians so basely treated by the white man and so ludicrously revenged when the vast oil strike was made on the arid Indian reservation to which they had been herded.

"Now, as the Whites talked, sometimes singly sometimes all together, I would interrupt. 'You mean actually Osage Indians in blankets and braids riding around in Pierce Arrow cars! You mean millionaire Indians living in wigwams!'

"'Why not?' said Bill White. 'They had been herded onto that reservation like cattle. It was the poorest piece of land in Oklahoma, you couldn't raise anything on it. The reason for that was the huge lake of oil that lay hidden underneath it—the richest oil land in America, and no one had known it. What a joke on a lot of political tricksters! Cynically and ignorantly they had given it to the Indian tribes to live on and die on and now it's theirs.'

"I had listened to all this literally open-mouthed. 'Why hasn't some one written it? What a novel! Bill, you've got to do it.'

"'Me! No, thanks! Why don't you do it?'

"I shivered at the thought. Show Boat had been a tough enough job. I wanted never to tackle another like it. 'No, the story of Oklahoma is a man's job. I want no more big canvases, no more open spaces, no more months and years of research. Let somebody else do the American background and foreground. From now on I'm going to write stories all about two people in a telephone booth . . . But how I'd love to have just a tourist's look at this Oklahoma.'

"'Done and done,' said the Whites. 'It's a bit too early now, the Oklahoma roads would be mud-wallows out in the oil country just now, but if you'll come back to Emporia in May, say, we'll all pile into the car and young Bill will drive us through Oklahoma.'

"And in May I went back to Emporia, and we drove into Oklahoma, and they stayed a week with me and then they left me there, an unwilling prisoner hugging her chains, slogging through oil fields, living in sky-scraper luxury hotels, talking to old-timers who had made the Run in the 1880's, sitting in a rocking chair on a hundred front porches while I listened to tales tall but true; reading musty old letters and annals and tiny newspapers, yellowed now, in the State Historical Library in Oklahoma City, dining at the improbable palaces of white oil millionaires.

"It was hot, it was exasperating, it was fascinating, it was seemingly endless, it was Cimarron."

It must have been that she riled some of the owners of some of the front porches that she sat and rocked on. Here is a piece that appeared in a Bartlesville, Oklahoma, newspaper:

"Edna Ferber is best remembered in Bartlesville as an extremely offensive personality garnished with a profusion of hair dye and egotism. In a group at a party one evening a gentleman of education and culture, well acquainted with the state volunteered some information that he thought she might use.

"'Never mind giving me facts,' she interrupted waving her highball as a token of her displeasure. 'I am a fiction writer and don't want facts.'

"'I thought,' replied the volunteer informant, 'that I might save you from appearing ridiculous in your story. Most folks who write about Oklahoma get their facts while passing through the state at sixty miles an hour and it occurred to me that you might want to know the facts from one who has done a few things in the state and knows about it.'

"'Say, Big Boy,' she blatted in that tone children of the Ghetto are apt to use after about the third shot of Oklahoma corn, 'I know my business. Folks will be reading my books ten thousand years after they have forgotten how to spell your name. I'll find some dumb publisher who will know as little about the state as I do and he will take my story all right.'

"So the lady passed on and put together a story she calls Cimarron and pronounces the last syllable as though spelled, 'roon,' a pronunciation she never acquired in this state. She fills the story with fantastic characters that could be fabricated only by a person as ignorant of the conditions of which she wrote as Miss Ferber and accepted for publication only by publishers as dumb-witted as she declared she would find."

Although this seems too ludicrous to be hurt by, it might have pricked her all the same. She prided herself on "research manners," and was so entirely misrepresented and maligned here. To her publicist, Dan Longwell, she made a show of "above it all" good sportsmanship:

"Well, Big Boy, I'll blatt to the cock-eyed world that I found a publisher as dumb-witted as myself. Even if Bartlesville doesn't like my little epic. Return this [the piece], will you Dan dear. I want to give readings from it. Kosher Edna."

Cimarron not only was read, but was worn. An ad in the paper said: "Cimarron" . . . A SUMMER MILLINERY NOTE–A supple straw, with a romantic Western name . . . but a Paris signature. $10."

Not only read and worn, but revered:

> "IT IS WITH SINCERE APPRECIATION THAT I WANT TO THANK YOU FOR CIMARRON. IF WE HAD MORE PEOPLE IN OUR COUNTRY TODAY WITH CIMARRON IN THEIR HEARTS AND MINDS THIS WOULD BE A HAPPIER COUNTRY TO LIVE IN. SINCERELY–CLARK GABLE."

Ferber, for all her seeming neutrality about hobnobbing with married couples, had a streak of "loved him, hated her" in her nature. In many cases she veered toward the men for solid companionship, and tolerated the wives. Examples stack up: William Allen White-Sallie White; Marc Connelly, Robert Sherwood-Madeline Connelly, later Madeline Sherwood; Leland Heyward-Margaret Sullavan Heyward; George Kaufman-Beatrice Kaufman; Harold Ross-Jane Grant Ross; and Louis Bromfield-Mary Bromfield, with whom she spent the summer of 1929 in Socoa, France.

Now, she attributes some of her best writing on *Cimarron* to the peace and perfection of that summer she spent with "dear Louis" and "dear Mary." In truth, she was hellishly depressed, got scant work done, and quarreled with Mary all the time. Her diary reveals what she really thought of "dear Mary."

Entry: "To Pergola with Louis and Mary. One of Mary's hysterical scenes."

Entry: "Little work done. Frightful headache because of that Bromfield woman."

In her novels, Ferber's women were of the highest caliber. In reality, she thought most of them were tiresome, prattling, and venal. The exceptional few, of course, were her friends for life. As for the others, off with their empty little heads.

In 1928, Ferber could well afford to be spiritually beneficent. Never was there such a sense of well-being in a woman made up of sizable angers. The reason breaks down into two successive nights. On December 2, 1927, Jerome Kern and Oscar Hammerstein's *Show Boat*—based on Ferber's 1926 novel—opened at the Ziegfeld Theatre in New York. On December 29, 1927, Ferber's and Kaufman's second play, *The Royal Family*, opened at the Selwyn Theatre in New York. Ferber's name was attached to two of the biggest Broadway hits of that, or any other, season. Old gal Ferber was rolling royally along.

First nights first. *Show Boat*, which Ferber referred to as her "oil-well," was a classic from the moment it dropped anchor on stage. It was a breakthrough in American musical theatre. Some consider it to be the first important American musical theatre production. It was not vaudeville; it was not operetta*; it was not a play with incidental music, or music and lyric with an incidental play; it was not a revue, nor a musical comedy. It was musical theatre. It was *Show Boat*.

Sorry, but never was there such a score. Brooks Atkinson thought so too:

"For such musical drama no tin-pan clatter of eclectic melodies suffices. In providing 'Show Boat' with a full complement of 'song hits' Mr. Kern has not violated his sense of the fitness of things. 'Old Man River,' sung by Jules Bledsoe, intones the silent mastery of a mighty stream. 'Can't Help Lovin' That Man,' in all its interpolations, is pure negro in its folklore mysticism. The rest of his score runs from the dry mockery of 'Life Upon the Wicked Stage' to the warm romance of 'You Are Love,' never hackneyed, always charming. Even the jazz tunes become integral parts of the score."

Possibly, I'm overreacting when I say that *Show Boat*'s score is a great one, instead of a wonderful score. I grew up on this music. Songs from *Show Boat* were my lullabies. My mother Janet used to select them for me according to my moods, or hers. No Band-Aids or aspirins or kisses were as soothing as those songs. Her favorite, and the one she knew every single word to, was "Can't Help Lovin' Dat Man." I used to think it was called "Fish Gotta Swim" because that was the opening lyric to the song. "Sing Aunt Edna's fish song," I would beseech my mother, having no understanding of the song's sultry syntax, or of the fact that Ferber didn't write it. I only knew that it worked wonders on scratches and bruises.

Then there was "Bill," which I used to think was written for my

* In the known style of Sigmund Romberg and Victor Herbert.

Uncle Bill, when he married Mina in 1949. Kids have little sense of time proportion. "Bill" was Ferber's favorite song, possibly because it echoed some of her own emotions for Bill White—although Hammerstein couldn't have known that when he wrote it. But some of the lyrics certainly evoke my vision of Bill White, and perhaps they did Ferber's:

"And along came Bill. He's not the type at all. You'd meet him on the street and never notice him. His form and face, his manly grace, are not the kind that you would find in a statue. And yet—I can't explain—it's surely not his brain that makes me thrill. It's 'cause he's . . . I don't know . . . It's cause he's just my Bill."

The word great implies immortality. I would say that the songs from *Show Boat* have a good crack at it.

I hear that when Helen Morgan sang "Bill" one would have been awfully hardboiled not to have wept. Said Ferber of Morgan, reflecting back on the Boston tryout, "Little did anyone know that the skinny girlie who hoisted herself up on the piano would become a star from this show."

Brooks Atkinson, often reticent with praise, and not given to grandiose statements, admitted that, "Show Boat becomes one of those epochal works about which garrulous old men gabble for twenty-five years after the scenery has rattled off to the storehouse . . . One is not disposed to pick trifling flaws in such a captivating production. Show Boat is woven of beauties."

It was Brooks Atkinson's year for being courtly. In his review, he assures Ferber and Kaufman that they were not wasting each other's time:

"After viewing the theatrical profession sentimentally in 'Show Boat' Miss Ferber has executed an about-face by viewing it ironically in 'The Royal Family,' written in collaboration with George S. Kaufman. Their play is one of the most enjoyable of the season. Nothing could make for completer exploitation of its theme than this collaboration of a fiction writer, primarily concerned with plot and characters, and a satirist remarkable for his neat, critical dialogue and his skill in play technique. After completing a play . . . even the collaborator is never quite sure of how much of the work is his . . . Whatever the sources of its capital humors may be, 'The Royal Family' molds them perfectly . . . Jed Harris, the high priest of 'Broadway' and 'Coquette,' has produced it."

"I saw the 'high priest' of low character's 'Coquette' twice,"

Ferber wrote to Fan, "and bellered as much the second time as the first. Helen [Hayes] does a beautiful job in it, doesn't she?"

Ferber was having as much of a whirl as she could permit herself. The *cognoscenti* were converging upon her. Jerome Kern named his new yacht *Show Boat* and asked her to christen it. She lunched with Gene Markey and dined with Woollcott. People flew East to see her: "Kathleen and Charles Norris here from San Francisco to visit lil ol' me. I call that custom service." She took part in hijinks: "I've just come from Woollcott's where I saw a motion picture of myself—the first I've seen—taken last Sunday when I was there at one of his Sunday morning breakfasts that begin at noon and last until six. The pictures were taken casually, sort of strolling one by one out on the balcony overhanging the river, and they're amusing. Woollcott, Alice Duer Miller, Ruth Draper, Charles MacArthur, Ben Hecht, Madge Kennedy, Kathleen and Charles Norris, Neysa McMein, all behaving rather foolishly, but not as cock-eyed as you'd think." She had soirees: "Tomorrow night Ray Long—editor of Cosmo—Woollcott, Faye and Walter Lippmann, Lynn and Alfred are coming to dinner." And went rather grudgingly to them—suddenly moral and questioning about the social mores of her time: "I may go to Conde Nast's for a half hour after the Guild play Sunday night, just to take a look. He always says, in his invitation, that he is giving 'a little dance' or a 'little dinner.' And there are always hundreds . . . I suppose social ambition is as worthy as any ambition, but it always makes me a little sick to see people elbowing and crawling and scheming to be seen with people who despise them, or care nothing about them." She staged a generous tribute: "I'm expecting the Hunters [Charles Hunter and Beulah Adams, of the James Adams Floating Palace Theatre] on Wednesday. They're the people who were so darling to me when I was down on their show boat. They haven't seen the show, and I'm sending them, of course, and getting seats for anything else they may want to see. And I thought I'd throw them one whale of a bash."

The Hunters were both showboat troupers; the owners and stars of a showboat in North Carolina. They were invaluable sources for Ferber's research, and without their showboat, there would have been no *Show Boat*. Ferber had jollied it up with all of the Hunters' friends and the acting company on their showboat, and she had promised them that when they came to New York—all expenses paid—they would meet her friends. That was some group of friends. She gathered every highlight of the theatre world that she could find, and put them together in a blazing glory of party giving. Gertrude Lawrence, Ina Claire, Constance Collier, Noel Coward, Helen Hayes, the Lunts, the Kaufmans, Moss Hart, Katharine Cornell, Marc Connelly, etc., and the Hunters, who, in their quiet way, went home bursting and sated—knowing that they'd seen the true Green Pastures.

This time of extraordinary recognition caused Ferber to be extraordinarily sentimental, drawing her family to her "brust," as Julia used to call breast. Slightly guilty, she tried to square her success and her love for them all in a letter to Fan. Knowing how Ferber and Fan ended up makes the letter seem almost a charlatan's.

"About families, Doll. No one is fonder of her family than I am. I don't string along with you when you say in your letter that you think 'families should see quite a lot of each other while life lasts for them.' I object to the should see', having a horror of just that kind of duty thing and dependence thing. I think it is nice for families or members of families to see as much as they want of those they are fond of. I happen to be cuckoo about you and Jan and Minnow. Unfortunately I have always been buried to my eyebrows in work that is pretty racking, so that it has been impossible, perhaps, for me to spend as much time or even thought on you (or with you) folks as I might otherwise have done. But I have comforted myself in the thought that maybe that work has made up in other ways to you all. As for mother—well I suppose I am fonder of her than any of her family is. It is true that she is difficult and nerve-racking, and that living together as we have for twenty years life has often seemed too impossible for me. There's a case where, if we had seen less of each other we would both have been happier in many ways. I know you know that I love you more than anyone in the world. Good night, Doll."

There is telltale proof that Ferber was somewhat relishing the fuss being made over her because she was deeply concerned about clothes and chic. To Fan:

"Farber is going over my mink coat and my old black mess. He is making me the collar for my red suit . . . and I am having a band of fur put around the bottom of my red velvet evening coat. It makes it simply magnificent and of course much longer. It is cool here and loads of people are wearing fur coats, especially caracul . . . fur coats seem to be no longer. Everyone is wearing their fur coats short, with the long dresses and tails showing beneath. Long fur coats are so clumsy and hick looking I think. I'm not having mine lengthened . . . All my shoes are taking a sun bath on the balcony, where the evening slippers look very queer, like old chorus girls that can't stand the daylight. I wish I could spend the day (or an hour) out there in the sun myself. But instead I have to go out and fit a corset and fit a blouse and fit a sport suit that is hideous and clumsy. I wish I could resign myself to being a complete frump. Then I'd be much happier."

More belle than frump, Ferber was extending, expanding, and enjoying herself more than she ever would again. She was drinking socially: "Had four highballs in a row. Felt no pain. Felt better than I have in years." She was staying up late: "I gave a little party, late, and asked Noel, Jerry and Eva Kern, Louis and Mary Bromfield, Dicky Rodgers and George Kaufman. It turned out so nice, with Jerry, Noel and Dicky at the piano. They stayed until almost four in the morning, and I enjoyed it so much that I actually didn't get sleepy for some strange reason."

She was having a high time during, of all times, the Depression. It must have been almost a "touch wood" philosophy that made her abstain from mentioning the suffering that was all around her. In a letter home she gives short mention—itemizing like a shopping list—who of her friends went broke:

"Herb Swope lost about seven million (which leaves him precious little, let me tell you) Gerald Brooks a million and a half, Al Barach his shirt, F.P.A. cleaned, Phil Barry pretty nearly everything."

But Ferb's band played on:

"A party at midnight at the Lunt-Fontannes—with only eight people asked and a five-piece Hungarian orchestra playing for us, like royalty, all during the evening. We had supper (blinis, which are those Russian pancakes with caviar and sour cream; and tiny chops and Julienne potatoes, and salad and ice cream and cake and coffee) up in the living room, with the orchestra playing anything we wanted to hear. It was divine. Woollcott, Thornton Wilder, Greta Kemble-Cooper, Dr. Eskell, Charlie Brackett, and the Lunts. We left at 5, me dying."

This time of life should have been a solo flight for Ferber; she should have soared alone. It wasn't and she didn't. She was constantly to be grounded, thwarted and bettered by Julia. She shared veiled bitchy feelings toward Julia with her confidante of the day, Fan:

"Mama is out to dinner tonight, tomorrow and Thursday nights and, I believe, Saturday. She wore your black satin and it looked very nice, but it was, I thought, a little low in the back for her. You have to have a flat fine back to wear a low cut dress like that. I hate to see older women in them. But mama had had it made over, and liked it very much, and the dress, as a whole, did look very nice on her. I s'pose."

Ferber would dance; Julia would dance till dawn. Ferber would win a game; Julia would win the jackpot. Ferber would have nine invitations; Julia would have ten—including herself in Ferber's nine, with one extra. Ferber would eat the oysters; Julia would string the pearls. Ferber would have aces; Julia, a royal flush.

Fanny Butcher remembers that in Chicago, when Ferber would be courted by a young man, Julia would assume that she was really the one who was being courted. Eventually, Ferber gave up and courted Julia herself.

There were reasons for this damaged devotion, or so Ferber was convinced. Because she had seen what shabby, emotionally empty young womanhood her mother had, she'd vowed to make it up to her. She must have thought she knew best.

MOTHER KNOWS BEST
1927-1911

"THAT FORCE of Ma Quail's, in terms of power units—amperes, kilowatts, pounds—would have been sufficient to light a town, run a factory, move an engine. The girl had had plenty of spirit, too, at first. But it had been as nothing compared to the woman's iron quality. If ever a girl owed everything to her mother, that girl was Sally Quail. She said so, frequently. So did Ma Quail."

The quote is taken from "Mother Knows Best," the title short story in a collection that Ferber had published in 1927. Briefly, the story concerns a relentlessly driving mother and her actress daughter, who come out of Wisconsin and go to Chicago and then New York, where the daughter gains fame and fortune. They are definitely a couple—mother and daughter—until one day the girl meets a young hoofer with whom she falls madly in love. The mother, threatened, destroys the relationship. The girl, dependent, lets her. It is the victory of the mother's life, and the tragedy of the daughter's, who dies an untimely death from a mysterious fever, which presumably links to an unmended heart. What happens on her deathbed is overdramatic, unlikely, and stirring:

"She sat up in bed as though she were strong and well again. All the little lines in her face were wiped out queerly, completely, as though by a magic hand. She lifted her chin a little with a shy upward eagerness and her fever-dried lips took on the tremulousness and the flexibility of the lips of a woman who knows that she is about to be kissed. Her arms were outstretched, her eyes fixed on something that she found wonderful and beautiful.

" 'Sally!' Ma Quail had screamed. 'Sally! What is it! What is it! Oh, my God! Look at me. It's Mother! Mother loves you!'

"And, 'Oh, I love you, too!' said Sally Quail. Her voice was a breath, a whisper."

The word was out that the story was patterned after the actress Elsie Janis and her "Mama Rose" of a mother. Ferber contended that the relationship was based on that suffered by actress-comedienne Mabel Hite with her bruiser mother. It was neither of the above. The nub of the story is pure Ferber and Julia, and is worked out at a level of bitter-sweet fantasy. Ferber, always wanting to have been an actress, never liking her stocky looks, has transported herself into an ethereal pastel-like creature of the stage. She has rendered herself harmless against her mother, but has allowed herself the love of her life—thwarted—but there in her spirit forever. She has unleashed deep-seated resentment and drawn the Julia-figure mother as a monster. It is the closest to psychological home that Ferber ever reached on paper.

Ferber attributed her writing of *Show Boat* to the well-known producer Winthrop Ames, who, for a producer, was unusually gentle and gentlemanly. To make good her thanks toward him, she dedicated the book: "To Winthrop Ames who first said Show Boat to me." Ferber elaborates on how from a so-so play a showboat sprang:

"Perhaps those bearded freudian gentlemen who hail from Vienna and who insist that our adult character and actions can be traced directly back to early childhood impressions could give me some information on how I happened to write a novel dealing largely with the Mississippi River. Certainly my knowledge of the Mississippi River amounts to practically nothing. I once spent two hours on it.

"The Viennese viewpoint, I suppose, would necessitate my peering back into the dim dark past when I was eight years old. At the age of eight I lived in Iowa. Gra'ma and Grampa Neumann lived in Chicago, Illinois. When you live in Ottumwa, Iowa (which I hope you don't) and your grandparents live in Illinois your visits to them necessitate your crossing the Mississippi River—on a train, of course. That Chicago-bound train undoubtedly passed through the usual midwest countryside; rich farmland, woodland, small towns.

But one thing, and one thing alone, remained in my memory. The River.

" 'When are we coming to it?' I would ask my mother.

" 'Pretty soon.'

"And then again. 'Are we nearly there?'

" 'Almost.'

". . . For some reason that I cannot explain the river had held for me a mystery, a fascination, a terror, even, that has stayed in my subconscious through the years.

"That early impression must have sunk deep, deep. For example, the novel Show Boat wasn't meant to be called Show Boat at all, for the excellent reason that when I first contemplated writing it I had never heard of a show boat. It was to have been a novel entirely laid around the old Chicago Clark Street gambling days. In the meantime, George S. Kaufman and I had written a play called 'Minick.' There were long hours of rehearsal, and weary nights of tryouts in small towns outside New York. It was to be brought into New York in September. The August preliminaries day after day, night after night, found us all weary, hot, depressed, as is usually the case. Mr. Winthrop Ames, the producer, said one day, 'Some day let's all run away and join a show boat troupe on the Mississippi and forget there are things like Broadway, and First Nights.'

" 'What's a show boat?' said I.

"He told me. And as he told me the Mississippi that had lain dorment in my mind all these years lashed out with her terrible tawny tail and with that one blow sent old Clark Street reeling back just about fifty thousand words."

Ames and Ferber, having been professional friends during *Minick*, were friend-friends ever after those two words were spoken; and a hot night in August, 1927, found her at his and his wife Lucy's house in Providence, Rhode Island, drinking "highballs, cocktails, champagne and gin fizzes steadily all the time."

In those early years of Ferber's and Julia's living in New York, Julia was still socially attached to Chicago, and would return frequently, for spells of mahjong playing and wedding and funeral going. This left Ferber free to take weekends with friends, such as the Ameses. She would report to Fan, via newsletter, the spectrum of these weekends—who-how-what for dinner—she didn't-he couldn't—knowing full well that Julia would be peering over Fan's shoulder. It wasn't so much that she tried to lord her good times over them, as that she wanted Fan and Julia to live them vicariously. Julia's being away made her slightly giddy. Her success in New York had not reached full throttle yet; and a weekend with people like the Ameses was big stuff. In a letter discussing the weekend, Ferber conveys the headiness and the confusion of being nearly at the top of the heap.

". . . After drinking a great deal I emerged feeling better than I have in a long time. I think I shall go in for drinking in a big serious way. (Shrieks of horror from Mrs. F.).

". . . The house is an old stone thing, too restful for words. The trees are huge English oaks, and there are great stretches of old lawn, and rose gardens, and terraces and fountains and pools, and yet it isn't at all the regular country place you see in Vanity Fair or House Beautiful, or that kind of garbage.

"The people who bought Mother Knows Best want now to make a part talky of it. I said that they would have to pay for it as much as they are paying for Ain't Nature Wonderful . . . and so they are paying an additional $1500, which is velvet.

"Also . . . Universal has made an insane offer which I would like your advice about. They want an option on the picture rights of my novel, sight unseen. They will pay whatever I ask for the option ($10,000 I suppose) and agree to pay whatever I ask for the picture if they want it after they have read the story, and to lose the option money if they don't want it. What do you think? It sounds cuckoo. I hear it's never been done.

"I sometimes wish I were back on the Appleton Wisconsin Daily Crescent.

"No, I don't either.

"Dear Mom, I shan't be psycho-analyzed—at least not until everything else has failed. But it seems to me I'd do almost anything to be un-nervous again, and not to look like a piece of cheese."

There never was a nerveless time for Ferber. She was unique, knew it, and paid the Freudian piper by wrestling with various tics and psychologically induced physical woes. One would think that she almost tried to birth an ulcer, for in 1927, her first possibility of an ulcer occurred. She treated it and herself to three weeks of bed rest, and recorded wryly in her notebook:

"I have been busy trying to get my life into some kind of shape.

It was running like a bride's first attempt at grape jell. I did quite a lot of thinking about one thing and another during my three weeks in bed. I rebelled and roared and tore at the bed clothes that first week. But then I calmed down and rather enjoyed it. I haven't had such a complete rest since I spent nine months in Mrs. Ferber's womb, and even that wasn't such a bed of roses, I should say, if I know that lady and if my memory serves me."

During her stay in bed, she kept a rather amazing notebook that is full of cryptic, epigrammatic, ironically enough, ulcerated thoughts. The contents of the notebook display a different Ferber than those of any other that has surfaced.

In her diaries there is an on-guard quality; in this special notebook there is an unguarded one. Some of the passages are bizarre, curdled—especially the ones dealing with men. Her stage of mind when writing this notebook seems to represent the woman forming into the Ferber. So here is a bit of the sickbed stream of consciousness of Edna Ferber—1927:

"There are these people who say, 'Come and take pot-luck with us. We won't put ourselves out a bit. I'll just put on an extra plate, that's all.' I hate them. I like the old-fashioned hostess. I like to know that she is scurrying around in the kitchen beating up a special sauce; sending out frantically for a half-pint of cream. Opening a can of mushrooms; jabbing at the bland cork of a bottle of fat ripe olives; gouging the puffy heart out of a grape-fruit. The casual pot roast, the family lamb stew, potted but unluckily, fill me with no anticipatory joy."

"He's the apple of my eye . . . Your eye! Your eye's an orchard."

"Why is it always the wrong man who sends you roses?"

"I don't want you to put your arm around me. I don't know you yet. It's like eating your dessert before you've had your soup."

"The masher: When he dies it will be of lipstick poisoning."

"My desire or will to power probably is satisfied in another way. I have very little desire to save young men from their baser selves . . . I've arrived at the age when boy flappers are supposed to appeal to me, but they don't. They bore me to death with their limpid eyes and their sex talk."

"Asked if in love with a certain man, 'I've often wondered about that.' When a woman wonders if she's in love, the chances are she isn't."

"This lethal sugar plum (Margalo*)."

"Stuffed prunes—Plumbridge—great prunes stuffed with lesser prunes, like cannibalistic creatures who eat their young."

"I'm so sick of getting up early and doing setting-up exercises and sitting in front of a typewriter and putting words down on paper. I'm going to buy a black lace nightgown and never get up."

"Collector's Item: He says he likes to see the reaction of his love-making."

"Middle-aged actress. Crepey skin. 'Crepey! It's acordion pleated.'"

"Bill White—Saves glass of water from overturning at dinner—is praised for it—'I only did what any loyal American would have done in my case.'"

"Wise people are generally unwise in their own lives. Socrates—the hemlock cup."

"I don't see why suicide is looked upon with such horror. Without the thought of it to sustain us many of us could not live."

There was a young writer spawned out of the forties named Tom Heggen, who wrote a novel called *Mister Roberts,* which was converted into a play and later a movie. This one property caused him enormous, overpowering success—and anguish. He couldn't meet up with his own talent again. He was unable to write anything substantial again. He killed himself. Tragic, but understandable according to Ferber. Upon hearing of his death, she flashed back to her "dais-time" of *Show Boat* and *The Royal Family*—when her success had reached its pinnacle—when if she did nothing more she could do no wrong, and the feeling of the awesome responsibility of having to perpetuate that success. It had been a gruesome time, where the pleasure lay in those who applauded her, and they, fickle beings, would condemn her if she didn't continue giving them pleasure. She said that to top extraordinary success was like scaling Everest twice. Ferber didn't harbor thoughts of suicide within herself, but she sanctioned them for others.

Ferber managed to overcome her success only because of her inviolate sense of privacy. When Hollywood beckoned her, giving her carte blanche to work on anything she wanted, she wrote to William Allen White: "I took two tablespoons of Castor Oil and shut the door to my workroom."

* Margalo Gillmore.

In her letters home, when she felt that she was having too good a time, she chastised herself saying, "I had the most crowded society day I've spent in years. I never do that kind of thing." She felt like a sneak thief when she took pleasure, but in 1927, pleasure was in abundance. She was like a teetotaler tossing off a jigger of scotch and then spitting out the last small bit, as though to keep her thumb on abstinence. The emotion in her letters to the "Foxies" is "Lookit me! I'm dancing!" but she qualifies that exuberance with "Lookit me—I'm limping from all that dancing. I shouldn't have danced." Some of the trots she reported to the Foxes:

"I took a plunge into English literary society yesterday, rather unexpectedly. Conde Nast gave a quick-call luncheon for Michael Arlen, who has just landed. I sat next to Arlen, and found him really fascinating, though I suspect a rotter . . . Nast's place is too lovely. The top floor and the floor below that at the corner of Park Avenue and 86th street . . . He has the whole roof, too, which he is turning into a garden with all kinds of awnings and fountains and things. He is giving a dinner and dance on the 22nd, to which I'm invited. After that I'll take off my toe shoes . . . Arlen was awfully amusing. His play, made from the Green Hat, is in rehearsal, with Katharine Cornell in the leading part. He said it would open in Stamford, Connecticut (pronouncing all the c's), and that from there it was going to Detroit, Illinois, and he pronounced Detroit Day-trwa, in the French fashion. It was grand! In the evening I went to dinner at Charlie Towne's and met Somerset Maugham, whom I like very much . . . I'm having myself a time, a thing I must stop . . ."

No such thing. The musical of *Show Boat* was being mounted, as were the parties and the gaiety. The social skein continued:

"I'm holding my breath about the Ziegfeld thing. I had just about given it up . . . when I had a letter . . . saying that contracts were to be signed in Ziegfeld's office . . . and that I would be given notice of the hour as soon as it was arranged. Kern and Hammerstein are starting work together tomorrow, contract or no contract, evidently. Kern outlined to me a perfect whale of a story, with the river and the show boat (and a show boat performance) in the first act, and modern New York in the second. Of course I refuse to believe anything until I see all the names on the contract. Until I see the opening performance, for that matter.

"Bea and George wanted me to drive out to the Swopes', but I didn't care to. Woollcott asked me to dinner and the theater tomorrow night, but it's nothing I care to see, and I'm through going to the theater just to be going to the theater."

Ferber took gleeful license in talking about spending time with people whom she didn't like. One such being the popular novelist Fannie Hurst, whose literary reputation—to most critics' ways of thinking—was parallel to that of Ferber's. Hurst was Ferber's favorite nemesis; her nails grew at mention of the author's work. There is a statement about Hurst that Ferber was reputed to have said, and although there is no evidence, it makes for a lovely if apocryphal slap: "When Miss Hurst's work is compared to mine I become incensed. When my work is compared to hers she becomes ecstatic." That Ferber was invited and accepted dinner at Fannie Hurst's is peculiar but documented:

"Miss Hurst's dinner was pretty darned terrible if you ask me. Her apartment is on the first floor . . . It must be dark as a pocket in the daytime. Her living room is a vast and quite lovely thing, if you like a room that looks like a Roman Catholic museum. Enormous red damasks and hangings on all the walls—sheets and sheets of them—prayer benches, prayer books, hanging lamps, priest's robes, pulpits, whatnots and whosises. I couldn't stand it. Her guests were a motley lot . . . Papa Hurst wasn't there. I think she only takes him when she goes to the theater, like a taxi. The dinner was abominable. Nothing well cooked, nothing hot (except the champagne). I blew at about 10:30 and staggered up to Woollcott's apartment a few doors away, where I had to be revived with a cracker and a glass of sherry. Then we went to Kit Cornell's party, which was very nice."

It is doubtful that before 1926 there were any baby girls being named Kim, for the name did not exist for a girl. Its coinage was Ferber's; its debut was in *Show Boat*; its owner was the daughter of the novel's heroine and antihero, who was born and raised on the showboat of the title. Ferber derived the name from the proximity of the states of Kansas, Illinois, and Missouri. The name went on to sizable popularity in the late forties and fifties. Kim Stanley, Kim Novack, and Kim Hunter are a few well-known ladies who sport it.

At the time of publication, *Show Boat* was not known for the name Kim as much as for the volatile subject of miscegenation, and the damage suit threatened by one Tom Taggart, a former United

States Senator whose name Ferber referred to in her novel as being connected with a gambling casino. Here are the reportorial facts that emerged from Ferber's fiction:

"Nelson Doubleday of Doubleday, Page & Co., publishers of Edna Ferber's novel, 'Show Boat,' announced today that all reference to Tom Taggart in the novel would be eliminated in future editions.

"This is believed to be satisfactory to Mr. Taggart, who threatened to bring suit for $100,000 damages for libel against the publishing house on the ground that he was mentioned in the book as a professional gambler.

"Miss Ferber also is agreeable to the change, Mr. Doubleday said. Miss Ferber, at her home, 50 Central Park West, refused to take any part in the controversy.

"Mr. Taggart, Democratic boss of Indiana and former United States Senator, claimed his character was damaged by a passage on page 303 of 'Show Boat' in which one of the characters said: 'Let's go down to Tom Taggart's and take some of his money.'

"Mr. Doubleday said the presses had been stopped and the name Tom Taggart changed to some ficticious name—Sam something. Sam was selected as having the same length as Tom and another name with the same number of letters as Taggart was substituted, he said.

"There are 135,000 copies of the first edition of 'Show Boat' already sold or in book stalls. These cannot be called in, Mr. Doubleday said. He added that using real names in fiction was 'bad stuff.'

" 'The use of Mr. Taggart's name was purely incidental,' he said. 'It was not essential to the story. Any other name will do just as well. We are only too glad to make the change and Miss Ferber is likewise agreeable.' "

Ferber's concession to Tom Taggart's demands was far from agreeable, but not for the obvious reason of humiliation. Her case of distemper was not directed toward Mr. Taggart at all, but toward Doubleday's negligence in allowing the reference to go to press—after she'd checked it with them. In her lashing letter to Nelson Doubleday concerning his company's behavior, she has not yet cultivated her asp's sting, but the rudiments are there:

". . . I want to say that I did not ask you for an alibi. You say you were out of town, and I am willing to believe you. I can scarcely believe, however, that the entire staff of Doubleday Page and Company was out of town. I only know that you were, during the Taggart matter, in town long enough at least to talk on the telephone to my lawyer, Mr. Morris Ernst, and to ask his opinion on the use of names of real persons (other than Mr. Taggart) in my novel. Long enough, also, to express to him the opinion that the use of these names was a bad thing. You had the manuscript of Show Boat in your office six months before the date of publication. If you thought the use of real names a bad thing why didn't you say so at that time, to me? For that matter, I have on file a letter from me to your firm, and a reply from your firm to me, touching on this same subject. I asked you if you did not think it wise to omit the name of Heywood Broun, as he was no longer a dramatic critic. Your answer was negative.

"As for the rest of the firm, first and last, top to bottom, you've shown yourselves the shortest sports in the history of the book publishing business. I hate to have to admit it, but it's true. Not one member of the firm . . . wrote me, telegraphed me, or spoke to me to offer advice or encouragement during the Taggart unpleasantness. According to the terms of my contract you were perfectly protected. You had, therefore, nothing to fear. You might, I should think, have made at least the hollow gesture of courteous concern. Certainly I know of no publishing house that would have behaved as you did. I do know a half dozen who have expressed surprise and indignation at your actions and attitude. The single statement issued from your office was one which, had the case come to trial, would have been the strongest legal point against me.

"I was under the impression that ours was a sort of partnership. I realize now that it is, on your part at least, a catch-as-catch-can affair. Sentimental old fool that I am, I hope I have learned my lesson. If strictly business is your motto, and devil take the hindmost, I can be as businesslike as the next one.

"Believe me when I say that the Taggart matter did not upset me half as much as the Doubleday Page matter. I had no false ideas about Mr. Taggart. Fifty people have said to me, in the last two weeks, 'Why did your publishers ditch you?' And I have said, 'I don't know.'

"I am delighted to learn that Show Boat is selling well. I note, however, that it sold 10,000 three weeks ago, 7500 two weeks ago, and 6000 last week. I wonder if this drop is due to the fact that there has recently been no advertising. Sincerely, Edna Ferber."

Ferber had gotton a plethora of information about showboats from Charles Hunter. She accredits him with almost everything—save for the actual writing of the book:

"When I'm ninety and toothless I'll remember still an April afternoon spent with him two years ago down in Belhaven, North Carolina. I had come down there espcially to see the show boat and to get the proper setting for the book. For three days (spent on the show boat as the guest of the company) I had tried to pin Charles Hunter down to a long talk. He knew show boats from stem to stern, from pilot house to cook's galley; he knew the river from Minnesota to the Gulf. But he was busy, what with rehearsing, acting, directing, for he was not only juvenile lead on this boat, but director and frequently author.

". . . Finally, one afternoon, just when I had despaired of cornering him for any length of time, he slumped his lean length into a rocker up in the bright cheerful bedroom off the balcony, forward, lighted the preliminary cigarette in a great procession to follow, and began to talk. He talked for hours. He talked until evening came on, and the hour for the night's performance approached. And as he talked I repeated a silent prayer, 'Oh, Lord, don't let him stop talking!' Tales of the river. Stories of show boat life. Characterizations. Romance. Adventure. River history. Stage superstition. I had a chunk of yellow copy paper in my hand. On this I scribbled without looking down; afraid to glance away for fear of breaking the spell.

"For those readers . . . who do not like the novel Show Boat as it now stands I crave the boon of another chance. For it seems to me that there is a fair-sized volume that could be made up entirely of rich bits told me by Charles Hunter that April afternoon and that, somehow, never got into the book at all."

That April afternoon of 1924 stretched late into 1925—via letters between Ferber and Hunter. There needed to be no lagniappe as far as he was concerned. He liked her and he liked to talk and when she pumped he spilled willingly:

"If you were here," he wrote to her, "it would be much easier to answer that battery of questions you have 'flang' at me . . . I enjoy talking to you much more than writing, in other words I like Miss Edna Ferber 'human' and not the name on the back of the book."

One of the most dramatic moments in *Show Boat*—book and musical—occurs when Steve, a white man married to Julie, a black woman passing for white, pricks her finger and sucks it, thereby mingling his blood with hers to give him a percentage of black blood. Intermarriage was illegal back in the 1870 days of life along the Mississippi. Steve's gesture not only stood for his love toward his wife, but of his total lack of prejudice. The creative incident was Ferber's; the source was Charles Hunter. One can see from his letter just how she derived her version from his historical background. Hunter had the cadence of a storyteller, and it's a shame that the material he provided Ferber never got into print on its own. To do service to him through her, I present the "Miscegenation" story:

"All Southern states have a miscegenation law, but very few Northern states—I know in my home town in Ohio there are quite a few cases of white women married to negro men, but I don't know of a case of the condition being reversed. In the South it would be a pretty hard thing to find a case of a white woman and a negro man, in fact I never heard of such a case. But I can't say as much for the Southern men. Between me and you there is plenty of mixed blood in the South and it isn't all confined to the lower classes by any means.

"The 'drinking blood incident' actually happened and I knew all the parties concerned. It happened about 20 years ago and it was in Charlotte, N.C.

"At the time I was a musician in the band with what was called a 'rag front' carnival. You see some of the carnivals at that time had elaborately carved wooden fronts to their shows, but the smaller outfits simply had painted banners pulled up on poles in front of their attractions, hence the name of 'rag fronts.'

"One of the attractions was The Old Plantation, or the South Before the War. All carnivals had one of these attractions in the old days, and still have. The show was an all negro one and consisted of songs and dances—something like a colored minstrel, but they all ended the same—that is with 'Uncle Eph's Return.' Uncle Eph would be the best dancer in the troupe, and he would be supposed to come back from up North after a long absence. To lead up to one sure-fire laugh, the old 'mammy' would introduce each of them as one of Uncle Eph's children grown-up, but there would always be one small 'pickaninny' hiding behind mammy's skirts and Uncle Eph would discover it last and when he would begin to question mammy about this one she would give him this answer . . .

"Eph . . . Mammy, who is dat button headed youngster hidin' behind you all?'

"Mammy . . . 'Why Eph! Dats dat postal card you sent me.'

"Well, 'our man' had one of these 'Plantation Shows.' His last name was Henry; I never heard his first name. He was a quiet gentlemanly sort of fellow, a big man with sandy hair. He knew that it was general knowledge on the show that he was associating with this 'yellow girl' so he never thrust himself on anybody.

"This girl, Bessie, was a good looking 'high yaller,' and the thing that I remember most about her was when the season was getting along in cold weather I would see her out on the 'ballyhoo'—this was a platform in front of the show where all the performers would come out and give the crowd a sample of what was to be seen inside. She would be on the 'bally' in an evening dress, low neck and short sleeves, and, of course, powdered until she was almost white, but wearing a short pair of red woolen mittens. I can see those mittens yet waving in the air, and hear her singing 'Can't You See My Heart Beats All For You.'

"Henry would be on the 'ticket box' watching her every move as he was violently jealous of the bass drummer.

"We had never known of him actually living with this woman until Charlotte, N.C. where he discharged one of his employes. It seems that he was living out in the negro quarter with her, and this man reported to the authorities. Henry was tipped off by one of his men that they were going to arrest him, and he knew what the penalty was in the South. The colored boy who did the tipping is the one who told us that he saw Henry take a needle and prick her thumb and suck the blood. For in the South, one drop of negro blood makes you a negro.

"Henry went on the stand and swore that he had negro blood in him. I didn't hear the case but they tell me that the Judge scorned him unmercifully, and told him that if he had sworn to a lie to evade the law he had worse than negro blood in him.

"Of course that settled his connection with the carnival, but we learned later that he continued to live with her as man and wife although they were not married, until she deserted him for a big black negro who worked for him called 'Capudine Bill'—from the fact that Bill would take a 25 cent bottle of Capudine headache medicine and drink it straight down to get a kick out of it.

"And that's that. I can't squeeze another thing in it to save me."

Ferber wanted to repay Charles Hunter for his superb help, and shortly after the manuscript was completed she sent him a whopper of a check. He wrote to her thanking her and saying, "If I ever need it I'll write and ask if it's all right to cash it. Who knows?"

Many years later the James Adams Floating Palace Theatre sank, destroying everything that Charles Hunter's life was made of. It was then that he cashed the check.

Always when Ferber had a book out that she was pleased with, she treated herself to travel, rest, insuredly good meals, and perhaps a bit of work. Feeling beneficent in the spring and summer of 1926, she treated Julia to the same, relinquishing that "bit of work," of course, for with Julia around there was no such thing as Do Not Disturb.

The only treat that counted of that day was to go abroad. Everyone who was anyone did, and Julia, by proxy, was certainly someone. The literati were represented on the ship going over. The cast included: Marc and Madeline Connelly, Russel and Alison Crouse, Robert Sherwood, Edna and Julia Ferber. Marc Connelly remembers that at meals Ferber would eat at a separate table with Julia. He shrugs it off as a simple mannerism of the two women—nothing to discuss behind menus:

"We were individualists all," he reminisces. "We recognized a fellow individual. Edna was an eternal maiden lady who traveled with her mother. That was all."

Ferber would have grimaced at his simplification of her complex situation. She grumbled to Fan about the first strain of their trip together—and they were barely off the boat:

"How dumb of me not to have sent you a cable when we landed. I always do when I'm alone, of course, but when mother says 'How foolish!' one sort of doesn't, as one of the things it's easier not to do than to fight about. There are so many things I have to do in spite of opposition that I suppose I haven't enough energy to last me for everything."

Golf was the sport of the gentry—both domestic and abroad, and although the picture of Ferber putting and parring is incongruous, she did just that in St. Jean de Luz, France, at the Golf Hotel. She wrote home about her golf swings temporarily replacing her written ones:

"I had a golf lesson this morning from a funny bony Scotchman who bawled me out from beginning to end. He taught me more in that hour than I had ever learned in all these years . . . I drove some awfully good balls . . . You've no idea how the days slip by, with nothing done in them. I always wondered what it would be like to be idle. And now I know. And I don't like it. Of course, it would be different, I suppose, if I were traveling with some one my own age, who played golf and walked, and all that. . . . I haven't done any work so far, but I'm going to start a short story now, if I can. This being with mama all day is too frightful. I feel as if I had had typhoid."

But she made the best of it, attempting to enjoy Julia's enjoyment:

"Yesterday mama and I drove to Biarritz and shopped and looked around, and had tea and came home. Mama has had a grand time running around the little shops of the village having brassieres made, and looking into antique shops. She likes it immensely. . . . We are planning a motor trip after leaving here, taking a car and chauffeur to Pau, Lourdes, Luchon—then on to Carcassone, then Nimes, Avignon, up to Geneva, and into Switzerland . . . After that I don't know what we'll do. Probably Austria and maybe Baden-Baden."

After a week of motoring together, both mother and daughter were in dire need of being massaged and restored at Baden-Baden, the famous spa. Ferber convinced Julia that a week's more restoration would do marvels for her, and took off, alone, for Paris, which she found in its postwar state to be less than desirable:

"Things are queer in Paris, and I have written mama not to come back here on her way home unless I write her that there is no danger of unpleasantness to Americans. The situation is fantastic beyond anything you can imagine. Envy and jealousy and spite against the Americans, because our currency is stable, and because we can't see why we should present France with her war debt, has turned into actual hate against us, so that we are the most unpopular nation on earth today. When I left Baden-Baden there was, in my train compartment at Strasbourg . . . a lovely American woman . . . She heard me speak German to the porter. We were the only Americans on the long train. It was packed jammed with fat Germans speeding merrily on their way to Paris to spend their marks. The American woman, hearing me, said, 'Oh, how fortunate you are to speak German. I wish I could.'

"I said that German wasn't much use in Europe, and that if she could speak enough French to get around, she was much better off. But she said no, that wasn't it. She meant that if she could speak German she would feel so much more comfortable in Paris. Can you beat that! And today I saw for myself that it is actually true. The Germans are much more popular here than the Americans. I saw three sight-seeing buses loaded with Germans today, all flying a small German flag, because that protected them. A few days ago a French crowd had set upon a bus load of Americans. Isn't that too grimly funny! In Paris!" And then, referring back to expansive home-book ground: "You'll be glad to know that the advance sales of Show Boat are very good indeed. They are getting out a first edition of between 75,000 and 100,000." And then ending in a twinge of guilt about the old lady whom she'd left at Baden-Baden: "I'm sailing on the France. I'd really feel more comfortable if mama sailed with me, and I've written her to do that if she wants to. Though she could comfortably sail from Hamburg or Southampton, and probably will."

The play *Minick*, produced by Winthrop Ames in 1924, was too gentle to be a hit. It didn't have—Ferber's pet word—enough "brio." It was based on one of her short stories called "Old Man Minick" and it had been George S. Kaufman's idea to dramatize it into the first play that they would write together. The *Herald Examiner*'s review did not exactly herald their togetherness:

". . . It is so 'natural' that you forget you are in the Playhouse. Sometimes you fancy you are at home. Sometimes you yawn, as you do at home . . . There is no 'love interest,' 'no sex,' not even rough language in 'Minick.' It is as natural as a pain in the back . . ."

To have their play compared to a twinging sciatic nerve was not an auspicious beginning. Even Ferber's friend Woollcott turned critic on her, giving the play short and violent shrift in his review for the New York *Times*. Ferber accounts—with a sort of low dudgeon—how she and Kaufman happened to do the play in the first place:

"I had a letter fom George Kaufman whom I knew slightly. He had a number of successful plays to his credit, written, for the most part, in collaboration with Marc Connelly. He had read my short story Old Man Minick. He thought there was a play in it. Would I care to collaborate with him in writing it?

"I didn't think there was a play in Minick, and I don't to this day . . . But if George had approached me with the idea of dramatizing McGuffey's First Reader I'd have been enchanted to talk about it. We met in the apartment up in 86th Street in which he and his wife Beatrice were living. George was still dramatic editor of the New York Times, a job he clung to long after he became spectacularly successful. That meeting between George, Beatrice and me has been followed by . . . years of friendship, full of ups and downs, with the ups definitely predominating . . .

"'Minick's a play,' George said now.

"'No. I don't think audiences would be interested in a play about an old man who comes to live with his son and daughter-in-law. But The Gay Old Dog—there's a story that would make a marvelous play.'

"Old Man Minick won. And I still think George was wrong and I was right."

Not to quibble. Out of the meager endeavor came three major gains: the continuing friendship and partnership of Kaufman; the estimable friendship of Winthrop Ames, who led her to the almost inestimable pleasure and profits of *Show Boat*.

The year 1925 was a prize-winning one for Ferber. The Pulitzer was given to her for her 1924 novel *So Big*. It was not quite won on the book's merit alone. There was a go-between—a self-appointed courier who brought affection to business. In the following series of letters the identity of the do-gooder is revealed as his quest for Ferber's Pulitzer unfolds:

DECEMBER 17, 1924: "My dear Mr. Fackenthall*: I shall look forward to the books you are sending with interest and check them back to you as soon as possible. Thank you so much for giving me this opportunity. Sincerely yours, W. A. White."

JANUARY 27, 1925: "My dear Frank†: Is Edna Ferber's 'So Big' . . . entered in the Pulitzer contest? I am one of the judges of that contest and have not received the book. I don't need the book; I have read it until I can sing it, but I want to know if it has been formally entered. Sincerely yours, W. A. White."

FEBRUARY 2, 1925: "Dear Mr. Fackenthall: Is Edna Ferber's 'So

* Organizer of the Pulitzer Prize committee.
† F. N. Doubleday, president of Doubleday, Page & Company, of Doubleday.

Big' on the list of novels entered for the Pulitzer Prize? I don't see it on the list submitted to me. I should certainly think that it should go in the first nine anyway . . . Sincerely yours, W. A. White."

FEBRUARY 10, 1925: "Dear Mr. Fackenthall: I seem to have forgotten the other members of my committee to consider the Pulitzer Novel Prize. I shall be glad to have their names and addresses. Sincerely yours, W. A. White."

After securing Ferber's position on the list, and the names of the two other members of the jury, White proceeded.

MARCH 7, 1925: "My dear Mr. Firkins: I have been looking over the novels of the Pulitzer Contest. It seems to me that not more than two or three are available. My judgement is that everything considered, Edna Ferber's 'So Big' is the best of the lot . . . Sincerely yours, W. A. White."

An exact duplicate of this letter was sent to another member of the committee, a Dr. Fletcher, to whom, on March 9, 1925, he wrote:

"Dear Dr. Fletcher: I feel somewhat as you do about the novels in the Pulitzer Prize contest. I believe I listed a few in a letter the other day—notably 'So Big,' Plume's and Hergesheimer's novel, which might be possible winners. But on the other hand, I wouldn't insist that either of those were an outstanding book, though I believe 'So Big' is a thing which tremendously needs to be said. If you and Mr. Firkins feel that the award should be abrogated for this year, I don't feel strongly enough for 'So Big' to make any serious objection.

"I am, however, a little bit fearful that our refusal to make an award will be misunderstood. The question will arise then: What becomes of the money? Will it be a two thousand award next year or will it go into the principal, or what? All these things will have something to do with my decision, although not a great deal. Sincerely yours, W. A. White."

MARCH 9, 1925: "Dear Mr. White: It is certainly time for us to get together, since the time limit is March 15th, only six days hence . . . I have not even seen 'So Big'; but if you put it first, we ought all to read it . . . As for the other books, I agree with you in dividing my interest pretty equally between BALISAND and PLUMES; but I prefer BALISAND . . . Between you and me agreement should not be difficult; Of Mr. Fletcher's feelings I know only that he likes none of the books well and is half disposed to renounce the project of award. Very truly yours, O. W. Firkins."

MARCH 11, 1925: "Dear Mr. Firkins: I am sending you on this mail a copy of 'So Big.' I wish you would give it a careful reading It is nothing in its favor to tell you that it has been on the list of the Best Sellers in America for the last ten months but that does indicate something in the way of appreciation of the average man . . . I feel as you do about Balisand, but I rather think 'So Big' is a better novel, though we won't have a quarrel about that. Sincerely yours, W. A. White."

APRIL 3, 1925: "Trustees of the Pulitzer Prize Fund: Gentlemen: I beg to submit the following report of the Jury consisting of Mr. William Allen White, Professor O. W. Firkins, and myself, on the prize for the best novel of 1924.

"The jury has come to no full agreement. The issue hangs, however between three novels: Joseph Hergesheimer's Balisand, Edna Ferber's So Big, and Lawrence Stalling's Plumes. Mr. White's first choice is So Big. Professor Firkin's is Balisand. For second choice both Mr. White and Professor Firkins name Plumes. If a positive choice by the Trustees is desired, I should prefer, myself, Balisand, but my greater preference under the circumstances would be to divide the prize between Balisand and So Big . . . Regretting that I am unable to present a more definitive decision I remain Sincerely yours, Jefferson B. Fletcher."

William Allen White was not a politician for nothing. The outcome—granted by default—was that the prize went to *So Big*. White traces for Ferber how this came about in his victory blessing to her:

APRIL 28, 1925: "Dear Edna: As you may or may not know, the judges in the novel contest were Professor O. W. Firkins . . . Professor Jefferson D. Fletcher . . . and your obedient servant. You remember last January when I was talking to you, I asked you when 'So Big' was published. I asked it because in looking over the list of the novels submitted, 'So Big' was not listed. I immediately wrote to Doubleday-Page and Company asking them to submit a copy which they did, but sent just one copy when they should have sent one to each of the judges. When it came to reading the novels, I wrote to the other judges saying that I was for 'So Big' for my first choice. Firkins had not received it. I bought a copy and sent it to him. Then when it got down to the last three, I was for you, the other two judges were for Balisand and Plumes had two second choices, mine and Firkins' as I recollect. It was not a unanimous decision and as I recollect it 'So Big' had one first choice, mine, one second choice, Fletcher's, and one third choice, Firkins'. So we arranged our grades like this:

	WHITE	FLETCHER	FIRKINS
Balisand	3	1	1
So Big	1	2	3
Plumes	2	3	2

"The rating was to be established on the book that got the lowest number of points. I received a letter from the Chairman of the Judges, Mr. Fletcher, indicating that we could not come to a unanimous decision and suggesting that I agree to 'Balisand'. I wrote him a letter of agreement and then I appealed from the decision of the judges to the committee which reviews that decision. My appeal won and 'So Big' was chosen.

"I am sending you, very confidential, all the correspondence in the case, thinking you would like to file it with the award. I am so proud and happy over the outcome.

". . . Give my love to Julia and tell her that she and I, at least, are equally proud of our angel child. Affectionately yours, Will."

A fitting postscript to the tale of the prize, and the maneuverings thereof, was what Ferber did with the money. A gossipy columnist covers the item sufficiently:

". . . She mightn't care to have me tell, but she did such a nice thing with it that I think the world deserves to know about it. The Authors' League of America has started a campaign to raise $5,000,000 as an endowment fund for needy authors. . . . Edna Ferber had turned over, in toto, and without any strings to it, the Pulitzer prize to swell the fund, which it will do not only to the extent of the money—$1,000—but immeasurable in the publicity which the act will receive."

For Ferber to have to get publicity for an act of charity was a second act of charity. She tried to shun the limelight when at all possible; but for a young woman having just won the most coveted writing prize in America, having a novel out that was sweeping this and European countries, having a movie released based on that novel, having just collaborated with George S. Kaufman, having the most enviable friends on two continents, and having a tongue that was becoming more celebrated than civil—it was no wonder that a reporter would want to bag an interview. And when she wasn't available, word-of-mouth stories about her hit the press anyway—such as an item in the Boston *Evening Transcript:*

". . . Mr. Russell Doubleday* will tell of dining in her apartment on a cold and snowy night, when she and another girl brought out an improvised ouija board and with eyes blindfolded, relayed thrilling messages from Nat Goodwin. Suddenly the girls pushed the board away, being tired, and went into a chamber to rest. She came out with the news that her friend was feeling ill, was greatly overcome by the spirit control, and she tenderly led her out and seated her in a chair, looking very pale and exhausted. It was only after the entire company had expended considerable sympathy that they discovered that the whole thing was a hoax, and that the pallor was powder skillfully applied by Miss Ferber."

She was featured in other people's literary work. Alexander Woollcott dedicated his book *Enchanted Aisles* to her. In a passage from it he draws a typical high-life party tableau, taking place at the studio of Neysa McMein, in which she is prominently featured:

"The population is widely variegated. Over at the piano Jascha Heifetz and Arthur Samuels may be trying to find what four hands can do in the syncopation of a composition never thus desecrated before. Irving Berlin is encouraging them. Squatted uncomfortably around an ottoman, Franklin P. Adams, Marc Connelly and Dorothy Parker will be playing cold hands to see who will buy the dinner that evening. At the bookshelf Robert C. Benchley and Edna Ferber are amusing themselves vastly by thoughtfully autographing her set of Mark Twain for her."

This Ferber played pranks, stayed up late, brunched and lunched, impulsively had her hair bobbed—"I always felt that I had a good line at the back of my head and I wanted to see for myself"—chatted more than expounded in interviews, laughed more than grimaced at life. This Ferber was young.

A typical newspaper description of the 1924 Ferber was: "Miss Ferber is small, with dark hair and big, brown eyes brimming over with life and fun, and her manner is absolutely natural and unaffected." All the positive adjectives that Ferber gathered had mostly to do with character. She would have surely traded the whole bundle for one "pretty," "glamorous," "fetching," or "lovely."

* Director of the editorial department, Doubleday, Page & Company.

But the "ingenuity" so often attributed to her led her, at least, to improve her looks.

The story predates the rage of rhinoplasty. One day Ferber was sitting under the dryer at Arden's salon, where she overheard a woman telling the manicurist about a Dr. Isaacs of Cincinnati, who had performed nose surgery on her. Ferber, who had always loathed her nose, leaned over and pumped the woman for information. Having been given what she wanted to know, she called the doctor and made an appointment, called Rebecca at home, telling her to pack a bag and bring it over, and left directly from Arden's to Cincinnati, Dr. Isaacs, and nose surgery. The job, being one of the first, was barely adequate compared to later progress. However, Ferber was always the better for having done it. It vastly improved her attitude, bringing her a step closer to one of her ravishing fictional heroines.*

Ferber tends to depict herself in those early days as being a vagabond—with her typewriter on her back, peddling words in exchange for shelter. When one halves the image, one sees a stylish middle-class young woman living in rather better than middle-class hotel-apartments. Ferber was never without her sense of drama—just as she was never without a decent home.

Because her fictional platform concerned the workingwoman, interviews with Ferber more often as not appeared on the "women's page." When she moved from the Hotel Majestic to 50 Central Park West, it was "apron" news. The piece captures a girlish voice—more Edna than Ferber:

"Have you ever lived in hotels for twelve years and then suddenly realise that you had signed a lease for three years for a real home? . . . I'm never going to give up this wonderful place. Never. They'll have to wheel old 'Gamma Ferber' out when they tear the building down. The very nicest thing, though, is to have a mattress that you know no one else has ever slept on. I never spent a comfortable night in a hotel bed, because the ghosts of the former occupants will hover around and disturb me.'

"We stepped over piles of sawdust, planks, beaming architects, plasterers and painters. All of the workmen seemed to catch the enthusiasm of Miss Ferber, and who wouldn't? We immediately de-

* This is the first version of how Ferber came to have her nose bobbed. The second version appears much earlier.

cided that nothing but a six-room apartment with eight windows overlooking Central Park, a Welsh sideboard, pewter candlesticks from Munich and a bedroom done in yellow and green would satisfy us.

"'This mantlepiece was adorned with writhing serpents and fat cupids, but now it's beautifully plain and with my pewter candlesticks it will be lovely,' said Miss Ferber enthusiastically.

"'The view is entirely too distracting,' said Miss Ferber. 'That's why I have my study in the back. Of course it's very nice to look down and see two Jersey cows grazing in your own front yard, but I know I wouldn't write two hundred words a day . . . At night this view is heavenly . . . all purple and black with little gold balls of light. My small niece said, "Why, it's just like the sky upside down," and it is.'

"Then the architect interrupted us for a moment and she was off to plan the arrangement of her mother's room. Miss Ferber laughed when we asked if Mrs. Ferber would be with her. 'Oh, yes; mother and I are inseparable, but I'm afraid I treated her rather badly this time. My wire was very much like 'Becky, come home. You're engaged,' for I never consulted her or anything. I just signed the lease, and then she had to come.'"

Things were not as blithe as the interview chirped them up to be. It wasn't a simple move; it was an evolution. It wasn't just a pleasant apartment to reside in: it was an offering to Julia, who had lived off and on between Chicago and New York and would now have a permanent address and daughter. Ferber was frantic. The graceful, ebullient new lease owner, cheering on the ever-helpful plasterers and painters, did not exist in her letters home to Fan. The misadventures now read like a screen vignette featuring the Marx Brothers and Margaret Dumont as Edna Ferber.

"The last day or two before mama came made a sort of hideous climax. I think I never was so tired and discouraged in my life. The things—nightmarish things—that could happen in one day were incredible. Things like having my bedroom set, for which I have waited four weeks, arrive painted a hideous putty color instead of apple green; having the telephone company send a man up to yank out the private phone which was here in the name of the previous tenant and which I had hoped to keep because it usually takes from six months to a year to get a private phone installed where there is a house switchboard already in use in the building; having the painters utterly ruin the top of my typewriter desk by having them set a hot pan of some mess right down on it, taking all the finish off it; by having them take a great gouge out of my piano; by having the hall floor so badly done that it has to be done all over again; by having none of the workmen accomplish anything at any time except destruction. I was reminded of nothing so much as an act I once saw in vaudeville of a man papering a room. It was a rather famous act and one of the funniest I ever saw. He got so hopelessly snarled up in the wall paper, the paste, the brush, the ladder, that the audience was screaming in a kind of hysteria when the curtain went down. Multiply that by six and you have the situation here in the last ten days."

It didn't stop there. Julia came, saw, and set her jaw—determined to give Ferber a harrowing time. And the thing of it was, it had little to do with bedroom sets.

"I didn't get my little apple green painted bedroom set after all," Ferber lamented to Fan. "You see I had got my bedroom furniture at wholesale, ordering the green for me and a deep ivory, almost golden for mama . . . A mixup occurred just the day before mama came. They sent the two sets but had painted mine putty instead of green. I sent it back but kept mama's set. They were to repaint mine and let me have it in three or four days. In the meantime mama hated her set, said she wouldn't have a painted one, raised hell, acted like a prima donna, and now I actually find myself with her set in my room, as the furniture people refused to take that back too. They kept the set I had ordered for myself and mama selected a hideous mahogany thing for herself. Strangely enough it doesn't make me angry. But it does rather frighten me to realize that any human being could be capable of such hideous selfishness . . . Some day I'm going to make somebody pay for all I've gone through with this mess."

Among other fond assessments, Franklin P. Adams called Ferber "an adroit self-kidder." She did have a knack of turning a beastly situation with Julia into a wry comment on her own life:

"Mama drives me frantic. Perhaps she is nervous and excited, or something. At any rate, I think I have never seen her so terrible. I was amused, Fan, at your cheery bit about tucking that mythical husband snugly away in a corner of my apartment. Believe me, Mrs. Fox, if I ever cared enough about anybody to marry him the first thing I wouldn't do would be to introduce him to the life I have to live. When I marry a gentleman, mother distinctly won't."

So Ferber was once vulnerable to the thought of marriage. Or perhaps she felt safe on the brink of resignation that she wouldn't ever marry, and so was able to toy with the thought—like a child with a loose tooth knowing that it will soon be out. For all the achievements that she did make, it's the question most asked—almost rhetorically—implying her womanly failure: "She never married, did she?"

The exhausted old stand-up joke: "Tell me, why did you never marry?" "Because nobody ever asked me" didn't apply to Ferber. She'd had gents "smit"—as she called the preliminary stage of passion—with her. She'd had suitors on bended knees; one of them, in Miles Standish fashion, even going to Fan for help with his nuptial intent.

"What was his name?" I begged of my grandmother.

"Oh . . . I don't . . . It was so long . . ." She sat very still with her eyes closed, like a clairvoyant straining for contact.

"Try!" I implored, feeling like Theseus with his ball of string.

"He was the handsome one . . . very debonaire," she said, the memory pushing through. "He was an editor . . . She met him when she first came to New York."

"His name. What was his name?"

"Oh . . . I don't . . .

"Yes, you do!"

Then, as though she had reached her hand back in the grab barrel of years, she brought it forth. "Boyden. Bob . . . . Bern . . . Bert. Bert Boyden."

"And what happened?" I prodded.

She opened the windows on the story. "Well, he came to me—I was living in Chicago—and he said, 'I love Edna dearly and I think she loves me. What can I do to make her marry me?' And I said, 'Nobody can make Edna do anything, but good luck anyway.' A while later he called me up and he said, 'Well, Mrs. Fox, that's that. I asked her to marry me and she said that we'd have to live with her mother. I'm too much of a man for that kind of nonsense.' And I said, 'You're so right and I'm so sorry.'"

"How utterly sad," I said to my grandmother, who nodded in agreement. Perhaps she was thinking what I was—of Julia's words on her deathbed: "Oh, Edna, I ruined your life—didn't I?—I did. I ruined your life."

Ferber's epitaph to Bert Boyden appeared in *A Peculiar Treasure*. In her description of him there is no inkling that he was a great love. But then, she was careful never to let her heart slip out.

". . . Bert Boyden . . . turned out to be a gay handsome young fellow—even young enough not to seem middle-aged to my twenties. He had brilliant white teeth and deep blue eyes and an overpowering zest for life and curiosity about it, as though he must quickly cram as much fun and experience and lavish generosity and friendship into it as he possibly could. He was right, or he was psychic, for the war killed him. I never have known anyone who was so genuinely and wholeheartedly interested in others. He never talked of himself; it was you, you, you. What are you doing? What are your plans? Where do you want to go? Do you like the theater? Have you ever seen Coney Island? Will you come to dinner? Whom do you want to meet? What do you like to eat? We went dancing at Reisenweber's in the Circle, and at the McAlpin and Castles in the Air. It was Bert who taught me the fox trot and the Castle Walk . . . Bert could hypnotize you into writing a story on schedule. He could make you feel that your next short story was the most important single thing that civilization could hope to evolve. He was a superb editor. He was a superb human being. When I last saw him he lay dying. He no longer had the strength or the will to raise his eyelids. They were closed over the sunken sockets. He spoke, though, in a whisper that was little more than a ghostly breath. I leaned closer. 'What are you writing? When . . . finished? Good? Good.'"

Boyden must have been all that Ferber said of him, for in his last letter written to her in 1924, when he was dying—and knew it—his only concern was for her. The letter—knowing the condition of its sender and his previous feelings toward Ferber—is the stuff that lumps in throats are made of.

"Dear Edna: You probably have heard—but on the chance that you may not I pass it on—that William Lyon Phelps one night last week in Brooklyn before an audience of 3000 said that E. Ferber's novel* was not only the best American novel of the year but so far and away the best that there was no other near. I don't know what

* *So Big.*

you think of Phelps or what prejudices you may entertain about Brooklyn but I assume that you have no objection to any one saying such a thing to any three thousand native or even foreign born.

"Don't bother to acknowledge this. If we don't meet here we'll do so often in Billy Sunday's heaven—one of the things that will make heaven heaven will be seeing all your friends all the time . . . I hope the play is progressing. Votre toujours devoué, Bert."

A slightly jarring counterpoint to the sincerity of Bert Boyden's tone is the outrageous and irreverent one of H. L. Mencken, another attentive friend in Ferber's life at this time. Here is a letter—out of many of the same kind—that delivers absolute nonsense, which Ferber needed a dose of now and again.

"To the trained mind, du bub'du, the whole thing is childishly simple. I see it all now. You're in love with an actress—probably Fanny Brice. This secret passion distresses you. You are ashamed of it. In your efforts to justify yourself in your own eyes you cast about in your mind for the most distinguished, irreproachable, balanced, dependable, and altogether delightful person of your acquaintance and try to imagine that person in a position similar to yours. Naturally, your mind at once fixes on me. You delude yourself into fastening upon me an infatuation of the kind with which you are obsessed. In so doing you lift your own burden of reproach. You feel justified in your own eyes. You are at peace. Oh, well—I have been very ill with the flu for four days. You probably will catch it after reading this letter. Then I, too, shall feel at peace. Immer deine, Gustav."

Ferber's concern about Fan's literary career was genuine yet somewhat lofty. She knew that she could keep Fan's initiative down, keep her by the home fires, by spoiling her. She would offer advice and encouragement with one hand, and monetary appeasement with the other.

"I'm as disappointed as you are, Orrea, to learn that the Delineator thing came back," she wrote to Fan, who was doggedly sending out short stories. "Did they return it with a note, or a printed slip? Where are you sending it now? . . . I keep thinking how O. Henry sent his 'Unfinished Story' out thirteen times. Kathleen Norris's first story she sent to every magazine in the country, had it refused by all of them, started all over again with it, beginning with the letter A, and had it accepted by the first one who had refused it months before . . . Don't get discouraged. After all, think of the years of newspaper experience that I had, slaving for three dollars, eight dollars, twelve and fifteen dollars a week, trotting all day, before I began to write outside stuff. Isn't it comic that I never even tried, or wanted to try? Perhaps I was too tired at the end of the day to think of anything else . . . I am returning that two hundred and will keep right on returning it, so you may as well make up your mind to that. Please don't be so silly."

Obviously Fan learned not to be so silly, and never did come into her author's own.

Nobody could outgive Ferber, but few realized to what a great extent she joyfully received. Her public front of disdain about Christmas and birthdays covered her fear of being forgotten. Nothing could point up her pride at having been given to as much as her letter to the "Foxies" discussing Christmas, 1923:

"We loved our Christmas boxes. I hope I'm right in using my velvet jacket for a smoking coat. It may be that it is a bed jacket, but I think it's too cunning, so I wear it over a black evening dress, and with a white one too, and it looks stunning. The dog collar is so different and becoming. I had never seen one like it. It was so darling of the girls to give their aunt nothing less than jewels. Altogether we had a grand Christmas, and your boxes were the nicest part of it.

"I gave practically no presents, and got millions. I can't begin to tell you what my living room looked like. Perhaps an Italian second rate prima donna's after her first appearance. Not that the flowers were second rate. No ma'am! I got exactly twenty plants and boxes of roses—six huge poinsettia plants, so that I massed them altogether on one table, and they looked like a florist's window display. It made things very festive and I felt popular and happy."

For a writer it was amazing how social she was, but she could never reckon with it—always suffering between her outgoing personality and her incoming muse. She was just beginning to deal with both phases of herself, but her social life often threatened to take the lead. She would rein it in only to have it gallop away with her again. One can distinctly see her pull between what was proper and what was pleasure. Edna, the party girl, wrote home of her doings:

"On Sunday I drove out to Neysa's with Irving Berlin . . . I like her so much . . . She's very plain—almost ugly—but with great poise and intelligence. The way she and I agreed about the Poison Squad* probably attracted me to her more than anything. After lunch we drove to Ring Lardner's for a minute. Then Berlin asked us all to have dinner with him at Voisin's. So we drove in and had dinner at about eight. He is such a sweet chap . . ."

And of her undoings:

"I woke up this morning with a little sore throat, but I've learned by now that that doesn't mean a really sore throat at all, but acidity. And that's my own fault. I went to the Barrymore party last night and drank two cocktails like an idiot, and two glasses of red wine. It was rather a nice party, and I met two or three niceish men of the architect and banking variety, one of whom asked me to go on to the Mayfair dance at the Ritz. Marc Connelly and Margalo were going, too. I said I'd go, though I rather wished I hadn't. But I was saved the trouble of regretting my decision because the gentleman proceeded to get so soused that I left him, hat in hand, wavering slightly, at the top of the stairs, and beat it from him with Marc, Margalo and some others, dropping most of them at the Ritz and going on home like a sensible person. For all I know he is still standing at the head of the stairs, waiting."

Ferber, the purist, wrote to William Allen White: "I'm unhappy as hell. Nothing to do with my work, and my heart's all right. I want serenity and peace. I'm black and blue all over."

A physical change seemed to be the answer. High altitude. Estes Park, Colorado Springs, the Broadmoor Hotel, which was the Arden's Maine Chance of that day where she could find "rest and recreation and peace." Complete retreat was impossible, for the places she chose were a combination of spartan-posh—in a word, chic. So she would arrive and walk and breathe the clear air and stumble upon Dicky Rodgers, Lorenz Hart, and various other muckamucks, and the gavotte would start all over again.

Several of her friends had vacation homes in the Colorado area—Estes Park and Longs Peak being the favored spots. House parties were *au courant*, and Ferber used the phrase "a whole bunch of us" often when discussing who else were houseguests. She would rarely find that she was the only guest; and the atmosphere that prevailed seemed like a long New Year's Eve party, with continuous verbal square dancing.

* The rudiments of what was to be known as the Round Table.

Luckily, Ferber's eye always maintained its equilibrium. A reviewer of her 1922 volume of short stories titled *Gigolo* wrote:

"Edna Ferber's world is full of stories. What her eye beholds her mind immediately knits up with a series of related incidents—and the story is there. She has a faculty for finding the salient mannerism, the essential characteristic, the right word that identifies a living character. Gene Markey tells how one day when he was walking with Miss Ferber they passed a garage where a mechanic was at work under a car. Miss Ferber stopped instantly, gazed at him and exclaimed: 'There's my man. I've been looking for him.'"

Bert Boyden, more enamored than critical, wrote a charming, if fawning, letter concerning *Gigolo:*

"Reveredand Only Edna: That book of yours is a marvel. Such a collection of portraits I haven't run into since I wandered in the Munich gallery. You say with words what Holbein and some of those other old boys did with paint. Such a glorification of the commonplace, such an appreciation of what an adventure this living game is for every one of us and such amazing observation of the varied forms it takes fills me with wonder love and awe . . . With my hat off and my head bowed I am yours proudly, Bert."

The quintessence of a Ferber short story was that it was about real folk. Her very ability to dramatize without taking away the dignity of "the average" was her pole vault into the charmed world of celebrity. How ironic, then, that the people she wrote about with their modest larders supplied her with her first ample bread and butter. In a piece that she wrote for *Liberty* magazine bearing the shucks, ma'am title of "Middle-Class, Middle-West Me," she explains, convincingly, why Middle Amurica was her heart line:

"While there has been no nation-wide clamor about it, there has been an occasional inquirer to say, boredly, 'Why do you always write about Chicago or some such Middle-Western wilderness? And why do you always choose commonplace middle-class people for your characters?'

"At first these questions gave me what is rhetorically known as a pause. I hadn't realized that I was confining myself to any section or stratum. A middle-class person living in Appleton, Wisconsin, or Chicago, Illinois, one naturally wrote about middle-class persons living in Appleton or Chicago. Never having been rich or poor, the rich and poor were strange fields and pastures . . .

A junior at Ryan High School, Appleton, Wisconsin. The blouse seems to be in trouble, but the hat (whipped up at home by sister Fan) makes up for everything.

The graduate, 1903.

The reporter for the Appleton Daily Crescent. *The pompadour was a success but not the four-in-hand. 1904.*

Ryan High School paper, The Clarion, *editorial staff, 1903.*

Edna in Ottumwa, Iowa, 1890.

Sisters Edna and Fannie Ferber, 1892.

Fannie Ferber in Kalamazoo, Michigan, 1888.

Jacob and Julia Ferber's "My Store," Appleton, Wisconsin, 1896–1909.

Jacob Ferber.

Julia Ferber.

Harriet Neumann, Ferber's maternal grandmother.

Louis Neumann, Ferber's maternal grandfather.

The house in which I was born.
Kalamazoo, Michigan. August 15, 1885
Edna Ferber.

"'But,' persisted the interrogator, with a tinge of distaste in his voice, 'do you like to write about them?'

"'Like? Like to—why, listen! No other kind of person fascinates and excites my writing sense. And that's the truth. There's no explaining it.'

"Still, perhaps at birth, one of those Bad Fairies who hadn't been invited came sneaking in and gave me a smart clip over the head with her magic wand, saying:

"'Abracadabra or wordstothateffect! Yours shall be the commonplace middle-class name of Edna. All your life you shall be cursed with the inability to be dazzled by the romantic rich or thrilled by the picturesque poor. Never shall you be seen wandering, wet-eyed, around the slums of the lower East Side looking for what is known (by people who don't write) as copy; and though you peer hungrily into the perambulators and limousines of Park Avenue it shall avail you nothing. Not A Thing. Always for you, a tough young garage mechanic on his afternoon off shall appear more interesting than a Van Bibber on a polo pony.'"

She ends the piece by excusing herself for living in New York, and vowing identification and allegiance with the humble faction of the human race:

"And, though now I live in the City of Sophistication, I'll never be more than an onlooker in it. First Nights, and Literary Teas, and Pomeranian Pups, and Sable Coats, and Roof Bungalows will always be things that I shall View With Alarm, mingled with a feeling of unreality. And when it comes to writing I turn back to the town with a little human awkwardness left in it."

Whall, whall, whall. Mebbee. Her comment to Fan about the above article was:

"I just finished and sent off my gosh-all-fishhooks piece for Liberty. I'm rather pleased with it, though."

She may have come from the norm and written about the norm for the norm, but as a young woman, as a successful woman, as a single (figurative, for there was Julia) woman in New York, she was changing. She was fluctuating from her original intent to forever be of the people, by the people, and for the people. The realization that she couldn't manage fame, industry, humility, Julia, and a love life began to root in the early twenties. She was miserable, but for the most part mustered up bravado. Occasionally, she was caught.

The "catcher" in one instance was a "dark horse" man in her life —Jay "Ding" Darling, the Pulitzer Prize-winning cartoonist and well-known conservationist, whom she had met when she was a slip of a girl reporter covering the National Democratic Convention of 1912. To my knowledge, there has never been any mention that he was sweet on her. His letter is to the contrary:

"What a man thinks about after getting home from an evening with E. Ferber—Gee—wonder what she meant when she said I was like an old slipper—And then raisin' the dickens about everything I said—She went and says herself that with the exception of a couple of weeks in the mountains she'd been miserable for a year—Then she gets all het up when I says nobody aint got no right to sucha monopoly of misery and she must have forgotten how to play or something—And she says nothing of the sort and didn't she look cheerful—And says I, yes, but she wasn't and something ought to be done about it—And she says how insulting—She wouldn't have nobody think she didn't seem the way she looked—Gosh I don't know."

The telltale part of the letter is the cartoon which he has drawn to accompany it: a man sitting on a bed with one shoe off, looking rejected and forlorn. Question marks are sprouting out of his head. The caption reads: "After thought—Beg pardon I'd forgotten you didn't like bedroom scenes."

Before 1921, Ferber had not yet formed her oeuvre as a novelist. She was a popular short-story writer, a women's club lecturer, and a definite personality. If one failed to notice her, one did not fail to hear her. At a dinner in Estes Park with the "old gelt crowd" the discussion turned to lineage. Ferber put hers in. "Having a Jewish heritage is like owning a beautiful back," she said regally, the statement greeted by instrumentals on the cutlery, "or front," she polished it off.

The writing, publishing, and reception of Ferber's novel *The Girls* was a watershed event in her career. It transformed her from storytelling puberty into a novelist's young maturity. It was her first work which dealt with generations—a theme that was to become her trademark. It was her first work that she was totally proud of, which was to become a rarity. It didn't make much profit, but it secured the start of her reputation as a major novelist—especially among writers and editors. Editor Gertrude Lane, for one, who bought it in four installments for serialization in her magazine,

Woman's Home Companion. H. L. Mencken for another, who was at that time editor and owner, along with George Jean Nathan, of a magazine called the *Smart Set.* Always astute—but usually Puckish—he was more pontificating Polonius in his praise of *The Girls:*

"Respected Mlle.: The Girls came in the other day, and I began to read it. Well, I may roast in hell forevermore if it [isn't] an A No. 1 piece of work. You have never done anything better . . . It is capital stuff—well imagined, swift moving, humorous, and full of sound feeling. The cleverness of it gives me a genuine thrill. Every time you run into a problem you solve it perfectly—and one after the other . . . The people in it are absolutely alive . . . The action is so probable that it seems inevitable. And if an old man may speak out boldly, I think there is constant ingenuity and brilliancy in the writing."

"Mama liked it so-so," Ferber reported to Fan. And then, "but Will White liked it so much and that makes up for just about everything."

"In general, what did Julia feel about Aunt Edna's work?" I asked my grandmother.

No hesitation. "She was jealous of it," came the answer.

In 1920–21 Ferber divided her time between a Julia life in Chicago and a hotel life in New York. When Julia came, for extended visits, she would stay with Ferber at the Hotel Majestic on West Seventy-second Street. In Chicago, Ferber would stay with Julia at 5414 East View Park—about which she said to W. A. White upon finding herself there in late 1920: "I'm thoroughly at home and almost happy, what with one thing and another. The lake's going on as usual, and things are green (you don't know what that means after six months of brownstone fronts) and burglars tried to break in last night, and it's the same old Chicago."

Her six-month shifts made visiting arrangements confusing. "Where, if any, are you?" she continued to White. "There is a rumor to the effect that you are coming to New York but I'm not buying in. I know that you never come to New York without first making sure that I'm in Chicago."

Earlier that year Ferber had had an abysmal failure which she took fairly philosophically. High hopes had not been there from the beginning. The venture was a play with the leaden title of *$1200 a Year,* which she collaborated on with a Chicago lawyer-playwright named Newman Levy. It was produced by the usually discerning Sam Harris, who discerned enough to close it out of town, allowing it to never see Broadway. It seemed to be the stumbling block between Ferber and getting on with her work on *The Girls.* Her correspondence with W. A. White chronicles the time span of the play, her need to write *The Girls* and her actual writing of *The Girls.* White was probably the only one in her world who could handle her playing the part of the damsel in distress.

Ferber to White: "The play, dear Will'um is now getting three coats of paint and a layer of varnish. I hate it so that I can't talk about it. Fed up. I'm so eager to get at 'The Girls.'"

White to Ferber: "I am coming to New York . . . I will be at the National Arts Club. I will phone you as soon as I get in town, and I will arrange to meet you somewhere at your convenience. I am simply telling you this, so that you won't be out of town."

Ferber to White: "Dear Will: I'm living in great magnificence on the tenth floor of the Majestic Hotel and wish you were the same. I hate New York this year for some reason. It seems so hideously crowded and dirty and the women's legs are so ridiculous sticking out in grey silk pudginess from beneath a scant ten or twelve inches of skirt. Then, too, everybody who is writing, excepting only E. Ferber, seems to be earning a minimum sum of $100,000 a year. I'm struggling with 'The Girls.'"

White to Ferber: ". . . For Heaven's sake, now take your time on that 'The Girls' novel. It is a good idea and if you will just take your time to work it out as you do in your short stories, you will have a great story there. But you are tempted to see a dollar and thirty-eight cents and grab for it. Stop it."

If there was one person whom Ferber could thank for changing the course of her human events it was Bill White. On her thirty-first birthday he sent her a present in the form of a letter. It's an odd, abstract thing for a love letter, but seeing that they did not share the "conventional" relationship, it's as passionate as anything he would ever write to her. It served to steer her in the direction of what she would become.

"Dear Edna: This letter is the only birthday present I can send you, and I couldn't send it except for my precious gift of rendering myself invisible and bringing it! They will not let me bring with me jewels or cloth or fabriced things so I have come with this. It is too bad—really too bad—that I could only bring this when the world is so full of a number of things I should like to take, and when even this you may never see. For perhaps only the dear little mermaids will see this letter and read it to the mermen and flash their tails in glee at it and you, for whom it is written as a birthday greeting may only feel it; may only feel it in the vague way one feels the truest things and wonders if they are true. You will recall—now that I have mentioned it—how you wondered on your birthday if I would remember. And there I sat in my gorgeous invisibility beside you with this letter in my hand—or maybe not in my hand; I think my hand is rather useless in my invisible excursions. And so is my head. I only take my heart. So we must say that I sat there by you with this letter in my heart wondering why you didn't look up and read it. And perhaps if the mermaids get it and you do not, you will always be sure that it was written and never be puzzled with the doubt that comes of having actually read it—the doubt that asks why it was written.

"If I was really sure you would get it I should not try to tell you why it was written. So I must give us the benefit of the doubt and set it all down. It was written I believe quite literally to help you; to cheer you up, as I told you where I brought it, though you wouldn't listen, quite deeply enough!

"You were a little blue about your work and were feeling that thirty one is tremendously old and that you should be further along. You are wrong. You have come a long way for 31 and you have much ahead of you. When I was sitting beside you in my invisible garb I could see far ahead into life for you. You are about to turn a corner. You are now ready to quit writing when publishers howl 'copy.' You are now ready to reap where you have sown. You have two big tricks in your bag: a sense of dramatic power, or values, and a gift of observation. Your last story was a far step ahead. It was an evidence of growth. It was tremendously a credit to you. But it was not your best. You will do vastly better, and that vastly better will come when you write your next long story. Write the short story all you will; it is splendid practice. But—in a year—maybe two maybe three—there will come to you the moving impulse, big and irresistible—to pour out your heart to break your alabaster box upon some new cause. The really splendid thing about Fanny was that you did work out a thesis—worked it clear out to a logical and beautiful conclusion and that you thought out all that you felt. You can do that again. But more than that the next time when you conceive a great idea, you are going to write it clear through—clear plumb through and send it to me (perhaps via the mermaids but still to me) and I am going to get out a perspective that you can not have and (even through the mermaids) I am going to insist that you revise it, and end it, in whatever way the theme demands and you are going to cut out your guide book stuff and stick to your theme.

"These things are clear to me. I know you are just beginning. What you have done will be known as your earlier work. And what you will do is going to be so much greater than what you have done that you will look back on this work as the work of another person.

"And that is what I have brought you in my heart for your birthday."

Ferber was, as White suggested, a bit of a money scout, and as a result the polarized themes of crass commercialism versus artistic merit plagued her all her writing and selling life. She cranked out short stories in order to: a) support herself, b) to keep Julia in the style that she was beginning to become accustomed to, c) to build a nest egg with which to settle back and write an "important" work.

She needed to write *The Girls* so she hied herself to Los Angeles —about which she said with "first-time" eyes: "This is the only town in the United States and Europe in which one could walk down the main business street at 10 A.M. attired in full evening dress with yellow riding boots, carrying a purple parasol and turning handsprings every tenth step and nobody would flap an eyelid."

Her sole purpose of being there was to sell her second novel, *Fanny Herself*, to the "moovin' pitchers," which she did by way of the wunderkind producer Irving Thalberg, who bought it for a modest sum. She leased a house, sent for Julia, and settled down to write her novel. What developed rapidly was a major case of ennui due to physical surroundings. "I don't like my sun this friendly," she groused; packed up, left, and finished *The Girls* in moody Chicago.

To have Franklin P. Adams put in his column:

"O Henry's name unless mistaken I'm

Goes ednaferberating down through time."

was not good enough. She was yet to offer the proof of the Ferber, but spent every waking (and sleeping—for she believed in subconscious achievement) hour working on it and worrying about it. She was able to keep her friends at a distance in the years of World War I, for, indeed, a great many of them were physically dispersed. H. L. Mencken was the Baltimore *Sun* correspondent in Berlin, but still had a moment for her writing: "Friend Feldman . . . Be prepared for news when we meet. I am so stuffed with scandal that my ears ring."

Alexander Woollcott, who was with the New York Times Bureau in Paris, found room to chat with her in a tone that was just like home:

"I might tell you about my hour with Barrie* in London. I went up to tea with him in his tower-like study above the Thames and found him a gentle, childlike person, who rolled around the room like an uneasy ball . . . Or I might tell you how Mrs. Patrick Campbell lost her temper in the midst of a 'Pygmalion' rehearsal the other day and shouted across the auditorium, 'Shaw, some day you'll eat a mutton chop and then God help all women!' . . . Is it true that you have been secretly married for five years to Rube Goldberg? Amoeba."

William Allen White, who was sent to France by the Red Cross, had many moments for her, writing her constantly and sending her his articles. It wasn't enough. She missed him sorely, and told him so in a pining paragraph:

"You may not have gathered how really bitter was my disappointment in not seeing you before you left. I have the most selfish kind of need of you. I think you know that when I slide downhill just about so far I can always get to the top again by hooking on a ride behind the W.A.W. upgoing vehicle. I wish you'd talk into a nice, round Edison record arrangement so that I could turn you on whenever I feel the need of some of your conversation."

The year 1918 found Ferber hurt, humiliated, bitter, and slightly vengeful. Eternally patriotic, always eager—in her words—to be a "piece speaking and writing fool," to be turned down from going to France for the Red Cross because of a Hungarian-born father was just not fair. She expressed her opinions to Theodore Roosevelt, who was a prodigious reader of her short stories, and was therefore particularly sympathetic in his response to her, saying: "I am mortified and angry that you should have lost out. I have had no hint as to the reason. That it is not a good reason goes without saying. I prize your letter. Faithfully yours, Theodore Roosevelt."

* James M. Barrie.

Quick to realize that indulging in self-pity was an antiwar-effort exercise, she got to work domestically—writing and making speeches for the Red Cross and the Liberty Loan Drive. She reported the end of her sour grapes to White:

"It's Sunday evening, and I've just come from a huge meeting in Oak Park. Twenty-five hundred people. I've been speaking in Illinois and Wisconsin, and all over Chicago, at huge meetings, and it has been glorious. I don't think I've had such a stirring experience since our campaign days. One morning in Monmouth Illinois I got up at six o'clock to see seven Monmouth boys go to war. The thing got me as no great pageantry of this war has got me. The thing was so real, so human, so microscopic, somehow. Those boys, in their plaid mackinaws, and their big boots, and with their little pasteboard boxes, marching down Main Street to the depot—" She closed with her special humor, which saved itself from being cute by a hair of self-mockery. "I'm reasonable happy, but not so werry husky, count late grippe and lingering laryngitis. I've a C'meel cough, and when I speak to a big house as I did this afternoon I find my voice cracking grotesquely like Teddy's* when he's falsetto."

Her extension and enthusiasm toward this man was very needing and real. Later, she kept up the same plucky/humble thing with others, but it turned into a professional front.

In the White-Ferber correspondence there is a startling piece of evidence. A revelation. An upset. A turn of events, showing a Ferber who had a love that was physical—or at least all the implications were there in a portion of a White letter to her:

". . . And tell me something more of your love affair. Is it the same man? I thought you had sent him away! They don't stay away. That's the whole trouble with man. We're a great nuisance. But I'd like to know about the man. Sit down, choke your squat legged demon of cold stoicism who hoots at you and your emotional rises, and write me all about the man—I mean in particular. He must be more than two thirds nice to appreciate you. Why don't you let yourself go—slam bang—and maybe you can! Emotion feeds upon itself. Try it. But throttle that Oriental that blinks out of your subconsciousness—Kill him and laugh at him; even if you know you're a fool. Be a fool. It will help. Too much wisdom is unwise."

* Theodore Roosevelt.

One would assume that she did not take White's advice, for there is not a clue to identify the participant in the affair. And in the years to follow she would often say, bristling and haughty, "No fool I."

Almost as an afterthought, in 1918 Ferber tossed off a collection of short stories titled *Cheerful, By Request,* which marked her first publishing liaison with Doubleday, Page & Company. She blithely called it a "new marriage" and didn't seem too concerned about the fate of the stories, one of the reasons being that she had a severe conscience about war, and felt her own work frivolous when men were dying.

Even the year before she was turned down from going to France she was doing moderate war work—with aspirations of going to France. To White she talks about her reception after reading her "deathless prose" to some soldiers at a Camp Upton in Yaphank, New York:

"If they don't like your stuff (and usually they don't) they simply rise AND—LEAVE! I gave them a minute-talk, and three short sketches, and they—God bless 'em!—put their fingers in their mouths and whistled their approbation, and I nearly passed on with joy. All kinds. All grades of intelligence. Princeton chap next to Ignatz Czernowski. I read, by the way, under the Y.M.C.A. auspices. And they are willing to let me go to France and do the same if I make good here. What do you think? I've got to get over there, somehow. I want to see this thing. It's been boiling in me for months.

"Isn't there a Red Cross job for me? If only for a few weeks? I could come back and talk about it to audiences, if nothing else. I can see things, you know. And I can make other people see 'em."

She certainly made other people see very clearly the character of Molly Brandeis, who appeared in her second novel, *Fanny Herself,* which was her last work to be published by Frederick A. Stokes Company, and which was the only work to be dedicated to William Allen White. The mother in the book about a Jewish girl growing up in Appleton, Wisconsin, was Julia Ferber in mufti. The daughter, Fanny Herself, was a patchwork version of Ferber herself. The critics realized that it was semiautobiographical, and gave it sweet, understanding, and rather patronizing reviews. Others, who knew Ferber better, realized that it gave vent to her maternal death wish

—for midway through the story, she killed off Molly Brandeis. Ferber, the fledgling novelist, regretted it for with Molly went the vigor of the tale. Ferber, the daughter, had purposely allowed it to happen.

Often one has to leave a cushy spot to get on with the stretching and learning process. Ferber's lucrative cushion lay under the head of her immensely popular fictitious character Emma McChesney, or, as she referred to her, Emma McChestnut.

The Emma McChesney stories appeared over a five-year period (1911–15) in the popular *American* magazine and *Cosmopolitan* magazine. They were also published by Stokes in three separate volumes: *Emma McChesney & Co., Personality Plus,* and *Roast Beef Medium.* They brought her national recognition, some very pretty pennies, and, eventually, to New York and "a room of her own."

Ferber's proverbial fame and fortune all came out of the suitcase of Mrs. McChesney, who happened to be a traveling saleswoman by trade, the first of her kind—fictitious or otherwise. Emma was just as much a major statement about and a breakthrough for women, as she was an engaging serial to follow (skirting the corners of what we now define as "soap opera"). Today Emma could be considered a feminist, but I would rather change that word into a bastard German: feminine *ist*—meaning feminine is . . . anything it wants to be. Emma's creator did not portray her as angry or frustrated or predatory. She was a divorced woman of a certain early middle age with a young son to support. Luckily, she had integrity, tenacity, and charm—as did Ferber. But it took considerable pluck to allow those traits to escape, breathe, and flourish in a man's world—which is where the feminist theme could creep in.

Necessity was the Emma of invention. She had to make her own living; there was no alternative. She had to support herself and her son, and chose to do it as a woman person instead of as a woman drudge. She wanted adventure, stimulation, and income—in that order, for she decided that that was the only order that would make her a successful human being.

Perils, usually in the form of discrimination, befell Emma, but she staunchly made her way—stepping over, and eventually diminishing, the sexist dragons. She had no enemies, nor any gender segregation among her readers. The only qualitative difference was that the women wanted her to continue doing very well without a man, whereas the men wanted her to go just so far and then to settle down. Theodore Roosevelt wrote to Ferber pleading the latter argument:

"Of course I have read all those stories, because I never let a story of yours pass; but I am glad to have them in a book. I wonder if you feel that I am hopelessly sentimental because my only objection to the last twelve pages is that I would have liked somehow to see not only the boy marry, but poor Emma McChesney at last have the chance herself to marry somebody decent with whom she was in love."

Emma became Ferber's mouthpiece in interviews. She realized that she'd started an upheaval, and decided to cash in on it—not just for Emma, but for women in general. She spoke out to the New York *Times Magazine* of 1915, saying things that we just came to terms with yesterday:

"I have no sympathy with the restless woman, the woman who takes time from her household duties to do something absolutely worthless. The woman who is domestic is capable in everything she does. These women who do all the shouting and haranguing, who go about vaguely 'uplifting' and making a mess of everything, are absolutely no good. They don't accomplish anything. The loudest Feminists don't seem to know how to make shirtwaists or even how to wear them properly. And they can't make cakes. Their cakes always fall, and their shirtwaists haven't the right slant somehow . . . It all comes to just this—a woman who is nothing but a housekeeper may possibly be domestic. But a housekeeper who also has a business or other serious interest outside her home is almost certain to be much more domestic. Did you ever hear a good, successful business woman, earning a thumping big salary, talk about her house and family? She actually loves it! The ordinary housewife does not talk about it with the same affection, for she does not regard it with the same affection. She is tired out, or indifferent, or bored. But the business woman talks about the new chest of drawers that she is going to buy and the new couch and the new portieres for the living room with a splendid fire in her words. She actually has a passion for domesticity. And that passion finds practical and efficient expression, too, let me tell you! There is nothing so thoroughly domestic as the successful business woman."

As the spokeswoman for the evolving woman, Ferber continued her discourse. It's surprising that her tract has not been utilized by advancement-for-women proselytizers of today. She uses Emma McChesney as a password for communication to and among women, who apparently understood that Emma was a symbol of their own egos:

"I think that Emma must be a type because so many people write to me claiming to be the original Emma McChesney. Every now and then some business woman sends me a letter saying, 'I am the woman you are writing about . . . how did you come to know so much about me?' She is a type, and she is a very young type . . . She is so new that she is worth talking about. But ten years from now a talk like this will be an anachronism. The idea that anyone ever questioned the propriety of a woman's going into business, or thought that such an act on her part was inconsistent with domesticity, will be obsolete as milestones.

"Of course there is some reason why all these good housekeepers are finding that something besides housekeeping is necessary in their lives. The reason is that the household drudgery that took up so much of their time and energy has been done away with by the vacuum cleaner and the telephone and the dumbwaiter and all the rest of the modern household appliances. And, then, the woman's attitude toward life has changed. Fifteen or twenty-five years ago the mother spent half an hour every day forming her little girl's hair into long, lank curls. Now she bobs the little girl's hair. And she bobs everything! She has taken the ringlets from the little girl's head, she has taken the ringlets from the furniture, she has taken the ringlets from her housekeeping, and what is most important, she has taken the ringlets from her mind."

Emma McChesney became Ethel Barrymore when the property was dramatized as *Our Mrs. McChesney* and produced at the Lyceum Theatre in 1915. The neophyte playwright was Miss Edna Ferber, who collaborated with the more experienced George V. Hobart, who did not prepare her for the mind-click ease that she would later find in working with George Kaufman. She and Hobart were completely dissimilar; her talent was young and his was only fair. Her ear was original; his was tin. She was impromptu; he was structured. She gives a sample of their daily taffy pull:

"'But they wouldn't do that,' I'd object. 'The audience never would believe it.'

"'They'll believe it if they see it before their eyes, on the stage.'"

But to have Ethel Barrymore do her play on Broadway seemed to suffice, and to appease the kind of artistic flare-up that she was to become known for. However, she certainly had her own ideas—none of which concurred with the production at hand. Foremost, she felt that the elegant Ethel Barrymore was miscast as the doughty Emma, and would overshadow the character with her star presence. She was smart enough, awed enough, to keep it to herself. She knew that if Barrymore ruined Emma it would be more of an honor than an average performance by another actress.

Her instincts were correct. Barrymore was wrong for the part but right for Barrymore and made the play a personal hit—and an artistic miss as far as the play's being the thing. The reviews were slavish with praise for the Divine Ethel, and threw small bones for the puppy playwright, Ferber. The *Daily Telegraph* read:

"Ethel Barrymore's 'following' . . . still worships at her shrine and it matters very little what she does, just so it is Ethel . . . She is very exquisite and splendid to see, is Miss Barrymore, made young and even handsomer than ever by a marvelous rejuvenation in her face and figure and a more thrilling enunciation of her varied charms, physical and spiritual. She is adorable as the brilliant woman of business, exquisite in the motherly instants developed and masterful in dexterous ways of making much out of nothing in particular.

". . . The sale of seats . . . is phenomenal, breaking all records, not only because Miss Barrymore is a tremendous favorite, but because Miss Ferber's stories are famously admired and applauded by the great and small readers of the world of reasonable taste in American humor and good, solid writing."

It was to Barrymore's credit that the play was a hit, but for the young Ferber, a first playwrighting credit—hit or no—meant that her curtain had gone up. She had arrived in the world that as a child she had staged for herself. She was Dorothy come out of Kansas into Oz; Ethel Barrymore was Glinda the Good Witch, and the Munchkins were her public.

And it seemed that with a mere three clicks of her silver slippers Europe exploded into war.

With the proceeds from the McChesney stories, she packed up Julia and off they went, on their first crossing, to the prewar Europe of 1914. They got out just in time. On the ship sailing home from Germany they found out that war had been declared. She writes:

"Well, it was all very exciting and dreadful, but it was their war and none of our business. It would all be over in a couple of months. I regretted having missed the chance to see a Europe plunged suddenly into war. Tourists abroad were scrambling wildly for American-bound boats—any boats, any sort of passage, second-class, third-class, steerage. I told myself I'd have stayed on to see the sights. The ex-newspaper reporter. My friends congratulated me on getting in just under the wire."

But, oh, what a carefree Europe that carefree Ferber saw. One of the reasons that it was such a positive experience was because she felt so on top of everything. Life was her "oerster," as she was fond of pronouncing it. She was finally able to give Julia an exotic treat instead of a new camisole; she'd had two vicarious blessed events with the births of Janet (Janno) and Mina (Minnow) born thirteen months apart—whom she continued to refer to as "the infants" well into their twenties. And, she'd been able to make a turning-point decision. Shortly prior to sailing, *American* magazine's rival, *Cosmopolitan,* sent her a blank contract for an unlimited number of McChesney stories at the price she named. Then and there she could have been a millionaire. Instead, she sent the Faustian contract back and went to Vienna to have *kaffee mit schlag* and nose surgery.

The second version of Ferber's nose bob is less entertaining but probably truer. Vienna, home of advanced pastry and medical procedures, was where Ferber chose to have her transformation performed. She didn't seem to have much trepidation about the innovative surgery. She breezed through it, writing home:

"My nose is healing nicely, though it won't really be thoroughly healed inside for a month. But it is its normally graceful shape now, and I can breath through the bad nostril like a regular person."

In fact, she felt like a special person. A privileged young woman with a new nose—not quite retroussé, but nice all the same—health, and spreading success. Her letters to what would become the "Foxies" but were then the "Fellers" are blithe to the point of silliness; joyful to the point of bursting. The mood of them parallels what she saw of the last blithe, bursting Europe:

VIENNA: "Fellers: Erstens, we love Vienna. Zweitens, we're staying at the Pension Atlanta . . . We have taken a bedroom and sitting room, so comfortable, and comparatively reasonable. Twenty kronen (a kronen is about twenty-one cents) a day for the two of us, of course including meals. Of course that doesn't mean anything as wild as a bathroom, or running water. A bath here is a distinct function, and is also a process strongly recommended as a means of relief from weariness after much traveling. That is, when we said, in Budapest, that we were tired after our strenuous month in Italy, one Barona suggested that we try a bath. We said we had tried it already, with great success. She said she often did too, so that made it nice all around . . . We spent three days in Budapest . . . We always walked in the Corso, the promenade lined on either side with benches, on which people sit and watch the gay Hungarian ladies flopping up and down in their French heeled slippers . . . The women are really stunning, but the men! They wear trousers that are wide and flappy at the bottom, like sailors' bell-shaped ones, and fierce collars and neckties, and socks . . . In the afternoon everyone in the fashionable world in Budapest goes to Kuglers, and there drink kaffee and eat cakes. There are gay officers roaming about back of the counters, and silk-hatted beaux, and nobility galore. Also, you should see Mama in the act of having her hand kissed. She purt nigh died the first time, but she's sort of hardened to it by this time. Fortunately for me, it's not generally done to the younger ladies, so that lets me out temporarily."

"Dear Fellers: . . . Let me address to you a few fleeting remarks on the subject of that mythical thing known as the chic Viennese. O, my children, my children! What a blow have I had! Mama and I have laughed ourselves into purple hysterics, and that we haven't been arrested for shrieking on the streets is still a source of mystery to me . . . The chic Viennese, my children, is a fat, waddling, triple-chinned person who is stuffed into a skin tight suit as a piece of smoked goose-breast is stuffed into its skin. She is a hideous and awful example of what kaffee and kaffee kuchen, not to speak of four other meals a day, will do to one. She wears her corsets only on the street, and never NEVER in the house, I can swear. And if she were to take an incautious breath, sudden-like, her buttons would burst like Peggotty's, and go rattling all over the street. She wears suits that we stopped wearing year before last, and her feet would make you think that Chicago girls must have adopted the Chinese fashion of foot binding . . . The women get up at noon and the husbands go to the kaffee häuser for Wiener Fruhstuck.

Then the women have dinner ready for their husbands, and in the afternoon they go to the kaffee haus and sit there for hours. Hours! From four in the afternoon until ten at night . . . Such faces! Dumm! Such types! Such fat ugly vicious looking women. Mama and I sit there and revel in it. We just pick out the juicy ones and have a grand time watching them."

(A memory of mine interrupts. I am six or seven. Aunt Edna and I are sitting on a bench in Central Park. Later, we will go to F. A. O. Schwarz Toy Store so that I can have a dessert-like splurge. But first we must assess the park people. New York's best and worst and funniest and saddest promenade by us, and by silent agreement we guess at their lives. Aunt Edna starts us off.

"Julie doll, what do you think of that chap?" she asks.

"I think his wife beats him up," I answer.

Aunt Edna smiles from one side of her mouth. "And what say you about this dazzling creature," she inquires about a lady who looks like she knows all about night work.

"I bet she cries when no one's looking."

Aunt Edna commends me on my ability. She says that I get an A in people watching. I ask her to tell my father so that perhaps it will make up for my low marks in math. She says not to worry about math; that keen observation is a talent that will see me through my life. She should know.)

VENICE: "The impressions crowd in so thick and fast that it is impossible to digest them, much less put them down on paper. Your friend Emperor William is here in the royal yacht, and also the King of Italy. We call the emperor Willie off the yacht. The flags are flying everywhere, and the balconies of the hotels and the palaces along the Grand Canal are hung with tapestries and velvets and rugs, and it all looks, not like a city of this age . . . This afternoon we took a gondola and had two and a half hours on the canals, and we also crossed to the Island of Murano where one of the famous glass factories is located, and where they showed us the process. We saw the nobility going to the king's reception in their private gondolas. All the gondolas are painted black, and the sensation you get, lolling about in them, floating past these wonderful palaces, is not to be described by a mere slang-thrower like myself. But I rise to state that Browning, Byron, Tennyson and them guys haven't exaggerated anything. It is strictly as advertised.

"Our hotel occupies three old palaces. Our room is big enough to make an ordinary Chicago six-room flat, and when we're in it mama and I have to call to each other in order to keep track of one another, and we're constantly discovering in it furniture that we never saw before. The ceiling is so high that we look like babies walking around."

PARIS: "We had lunch at a restaurant whose hors d'oeuvres are so good that you can't eat anything else. You eat quarts and quarts of artichoke hearts, and smoked salmon, and radishes, and cucumbers, and foie gras, and sardines, and tomatoes and sausage, and then you haven't room for any real food. The food here isn't half as cheap as in Berlin, where we were spoiled by being fed lobster and caviar and squabs and salad and pastry and strawberry-bowl, and charged a dollar and a half.

"Paris, my children, is plumb, stark crazy. Compared to this, Chicago is a sylvan glade. The people jump about like fleas, and the streets swarm with taxis like an ant hill with ants, and mama will never leave this town unmaimed, I'm sure."

MUNICH-NÜRNBERG: "Mama and I are both mad about Munich. One could live here for a year. It has that atmosphere which Vienna seemed to lack . . . We went to see the dancers Sacharoff and Clothilde Von Derp last night. It was the most grotesque sort of dancing, but interesting, and there was a semi-riot of students when one of the numbers danced by Sacharoff struck them as being too effeminate.

"This morning mama and I went to the Deutsches Museum, then to the Hofbrau, a sight not to be described with a pen. If I had my Remington here I'd do it for you. We spent the whole afternoon until seven o'clock at the May fair, where, once a year, are all sorts of things—furniture, china, silver, pewter, peasant dresses, hundreds and hundreds of booths. We bought a black silk lace shawl for mama, three wonderful old pewter plates a hundred years old, hand-chased, two old pictures. It's sort of a glorified rummage sale and we had a grand time.

"We hate to leave München. It's a fascinating place. And as for the shops! You can't tear away from them. We went into an establishment that sells only antiques. But not as we think of antique shops at home. It is a succession of beautiful rooms, furnished to the last detail with these exquisite antiques. Such tables, such chairs and chests and rugs and beds, all as they should be in one's home. It was a real fairyland . . . Poor little Minnow! I'm all for her, poor little old fing. And when I get back I'm going to sperl her and you can all fuss over Fiendy."*

"Fellers: We left München with real regret . . . In our compartment today, from München to Nürnberg were two German women—young, well-dressed (for Germans) and nice looking, and well educated. But you should have heard them on the subject of America! They have the wildest notion of it. They announced that all Americans drink camomile tea after each meal, and nothing we could say would shake them. Also, we ate soup for breakfast (Quaker Oats is soup to them, and they were firm in the belief that we ate it regularly). They wanted to know if the sky-scrapers didn't rock and tumble if the wind blew. We gave up at last, in despair . . . The chief charm of Nürnberg is its quaint old streets and buildings and city wall and moat and castle and all that . . . Mama sends love. She is now sitting by the window bewailing the fact that she had bock beer and sandwiches this morning and coffee and cake this afternoon. As for me, I can't hook my clothes."

ON BOARD THE HAMBURG SAILING FOR NAPLES: This is the last day of our voyage . . . not one storm, and no one seasick during the entire time. Did you ever? . . . We stopped in Algiers yesterday and had a wonderful morning . . . We had a chief guide. It is absolutely necessary when going through the Arabian Quarter. It is another world and you are taken back centuries and centuries. You walk through unbelievable streets, so narrow that two people can scarcely pass, and lined on either side with tiny, black, awful shops . . . We saw the funniest Arab school, with everyone squatting on the floor, including the turbaned, spectacled, bearded teacher. They all recite or study at the top of their voices . . . The women were all in baggy Turkish trousers, and veiled to the eyes . . . One thing that I have loved is the flower-vendors who swarm up the boat and at the quay, and all about with wonderful flowers. We bought a huge basket containing hundreds of violets, roses, pansies, fresia, hyacinths, basket and all, for twenty-five cents.

"It's luncheon time. I shall now go down and eat quarts. The food is marvelous. For dinner last evening, just for example, we had all sorts of canapes—caviar, sardellen, smoked fish etc.—soup, deli-

* A nickname for Janet.

cious fresh Mediterranean bass, filet with vegetables (not just plain vegetables but marvelous things with marvelous shapes and sauces) then French artichokes with butter sauce, squabs, salad, compote, peche melba, cake, fruit, cheese etc. Cooked perfectly and perfectly served. I've just been weighed and to me horror find that I've gained five pounds in two weeks! Mama gained six!"

NAPLES: "Everyone is a cut-throat, a low-life and a robber here. You bargain for your very street-car fare."

ROME: "This is supposed to be a birthday letter, dear Sis. You'll never know what I wish you, or how much I wish it. I'd give anything to know that you are well again. That's the main thing. You have that darling Jack for a husband—he's the nicest man in the world, and you'd realize that if you saw all these other men. And you have the Snooties, and that's more than I'll ever have."

(Young as she was, what she does at this point in the letter indicates the fierce dictatorial streak that she would improve upon later.)

"We are sending you money instead of presents. This is the arrangement:

"Mama's check—$25 for you Fan, $5 for a present for Jack, $5 for a present for Uncle Julius's birthday.

"My check—$30 for Fan: $25 for a suit or something, and $5 for matinee tickets.

"I wish I could tell you about our funny experience at the Colosseum. We wanted to see it by moonlight, as is the custom. So we made up a party of five women, and ventured forth. We thought it was a rather devilish thing to do because the Colosseum is a great scary place even in daylight, and it might conceal whole armies of robbers and bandits. So we took about two lires each, and left our jewelry, pocketbooks and all that behind, and ventured forth—sh-sh-sh!! like that. When we reached there at about 9:30 the place looked like Grant Park on band nights. It was packed with moonlighters who were saying, 'Aint it grand!' (Americans); and 'Ptachtful!' (German tourists) and 'Charmante!' (French tourists). You could hardly find a ruined Roman stone to perch on, and the crowds tramped about in the moonlight like a herd of buffalo. Romance! I shrieked, it was so funny."

LONDON: "We're wild to get home, now that we're really off. And Mrs. Fox, if e'er I see your kitchen portals again, will you please ask me to dinner, serving for same: Noodle soup. Celery. Pot roast. Real potatoes. Spinach with aig sitting. Maybe apple sauce though I can't expect too much. Salad. Somepun grand fur dessert. I just tried on my Paris dress and it makes me look huge in the rear, being built simple."

Short stories, family, food, clothes, and covering Chicago's Democratic and Republican national conventions for the George Matthew Adams Newspaper Syndicate were Ferber's priorities in late 1912. She was assigned as fifth on a work team made up of four men: Jay Darling and Harold Webster—cartoons; George Fitch—humor; William Allen White—political. It was her first meeting with White, and perhaps that time they spent together was the greatest mental-humor-food fling that they were ever to have. Years later White reflected back, capturing for her that first Ferber he knew:

". . . She was just a child . . . and had published only two books . . . I knew her when she had little fame . . . She was my friend; I was proud of her even before she struck twelve. And it has been one of the great things of my life that I have been privileged to be her friend, that many times she turned to me for council, for friendship, for sympathy, for understanding, and I hope that I have never abused the rare privilege she has given me. And now that I am a puffy, fat, watery eyed, unsure old man, who is not wholesome to see, I am glad to look back on the time when I was strong, and full of life, and she was young and to my eyes a most beautiful woman, and we were good friends, and I hope she will ever know how I have always respected her, and honored her and admired her, and enjoyed her."

In early 1912, Woodrow Wilson might have held the winning ticket for the Presidency, but Ferber gripped the winning ticket out of Chicago and to New York—and to her introduction to high-writing society.

Stokes had published her second book—a volume of short stories titled, *Buttered Side Down,* because she felt that slices of life and toast didn't always come out right. Each story reflected the title; and each Chicago critic reviewed the stories as reflections of O. Henry's style—hence, her O. Henry mantle.

She found herself a local celebrity, and, as such, began to be sought for local interviews—not the flash-bulb-popping variety, but the cozy, coffee klatch sort. During one of these she met a young book reviewer from the Chicago *Tribune* named Fanny Butcher, who turned into and remained a friend for life. "It was a continuous live river without any rapids in it," she says of that friendship. And Fanny Butcher remembers how it all came about through a turnabout:

"I remember that interview with her vividly. When I left, after a couple of hours of talk that was so exciting that neither of us was aware that hours were passing instead of minutes, I realized that I hadn't anything to write about concerning her work . . . I had only impressions of her . . . Instead of my interviewing her she had been interviewing me, finding out what I thought, what I wanted to do with my life, what I had done so far, and why. I realized then that the true story teller's instinct is to find out more than to give out."

There is a clue dropped by Fanny Butcher that later was to help with the understanding of Ferber's self-proclaimed savior and, at the same time, Achilles' heel—her spinsterhood.

Enterprising Fanny Butcher not only was a book reviewer, but owned and ran a bookstore, in which she employed another young woman named Kate Sproehnle, who was absolutely ravishing. In a letter to father confessor White, Ferber summarizes Kate Sproehnle as though she would like to smite her:

"Along comes this Kate Sproehnle. And besides being built on the general lines and coloring of a goddess she's got an appreciation of humor (and a pretty wit of her own) that you meet with only once or twice in a lifetime. I know when I'm licked."

Indeed. For Kate Sproehnle had a beau, whom Fanny Butcher felt Ferber cared a great deal about. He married Kate Sproehnle. Ferber axiom: goddess girls got the beaux; homely girls turned to books.

Bert Boyden, an editor on *American* magazine, didn't think her prose was homely, or, when he met her, that she was either. It was after the McChesney stories had taken off—via *American* magazine and the Stokes book publications—and were the rage that Boyden and Frederick A. Stokes paged Ferber to go to New York and balloon her reputation.

She went—from the Vincennes apartment-hotel on Chicago's South Side to the Belleclaire Hotel on Manhattan's West Side. It was just a visit; a short courtship; an enchantment; a taste of good white wine when cider is still preferred. She met the kind of people she would later thrive on:

". . . Dinner at Bert Boyden's apartment in Stuyvesant Square . . . was best of all. I never had seen a bachelor apartment until I came to New York, and I was naively astonished to find that a man could live in such comfort, unwed. Here were tasteful charming rooms; delicate china and glass; candles, cocktails, wine, delicious food beautifully served; gay, witty, friendly dinner companions . . . Here I met . . . Lincoln Steffens, Kathleen and Charles Norris, Rube Goldberg, Fontaine Fox, Charley Towne, Kate and Grantland Rice—scores of people who were writing or acting or editing or publishing. There was good talk. I didn't try to meet Names."

Contrary to Thomas Wolfe's philosophy, she went home again. For a while.

Children ask: "So what happened after that?" Well, Edna Ferber the writer happened after that. But what happened before, in 1911, made it all possible.

Julia Ferber proved that Mother knew best by giving birth twice to the same daughter—once to an Edna, and once to a writer.

EDNA
1911-1885

"To My Dear Mother who frequently interrupts And To My Sister Fannie who says 'Sh-sh-sh!' outside my door" was the dedication of Edna's first novel, *Dawn O'Hara, The Girl Who Laughed.* It was published by Frederick A. Stokes, and did fairly well—earning decent reviews and selling ten thousand copies off the bat. Edna hated it. She thought it mushy, maudlin, sophomoric, and undeserving. She'd said to herself, ". . . it isn't good. It isn't as good as you are this minute." But she'd taken it to an agent named Flora May Holly, who had taken it to Stokes, who had taken it to press. It was all by default. She'd applied for a position as a reporter on the Chicago *Tribune,* who turned her down. They didn't use women. Stokes published women. There seemed to be no other choice than to accept the fact that suddenly she was a woman writer.

The inception of the book's progress began in 1910, with the quick eye and hands of Julia Ferber.

Jacob Ferber was dead. The dry goods store called, touchingly, "My Store," which he had owned but which Julia had run for thirteen years in Appleton, Wisconsin, was sold. With the sizable profits from the sale of their house and the store, Julia had decided to move herself, Fannie, and Edna to Chicago, where they had family, and where they could have new hope.

As they were selling off the things in the house, and packing up the ones they would retain, they took trips down to the furnace to throw out the things nobody wanted. Edna was about to include the manuscript of *Dawn O'Hara* in the discarded-about-to-be-burned pile when Julia noticed. Ferber recalls the moment:

" 'What's that?'

"Suddenly I felt embarrassed. Failure always embarrasses the unsure. 'Oh, just that—uh—book thing I was trying to write last winter. It isn't any—'

"She took it out of my hands and put it to one side, neatly. 'I wouldn't burn that if I were you. Keep it.'

" 'Nobody wants it.'

" 'You never can tell. Maybe you haven't sent it to the right person.' "

Wouldn't most mothers save their child from the furnace? Most mothers would try.

Julia was very strong. As her years grew it was called headstrong, and then indomitable. One could say the same about Ferber. But Edna, in early 1910, was not so strong. She was recovering from what was delicately termed a "nervous collapse." It is difficult to decipher which came first—the physical chicken or the emotional egg. The fact of her condition was severe anemia, but it was surrounded by emotional complications.

Since her graduation from Ryan High School she had been working to help support a family whose father could eventually barely eat bread no less win it. The roles had been defined early. Jacob was the invalid—sweet, soft, and needy. Julia was the man of the family—productive, seemingly tireless, and emotionally muscular. Fan was goody-domestic-shoes—tame, pretty, a household genius. Edna was goody-work-shoes—smart, industrious, adventurous. Hers was the most complicated role. She was never allowed, nor permitted herself, to be a daughter. With Julia as head of the household, she suffered a reversal, and became the "No. 1 son" to her mother's masculine stance. "Ed can do it." "Ed will do it." "Good for Ed!" was the hum all around her. They even called her Ed, as though she were a tough little guy.

She had been working as a reporter on the Milwaukee *Journal* until early 1909—sending home a healthy portion of her sickly salary—feeling exhilarated at being away and guilty at having left. News of her father's progressively worsening condition wormed away inside of her the harder she worked. He was totally blind and dying; she was free and young. Fan was a slave to hospital corners; putting up pot roasts, marinating red cabbage, grating potatoes for pancakes; trimming old hats into new millinery. Edna was whirling in a social life, meeting bright young men. Julia was running the store singlehandedly—the accounts, the ordering, the banking—and administering to a husband who had no life. Edna was interviewing Governor Robert La Follette, and going to the theatre.

In a dramatic act of contrition, Edna fainted before going to work one morning, and Julia, with burdens enough, had another invalid on her hands.

Back in Appleton, Edna played "Camille" for the first act—being treated by Fan to: "frothy eggnogs . . . tempting trays decorated with snarls of mayonnaise, curls of parsley, jewels of jelly . . ." and then rallied for the second act to play herself. She bought a second-hand seventeen-dollar typewriter and between clandestine work on *Dawn O'Hara,* turned out a short story—her first—called, "The Homely Heroine."

After her chores were done, and Jacob had been walked, she would retire to her room (the porch, a circular affair, was too distracting with the town walking by on three sides) to make her two-finger staccato sound. That two-finger process lasted her forever—a process that newspaper people know well.

Julia: "What's Ed up to?"

Fan: "She's doing her typewriting."

Her "typewriting" of "The Homely Heroine" sold to *Everybody's Magazine* for $50.60. A first sale for a first story. Nobody tells about her successful moments better than Ferber:

"My decision to send The Homely Heroine to the editor of Everybody's was arrived at simply enough. It happened to be the one magazine on the living-room table. Its address was printed on the index page. Off went the story, badly typed and minus return postage.

"In an unbelievably few days the answer came back. I can still see Julia Ferber as she appeared at the corner of Morrison and North streets. I was lolling on our front porch. 'Yoo-hoo!' she called with a note of hysteria in her voice; and held an envelope high in the air. The letter was from . . . the fiction editor of Everybody's. They had accepted . . . my first short story, and enclosed please find their check for $50.60.

"I was furious. I'd never had so large a sum presented to me at one time. Of magazines and national magazine prices I knew nothing. I didn't feel elated over the fact that my first short story had been accepted by the most popular magazine of its kind in the

United States. I only knew that $50.60 wasn't an adequate price for an acceptable short story: and more than anything, that sixty cents rankled."

On September 30, 1909, Jacob Ferber died, and Edna began to fill the shoes he never wore.

Julia Ferber always turned herself out. She had thrift, chic, and good looks, which made for a fine "figger" of a woman. Living so long with an appendage instead of a man seemed to make her flourish in a singular way. But she had terrible contempt for her albatross husband; a contempt which both Edna and Fan caught and carried with them in their life-viewers. Women were potent; men not so much.

Every Ferber heroine had the young Julia's qualities. Almost every Ferber fictional male owned Jacob's deficiencies. That no Ferber novel was built around Jacob was not accidental. That Emma McChesney was a glorified Julia Ferber was deliberate. Even Julia nodded openly at her alter-image. "Julia McFerber," she called herself—preening like a woman who approves of her painted portrait.

Julia was shrewd bordering on perception, not in the least analytical and unsympathetic to her failings. Edna was entrusted with the sympathetic vision that her mother couldn't afford. Edna felt all of the pain that Julia left by the wayside.

One failing of Julia's was not her fault, much like being a "little bit pregnant," she was not quite accepted in Appleton's social circles. It had nothing to do with her being Jewish. That they could accept gracefully. What was not "kosher" at that time in the small Middle Western town was a woman who worked, who supported her family, who ran a business, who made decisions. A woman was just not dominant. Better to cuckold her husband than to be dominant. Julia was regarded as somewhat of a freak; and although the townsfolk happily traded with her and joked with her on her own turf, they did not invite her to toddy parties and weddings and funerals.

Since Julia was too busy being practical, it was Edna who bore the brunt of this snub. It was then that future promises to Julia began to be made. And as soon as she was of age, upon graduating from high school, she too joined the ranks of the workingwoman. Securing a job as a reporter on the Appleton *Daily Crescent* was as good as thumbing her nose and saying, "See, it runs in the family. Now, there are two of us."

Julia Ferber kept a journal during the first ten years of the twentieth century. Most of the entries are concerned with store-keeping and buying trips to Milwaukee and Chicago, but some are personal, and eerily familiar: "Unbearably weary," she records. "A dreadful day." "So many burdens." "Horribly weary." "A ghastly fight between Fannie and Ed." Blood yells.

Edna referred to her three-year stint in Milwaukee as an "interlude." In a sense it was a reprieve from genetic overkill. She was able to see and feel things all by herself without the beneficial/detrimental slant of Julia. She didn't have to be reminded that Fan was the prettier one, that her father was the weak one.

Having no opportunity to go to college, the "interlude" lent itself to a form of higher education. Milwaukee was her campus; the newsroom was her homeroom; the rooming house where she stayed was her dorm; her assignments were her courses. She was later to say that it was the toughest and best education that she could possibly have had.

She was taught the basic hardships of being a writer—a code that she honored all of her life. She was taught that she couldn't afford mistakes in her research. The research part she got down pat, but she never could quite forsake her embellishments. "I'm adjective-noidal," she would admit of herself. Prone to flights of romantic embellishment, she was taught to cut it out and write clean, terse, accurate copy.

It was at the Milwaukee *Journal* that she found an "early influence"—first in name only, and then in person:

"Years before I came to work on the Journal there had been on the reportorial staff a woman whose name was now constantly held up to me as a model. I grew to hate the sound of it. From Milwaukee she had gone to work on a New York paper. From this she had graduated into a highly successful fiction writer. Her name was Zona Gale." Years later Ferber said that Zona Gale reminded her of pale sunshine. Woollcott countered the metaphor with his own: "more like filtered light," he said. "It sounded to me made-up and affected. Then, one day, there was a great to-do down the hall. One heard the voice of Campbell, usually harsh and grating, now dulcet as a dove. He appeared, hovering calf-eyed over a fragile and lovely creature whose skirts rustled silkenly as she moved.

"She had great dark tragic eyes in a little pointed face; the gentlest of voices; a hand so tiny that when one took it in one's grasp it felt like the crushing of a bird's wing. I was introduced and mumbled something inadequate. This was the first real writer I had ever met. I wasn't envious. I was impressed. I never had remotely thought of becoming a writer outside newspaper work.

". . . At the desk behind mine sat Jean Airlie, who conducted the People to the Journal column. She had known Zona Gale in her reporter days. They talked together now, the successful fiction writer and the weary-looking newspaper woman. Blandly I listened.

" 'Tell me the name of a good writer's agent,' Jean Airlie pleaded.

"Zona Gale mentioned a name. It sounded highly floral and faintly improbable.

" 'Send your stories to her,' Miss Gale said. 'She placed my very first things, years ago.'

"Tidily I tucked the name away in my memory and closed the door on it."

No fool Edna. The name of the agent was Flora May Holly, the woman who sold *Dawn O'Hara*.

In 1905 Edna had left for Milwaukee. It was not an easy parting. She set it down in a small, painful paragraph.

"My farewell on going to Milwaukee to work regularly. As I look back on it now it was the only sheer act of brutality I have ever committed. I see him now, in his nightshirt, his spare shanks showing beneath it. 'I'm going,' I said. I think it must have been a terrible statement for him to hear. I must have shut my eyes to his stricken face."

She called him "Popsie" when she didn't call him "Bill." He always called her "Pete." They were less father and daughter, more tender friends—for he never dispensed discipline, and as far back as she could remember, he needed her. She felt sorry for him, and, in many ways, older than he. He was like a wounded pet entrusted to her care.

In *A Peculiar Treasure* Ferber berates herself for not finding out more about Jacob: "I wish I had talked to him about his childhood and his youth in Hungary, and his high hopes as he crossed the ocean, a lad, to find fortune and happiness in this golden new land. But I didn't."

What she did do was to pay more attention to him than anyone else in the household. She would joke with him, read to him for hours, walk with him on the shady sides of the Appleton streets, for she didn't want the sun to hurt his failing eyes.

When, as a cub reporter for the Appleton *Daily Crescent*, she had to cover a story and couldn't break away to take him for his walk, she would recruit Arthur Howe. Sweet, dumb, non-Jewish Arthur Howe, who worked as a stock boy for the Ferbers in My Store, and who was resigned to Julia shouting, "Gonif, gonif!" to him when a customer came into the store needing help. Just as he did Julia's bidding, he did young Edna's, and would dutifully and carefully walk with Jacob when she couldn't. For this favor, in years to come, she saw to it that he was sent autographed first editions of all of her books.

Eighteen and jobless. Edna had been told that her services were no longer required at the Appleton *Daily Crescent*. Appleton rumor still has it today that the chief reason was because she wrote fiction in lieu of journalism—that she bent the facts to suit herself. It was a most fortuitous firing, although she didn't know it at the time. She was crushed, snuffed, all washed up. She'd known that it was unheard of for a girl to be a reporter. "Never been done before," they told her—unanimous heads shaking. But she'd been hired, and there she'd been all the time thinking herself a pacesetter doing a top-notch job, showing 'em all, when all the while the staff had regarded her as an interloper, doing a not good enough job. Yes, but what about her piece on the fashions of 1905? Her notes show that even with a subject as loose-weave as fashion she embroidered:

"Princesse gown of sage-green velvet and handsome ecru lace, metal buttons—ecru lace all down the front . . . Dinner waist of black dotted lace over pristine white . . . Silk moire mull and English embroidery, dressing sash of cashmere, velvet cuffs topped with cream lace . . . Evening coat of chalk-color with handsome ivory lace band over satin collar . . . Hats—structures set on pompadours tipped up in back and down in front. Ribbons. Feathers. Roses. (cache-peigne?) Whole birds as large as hens."

Her two years at the *Crescent* had been fruitful while they lasted. After all, she hadn't even intended them. She had chosen for herself a life on the stage—her fantasies pirouetting into curtain calls, deep bows, and long-stemmed roses after winning the Wisconsin state declamatory contest in her senior year of high school. She'd had it all mapped out. She would go to the Northwestern University School of Elocution, in Evanston, Illinois, and then, somehow, to the footlights. It was as simple and clear-cut as dreams are. The reality was simpler. The Ferbers couldn't afford it, thereby forcing Edna to replan her life.

Upon obtaining her reporter's job, she got her first whiff of publicity when her own newspaper gave her a plug:

"One of the brightest young women of this city, Miss Edna Jessica Ferber, gives promise of becoming one of the best newspaper women in the state. Miss Ferber is but eighteen years of age, a graduate of the Ryan High School in this city, and had an intention of taking up elocution, but was disuaded and went into journalism instead. There she met with instant success."

The curtain calls and long-stemmed roses receded.

Edna, the actress, was last seen—until almost four decades later—playing Suzanne de Ruseville in *A Scrap of Paper*, performed in the auditorium of Ryan High School. It was the first and last time she was ever wooed on stage, and perhaps the only time—onstage or off—that she yielded. An excerpt from the synopsis of the play reads: ". . . and the play ends happily by Suzanne, the invincible, yielding to the love of Prosper."

Edna was a sunny person during her years at Ryan High; the thunderclaps were kept under tight supervision. She felt herself ugly, and knew that that alone wouldn't get her very far. She chose the road of least resistance: a winning personality. She was charming, friendly, bright, curious, witty, and altogether colorful. Even then she knew that the key to life was character, and refused to be short-changed on that score.

She changed the criteria of what was popular for young girls. At that time it was docile, dimpled, and domestic. Edna, with her hair bow askew, glasses, and a dumpy kind of plumpness, was outspoken, emotional, imaginative, and achieving. Fan, three years older, compared their high school careers: "I was the pretty one, but Edna had the beaux," she said.

Two of Edna's girlhood friends provide testimony of her winning ways:

BEATRICE FRANK: "Here in this area you had to develop yourself. Edna was a very busy girl doing just that. She was editor of the school newspaper, The Ryan Clarion, and was always on this committee or that. She certainly was an exciting child. She was a stimulant."

MIRIAM ELKAN HEART: "Edna's mother was a friend of our mother and that's how we got to know Edna. My older sister, Belle, was the one who really knew her because they were the same age . . . During our girlhood, Edna had an imaginary boyfriend named Joe, and she told wonderful stories about him in an Italian dialect. Oh, she was always very lively—full of talk—lots of humor. She was a real storyteller. She was popular with people in general, but she didn't like to be crossed . . . I was a good deal younger than Belle and Edna, but was occasionally permitted to tag along with them. I remember going to the beach with them one afternoon, and they began to discuss psychoanalysis, which was an ultra-modern and racy subject at that time, and Edna said, 'Well, I'll never need it.' . . . She was so very alive with a perfectly lovely curiosity . . . Her success derived from the fact that she wrote about things she'd known all her life, and for all her lack of schooling, her natural intelligence was brighter and carried her farther than most people's . . . She would always say to my sister Belle, who wanted to write and never made a success of it: 'If you want to write, just sit down and write.'

"The last time I spoke to Edna was in 1964 or '65 when she came to Chicago for a visit. She phoned and asked me had I heard a big noise at around two in the afternoon. I said no and asked why. Well, she had gone out to Graceland Cemetery to check on the upkeep of her mother's and aunt's plots, and had found the conditions deplorable, and had made a commotion. 'I bellowed,' she told me. 'Just thought you might have heard it.' When we were girls she didn't bellow, but we knew that some day she would."

Before moving to Appleton, the nomadic Ferbers moved from Ottumwa, Iowa, to Chicago. Jacob was failing—in business and in health; Julia was disconsolate; and the girls were beginning to feel dislocated from so many relocations. This time they all landed on the traditional, familial security blanket—the grandparents; Julia's mother and father, Harriet and Louis Neumann. These two kindly people had also taken in the other family strays, known to Edna and Fannie as: Aunt Jo, Uncle Isidore, Uncle Ed, and Uncle Julius.

Jacob, with Julia's ever-strengthening hand guiding him, decided to stay in Chicago until he could decide what to do. Eventually, that decision was to move to Appleton, and it was Julia's. Meanwhile, the Neumanns roofed them with temporary stability, a sense of the *gemütlich*, mouth-watering rich German-Jewish cooking, and regular outings to synagogue and to the theatre. It was here that Edna began to develop her appreciation of food and theatre—later to become Ferber passions.

Among Ferber's autobiographical notes are found impressions of her grandparents. They are from Edna's misty, adoring standpoint:

"Grandma Neumann: Her house was always full of friends and relatives and the dining room table in the three-story and basement house on Calumet Avenue always was stretched out to accommodate at least twelve. The soup was served in a tureen. The meat and vegetables were served at the table. I can see the cover coming off the big oblong cream china soup tureen with the leaf pattern and the steam and the aroma of noodle soup. I wonder if that wasn't an excellent custom because of the message that the eyes sent to the stomach. 'Get ready!' it said to the gastric juices. 'Gather all ye juices. Make ready to welcome a succulent meal. Here comes the soup. Smell it! Here is the crispy nut brown fowl, its slicing melting away from the carving knife.'" (Interesting that she titled this gastronomic experience as a portrait of Grandma.)

"Grandpa Neumann: In fiction and history old Jewish gentlemen are always shown as being patriarchs and scholars, full of culture, wisdom and sayings from the Old Testament and the Torah.

"Grandpa Louis Neumann was a scholar and a gentleman, certainly. White mutton-chop whiskers, a gentle blue eye, gold rimmed glasses and a knowledge of French, German, Spanish and Italian. He was a darling old man. Now that I think of it, he wasn't old at all, yet he seemed an ancient to me . . . A gentle cultured straight-standing man. He had a gold-headed cane and walked with a little trot. I wish he were alive so that I could talk to him now."

The house of Neumann served as a recovery room for Edna. Two years of healing after seven of being wounded. The town of Ottumwa, Iowa, was her flagellator.

For seven of her formative years she fought against being twisted out of shape in an atmosphere that had nothing to offer and much that was ruinous. It was not so much that the physical surroundings were hideous; or that Jacob began to lose his sight; or that Julia began to take over; or that Fan became prettier. Edna had a strong constitution; those things could be digested. What rendered her powerless, what made her emotionally queasy, was that Ottumwa, Iowa, was a Jew-hating, Jew-baiting town. The Ferbers were victims of the kind of rabid bigotry which this country has learned to know so well, and to deal with so badly. The only way they could fight back was to keep a straight back. They didn't cower and huddle. They suffered proudly. That in school Edna learned the three R's was elementary. The real lesson that she learned to pass with flying colors was how to hate people who hated.

The climax of the Ferbers' degradation in Ottumwa came at what Edna referred to as The Trial. There was a girl working for the Ferbers in their store, who had been pilfering items over a long period of time. Although finally detecting it, the unpopular Julia and Jacob were helpless. It was the girl's good Christian word against their smirched Jewish one. What looked like a miracle of justice came their way when several of their customers agreed to testify in their favor at the trial. With dignity and confidence the family marched into the courtroom. They were quickly stripped of that dignity and a great deal of money. The supposedly friendly witnesses vowed that they'd seen no evil, heard none, and would speak none against one of their own kind. Julia and Jacob Ferber were judged guilty of slander and lost the suit. What they gained was the impetus to leave Hades/Ottumwa, Iowa.

The sense-memory of Edna's time there never left her. In recalling it, her notes scathe:

"Ottumwa, Iowa was a wretched coal-mining town. God knows by what miracle of bad judgement my father had chosen it of all the towns in the United States. My sister Fannie and I were parked in Chicago while my parents went about looking for what they called a location . . . I don't think there was a day (in Ottumwa) when I wasn't called a sheeny. It must have been a very backward little town and I still feel an absurd and deep hatred of it. And yet not absurd. It must have left its mark on a sensitive child . . . The hanging on Main street. Elocution lessons at Miss Lang's. God knows what I learned . . . The loafers—those boys, idle, sullen, resentful, ignorant, sitting perched there on the drugstore corner with their heels hooked round the railing were the Nazis of that little

Iowa town. Here was something they could bait; here was a small helpless human thing, powerless.

"It wasn't so much what they said as their vacant evil obscene faces. I hope they were all very hungry, ill and in a good deal of quite unbearable pain before they died.

"My other cheek was all worn out long before I grew up."

It wasn't all bleak sights and black hats. Edna discovered that books were balm for the sagging spirit, and wrapped herself in a book a day. And they went to the theatre, the Ferbers, or to anything resembling a performance level—whether it was a play, a minstrel show, or a public speaking contest. Wherever there was an alternative to reality, there were the Ferbers attending it. Edna would retain all that she'd seen, and would regale the family for weeks afterwards with imitations and recitations. She didn't just keep it in the family. She took her histrionic wares to the streets, where she drew standing room only:

"I spoke pieces under the lamp-light—the gas lamp," Ferber recalled of her child-self. "Whenever they went to look for me there was a crowd round and I was reciting."

Ottumwa was a leavening time, and Edna, a small lonely extrovert, somehow knew how to rise.

Like a lost tribe, the Ferbers, in 1888, wandered out of Kalamazoo, Michigan, and into Chicago, where they stayed with the Neumanns until more permanent sights were set. At ages three and six, Edna and Fan adapted well to their grandparental environment. They were not totally aware yet of Julia's restlessness, or of Jacob's incapabilities. They knew only of a sprawling house that abounded with good food smells, and Mozart's *Don Giovanni*. It was a place for children to be happy, and Fan remembers that Edna was a determined-to-be-happy little girl.

Kalamazoo, Michigan. An early memory. Fannie speaks:

"I have a picture of Edna sitting on mama's knee, and mama singing 'Champagne Charlie' at the top of her voice, and Edna reaching up—not toward mama's face—but up, higher—her palms spread out. It was as though she expected something."

At 1 P.M. on August 15, 1885, Julia Ferber gave birth to her second child. She'd wanted a boy, and would have named him Edward. It was a girl. She called her Edna.

INDEX